THE
PRISONER
KING

THE
PRISONER
KING
CHARLES I IN CAPTIVITY

JOHN MATUSIAK

The
History
Press

For Bella and Genevieve

First published 2017

The History Press
The Mill, Brimscombe Port
Stroud, Gloucestershire, GL5 2QG
www.thehistorypress.co.uk

British Library Cataloguing in Publication Data.
A catalogue record for this book is available from the British Library.

ISBN 978-0-7509-6768-6

Typesetting and origination by The History Press
Printed and bound in Malta by Melita Press

God sees 'tis fit to deprive me of Wife, Children, Army, Friends and Freedom, that I may be wholly his, who alone is all.

Eikon Basilike

CONTENTS

1   Last Liberty and Refuge   9

2   Flight to Captivity   30

3   Marriage or Conscience?   56

4   To English Hands   80

5   More Congenial Custody   106

6   'To Seek My Safety'   130

7   'Made Safe From Stirring'   153

8   'Miserable Distracted Kingdom'   175

9   'Extraordinary Incidents' and 'Guileless Stratagems'   197

10 'Sweet Jane Whorwood'   218

11 'A Business of Action & Not of Words'   245

12 'Neither Peace Nor Honour'   269

13   Mischief, Blood, Abduction, Defeat   295

     Epilogue   312

     Index   315

1

LAST LIBERTY AND REFUGE

'Another city Lost! Alas poor king!
Still future griefs from former griefs do spring!'
Alexander Brome, 1620–66, Royalist poet

As the nearby clock of St Peter's struck three mournful chimes in the early morning stillness of Monday, 27 April 1646, Oxford's East Gate was cautiously opened by the city's governor, Sir Thomas Glemham, to release three cloaked fugitives into the night. Among them was Dr Michael Hudson, most trusted of all the king's chaplains, and the long-serving courtier, John Ashburnham, who had previously represented Hastings in the Long Parliament, only to be 'discharged and disabled' for remaining staunchly faithful to the Royalist cause when the time of reckoning duly arrived. The third, however, was an altogether more intriguing individual, whom Glemham self-consciously hailed as 'Harry' as he bade his farewell, locked the gate once more and left the travellers to the darkly looming world beyond the city walls. Earlier that evening, in the presence of his cousin the Duke of Richmond, the locks and beard of this same 'Harry' had been crudely lopped by his close friend Ashburnham, who, in response to the gravity of the occasion, had no doubt abandoned his familiar lively air. For 'Harry' was none other than the sovereign master whom the courtier had served for eighteen years as Groom of the Bedchamber, and more latterly as Treasurer to the vanquished royal army, which now lay in tatters under the grinding onslaught of its enemies. Reduced to anonymity and finally taking his leave of Oxford in the guise of a Roundhead serving man, King Charles I – ruler 'by the grace of God

of England, Scotland, France and Ireland' and 'Defender of the Faith' –
thus rode over Magdalen Bridge, up Headington Hill and away from
the previously safe haven that had succoured him as capital, headquarters and refuge since the early days of the English Civil War.

Only four years earlier, England's second Stuart ruler had entered the
same city to a hearty welcome, fresh from the field of battle at Edgehill,
proudly accompanied by his three beloved sons and brandishing before
him some sixty or seventy colours seized from his Parliamentary foes.
At that time, Edward Hyde, Earl of Clarendon, described Oxford as the
only city in England which the king held 'entirely at his devotion', but
the broader enmity of the outside world appeared of little consequence
as the mayor presented him with a bag containing £250, and the university's deputy orator rendered praise and thanksgiving for his safe
deliverance in suitably reverential tones. Taking up residence in Christ
Church, as his foot soldiers found billets round about, King Charles
could, it seemed, look forward to the future with not a little self-confi-
dence as his budding military base and newly established Court steadily
took shape. Before long, his cavalry headquarters was securely installed
at Abingdon, the best and most trusted of his generals, Prince Rupert,
was comfortably lodged at St John's, and his privy council, too, was
at business in Postmaster's Hall opposite Merton College, where the
Warden's lodgings were being carefully prepared for his French queen.
Nine months later, moreover, when the indomitable Henrietta Maria
finally arrived at her husband's side, flowers were strewn before her and
she too was treated, amid 'loud acclamation', to a purse of gold from
the city's mayor at the spot called Penniless Bench.

The queen's arrival after a long and painful parting could not, indeed,
have been anticipated more eagerly by her husband. For in August
1642, when the English Civil War finally erupted, she had found herself stranded at The Hague, fund-raising on the security of the royal
jewels and attempting to persuade the Prince of Orange and King of
Denmark to plumb their coffers liberally. For much of that time she
had been unwell – from toothache, migraines, coughs and colds – and
her negotiations had been anything but easy. The larger pieces of jew-
ellery, in particular, were not only too expensive to be sold easily, but
carried the additional liability for any potential buyer that they might
later be reclaimed by England's Parliament. In the event, the queen
proved only partially successful, not only with items like 'the great
collar' – which she believed carried some malediction, since no one

would touch it – but even the smaller pieces like Charles' precious pearl buttons. 'You may judge,' she wrote bitterly, 'now that they know we want money, how they keep their foot upon our throat. I could not get for them more than half of what they are worth.' And, as if to seal the queen's frustration, her existing unpopularity as a Catholic had been compounded by further accusations in news-sheets and pulpits alike that 'the popish brat of France' was busy mortgaging the crown jewels to foreigners for no other reason than to buy guns for a religious conflict of her own design. 'If I do not turn mad,' she had complained to her husband, 'I shall be a great miracle.'

Nor had Henrietta Maria hesitated to harangue the king more personally when occasion demanded. She had come to England in 1625 at the age of 15, ignorant of the language and institutions of her new country, undermined by her greedy French entourage, blocked by the resplendent and seemingly almighty Duke of Buckingham and weighed down by instructions from the Pope to protect the Catholics of England. But by now, as her husband well appreciated, she was a force to be reckoned with. The town of Hull, she told him in her letters, 'must absolutely be had', since it was vital to have an east-coast port to which money, military supplies and letters could safely be sent. She pressed him, too, about the security of the code in which the couple were obliged to communicate: 'Take good care I beg you, and put in nothing which is not in my cipher. Once again I remind you to take good care of your pocket, and not let our cipher be stolen.' And when news reached her of a possible 'accommodation' with Parliament, she had reacted with the kind of vehemence that appeared to reduce her husband to shambling inconsequence. 'For the honour of God, trust not yourself to these people,' she insisted. 'If you consent to this, you are lost.'

Yet the queen's conviction that she alone could stiffen her husband's backbone – 'for you are no longer capable of protecting any one, not even yourself' – had done nothing to quell his ardour or curb, for that matter, his ongoing indulgence of her whims. 'When I shall have done my part,' Charles assured her, 'I confess that I shall come short of what thou deservest of me.' And when, on another occasion, there had been nothing from her in the 'weekly dispatch', he confided sadly how 'I would rather have thee chide me than be silent'. Plainly, the king's unconditional love manifested itself all too often in what appeared to be a fawning self-deprecation, and in the process merely served to reinforce on his spouse's part that unbending faith in the superiority of her judgement that might, in the words of the Venetian ambassador, do 'considerable mischief in the successful conduct of affairs'. During her five-month return journey she had, after all, faced storms of unprecedented ferocity off the Dutch coast, and sustained her terrified ladies by assuring them that Queens of England were never drowned. Ultimately, indeed, it had taken three attempts before she landed at Bridlington in February 1643, and even then her trials were not over, for the small house in which she initially prepared to spend the night became the target of Parliamentarian ships, and she was compelled – dressed 'just as it happened' – to take shelter in outlying fields and hedges for two hours while cannonballs, as she herself put it, 'were singing round us in fine style, and a serjeant was killed twenty paces from me'. Thereafter, she returned to her lodgings, 'not choosing that they should have the vanity to say they made me quit the village', and calmly consumed her supper – 'having taken nothing today but three eggs'.

This, then, was manifestly not a woman to be taken lightly. Indeed, for all her 4ft 10in, the little queen immortalised by Van Dyck as hardly more than a doll-like ornament, had proved herself more than capable of striking hard-nosed bargains with artful diplomats and money-grubbing arms dealers alike. When, moreover, the queen and the others on board the *Princess Royal* were carried ashore at Scheveningen in varying degrees of prostration after her first unsuccessful attempt at crossing the heaving North Sea to her waiting husband, she had remained undaunted. Though her clothes and those of her ladies – stiff and sodden with sea water, vomit and excrement – had to be peeled off and burnt, she ignored all advice to postpone her next journey until spring 'when the strange conjunction of planets' was likely to have corrected itself. And by the time she was eventually met at Stratford by her husband's nephew, Prince Rupert, on 11 July, her journey had become nothing less than a triumphant march in its own right. Eagerly assailed by new volunteers for the king's cause and laden with munitions she had brought across the storm-tossed waves from Holland, the queen was accompanied by 2,000 well-armed infantry, 1,000 horse, six artillery pieces and 150 baggage wagons, crammed with supplies in case of attack. The Earl of Newcastle was her escort and the dashing Sir Henry Jermyn her commander-in-chief, while she herself, as she wrote exultantly to the king, stood out as her very own 'generalissima' over all – an impression that was more than fortified by the 'magnificent' reception awaiting her at Oxford after she had first met her husband, appropriately enough, at Kineton Vale below Edgehill.

Throughout her arduous journey, as she was later to tell Madame de Motteville, she had put herself at the head of her troops – always on horseback, *'sans nulle délicatesse de femme'* – and lived among them as she imagined the great Alexander must have done before her. She had supped in their company on boggy roads and byways, employing no ceremony, and treated them like brothers-in-arms, for which she had gained their firm devotion. At her journey's end, the streets of her husband's new capital were lined with soldiers, and its houses packed with spectators as trumpets sounded and heralds rode before her. At Carfax, Timothy Carter, the town clerk, intoned the obligatory eulogy, while at Christ Church, the Vice-Chancellor and Heads of Houses welcomed her in their scarlet gowns. Students read verses in Latin and English, and in addition to her purse of gold from the city authorities, she also received the university's traditional gift of gloves. To crown all, there was further joyous news before the month was out when Bristol fell to Prince Rupert, consolidating her husband's control of the south-west and compounding the annihilation of Sir William Waller's Parliamentarian army at Roundway Down, just north of Devizes, on 13 July.

The queen's return brought with it, too, an influx of fashionable visitors, as she and her attendants, 'half-dressed like angels', amused themselves with music and dancing, staged gay little supper parties, and teased and scandalised elderly dons like Dr Fell, who declared to Lady Anne Fanshawe that though he had 'bred up here' her father and grandfather and was loath to 'say you are a whore', she was nonetheless behaving like one. Before long, indeed, Oxford had become a veritable home from home for all the royal family's adherents – a bustling loyalist microcosm where the king could weave his dreams of ultimate victory and comfortably plan his return to the true capital from which he had been so rudely ejected. Jesus College, on the one hand, was soon accommodating 'persons of quality' from Wales, while the French ambassador took up lodgings at St John's, to confirm the impression of carefree continuity. By June 1643, the limited space at Pembroke College was also crammed with no less than seventy-nine men, twenty-three women and five children, as Prince Rupert prudently deigned to relocate from St John's to take up residence with his brother Prince Maurice at the town clerk's house, which probably lay at numbers 10 to 12 of the modern High Street. Sir Anthony Wood's family, meanwhile, moved out of their house in Merton Street to make way for Lord Culpepper, Master of the Rolls, as the more prestigious Royalists chose to gobble up the remainder of the best houses on offer. Noblemen, knights and gentlemen settled snugly into the parishes of All Saints, St Mary's and St Peter-in-the-East, and St Aldate's alone was soon housing a total of three earls and three barons, besides several baronets and knights. Somewhat less ostentatiously, smaller dwellings too became the nesting places of humbler Royalist fry, including the king's barber, tailor and seamstress, his surgeon, Michael Andrewes, his apothecary, Johann Wolfgang Rumler, and a variety of more menial servants who took up residence mostly in St Ebbe's.

As the second winter of war set in, then, life at the king's new home had assumed a cosily deceptive air of normality, as Charles himself played with Prince Rupert at 'Mr Edwards' tennis court', hunted as far away as Woodstock and even did his best to celebrate the marriage of his dear 'Jack' Ashburnham to the reigning beauty of the exiled court. A beagle pack, it seems, had also been smuggled through the enemy blockade for his amusement, and while fashionably dressed ladies strolled in college gardens or watched the new recruits marching down the High Street and out to the New Parks for military training, the king strove as best he could in other ways to maintain the splendour of what had once been the most formal court in Europe. The Master of the Revels organised elaborate entertainments, William D'Avenant continued to write verse and William Dobson, 'the most excellent painter that England hath yet seen', went on painting court portraits. Even humdrum domestic issues served to distract the king from the tightening net around him. Prince Charles, his heir, fell victim to the measles, while Prince Maurice was stricken rather more seriously by an attack of the stone, which appears to have worried his mother more than the war itself. For his own part, the king lacked stockings and other small necessaries, and sent to Whitehall for their delivery, leaving MPs to determine by a gracious vote of twenty-six to eighteen that a servant should indeed be allowed to carry them to Oxford.

But if warfare might, for one brief season at least, remain on comparatively genial hold, neither the king's daily routines nor the familiar faces round about could mask a deeper, more troubling reality. For while a stream of orders – raising money, appointing captains, sequestering brimstone and saltpetre, dispatching ordnance to Monmouth, confiscating rebel lands in Somerset – flowed steadily from the royal pen, and Charles continued to inspect Oxford's defences with such regularity that an enemy sniper could have set his watch by it, there was also rivalry, dissent and brooding gossip among his own followers, all too much of which centred upon the queen. There were many, after all, who resented her determination to re-establish herself as her husband's confidante and mentor, and those who had enjoyed unrestricted access to the king during her absence did not now wish 'to see the court as it had been, or the Queen herself possessed of so absolute a power as she had been formerly'. Lord Digby, one of her favourites, was at odds with Prince Rupert, while Henry Rich, Earl of Holland, who had begun the war on the other side, now spent far too long in her elegant drawing room at Merton – frequently in the afternoons when Charles himself was visiting. Refusing to countenance his previous disloyalty, the king would not restore him to favour, in spite of his wife's wishes, and the earl was duly forced to return to London, leaving Henrietta Maria, it seems, to nurse a residing sense of grievance. In particular, she resented Prince Rupert, whom she considered too young and 'self-willed', and suspected of conspiring to 'lessen her interest' with the king, though her bullying of her husband seems to have remained undiminished right up to the time of her eventual departure from Oxford in the spring of 1644 when another burdensome pregnancy at the age of 34 finally sapped her of any will to remain. 'If a person speaks to you boldly, you refuse nothing,' she had told Charles not long before her sad little party set out with him through the city's East Gate towards Abingdon, at which point the king and his two eldest sons returned to Oxford while she made her way to the West Country alongside Henry Jermyn on a journey that parted her from her husband forever.

By that time, however, even domestic pangs of this more painful kind were taking second place to other pressing matters, as the distant rumblings of war and the political strife that generated them began to assail the king more and more insistently. On Maundy Thursday 1643, Henrietta Maria's chapel in Somerset House had been ransacked, leaving the peerless Rubens altarpiece and image of Christ crucified in ruins. Two months earlier, preparations for the renewal of conflict had been stepped up markedly in Oxford itself as metal-working shops were commandeered, and the citizenry's brass kitchenware was collected and melted down for ordnance. By then, twenty-seven cannon were parked in Magdalen Grove and grain was being stockpiled in the Law and

Logic schools, whilst New College was storing fodder for the king's
cavalry and Christ Church's quadrangle had been rudely converted
into a stockyard for 300 sheep. No less incongruously, New College's
tower and cloisters now housed teams of armourers and local gun-
smiths, supplied by foundries cited both at Christ Church and Frewin
Hall, and even Oxford's Music and Astronomy schools were being put
to good military use, serving as factories where cloth was duly cut for
soldiers' coats before being carried by packhorse to nearby villages for
stitching by country seamstresses.

And while craftsmen and women geared for war, Oxford's steady
fortification also served as one more grim reminder that the king's
long-term freedom was now increasingly at a premium. Together, the
Thames and the Cherwell surrounded the city on all sides except the
north, and the king had high hopes, too, that communications with
Reading, which the Royalists held, might be kept open by garrisons
at Wallingford and Abingdon. But at East Bridge, the High Street was
nevertheless blocked by logs and a timber gate, and a bulwark constructed between it and the Physic Garden wall to support two pieces
of ordnance. Likewise, loads of stone were manhandled up Magdalen
Tower to fling down upon the advancing enemy, and plans were also
laid for the digging of trenches at vulnerable points between St John's
College and the New Park, as well as Christ Church Meadow, though
only twelve of the 122 townsmen ordered to work on the defences
north of St Giles actually did so, leaving the king with little choice but
to address the citizens personally and order that everyone over the age
of 16 and under 60 should labour on the foundations for one day a
week or pay the sum of 12*d* in default.

And this was not the only sign that even hardy Oxford might
eventually come to wilt under the strain of war. For while the soldiers' daily allowance of 1lb of bread and ½lb of cheese seems to
have been maintained, bad food for the general populace eventually
spawned the '*morbus campestris*' which infected the city in 1643, and
when the king first asked for money in January of the same year, he
was told in no uncertain terms that only £300 was available. Even
so, the order went forward in February that Oxford's citizens should
provide £450 a month, and in June the king asked for a further
£2,000, causing bitter acrimony over apportionment. Worse still, at
the end of May 1644, Parliamentarian forces under the Earl of Essex
and William Waller began a determined effort to trap the king, and

on 6 October 1644, much of the western part of the city was burnt in a fire.

As increasing numbers of soldiers became concentrated in the city from 1645 onwards, moreover, tension between troops and townsfolk mounted. On 18 March 1643, a 'common soldier' had been hanged at the Carfax gibbet 'for killing in a desperate passion, a poor woman dwelling in the town', and more minor disorders, mainly involving duelling and drunkenness, had continued to rankle. Prince Rupert himself, it seems, had at one time forcibly parted two of his officers with a poleaxe after a heated dispute over a horse, and on another occasion an inebriated trooper appears to have run amok in Trinity College, breaking an hourglass belonging to a certain Dr Kettle. Many of the latest newcomers were Welsh, and the language problem now became an additional cause for concern. Pillaging, too, became increasingly common, caused mainly by the wives of Irish and Welsh soldiers, who were more greatly feared, it seems, than their husbands. As conditions deteriorated by the day, Charles ordered that his men should attend church regularly and be fined a shilling for each obscenity uttered. Yet the effort was unavailing, and in February 1646 there was finally no choice but to impose a general curfew.

Nor, of course, was the steady influx of Royalist soldiers prior to this time coincidental, for, as the war went steadily from bad to worse, so the king's armies had been falling back on all fronts. The splendid gold coin produced at the Oxford mint by its master, Thomas Rawlins, to celebrate the 'victory' at Edgehill had in fact masked a deeper truth, for even Charles, as he confessed to the Venetian ambassador who visited him at Christ Church, was aware of the engagement's limitations. If the cavalry had not overcharged and thereby returned to the field too late to do further battle, he admitted, it would have been a great victory. In the broader scheme of things, however, the Royalists themselves had lost some 1,500 men in all, and as the physician William Harvey recorded, the figure would have been higher still if the frost had not congealed the blood of the wounded who lay untended on the battlefield overnight. In the wake of the fray, moreover, Charles had failed to exploit his opportunity while the Earl of Essex was moving off to Warwick and the way to London lay open. When, indeed, Prince Rupert had proposed to the Council of War that a flying column of 3,000 horse and foot should immediately march on Westminster to take the capital by surprise, he had found his king, already 'exceedingly and deeply grieved' at the loss of life so far, unwilling for a further confrontation. Instead, he marched to Banbury and captured Broughton Castle, where he procured supplies of food and clothing for his men, but thereby afforded the Earl of Essex a leisurely escape.

In doing so, Charles had perhaps already lost the war before it had truly begun. A single unconvincing attempt to march on London had been made in the wake of Edgehill when Rupert, on 11 November, had taken and briefly held a Parliamentary outpost at Brentford. But the London trained bands, 24,000 strong, had streamed out to protect their city at Turnham Green. 'Remember the cause is for God and for the defence of yourself and your children,' their general, Philip Skippon, reminded them, with the admonition to 'Pray hearty and fight hard', which they duly did, outnumbering the king by two to one and forcing his withdrawal. Whereupon, though he might have crossed into Kent and Kingston and enlisted support, Charles' campaigning season was effectively over and Oxford proved the more attractive option. Thereafter, though it would take at least two years and more before the full scale of his predicament became clear, the king was on borrowed time: tightly confined by cast-iron circumstances, partly of his own making, and increasingly firmly caged by the military, political and, above all, economic bars being steadily erected around him by his enemies.

In the country at large, just as at Oxford, there had initially been grounds for hope of a kind. At the end of 1642, a majority of the House of Lords and some 40 per cent of the Commons supported the Royalist cause – a figure considerably higher than the behaviour of either House had indicated in the rumbustious early days of the Long Parliament. Indeed, most of the 236 or so Royalist MPs had joined him at Oxford, leaving only 302 at Westminster. Though the industrial towns – especially the clothing centres of Lancashire – were firmly for Parliament and Puritanism, the surrounding areas, which contained many Catholics, remained loyal by and large to their sovereign. Not without justification, Charles laid great faith in the North, while in Cornwall, the Marquis of Hertford and Ralph, Lord Hopton, were in virtually complete control. If Parliament retained what would ultimately prove to be the decisive advantage of London, Kent nevertheless remained largely his, as did Wales and significant pockets of the Midlands.

In the event, it remained a matter of some puzzlement to Charles that his enemies wished to fight at all. Had not Edward Hyde, for instance, often told him that the majority of his subjects remained indifferent – a view echoed, albeit somewhat more cynically, by Thomas Hobbes, who was convinced that most would have taken either side for pay or plunder? The constitutional government that the Long Parliament craved had, in any case, been secured in the summer of 1641, and the long list of past 'abuses' addressed: the forced loans, the monopolies, the lack of preferment at Court or in office, the enclosure and forest fines, the knighthood fees, the tonnage and poundage, and the Ship Money that had financed the navy now in Parliament's hands. Why, then, at this stage did the king's enemies not accept that their calls for control of the militia and abandonment of the episcopacy could never be tolerated by any right-minded ruler? And were they sufficiently deluded to believe that he really was so lukewarm in religion, or so heavily influenced by his wife as to consider conversion to the Church of Rome? Did they, for that matter, genuinely consider for one moment that his relations with Spain were anything but opportunist, or that he had actively encouraged the Irish rising in 1641? And did they not appreciate, above all, that government by the king was no more expensive than government without him? For when John Pym met with a poor response from the City in 1642 in response to Parliament's calls for money, he had already talked of 'compelling' Londoners to lend – a move which resulted at once in the erection of street barricades. Certainly, declared Sir Simonds D'Ewes, 'if the least fear of this should grow, that men should be compelled to lend, all men will conceal their ready money, and lend nothing to us voluntarily'.

Many people, indeed, continued to believe that the only long-term outcome of continuing the quarrel with the king was the harrowing prospect of outright anarchy. The Venetian ambassador, for instance, was acutely aware of general apprehension lest an attenuation of royal authority 'might not augment licence among the people with manifest danger that after shaking off the yoke of monarchy they might afterwards apply themselves to abase the nobility also and reduce the government of this realm to a complete democracy'. Nor was it without significance that Sir John Hotham had explained his reversion to the king's cause after the fighting had started by citing his fear that 'the necessitous people' of the kingdom would rise 'in mighty numbers, and whatsoever they pretend for at first, within a while they will set up for themselves to the utter ruin of all the Nobility and Gentry for the kingdom'. It was this spectre of anarchy, too, as Sir Edmund Waller pointed out, that served as the prime justification for maintaining the episcopacy, which acted as a 'counterscarp, or network, which, if it be taken by this assault of the people … we may, in the next place, have as hard a task to defend our property as we have lately had to defend it from the Prerogative'.

It was not only the king's perspective, therefore, that government of any kind was necessarily oppressive in some degree, and that a well-intentioned ruler was best able to moderate its harshness – as, indeed, an incident of October 1642 had already illustrated all too graphically. For when a lawyer named Fountain had appealed to the Petition of Right upon refusing a 'gift' to Parliament and was told in no uncertain terms by Henry Marten that the Petition was intended to restrain kings rather than Parliament itself, he was subsequently consigned to prison. Yet the broader constitutional implications of the war in progress continued to elude not only most MPs but, more importantly still perhaps, the serried ranks of humbler folk left behind by economic developments and thirsting inevitably for an improvement in their lot. Try as Charles might, therefore, to fortify himself with the morality of his cause and immure himself at Oxford, a reckoning could not be postponed indefinitely – all of which rendered events in Scotland and Ireland absolutely critical.

Even before Charles had raised his standard in August 1642, his worsening relations with Parliament had greatly alarmed the Scots, who sought to protect their Presbyterian Kirk and hopefully avoid further embroilment in war with England – notwithstanding the fact that their soldiers were already occupying the kingdom's most northerly counties and charging Englishmen a grand total of £860 a day for doing so. When Scottish offers of mediation were forthcoming in February 1643, meanwhile, they were curtly brushed aside on the grounds that 'the differences between his majesty and the Houses of Parliament had not the least relation to peace between the two kingdoms'. But regal bravado was no substitute for hard policy, and the ensuing months had demonstrated that the neutrality of Scotland's Presbyterian 'Covenanters' could not be guaranteed in the longer term. Indeed, by 25 September 1643, the Scots had duly signed the Solemn League and Covenant with Parliament, committing MPs, or so the Scots believed, to the establishment of Presbyterianism in England in return for military assistance.

Ten days earlier, however, the news from Ireland had at least appeared to provide consolation of sorts for the king. Under fears of impending invasion by the Long Parliament and Scots, the Irish Catholic gentry had already attempted to seize control of the English administration in October 1641. Yet Charles had continued to harbour hopes that the Irish rebels might supply much-needed military support for the Royalist cause, and a truce was accordingly agreed on 10 September – albeit much to the chagrin of his main agent in Ireland, the Marquis of Ormonde, who fully appreciated the damage that an accommodation with Catholic rebels would wreak upon the king's reputation at home. For while Parliament's alliance with the Scots, as Charles fully appreciated, was likely to founder upon mutual recrimination and distrust, the Presbyterian Scots were neither so feared nor distrusted as their Catholic Irish counterparts. Nor, for that matter, were they nearly so valueless in practical terms, since Parliament controlled the navy and hence the seas by which any Irish aid would have to arrive. If Charles believed, therefore, that God would truly punish the 'undutiful thoughts' of 'our most malicious enemies' who had chosen to lie down with Scottish invaders, he would prove sorely mistaken.

Ultimately, it would take four years of fighting and the destruction of some 300,000 persons – or around 6 per cent of the English population – before this painful truth sank home. But by the time of his return to Oxford from a second season's campaigning on 23 November 1644, the king's military options, along with his army, which was at that point less than 10,000 strong, were already contracting steadily. There had, it is true, been notable victories earlier that year – not least of all at Cropredy Bridge and Lostwithiel, where Charles had exercised personal command – but Marston Moor had seriously dented Royalist hopes. When he returned to a dank and cheerless Oxford that winter, with the leaves falling from the trees and the mists rising from the meadows, the contrast with the triumphant scene two years earlier could hardly have been starker. By now the Court had shrunk, the courtiers' gossip was more muted and the students had departed. Merton College, too, was quiet once more, and no one trod the private way from the queen's lodging to Charles' own. For his wife was now in Paris – the guest of her sister-in-law, who had become Queen Regent during the minority of the 6-year-old Louis XIV – and once more preoccupied with fundraising for her husband after another decline in her health earlier in the year when she had suffered breathless panic attacks, described as 'fits of the mother', and 'a violent consumptive cough', which left Charles pleading abjectly with his physician. 'Mayerne,' he had implored, 'if you love me, go to my wife.'

Yet for all his woes, the king remained resolute. At the beginning of 1645, his old friend Archbishop Laud had finally experienced the fleeting hospitality of the gallows after a trial lasting some ten months, during which his accusers had casually wandered in and out of court, rarely caring to devote their afternoons to hearing the elderly prisoner's case as he laboured in vain to save himself under the blast of William Prynne's hateful invective. But Laud's fate had, if anything, only reinforced the king's determination to fight on, and the Uxbridge peace proposals presented by Parliament thereafter were met with every appearance of steely single-mindedness. He had been asked both to accept the establishment of Presbyterianism and to subscribe to the Covenant itself, and when Parliament's commissioners read out the list of Royalists to be excluded from pardon, the names had included both Prince Rupert and his brother Maurice. But the king's unyielding response was bold enough, it seems, to banish once and for all any residing doubts about his obduracy in defeat. 'There are three things I will not part with,' he declared decisively, 'the Church, my crown and my friends; and you will have much ado to get them from me.'

Nor, on this occasion at least, did his stridency spring merely from wounded pride. For while Parliament continued its plans for remodelling its army, the first fruits of which appeared in the New Model Ordnance of January 1645, the Catholic Irish appeared at last to be primed for action. Until now, Charles' foreign contacts had been failing one by one. His uncle, the King of Denmark, had remained inactive, and the French in their turn made no response to the importuning of his wife. In the meantime, the Prince of Wales had been offered as husband to the daughter of William III, though the marriage no longer seemed worth the expense. William, indeed, had informed the ubiquitous Henry Jermyn that the best course for his king would be to make peace with his subjects at any price. But now Charles was deep in intrigue with the Catholic Earl of Glamorgan to offer the Irish a mitigation of the recusancy laws – to be followed later by their total repeal – in return for 10,000 troops, who would land in North Wales, and a further 10,000, who were to be joined in South Wales by loyal Welshmen. At the same time, French soldiers, endorsed by the Pope, were to land in England's eastern counties.

That Glamorgan would ultimately disobey Charles' orders and lay down terms with the Irish rebels independently of the Marquis of Ormonde's own negotiations would prove a costly error. But the further victories of the Earl of Montrose in Scotland bolstered the king, and by 11 May, he had managed to avoid the troops of Oliver Cromwell, who were harrying the country around Oxford, in order to meet with a Council of War at Stow at the head of 11,000 men. The resulting plan was for General George Goring to march westward to confront Sir Thomas Fairfax, while Charles and Rupert would head north – at a leisurely enough pace, it seems, for young Richard Symonds, a trooper in Charles' lifeguard, to record the journey for posterity. Like so many of his generation, a member of a divided family after his brother had enlisted with Parliament, Symonds duly proceeded to fill his notebooks with picturesque details of the countryside through which the Royalist army now passed. The black earth which people cut into the earth above Uttoxeter, curiously wrought alabaster statues in a local church, 'a flowery cross', 'a private sweet village' still untouched by the ravages of war: all were carefully and innocently documented.

But the harmless jottings of a Royalist trooper enjoying the early stirrings of summer belied the much more ominous truth. For on 7 June, Charles learned that his opponents, like him, were heading for a fateful engagement at Naseby, where 14,000 Parliamentarians would face a Royalist force barely half that size – with all too predictable consequences. Seized by the kind of lethargic belief that all was well, or would ultimately become so, which sometimes overcame him in times of stress, Charles duly reviewed his men from one of the serrated edges of higher ground, separated by broken land of furze and scrub, which would prove the scene of carnage. His army, we are told, was a splendid sight: the regiments in the colours of their individual commanders, banners fluttering, horses groomed to a peak of perfection. As Charles drew his sword and paraded before them in full armour in the early morning sunlight of 14 June, swollen with pride and a very picture of martial prowess, he showed no inkling of the prospect before him – duly taking his place at the front of the reserve of horse and foot stationed immediately behind Sir Jacob Astley's infantry. For across the field of battle lay Oliver Cromwell, his nemesis, who, upon seeing the enemy army, uttered involuntary words of admiration at its grandeur.

Before the day was done, however, this same admirer had become the Lord's chosen instrument of destruction, for that evening 1,000

Royalist soldiers lay dead and 5,000 captive, including 500 officers. Covering an area of 4 square miles, the corpses lay thickest upon the little hill where Charles himself had commanded. The royal standard was taken, along with the queen's colours and the Duke of York's, and the banners of every regiment of Charles' infantry, which had suddenly ceased to exist as a fighting force, were with the enemy. To compound the disaster, the king's artillery train, powder, arms, baggage and wagons – including his own coach, in which he kept copies of his correspondence and private papers – had also fallen to the enemy. In consequence, some thirty-five letters, including one to the Duke of Buckingham about his wife's 'Monsieurs' and many of personal endearment to her, were now in the hands of his enemies and ready for publication. Even more disastrously, the same letters also revealed the plans for military assistance that Charles had been discussing with his wife: the intended landing of French troops at Selsey or thereabouts; the planned rising in Wales to coincide with the arrival of Irish troops; the schemes of the Earl of Glamorgan; the royal offer to suspend, and ultimately repeal, the penal laws against Catholics.

Yet despite the calamitous outcome of Charles' 'battle of all for all', still he refused to countenance any talk of peace – even from his most trusted counsellors. 'There is such a universal weariness of the war,' wrote Lord George Digby to Henry Jermyn in Paris in the aftermath of Naseby, that 'I do not know four persons living … that have not already given clear demonstrations that they will purchase their own and, as they flatter themselves, the kingdom's quiet at any price to the king.' Even so staunch a proponent of war to the limit as Prince Rupert was now advising his uncle to swallow the bitterest pill of all. 'His Majesty hath no way left to preserve his posterity, kingdom and nobility but by a treaty,' wrote Rupert from Bristol, which he was now holding against heavy odds for the dwindling Royalist cause. 'I believe it a more prudent way to retain something than to lose all,' he urged his uncle. But, as the king retreated to Raglan Castle during July to recover from his disappointments, in the company of the Marquis of Worcester – playing bowls, attending church and enjoying conversations about poetry – he remained both adamant and blind. 'I have such good hope of my Welsh levies,' he wrote, 'that I doubt not (by the grace of God) to be in the head of a greater Army within this two month than I have seen this year.' Though Rupert had also made clear that the king's further hopes for an alliance between Montrose and the Covenanters against Parliament were utterly hollow, Charles' mind remained closed. 'Speaking as a mere soldier or statesman,' he replied, 'I must say that there is no probability but of my ruin; yet as a Christian, I must tell you that God will not suffer rebels or traitors to prosper.' Therefore, he urged, 'I earnestly desire you no way to hanker after treaties', and proceeded to stake all upon the relief of Bristol.

The surrender of England's second city to Sir Thomas Fairfax's besieging army was not, however, long in coming. Outnumbered seven to one, with Fort Prior, a key bastion, lost and its garrison massacred, Prince Rupert duly accepted favourable terms from his opponents on 10 September, and in doing so shattered his uncle's congenial optimism at a stroke. He had promised to hold at any cost, only to commit what the king would construe as the ultimate act of treachery. Indeed, for three days after what he termed the 'monstrous intelligence' of Bristol's fall, Charles could do nothing but turn in upon himself to try to explain his most trusted general's 'strange and inexcusable behaviour'. The news of Bristol's loss, he wrote, 'hath given me more grief than any misfortune since this damnable Rebellion', and the fact that the deed had been done by the prince 'who is so near to me in both blood and friendship' rendered the blow all the more grievous. When Rupert's father, the Elector Palatine Frederick, died suddenly at the age of 36 in 1632, Charles had promised that he would 'now occupy the place of the deceased' and went on faithfully to send his sister money for the upbringing of her family. By the time that Rupert had eventually matured into a master military tactician and administrator, moreover, the king's reliance on him was unmatched. 'I must observe,' Charles told him in 1644, 'that the chief hope of my resource is, under God, from you.'

But now, in the words of the Cavalier Henry Varney, Charles had been left 'in a most low and despicable condition', and his orders that Rupert should at once resign his commission reflected his desolation. 'Tell my son,' he declared to his secretary Sir Edward Nicholas, who was on his way to Oxford to arrest Rupert's friend Sir William Legge for alleged treason, 'that I shall less grieve to hear that he is knocked on the head than that he should do so mean an action as is the rendering of Bristol castle and fort upon the terms it was.' In the wake of Naseby, furthermore, there had been other crushing reverses – defeat at Langport, the surrender of Leicester, the mutiny at Newark, the rout at Philiphaugh, the loss of the Highlands – and in the process Charles had been stretched to the limit of both his physical and psychological resources.

The king, after all, had now been on the move, almost incessantly, for six months, either on horseback or on foot, covering more than 1,200 miles of difficult country in long marches, sometimes from dawn until midnight, whose rigour can be judged from his men's descriptions: 'a cruel day', 'a long march over the mountains', 'dinner in the field', 'no dinner'. His longest stay in one place was for eighteen days at Newark, where he had witnessed the court martial of Prince Rupert – who was unanimously deemed 'not guilty of any the least want of courage and fidelity' – and found himself entangled in an ugly scene involving the prince's close friend, Sir Richard Willis, and some thirty Cavaliers who burst in upon him at supper and refused to leave when ordered. In the Welsh mountains, meanwhile, where for long stretches, as Trooper Symonds recorded, the soldiers 'saw never a house or church' and 10 miles felt like 20, Charles was even obliged on one occasion to share his cheese with fellow-travellers at a local inn. Far worse still, at Rowton Heath on 24 September, he had watched from the city walls as the leader of his Lifeguard, young Bernard Stuart, whom he had recently created Lord Lichfield, sallied forth to be slain amid fearful carnage. The king, wrote one admirer, 'was very fearless in his person', and his physical strength and fitness had so far stood him in great stead, for he was never ill 'throughout all the fatigues of the war'. But Oxford now had finally become his only recourse and refuge – and a temporary one at that. For when Charles finally decided to head back to his war-weary Royalist 'capital', Parliament's forces were already mopping up any remaining fragments of resistance in the West and Midlands.

To escape detection, a small party therefore left Newark at 10 p.m. on 3 November, reaching Belvoir at 3 a.m. on the 4th and pushing on throughout the day. By then, the king was so weary that he was compelled to sleep for the space of four hours in the village of Codsbury, a few miles north of Northampton, though at 10 p.m. he and a handful of close associates renewed their journey and before daybreak were past Daventry, reaching Banbury shortly before noon on 5 November, at which point a party of horse from Oxford escorted them to the city. It was nearly a year since the king's last return, and this time there were no victories of any kind to cheer him. Indeed, the city was now greyer, sadder and more still than ever. There remained, it is true, around 2,000 dragoons in the city, according to Parliament's own estimates, and the king was in no immediate danger. But the force at Charles' disposal remained nothing more than a broken remnant. 'There were yet some garrisons,' as the Earl of Clarendon observed, 'which remained in his obedience, and which were like, during the winter season, to be preserved from any attempt of the enemy.' They lay in the South-West, Wales, the West Midlands and in particular Worcester. 'But,' Clarendon reflected ominously, 'upon the approach of the spring, if the King should be without an army in the field, the fate of those few places was easy to be discerned.'

Almost every messenger, in fact, who somehow managed to slip through the enemy lines into Oxford brought further bad tidings. The Cornish militia would not leave their county, and as a result Prince Charles had arrested their leader, Sir Richard Grenville, for insubordination. Goring, meanwhile, had failed to take Plymouth and was constantly drunk. Even loyal Wales, for that matter, was denuded of recruits, and Archbishop Williams could not hold Conway castle much longer. Carmarthen, Chepstow and Monmouth had all fallen, while Beeston castle – down to its last slice of turkey pie and uneaten peacock – was finally starved into submission. From the West Country, Buckinghamshire and Bedfordshire came news of further 'troubles and dangers of these times', as so-called 'Clubmen', who wanted both sides to leave them alone to live their lives as best they could, became an emerging force. 'If you offer to plunder or take our cattle,' threatened one of their banners, 'be assured we will give you battle.'

In the event, the last gasp of the Royalist cause was to be rendered in hand-to-hand fighting in the streets of Stow-on-the-Wold on 21 March 1646, as 67-year-old Sir Jacob Astley staged a characteristically bold last stand for a hopelessly lost cause. Intercepted by Roundhead troops on his way to Oxford at the head of a ragbag force, Astley drew up the last Royalist army to deploy in battle array on a hill to the north-west of Stow, straddling the modern-day A424 highway, at around 6 a.m. But though the king's men 'stood stoutly to it' and initially repulsed the enemy's infantry, an attack by Colonel Thomas Morgan's 400 horse and 200 firelocks proved decisive. Falling back on the nearby town in a fighting retreat, Astley's men had nevertheless been 'totally routed' and cut down by opposing cavalry before the battered remnant was hopelessly surrounded in the marketplace. Ultimately, the battle had cost the Royalists about 100 dead, with sixty-seven officers and 1,630 men taken prisoner.

'His Majesty hath no army at all,' wrote Sir Edward Nicholas in the aftermath. Hereafter, it seems, the king himself recognised as much. 'Our condition,' he told the Marquis of Ormonde on 26 March, 'is now very low and sad … by the defeat given to the Lord Astley and the forces he was to bring from Worcester to join with such as we have in these parts, so as we have no face of an army left.' Accordingly, just over one month later, on May Day 1646, the all-conquering cavalry of the New Model Army was sighted in the hills east of Oxford, ready to begin the final conclusive siege. With typical bravado, Prince Rupert, in the company of nearly 100 cavalrymen, had nevertheless chosen 'to take the air' outside the city and was wounded in the right shoulder for his trouble, though the shot, we are told, 'pierced no bone'. Not long afterwards, the first warning cannon shot of the besiegers fell harm-lessly in Christ Church meadow as Sir Thomas Glemham prepared a typically heroic last stand on his absent master's behalf.

For by that time, of course, the king was already long departed and gone forever – to the Scots at Newark, to whom he had finally turned after his desperate flight from Oxford on the critical night of 27 April. Faced with the certainty that he had 'neither force enough to resist, nor sufficent to escape to any secure place', and that 'mere necessity' was now his only master, he had eventually staked all on a perilous escape to the Scottish Covenanters as the lesser of evils after his wife had opened talks with their envoy in Paris, and by the spring of 1646 was pursuing a treaty 'with all diligence … very confident it will succeed'. Certainly, the French government favoured such a solution, fearing the power of any newly established English republic just as much as the Scots them-selves, and if desperate times required desperate measures, there had never been a more appropriate juncture to grasp the nettle.

In the meantime, however, Oxford would at least be spared the final sacrifice. For on 18 May, some three weeks after his departure, Charles' Parliamentarian enemies finally intercepted the following note that the king had dispatched to Glemham not long before:

Trusty and well-beloved we greet you well. Being desirous to stop the effusion of blood of our subjects, and yet respecting the faithful services of all in that City of Oxford which hath faithfully served us and hazarded their lives for us, we have thought it good to command you to quit that City, and disband the forces under your charge there, you receiving honourable conditions for you and them.

In effect, it was a long-overdue gesture of realism from a king whose stubborn resistance to harsh realities and unpalatable truths had emptied his enemies of all respect for him. But it heralded too, in its way, the starting point of something altogether more profound: nothing less, in fact, than what was to become by turns a remarkable odyssey of self-discovery involving both a nation and a fallen ruler who had already, though he did not yet appreciate it, lost his liberty forever.

2

FLIGHT TO CAPTIVITY

'From Newcastle by Letters that came this day we are informed that the King is brought thither, neither Drum, nor Trumpet, nor guns, nor Bels, nor shoots of people once heard, but brought in far more like a prisoner.'

Kingdomes Weekly Intelligencer, No. 149, May 1647

In the wake of his defeat at Stow-on-the-Wold, Sir Jacob Astley had accepted the inevitable philosophically. 'Being somewhat wearied from the fight', we are told, he was given a drum to sit upon by his captors, before sharing a wistful observation with them. 'You have done your work, boys, and may go play,' he reflected, 'unless … you should fall out among yourselves.' Though uttered in full knowledge of the final collapse of the cause for which he had fought so tenaciously, the weary old general's proviso was nevertheless both telling and deeply prophetic. For Parliament and its army, not to mention their uneasy Scottish allies, would soon be painfully at odds, as would Presbyterians and so-called 'Independents' within the opposition ranks. It was this, above all else, upon which King Charles himself was counting as he headed into the night from Oxford in the company of Dr Michael Hudson and Jack Ashburnham in April 1646. Soldiers and civilians, religious independents and sectaries too, mostly of the poorer sections of society who had not received the benefits from the war that they had anticipated, were already becoming daily more restive. Successive years of conflict had increased taxation and disrupted trade, and many who had turned away from the king's Anglicanism were now finding in Parliament's Presbyterianism an equally rigid and intolerant form of ecclesiastical authority. Troops were unpaid, the press muzzled more tightly than ever and, for those who dared demur, there was summary justice – not from the Star Chamber or the High Commission, but from the very parliamentary committees that had replaced them.

Well before the king's flight, in fact, opposition to Parliament had been hardening and increasing numbers of men and women were responding to the calls for liberty from men like John Lilburne. On 7 January 1645, Lilburne had addressed a letter to William Prynne attacking the intolerance of the Presbyterians and claiming freedom of conscience and freedom of speech for the Independents, who balked at any form of state religious control. In October, moreover, Lilburne published from a secret press *England's Birthright Justified*, in which he continued not only to defend religious liberty but the more general 'freeborn rights' of every human being. True to these same principles, Lilburne had already refused in April to swear to the Solemn League and Covenant, on the grounds that those who were forced to do so, and in particular those dissenting members of the Parliamentary army, were being deprived of their freedom of conscience. It was not long either before 'Freeborn John' and some of the leading Independent leaders were indicating that, in return for religious toleration, they might be prepared, with the support of the army, to yield a greater control of government to the king than any terms yet proposed by his other opponents.

But on the eve of his escape from Oxford, Charles was still as yet unprepared to sup with this particular devil, and had already chosen on 5 December to request safe conducts from Parliament for the Duke of Richmond, the Earl of Southampton, Jack Ashburnham and Jeffrey Palmer, so that peace talks might be initiated at Westminster. Even so, by mid-January, MPs had rejected not only this but four other similar communiqués, and convinced Charles in the process that 'nothing will satisfy them but the ruin, not only of us, our Posterity, and friends, but even the monarchy itself'. In the words of one contemporary, he had offered terms 'as low as he can go with preserving of his conscience and honour', and in an attempt to sway public opinion, he had also published *A Collection of His Majesties Most Generous Messages for Peace*. Yet well-grounded fears that he was playing his favoured game of divide and rule left his enemies wholly unconvinced of his intentions. 'Cajole the Independents and Scots,' he secretly advised the Duke of Richmond, and had expressed similar feelings to his wife. 'Knowing assuredly the great animosity which is between the Independents and Presbyterians,' he informed Henrietta Maria on 18 January 1646, 'I have great reason to hope that one of the factions would so address themselves to me that I might without great difficulty obtain my just ends.' As a result, his last-ditch attempts to stir up fears that Presbyterian MPs would stamp out all radical sects as readily as they would Anglicans continued to fall on deaf ears, as did his other overtures to the enemy army. For they too remained reluctant at present to accept that the man whose intransigence had spawned four long years of gruelling blood-shed could be trusted to offer any better alternative to their faltering parliamentary paymasters.

Nor was the Irish option by now of serious interest to the king. The publication after Naseby of his letters to Dublin offering peace to the rebels 'whatever it cost' had provoked widespread outrage and unset-tled even his own supporters like George Digby, who admitted that the treaty engineered by the Earl of Glamorgan had alienated all good Protestants, since it lent credence to claims 'that all along the king had instigated the Irish rebellions, had the blood of thousands of innocent settlers on his hands, and was himself a secret papist'. That Charles had signed other letters to the Pope on the same issue as 'your very humble and obedient servant' had hardly helped his case. But it was rather the anger of a spurned suitor than guilt at what most perceived as outright treachery that seems ultimately to have terminated the king's court-ship of his would-be Irish rescuers. The tempting prospect of vigorous Irish support had been consumed by endless delay and inaction, and the king would no longer countenance such shabby treatment. 'I am as little obliged to the Irish,' he confided to his wife, 'as I can be to any nation, for all this last year they have only fed me with vain hopes, looking upon my daily ruin.'

Much to the queen's satisfaction, then, her husband was left with little option other than to lie down with the Scots. Appropriately enough, the French ambassador, Jean de Montreuil, had arrived in Oxford in the New Year of 1646 to oil the necessary wheels. Henrietta Maria's entreaties, as well as the possibility that a Parliamentary victory might free the New Model Army to intervene on the Continent, had prompted France's intercession. But Montreuil's hopes that the king's predicament would result in the swift conclusion of all business found-ered at their very first meeting on 2 January, when Charles declared that while he would tolerate Presbyterianism, he could never accept it as a satisfactory model for the established church. For, as the ambassador informed Cardinal Mazarin in Paris, the king would 'rather lose his crown than his soul'. When Montreuil had pressed forward with 'many arguments' that without a Presbyterian settlement 'nothing could be done in order to an agreement with the Scots', Charles remained bound to 'his conscience'.

Not even the queen's desperate letters, it seemed, could move him. Imagine if their positions were reversed, he pleaded, 'wouldst thou give ear to him who should persuade thee, for worldly respects, to leave the communion of the Roman church for any other? Indeed, sweetheart, this is my case.' 'For God's sake,' he went on ' ... consider, that if I should quit my conscience, how unworthy I make myself of thy love.' And such was his perplexity that he was even prepared on this occasion to lecture his wife – with an awkward lack of forethought and finesse that demonstrated his apparent turmoil. Calvinism, he told her, was no better than papism, and designed 'to steal or force the crown from the king's head' – a tactless conflation of Rome with Geneva, which naturally provoked a quarrel in its own right, and the following anguished response from Charles. 'I am blamed for granting too much and not yielding enough,' he remonstrated, 'but I plead not guilty to both.'

Yet even the hard rock of a king's conscience might ultimately prove susceptible, as events would now demonstrate, to the delicate manipulation of a diplomat's exquisite touch. For by means of the slightest hint of concession on Charles' part, qualified by a glaring loophole and condition, Montreuil was nevertheless able to push forward. Faced by the utter obduracy of Parliament and what he perceived as a growing wish on behalf of some MPs to eradicate both him and his family, Charles was therefore finally persuaded to write to the Scottish commissioners in London requesting assurances that, in the event of his seeking the protection of their army, 'we shall be secure both in conscience and honour'. In return for what he fondly believed would be a safe haven, he duly promised 'as soon as I come into the Scots army' to be 'very willing to be instructed in the presbyterial government'. However, in this, of course, resided both the short-term breakthrough and long-term sticking point, since 'instruction' and conversion were plainly different things, as the king made clear when he concluded predictably that he would strive to content his hosts 'in anything that shall not be against my conscience'.

Superficially, at least, it was a potential masterstroke on Montreuil's behalf in reconciling square pegs with round holes and conjuring the semblance of progress from utter deadlock. It was on 1 April, appropriately enough, that the Scots proffered an equally vague response via the ambassador that they would receive Charles 'as their natural sovereign' and assist 'in recovery of his Majesty's just rights' and 'in the procuring of a happy and well grounded peace'. But while Royalists, as Clarendon observed, were heartened at the 'excellent news', their optimism was entirely premature, since the issue of religion remained as intractable as ever. 'As for the church business,' Charles informed the Marquis of Ormonde, 'I hope to manage it so as not to give them distaste, and yet do nothing against my conscience.' At the same time, he would attempt to render the Scots and Parliament 'irreconcilable enemies' and thereby forge an equally unlikely alliance of Covenanters, Ulstermen and Highlanders to pluck 'an honourable and speedy peace' from a position of utter military defeat. The thorny issues of 'the militia, Ireland and my friends', meanwhile, were to be conveniently shelved until some later unspecified date.

It was duplicity and self-deception on a grand scale, and presaged precisely the kind of wholesale disillusionment that swiftly followed. Though he acknowledged that there was still no formal peace treaty with the Scots, he had nevertheless 'resolved by the grace of God to begin my journey thither upon Monday or Tuesday next', he informed his wife on Thursday, 2 April. Yet eleven days later he was still in Oxford, 'ready to go at an hour's warning', and growing increasingly frustrated. He had 'not heard one word from Montreuil since he went', Charles complained to Henrietta Maria, and thereafter – 'closed upon all sides' by Parliamentarian armies making escape more difficult than ever – he became 'much troubled' not to be 'parted hence'. One week later, moreover, his perplexity had become overwhelming. Acknowledging by this stage that he was 'in very great straits', he duly admitted to Montreuil on 19 April that, with the barest encouragement from the Scots, 'I have resolved to run any risk to go to them'.

Nonetheless, there would be seven further days before Charles at last received the Scots' reply, and its content proved even more galling than the tardiness of its arrival. 'The Scots,' Charles declared to his wife on reading their response, 'are abominable relapsed rogues, for Montreuil himself is ashamed of them, they having retracted almost everything which they made him promise me.' Their army, on the one hand, now refused to recognise the agreement made with their commissioners in London, and any intent to fight on the king's behalf appeared to have evaporated without trace. Furthermore, Charles would only be permitted to join the Scottish army at all if he pretended to arrive without prior arrangement, for fear of offending the English Parliament. Most reprehensibly of all, he must establish Presbyterianism in England 'as promptly as possible'.

Such, then, was the offer of the 'perfidious covenanters', which left Charles, as he openly confessed to Henrietta Maria, 'much worse than ever' and hopelessly perplexed at 'the difficulty of resolving what to do'. Like a man on the brink, he sent Sir Thomas Fairfax a vague offer the very next day suggesting that he would accept whatever conditions Parliament might offer, in return for his life and continued acceptance as king. But its prompt rejection was a foregone conclusion and the ultimate proof that his only recourse was escape from Oxford, perhaps to King's Lynn on the Norfolk coast, where he might take ship and thereby somehow muster sufficient forces 'to procure honourable and safe conditions from the rebels'. In Scotland, meanwhile, the Earl of Montrose was attempting to raise a new army for him, and if Montrose was not ready, Charles was also prepared as a final resort to seek shelter abroad, though he considered it unbecoming 'to quit his party that way' and was 'not yet resolved' in any case whether Ireland, France or Denmark was his best option.

The dithering, it seems, continued uninterrupted as the king laid smokescreens, telling his Council of War that he was making for London, and sent Lords Lindsey and Southampton to Colonel Rainsborough to discuss surrender terms. Certainly, as midnight approached on Sunday, 26 April, and Charles went secretly to the apartments of John Ashburnham to make good his departure, his direction of flight appears to have remained a matter of conjecture. Ironically, the camp of the Scottish Covenanters at Newark was still in his view no more than an abject last resort, and in the warmth and comfort of Ashburnham's chamber, he had not yet entirely discounted a bold descent upon London, where he might negotiate with Parliament in person. Though shorn of his flowing locks and disguised as Ashburnham's Roundhead serving man beneath a woollen soldier's cap with flaps around the ears and a hat on top, he remained, after all, King of England and under God's protection and guidance. In Ashburnham, moreover, he had beside him, in Montreuil's words, 'the person in whom the King of

Great Britain has now the greatest confidence', and in Dr Michael Hudson the services of a man who 'told him his mind when others would not'.

So as Sir Thomas Glemham bade 'Farewell Harry' to his sovereign master at the city's East Gate in the small hours of 27 April, and ordered that no further persons be allowed to 'pass in or out of Oxford for five days', the king's direction was initially south-east – under the guidance, appropriately enough, of Hudson, who had served until 1644 as scout-master to the army under the Marquis of Newcastle, in charge of reconnaissance and intelligence-gathering. Well known as 'a very skilful guide', he is said to have 'understood the by-ways as well as the common', which made him indispensable for the secret journey to come. But it was not only Hudson's knowledge of the land or even his 'plain dealing' and well-known want of reserve that on this occasion made his presence so important. For the journey ahead was as hazardous as it was arduous, and the chaplain's loyalty and courage were impeccable. A former tutor to the king, he had joined the Royalist cause at once upon the outbreak of war, and renewed his acquaintance with his erstwhile pupil at Oxford in the wake of the Battle of Edgehill. By the time that Charles had arranged a Doctorate in Divinity for him at some point during the winter of 1642/43, moreover, he had already lost the entirety of his estates, leaving his widow – whom he had married as Miss Pollard of Newnham Courtney, Oxfordshire, around 1630 – to eke out a meagre existence for herself and her family upon charity.

Henceforth, in fact, Hudson's life would become an almost uninterrupted exercise in self-sacrifice on his master's behalf, as arrests, interrogations, escape attempts, madcap projects to rescue the Royalist cause and feats of heroism followed one upon another. In June 1646, imprisonment at London House awaited him after his arrest at Sandwich en route to France, and later that month he would be examined by a parliamentary committee about his wanderings with the king, only to escape on 18 November and thereafter convey letters from Charles to Major-General Laugharne in Wales. By that time notorious in parliamentary circles, he would be captured again in the following January – on this occasion at Hull – and imprisoned in the Tower of London, where he employed himself chiefly in writing and in devising an unsuccessful scheme to deliver the Tower into Royalist hands.

Ultimately, however, it would be the ending of his life that eventually established Hudson's true credentials as a largely unsung hero of the Civil War. Escaping once more in early 1648 – this time in disguise with a basket of apples on his head – and returning to Lincolnshire, he would proceed to raise a party of Royalist horse, in order to rouse the gentry of Norfolk and Suffolk on the king's behalf. With the main body of those who had taken arms under his command, Hudson then retired to Woodcroft House, Northamptonshire, a strong building surrounded by a moat, where he and his followers were attacked on 6 June 1648 by a contingent of enemy soldiers. By then bearing a commission as a colonel, he is said to have defended the house with exceptional courage until the doors were finally forced, and to have staged a fighting retreat to the battlements – yielding only on a promise of quarter, which was subsequently rescinded. Finally flung over the battlements in retribution, Hudson nevertheless managed to support himself upon a spout or projecting stone until his hands were cut off and he fell into the moat beneath. Whereupon, in reply to his request that he be allowed to die like a man on land, a Roundhead trooper named Egborough killed him with a musket blow to the head before another cut out his tongue and carried it about as a trophy, leaving the body to be buried at Denton, Northamptonshire.

This, then, was no ordinary chaplain, and his uncommon valour could not have equipped him more admirably for the journey into the unknown from Oxford that he now made at his sovereign's side. For, as events soon demonstrated, the king was fleeing from his problems rather than following any coherent plan for their solution, and swiftly descended into passivity and indecision once the journey was underway. It was Hudson, therefore, who first determined upon a curious route in the direction of London – passing through Marsh Baldon, Dorchester, Benson, Henley and Nettlebed – with a view to confusing prospective pursuers. Though the secrecy of the king's departure was such that no pursuit eventually took place, his passage through enemy territory was soon resulting in various close encounters with the enemy. If challenged, it had been agreed that the party was to employ a pass bearing Fairfax's signature, which had been obtained from a Parliamentarian soldier on leave for the capital. By 10 a.m. that day, when all three finally reached Hillingdon, the considerable risk involved in the entire enterprise was already apparent. In one village there had been a guard of Parliamentarian dragoons, which, Hudson recorded, the group was lucky enough to avoid 'without any difficulty or examination'. A few miles further on, however, they were met by Roundhead cavalrymen who, upon noticing that Hudson and Ashburnham wore pistols in their belts, 'asked us to whom we belonged', to which the king himself 'answered "to the House of Commons" and so passed'. This was still merely the beginning, for at Henley-on-Thames they were stopped once more before managing to proceed 'without any question' after 'showing the pass to the corporal and giving 12*d.* to the guards'.

Stopping finally at Hillingdon, some 20 miles from London, in order, as Hudson put it, 'to refresh ourselves', the fugitives then found themselves in a crisis of another kind, generated not only by fatigue but by the onset of a further wave of indecision on the king's behalf. They had not slept all night, and for three hours or so made no move while Charles, 'much perplexed', appears to have agonised once more over 'what course to resolve upon – London or northward?' There were those of the opinion, after all, that Parliament would show 'much more moderation' if he was directly present rather than at a distance, since MPs themselves continued to fear that his arrival in the capital might well 'arouse the respect and affection of the people'. In light of this, might the king not be able to slip into London incognito and emerge from hiding, at an appropriate time, to lead the growing number of citizens who resented Parliament's exactions and feared the army's rising power? Had not the Lord Mayor himself, for that matter, escorted him into the city in person in November 1642, and might not history yet repeat itself in such distracted times? For a man like Charles – desolate, desperate and deluded – any crumb of hope was apt, it seems, to be snatched and savoured at this critical juncture.

But time was pressing, the net closing, his companions increasingly restless and his contacts within the capital plainly unresponsive, so that by afternoon Charles was on his way again, turning northwards in a wide arc through Harrow and St Albans to Wheathampstead, where he spent the night. His thoughts as he turned back to look upon London from Harrow's high hill can only be imagined. During the previous decade, it had been the scene of so much personal happiness, only to descend by turns into a seemingly bottomless cockpit of dissent, treachery and rebellion. It was the prize, too, that he had never been able to regain over four long years of bloody slaughter, and, above all, the financial stronghold that had resisted and then broken his faltering cause. Not altogether surprisingly, Charles would stubbornly refuse to discuss his thoughts at this time when later offered the opportunity by his confidants. In all likelihood, the memory of the fear and uncertainty, not to mention the crushed hopes and strains of flight, were simply too painful to revisit. But for the present – and whatever the risks – he was making for King's Lynn, a town he had never visited and 'where he was least known'. There he could wait upon events – in the reassuring knowledge that a boat for the Continent could safely be had – while Hudson sallied forth intrepidly to parley with the Scots in Nottinghamshire.

In the meantime, however, the danger for the king and his associates remained ever-present, for only a mile beyond St Albans, an old man armed with a halberd demanded to know the travellers' identity. Though the response 'From Parliament', coupled to a sixpenny tip, seemed to placate the interrogator, it was not long, Hudson tells us, before two horsemen came 'galloping after us very fast'. Once more, as it transpired, the threat was groundless, since the riders were none other than a gentleman – 'very drunk' and thirsting now for merry conversation – and his servant. Yet there were still more than 90 miles between the king and his hoped-for destination, and by the time that he was slipping past Cambridge by night, through ill-kept Fenland back roads, news of his escape was out. By the time that Charles arrived at Downham Market – where Hudson had family connections – on 30 April, therefore, the pressure was mounting incrementally, though there remained no other choice than to wait for all of four days at the Swan Inn while Hudson sought news from the Scots. In doing so, the king caused further suspicion, first by asking for a fire in his room – despite the comparatively warm springtime weather – with the intention of burning his papers, and subsequently by requesting that the town barber mend as best he could the damage done to his hair by Ashburnham's unskilled hands back at Oxford.

Hudson's eventual return could not, therefore, have been more timely, though the news he bore was once more altogether less heartening than Charles had been depending upon. For while the Scots offered vaguely 'to secure the king in his person and in his honour' and press him 'to do nothing contrary to his conscience', their commitment was palpably less than wholehearted. In the first place, they would put nothing in writing and their 'offer' had in any case not been delivered to Hudson face-to-face, but by Montreuil acting as intermediary. As such, the ambassador's further assurance that the Scots would apparently 'declare for the King', if Parliament refused to restore him, 'and take all the King's friends into their protection' remained uncomfortably frail. All hinged, after all, on what amounted to a string of Chinese whispers derived solely from a paper drawn up by the French ambassador and the ambassador's reading of Scottish intentions. There were no firm grounds either for explaining why the Scots should be any less concerned about offending Parliament now than they had been earlier. Indeed, if Hudson himself had not been won over so wholly by Montreuil at their meeting, there is every reason to believe that Charles might well have been persuaded by Ashburnham's alternative suggestion that he set out by sea in search of some much-needed temporary respite.

But with Downham Market's citizens already murmuring in corners and the king 'destitute of any other refuge' after Hudson had made unsuccessful enquiries 'for a ship to the north', there remained no option. As early as 11 May, Miles Corbet, MP for Great Yarmouth, and Colonel Valentine Walton of Great Staughton in Huntingtonshire – both of whom would later sign the king's death warrant – were in a position to report the fugitives' movements to the Speaker of the House of Commons, William Lenthall. 'Wherever they came, they were very private, and always writing', it was noted, and there was further mention not only of Hudson's vain quest for a ship, but that the king had acquired a new hat into the bargain from one of Hudson's friends. Under such circumstances, even Charles had been unable to hesitate further. Against his better judgement, he would deliver himself after all to those who 'first began my troubles' and join the Scottish Covenanters. In the meantime, he would smother his suspicions, as always, with that familiar coating of naive optimism that served so often as a substitute for hard policy when alternatives vanished. Perhaps despite all, he reflected, 'my rendering my person to them may engage their affections to me, who have oft professed "They fought not against me, but for me"'.

For the moment, however, Charles could at least distract himself further by making his journey north as pleasant as possible. Next morning, now disguised as a clergyman in 'a black coat and long cassock', and assuming the identity of 'the Doctor', he moved from Downham Market to an obscure village alehouse before heading secretly and by night for Little Gidding, a place of special charm for him, still untouched by war and housing the humble Anglican religious community established by Nicholas Ferrar in 1626. Such were its attractions, indeed, that Charles had visited the village, some 30 miles east of Cambridge, on two previous occasions, and en route he now took the opportunity to ride past Hinchingbrooke House at Huntington, scene of many a glorious hunt in former days. Throughout, he continued to traverse the most secret and circuitous routes, looping down through Huntington and the marshes round Ely, crossing the Nen and the Welland to Melton Mowbray, doubling back to Stamford and then heading north-north-west, skirting Grantham, over the Trent to Southwell and on to the house of the French ambassador, where he arrived at 7 a.m. on 5 May. His journey had taken all of ten exhausting days, 'having passed through fourteen guards and garrisons of the enemies' and being obliged at one point to spend the night at Coppingford on an ale house floor in the company of its keeper and his family. But now at last the Scottish camp besieging Newark was in touching distance, less than 8 miles away.

And though his liberty was soon to be surrendered forever, his enemies at least remained implacably divided. For this was truly, as Oliver Cromwell observed, 'a quarrelsome age', and the monarchy still, to all intents and purposes, the only rock upon which stability could ever be re-established. Since the start of the year, further rifts had arisen in London between Independents and Presbyterians over disbandment of the army and the terms for ridding England of the Scots. Only the day before Charles' arrival at Southwell, moreover, William Sancroft, the future Archbishop of Canterbury, had been hoping against hope for the king's appearance in London to cow the 'faction that hath the vogue at Westminster'. Writing to his father in Suffolk in one of his regular newsletters, Sancroft was convinced that the king's presence 'will attract hearts and animate many of the members to appear for him with open face who now mask under a visor, and sigh to see a party they like not carry all before them'. There were certainly high hopes among the London citizenry that the king's restoration might herald a long overdue return to normalcy – a feeling echoed also amongst many Presbyterian MPs, in expectation that the king might yet be persuaded on the need for religious change.

The Scots, meanwhile, were increasingly alienated from Westminster's leadership, though even they were in the throes of internal division as a moderate Royalist party led by the Duke of Hamilton emerged to fill the vacuum left by the defeat of Montrose's ultra-Royalist Highlanders at Philiphaugh the previous September, and subsequently challenge the dominance of the Earl of Argyle and the Kirk and their supporters among the Lowland towns and gentry. As Charles faced his imminent encounter with the leaders of the Scottish army, he knew that they too, therefore, were wholly aware of the potential benefits accruing from his reinstatement. For his deliberate decision to stay and negotiate, rather than flee into exile, had actually made it more difficult to get rid of him, and though there was some desultory talk of deposition, his added precaution of sending Prince Charles overseas rendered such a course largely impractical. No less important in the longer run was the king's sheer obstinacy in attempting to win the peace after losing the war. 'You cannot do without me,' he would maintain doggedly, 'you will fall to ruin if I do not sustain you.'

At the same time, the king's refusal to concede was backed, it seems, by two further considerations: his readiness on the one hand to suffer martyrdom for his principles, and an equal preparedness on the other to behave as disingenuously as circumstance might demand in defence of those self-same principles. 'I have already cast up what I am like to suffer which I shall meet (by the grace of God) with that constancy that befits me,' he would tell Ashburnham and others in July 1646, and throughout the ensuing negotiations with the Scots, he rarely missed an opportunity to remind his protagonists of this fact. As the chess player that he was, Charles therefore convinced himself that he could yet achieve mate from a position of apparently complete inferiority, or at the very least a last-gasp stalemate as his enemies were thwarted by the prospect of an ultimate step they could never countenance. While they dangled hopelessly, or so he believed, on a hook of their own making, he could resort to any immoral means – be it innuendo, subterfuge, provocation or outright falsehood – to achieve his ends, since in dealing with 'damnable' enemies any damnable expedient was ultimately permissible. This, after all, was the ruler who had promised to 'never abandon Ireland', only to persuade himself that because the Irish had forsaken him he could break his word with impunity. A guarantee made to a treacherous enemy, he would tell the Marquis of Ormonde, 'is as a reed, and the more you rely on it, will run into your hand the deeper'.

In the meantime, the king's arrival at Newark would both please and astound the Scots. Soon after his appearance at Southwell, numerous Scottish lords were making their way to the French ambassador's lodging, though they hurried forth laden with disavowals rather than welcome tidings of support. While professing their gladness at his arrival, they not only affirmed that they had no prior knowledge of his coming, but claimed to have heard nothing of any terms agreed with their commissioners in London. As such, they could not honour them. Worse still, before Charles had 'either drunk, refreshed or reposed himself', his Scottish visitors were issuing new demands of their own. Firstly, he must order the surrender of Newark to the English Parliamentary army that was also besieging the town. Secondly, he must command the Earl of Montrose to lay down his arms once and for all. Finally, and most gallingly, he must abandon the most fundamental of his sacred principles by signing the Covenant and imposing Presbyterian practice throughout England and Ireland.

The impact upon Charles of this greeting may well be imagined, and to add to his dismay he found himself lodged that night under strict guard in the Scottish military headquarters. Having forced the question of religion 'so ungraciously', as Montreuil put it in a letter to Cardinal Mazarin, there was now no trace of 'affection or dependence' in the Scots' behaviour. On the one hand, Alexander Leslie, 1st Earl of Leven and commander of the Scottish forces, asked no orders from the king and chose instead to forbid any army officers to see or speak to him. Nor did he make any attempt to discourage the flow of visitors determined to browbeat the king and press him to 'things ... most averse to his conscience and honour'. Such, indeed, was the general level of disrespect that Charles even briefly considered escape to the Parliamentary army on the other side of Newark. But he had no messenger to send, and any remaining doubts that he was indeed a prisoner quickly evaporated when he initially resisted the surrender of the town and was removed at once to Kelham House and summarily forced to comply – 'on very hard terms for those within'.

The document confirming Newark's surrender was signed, in fact, at Colonel Rossiter's headquarters in Balderton at midnight on 6 May, only a little more than twenty-four hours after the king's arrival at Southwell, and though the personal safety of all inhabitants was guaranteed, the town's Royalist governor, Lord Belasyse, wept at its acceptance. Since the siege began on 26 November 1645, Newark had lost one-sixth of its buildings forever and been reduced in the process to 'a miserable stinking place that could spread infection in the adjacent villages and towns'. So severe indeed was the scale of infection, that plague deaths reached a peak during June and July in the wake of the surrender and continued ultimately until the end of the year. Yet both Belasyse and the town's mayor had wished to continue the fight, fully aware that Newark remained a last defiant bastion, and knowing too that their stronghold was still comparatively well provisioned, with a good store of corn, butter and cheese, 'some plenty' of salt meat and many barrels of beer and wine. When, moreover, the Royalist garrison finally vacated the town, they would also leave behind them some 4,000 muskets, carbines and pistols, sixty barrels of gunpowder, a great store of match, ball and ammunition, and no less than twelve cannon, including the infamous 'Sweet Lips', named after a notorious Hull prostitute.

Yet further resistance on the king's part was never an option when the Scots themselves were increasingly fearful of attack from their Parliamentary 'allies' and seeking satisfaction at once. For as soon as the initial panic of the king's flight had abated and his new whereabouts was known, Parliament had lost no time in ordering the Scots to send him to Warwick Castle, and the threat of an outright fracture was already real and present. Under such circumstances, breathing space was essential for Charles' Scottish captors, allowing all options to be pondered at a safe distance from any prospective attacker. Apart from selling him to Parliament for a handsome dividend, there was also the more adventurous possibility that he might be employed at the head of an Anglo-Scottish force to attack or weaken the New Model Army, which had recently dealt the Royalists such heavy defeats and whose successes now made the Scots increasingly uneasy when looking south. In any event, Newcastle was the obvious safe vantage point from which to ruminate upon their options, and the Scots would make their way there within the week, along with a king who in spite of all remained compliant – seeking solace as always in his enemies' divisions and enticed all the while by the promise that a new group of Scottish commissioners would be waiting for him who might honour the conditions arranged by Montreuil.

Any hopes of relief that Charles may have been harbouring were soon quelled, however, upon his arrival in Newcastle at about 5 p.m. on Wednesday, 13 May. Since 1644, when the Covenanters had first joined the war against the king, the town had been under Scottish occupation, while the nearby villages starved under the burden of hungry cavalry regiments treating them, in effect, as so much booty. On Newcastle's high stone walls, therefore, Scottish sentries in baggy blue bonnets and red wool coats now kept grim watch, cursing their current circumstances and wishing, no doubt, for home. For after three years' service in a cause that had long since ceased to compel, they were in 'ragged and naked condition', though, if their clothes betrayed their predicament, their heavy muskets nevertheless stood ready for use. From the leather bandoliers slung over their shoulders dangled powder horns and pouches of shot, while at their sides were swords and dirks, and beneath the crenellated towers from which they peered stood other Scottish troops, Lowlanders to a man, who guarded the gates that were firmly locked each night, since neither man, woman, nor child could enter without an official pass. This was not all, for on the high ground round about stood cannon ready to repel any enemy force – which by this stage could only be Parliamentarian.

When Charles and his associates finally approached their destination, therefore, the whole place was still 'in a condition to resist any army however powerful'. Nor could the solemn procession of which the king formed part have reflected his straitened circumstances more aptly. From Gateshead onwards, in fact, the road was lined – by order of the town's governor, Sir John Lumsden – with musketeers and pikemen, and neither civic dignitaries nor the numerous Scottish lords who had arrived in advance were on hand. Indeed, Charles entered, as one eyewitness described it, 'in a very silent way, without bells ringing, or bagpipes playing or mayor and aldermen'. As the king crossed the Tyne, no cannon fire – 'neither by land, nor by water' – greeted him 'by way of triumph', and the numerous news-sheets of the day, both Scottish and English, were agreed that the general populace was eerily absent. 'There was not any extraordinary concourse of people,' reported *The Weekly Account*, 'neither was there any noise, or sounding of Trumpet.' Instead, as Montreuil reported to Cardinal Mazarin in Paris, 'the Scots not only failed in paying the honours required of them, but they prevented other subjects from rendering those they owed to him'.

All the while, Charles rode in the midst of 300 cavalrymen, with 'his lock cut off and his head rounded', wearing 'a sad-coloured plain suit', as those directly around him, including the Earl of Leven and various other Scottish officers, all 'rid bare'. 'Nor did they,' recorded one observer, 'in any solemne manner take notice of his Majesty.' When a solitary shout pierced the silence after the king had passed under a stone gateway and along an avenue of trees towards the house where he was to reside, the response could not have confirmed the king's predicament more decisively. For the lone cry of encouragement was enough to provoke a proclamation stipulating that none of his adherents were henceforth to have access to him, ensuring in effect that the so-called Anderson House – 'one of the bravest houses in the town' – in which the king now found himself was about to provide him with his first undiluted taste of captivity.

Ironically enough, it was at the gates of this grand Elizabethan manor house, just outside the town walls, that Charles had reviewed his troops in 1639 on their confident northward march to Berwick. But now, though technically entrusted to the mayor's custody, he found himself hemmed in by a guard of musketeers, while 'inhabitants of trust' from the local citizenry were appointed to act as further sentries round about. Outside the mullioned windows, likewise, Leven lost no time in ordering 'that some of the ancient men of the inhabitants of the town should constantly sit at every passage' within the Anderson House 'to examine and take notice what persons came in or out'. Any prior indications that the Scots might proffer support against the king's opponents in London were further quashed when Leven duly issued a proclamation 'by beat of Drum and sound of Trumpet', that 'although His Majesty was come thither, all persons should yield obedience to the ordinances of Parliament'. For only one day after Charles' initial arrival at Newark, the Scots had written to Westminster expressing the hope that 'none will so far misconstrue us' as to believe that it was their wish to exploit the 'seeming advantage' that had fallen their way so for-tuitously. Though, as all realised, the Scots' assurance was hollow, it was equally plain from what transpired that it was Parliament rather than the king that commanded their greatest respect.

Even so, it was clear that Charles would have to be offered some modicum of comfort commensurate with his status in order to make his stay at Anderson House more or less tolerable. Though Parliament had requested the apprehension of those who had assisted the king's escape from Oxford, the Scots also remained keen to assert some inde-pendence, and both Ashburnham and Hudson were actually allowed to make good their escape with minimal difficulty – the former after a visit to Montreuil's house on 16 May, and the chaplain a day later after cursory interrogation by the Deputy Mayor. In their stead, moreover, the king was allowed access to certain 'noble and faithful gentlemen', who though carefully vetted, proved not unworthy of their duties. Lord Lanark, for example, was appointed to act as his secretary, while William Murray and James Harrington, a friend of his sister, attended him as grooms of the bedchamber throughout the greater part of his stay. He was allowed, too, a groom of the privy chamber, named Tobias Peaker, and a page of the back stairs by the name of Levitt, along with a night-time companion in the Earl of Dunfermline, who slept constantly in his bedchamber.

The king's diet, meanwhile, was described as 'princely' and consisted of '15 dishes of English diet every meale'. Nor, it seems, was the prisoner entirely deprived of funds, for a certain Francis Crosse, in his examination of 8 June 1646, estimated the king's expenditure at the amount of £100 per month. At the same time, there was also no shortage of coal for Charles' needs, provided by the town corporation, and he was not only allowed to play golf and chess, but even afforded opportunity for an occasional visit to Tynemouth Castle, though a trip by barge on 21 May in the company of Lords Lothian, Dunfermline and Balmerino would hardly have lifted his spirits, since he was treated once more with barest ceremony – 'the most solemnity of his entertainment' being, we are told, 'three pieces of Ordnance fired at the Castle, and some fired by the Collier ships that rode in the Harbour both as his Majesty went and returned'.

Day trips and wholesome fare could not, in any case, make good the increasing disdain and indignity to which the king was subjected. Far from honouring the arrangement brokered by Montreuil, the Scots merely intensified their pressure, demanding Charles' 'full concession' to the peace terms that Parliament had offered him in their 'nineteen propositions' of 1642, which demanded, among other things, parliamentary control over both church and the militia. In pressing their case, the Scots were wholly prepared to subject the prisoner to what he himself termed 'barbarous usage', even hotly pursuing him on one occasion with demands that he accept the Covenant after he had retired weeping to his bedchamber on or about 15 June. Each day, he told his wife, was 'never wanting new vexations'. 'I have need of some comfort,' he informed her, 'for I never knew what it was to be barbarously baited before … there was never man so alone as I … no living soul to help me … all the comfort I have is in thy love and a clear conscience.' 'I hope God hath sent me hither,' he continued, 'for the last punishment that he will inflict upon me, for assuredly no honest man can prosper in these people's company.' And though in Montreuil's opinion he accepted all 'with an equanimity that I cannot enough admire, having a kindly demeanour towards those who show him no respect, and who treat him with very little civility', the personal impact of his treatment was particularly visible to one eyewitness who described him as 'melancholy' and 'very gray with cares'.

But it was not only ill-mannered Scottish lords and generals, and rough-bred common soldiers, who stood 'continually smoking' and bare-headed in his presence, that jarred the king's sensibilities. For only four days after his arrival in Newcastle, Charles was subjected in his own dining quarters to a long-winded and patronising sermon delivered by Robert Douglas, Moderator of the General Assembly of the Kirk, instructing him in the 'wholesome doctrine' of Presbyterianism. Thereafter, whether at Anderson House itself or in those town churches that he was occasionally allowed to attend, the same theme was unrelenting. Advised comparatively respectfully by Douglas 'to dispose his spirit to peace and unity', there was also altogether blunter, harsher advice for Charles to endure at the hands of the rougher brand of Presbyterian pulpiteer that the Scottish Kirk seemed to produce so readily. 'Thou piece of clay,' intoned Andrew Cant before his king on Sunday, 5 July, 'where thou sittest, think of thy death, resurrection, judgement, eternity', and place all hope in 'mercy upon repentance'. The preacher's text, Psalm 9:7, made free reference also to the previous verse – 'O thou enemy, destructions are come to a perpetual end: and thou hast destroyed cities; their memorial is perished with them' – amid allusions to the many deaths that Scotland had suffered as a result of the war.

Yet while Charles' countenance was observed to change 'more than once' during Cant's vigorous onslaught, he had nevertheless been sufficiently composed thereafter to invite the preacher and other ministers in attendance to discuss 'a case of conscience that he would put to them'. He had shown even greater resilience in late May and early June when locking horns in public debate with Alexander Henderson, Rector of Edinburgh University and a leading Presbyterian theologian, who had been largely responsible for the final wording of the Solemn League and Covenant. Predictably enough, the king's opening gambit was a profession of faith in the Anglican Church and the need for bishops – two beliefs, he asserted, that had been taught him by his father. Though Henderson's retort was equally astute, it was unavailing. Henry VIII himself, the Scotsman argued, had altered his religious views, and Charles' father would now surely approve of a Presbyterian settlement that at last perfected the Henrician Reformation by purging the Church once and for all of any papist remnants. At which point, the king responded by reminding his protagonist in no uncertain terms that he knew better than any the likely response of James I to the Covenant. 'I had the happiness,' he declared crushingly, 'to know him much better than you.'

And so the exchanges continued – over a total of eight papers in which neither side showed the slightest inclination to concede. On their knees, in fact, the Covenanters implored Charles to convert, but he remained obdurate until, on 3 August, Henderson became too ill to continue his efforts. One week later, indeed, the collapse of Henderson's health had become so complete that he was forced to return to Scotland by sea: a mortally sick man who would be dead only nine days later. He had found the king, in his own words, a 'most intelligent man', while Charles for his part showed no trace of triumphalism at Henderson's indisposition. He had, of course, been treated to what he himself perceived as the ultimate indignity – an attempt not only to undermine his sacred coronation oath to uphold the Church of England, but to compromise in the process the very prospect of his eternal salvation. Even so, he visited the Scot in person at his sickbed before his departure, and appears to have behaved with equanimity when the dying man 'wept to his Majesty and desired him to hearken to counsel'.

To Charles' credit, it was a generous act carried out at a time of unremitting anguish and anxiety, as he toyed aimlessly with the notion of escape, bemoaned his decision to submit himself to 'the false juggling of the Scots' and found himself increasingly an object of contempt, even for some local townsfolk, who appear to have found him 'not only weak but very wilful and obstinate'. 'Nothing can we see in him,' declared the same commentator, 'tending to a true Christian or the power of godliness.' Outwardly at least, he retained his composure. 'Never man saw him passionately angry or extraordinarily moved,' observed a Presbyterian theologian who had often engaged him in debate. But to Henrietta Maria he gave free vent to his frustration at the 'fools and knaves', who were now the only people he ever saw, and 'the base usage that I have had since I came to this army'. 'I care not much for others', he told her, before adding that 'all the comfort I have is in thy love'. 'Thy love preserves my life,' he confided in the special cipher he kept hidden under his pillow.

Above all, perhaps, Charles feared not only for his own safety but that of his children. Following the surrender of Montrose's Scottish forces and the loss of Oxford on Charles' order, James, Duke of York had been taken under restraint to London, where he joined his siblings Elizabeth and Henry in parliamentary custody at St James's Palace. Thereafter only Prince Charles retained his freedom, though after commanding the last of his father's forces in the south-west of England, he had been forced to set sail, first for the Scilly Isles and then for the Channel Islands. Until the heir to the throne was safely ensconced with his mother in France, however, there could be no guarantee of his liberty, and throughout the early days of the king's stay at Newcastle he was racked with concern – not least because the liberty or capture of the prince represented 'either my greatest security, or my certain ruin'. 'Your going beyond sea is absolutely necessary for me', Charles informed his son, and would 'make the rebels hearken, and yield to reason', so long as the young man avoided all temptation to compromise his religion, 'neither hearkening to Roman superstitions nor the seditious and schismatical doctrines of the Presbyterians and Independents'. 'For all other things,' wrote the king, 'I command you to be totally directed by your mother.'

By June, however, Prince Charles was indeed in Paris, though as one cloud lifted, the gloom continued to descend on all other fronts. Within a fortnight of reaching Newcastle, the king had begun to expect the worse. The queen must not be deceived by false hopes, he told her, for the new peace proposals expected from Westminster were bound to be 'such as I can never yield to'. In consequence, his one desire was 'to go from hence to any other part of the world'. 'And, indeed, to deal freely with thee,' he added ominously, 'my condition is such that I expect never to see thee, except … I find means to quit this wretched country … If I stay any time, I am lost.' Yet while Charles had apprehended both his predicament and its solution plainly enough, he was still stricken by inertia and refused, in particular, to make good any escape attempt without the queen's approval, begging her to think 'seriously and speedily' about his proposal, 'for upon my word it will not admit of long delay'. Once again, he was right, for his failure to come to terms with the Scottish Covenanters had drained their patience and emptied their options, leaving him increasingly at Parliament's direct disposal. With no prospect of an accommodation and ongoing unease about their own security, the Scots were indeed already contemplating their ultimate course of action – the sale of the king for a healthy down payment of £100,000 – while both Henrietta Maria and her protector,

Harry Jermyn, were urging him to stay put, emphasising 'the danger of the attempt, and the provocation given to the Parliament if successful'.

Nor, of course, was the arrival of a parliamentary commission in Newcastle long in coming. For on 13 July, Charles was duly presented with a series of propositions for a 'safe and well-grounded peace', which demanded not only that he become a Presbyterian, but forsake control of the militia for twenty years and, almost as intolerably, abandon a number of named Royalists, including Prince Rupert and Jack Ashburnham, from pardon. Papists and Independents alike were to be persecuted according to the dictate of Parliament, all parliamentary ordinances enacted during the war were to hold good and, as a final indignity, there was even a clause in the propositions recommending once again that the king sign and swear to the Solemn League and Covenant, 'according to the laudable example of his Royal father of happy memory'. There was to be no scope for meaningful discussion, and in the meantime Charles' Scottish captors, more desperate than ever to settle matters before heading north once more, would continue to apply the same unremitting pressure. 'It is almost incredible,' Charles informed Henrietta Maria, 'with what impudence I have been assaulted to yield.'

Even as the commissioners were approaching Newcastle, however, the king had determined that he would not yield 'one jot'. Indeed, when the commissioners first presented Parliament's propositions on 30 July after a typically exhausting journey up the Great North Road, he lost no time in deriding the very nature of their mission. Since they were not empowered to negotiate but had arrived only for the purpose of submitting Parliament's demands, their journey had, as Charles made all too clear, been largely redundant. 'An honest trumpeter,' he declared, 'might have done as much.' And such was his resolve that he was even now, or so he claimed, preparing for the ultimate sacrifice in defence of his just rights and those of his heir. 'No threatenings, no apprehensions of danger to my person' or 'misplaced pity', he had informed Jack Ashburnham and Lords Jermyn and Culpepper on 22 July, should make them waver even slightly 'from any foundation in relation to that authority which the Prince of Wales is born to'. 'I have already cast up what I am like to suffer,' the letter continues, 'which I shall meet (by the grace of God) with that constancy that befits me.' His followers, therefore, were to continue in 'unspotted faithfulness' and display that same constancy 'which you command in me', since the royal cause was 'so just' that 'I shall never feint in it'. As for the Church, Charles concluded, there was to be no surrender to Parliament over the Covenant, 'since people are governed more by the pulpit than the sword in times of peace'. Indeed, he would 'less yield to this' than over the question of the militia, 'my conscience being irreconcilably engaged against it'.

Yet it was plain, too, that the king's intransigence would need to be tempered for the time being by a prudent recognition of his current weakness. The Covenanter leader, the Earl of Loudoun, was only one among many who had taken umbrage at Charles' opening riposte to the negotiators, warning him in no uncertain terms that if no change in attitude was forthcoming, 'all England will join against you as one man … and depose you and set up another government'. Under the circumstances, therefore, there was but one option for the king: to play for time as best he might. 'All my endeavours,' he wrote to his wife, 'must be the delaying my answer.' And accordingly, on 1 August, he informed the Speaker of the House of Commons that Parliament's propositions 'do import so great alterations in government in the Church and kingdom, as it is very difficult to return a particular and positive answer, before a full debate, wherein these propositions, and the necessary explanations, true sense and reasons thereof, be rightly weighed and understood'. Parliament, after all, had 'taken twice so many months for deliberation, as they have assigned days for His Majesty's answer'. It was only after due and painstaking consideration, therefore, that 'all issues of blood may be stopped, and these unhappy distractions be settled'.

But if the king's case was superficially credible, the manoeuvre which underpinned it was nonetheless manifestly transparent, and neither his initial request nor a second evasive reply made in December met with any response. In the interim, Charles was left to fill the stony silence with idle threats and empty accusations against his enemies, and equally unwelcome declarations of resolve to those dear to him. Take it from me 'as an infallible maxim', he told the Prince of Wales on 26 August, 'that as the Church can never flourish without the protection of the Crown, so the dependency of the Church upon the Crown is the chiefest support of regal authority'. At all costs, therefore, the prince was to 'hinder the growth of Presbyterian doctrine, which cannot but bring anarchy into any country, whenever it shall come for any time'. By early September, moreover, another familiar note was being struck as Charles berated the Scots for failing to set an example by refusing to make the slightest concessions at a time when further talks were sure to be most fruitful. Two weeks later, by contrast, he returned to threats by warning that Scottish recalcitrance might lead him to deal with the Independents, which he did indeed begin to do at the end of the month when sixty leading Independent divines met him for discussion.

As the Scots well knew, however, the king's bold rhetoric was at that moment little more than empty bluster. He was tied and trussed, and dangling at his enemies' whim, sustained only, ironically enough, by his very impotence, which had until now inclined the opposition to a modicum of toleration. 'I am daily more threatened from London', he complained to his wife in August, and one week later, Jermyn, Culpepper and Ashburnham wrote from France begging that he make concessions. His 'piety, courage and constancy' in standing by the episcopacy were to be praised, they acknowledged, but he had now reached the point where he could only save the bishops by saving himself. 'Presbytery or something worse will be forced upon you whether you will or no,' they argued, and he was not obliged 'to perish in company with bishops merely out of pity'. Instead, he should remember that 'a disease is to be preferred before dissolution', since 'the one may in time admit of remedy, the other is passed cure'. 'How can you think it possible for me to find joy in anything after this?' came the reply, though the queen was equally adamant and pressed him to accept that it was control of the militia rather than defence of the Church that would allow him ultimately to defeat the 'anti-monarchical party'. 'Keep the militia, and never give up, and by that everything will return,' she urged.

And in the meantime, as Charles continued to pin his faltering hopes upon the arrival of 'a strong visible force' from abroad to make the Scots 'hear reason', the queen herself knew beyond all doubt that such a force was nothing more than wishful thinking: a weary phantasm of a sorely deluded man once again too weak to adapt to grim realities. Had not her own father shrewdly abandoned his Protestant faith and converted to Rome in order to obtain the throne of France? And had not Paris indeed proved 'worth a Mass', as he declared at that time? To Henrietta Maria, her husband's claims that 'religion is the only firm foundation of power' and 'that cast loose, or depraved, no government can be stable' were incomprehensible. What she now recommended, after all, seemed so much less than this: nothing more than the exchange – and a temporary one at that – of one form of heresy for another. Her husband's professions of 'inexpressible grief and astonishment' at such manifestly sound advice seems merely to have compounded her frustration. 'The queen will break my heart if she anymore undertake to obtain my consent for Presbyterian government,' he had continued to tell her.

But there was sometimes sharpness as well as dolour in the king's responses, which added salt to the wound. Though she had told her husband that she was willing 'to endure all, if you think it for your service', she also made clear that only her 'passion' for him might prevent her retirement to a nunnery, were he to reach an 'accommodation' with Parliament. She could never, she told him, trust herself 'to those persons who would be your directors, nor to you, since you would have broken your promise to me'. This, it seems, was enough to provoke the king at last to snapping point. 'For God's sake leave off threatening me with thy desire to meddle,' he rejoined, 'as thou lovest me give me so much comfort (and God knows I have but little, and that little must come from thee).' Nor was this the last of Charles' outbursts. For when the poet Sir William D'Avenant was dispatched by the queen to Newcastle in early November, her beleaguered husband gave vent to his hurt and anger much more forthrightly still. Told by D'Avenant that all his friends had now accepted the need to abandon the episcopacy, Charles at once asked for specific names, and Culpepper and Jermyn were subsequently cited. The result was a counterblast that amply embodied the king's despair. Jermyn, he declared, knew nothing about religion, Culpepper had none and D'Avenant must never again enter his presence.

When, moreover, the poet related the incident to the queen a few weeks later in Paris, her response was telling. 'There is nothing in this world I love equal to thee', Charles had declared to his wife in begging her not to enter a nunnery, assuring her in the process that 'both I and all my children are ruined, if thou shouldst retire from my business'. Yet still he was immovable on this self-same 'matter of conscience' that threatened to consume both him and his entire family. Plagued by his abandonment of the Earl of Strafford almost a decade earlier, he would not, he declared, repeat 'that base sinful concession' and compromise his principles again, 'thereby to salve state sores', since he had already been 'most justly punished' for his infidelity on that occasion, and 'a new relapse' was now sure, he insisted, to 'procure God's wrath upon me'. Rather than submit, he would, it seems, pay any price: though whether he knew at the time that this might include the loyalty of his wife seems unlikely. For the queen's frayed patience was also at breaking point. 'I do not cease to labour for your affairs,' she had once told him while struggling to raise funds in Holland, 'provided you do not spoil what I do.' By now her barbed proviso was assuming new weight, for when D'Avenant concluded his account of his fractious meeting with the king, she is said to have expressed 'more fear than hope'.

3

MARRIAGE OR CONSCIENCE?

'Only I must tell thee, that the queen will break my heart if she any more undertake to obtain my consent for Presbyterian government (to which end I know all possible art and industry will be used); for if she once should openly condemn me of wilfulness, but in one point, I should not be able to support my daily miseries.'

Charles I to Queen Henrietta Maria, 31 August 1646

As storm clouds continued to descend upon the king's prospects from all points of the political compass in the late autumn of 1646, so the shadows lengthened too upon his marriage. Twenty-one years earlier, 'sitting upon the very Skirts of Womanhood', the young Princess Henrietta Maria had bid a tearful farewell to Paris amid a 'countless throng of people' and a colossal baggage train of ladies, priests, nurses, maids and sundry other servants – some 200 in all – on her way to Boulogne and a Channel crossing towards her husband-to-be. Among those present all the while was Henry Rich, Viscount Kensington, the 34-year-old English ambassador who had brokered long and hard over fifteen solid months to bring the couple together, and his Gentleman in Attendance, young Henry Jermyn – tall, broad-shouldered, elegant and refined – who, like his master, epitomised the courtly grace and panache so beloved of the French court. Possessing, at only 20 years of age, what the poet Abraham Cowley would describe as 'a soul composed of the eagle and the dove', Jermyn had arrived at the Louvre in February 1624 as a callow subordinate to his handsome, refined superior, only to emerge by June of the following year as a bold, self-confident, worldly wise and watchful man of the moment. When young Henrietta, whom he had already befriended, finally came up the steep hill to the forbidding edifice of Dover Castle, where King Charles awaited her, he was close at hand. He was there too when, after a short and awkward embrace with her intended, she burst into tears of anguish. As the darkness gathered later that evening outside the dank Great Hall of St Augustine's Abbey in Canterbury, 'Harry' Jermyn stood solemnly with the rest of the congregation in the nave to witness the wedding itself. As the soft June rain pattered on the richly decorated royal barge bringing the newly-wed couple back from Gravesend to London, Jermyn too was coming home with them as Gentleman Usher of Queen Henrietta Maria's Privy Chamber.

From the outset, the new queen's experience of married life in a strange and foreign country left much to be desired. Though Charles emerged from his wedding night 'jocund' and unusually talkative, Henrietta Maria, by contrast, is said to have appeared 'very melancholy'. The extreme formality of the English court, which, as Alvise Contarini, the Venetian ambassador, reported, was 'so different to French custom and familiarity', was soon causing her to lead 'a very discontented life'. Subjected to a crash course in English, she was only allowed to speak and write in the presence of her English ladies, which led to several 'angry discussions' between the royal couple, and when Contarini met them both at Nonsuch, he found Henrietta Maria still inclined to shed tears when in conversation with anyone sympathetic to her homeland. 'The queen continues in affliction as usual,' the ambassador wrote later, 'more especially as she is watched by the argus eyes of those in whom she has little confidence': a scarcely veiled reference to the Duke of Buckingham, who both feared and resented Henrietta's potential rivalry, and guaranteed, amongst other things, that she slept in the presence of his niece, Mary Hamilton, whenever the king was absent on one of his continual hunting trips.

Knowing full well that maintaining his monopoly of influence over King Charles might prove altogether more problematic than it had been under the distinctly bisexual James I, Buckingham made every effort, indeed, to weave a particularly spiteful and devious web with which to ensnare the interloper. Pointing out how damaging it was for the country that Henrietta Maria would not attend either the State Opening of Parliament or the Coronation, on the grounds that the ceremonies were Protestant, Buckingham also suggested that the presence of the queen's priests was stoking fears that Charles himself would become a Catholic. As well as her Grand Almoner, the Bishop of Mende, a close relative of Cardinal Richelieu, her chaplains included twenty-four Oratorians who enjoyed apparently unrestricted access to Henrietta's apartments. There were other, albeit pettier but no less pernicious, snipings for her to contend with. The members of the queen's French household, for instance, were said to be treating English courtiers with contempt, and there was even disapproval for the more exotic clothes that she preferred to plainer English fashions.

Yet the king's wife was disinclined, it seems, to accept her ill-usage passively. Certainly, she required no interpreters to make clear her feelings when one Englishman, who had joined the throng at Whitehall to catch sight of the diminutive 16-year-old at dinner, noted that 'howsoever little of stature', she was nevertheless of 'spirit and vigour' and appeared to be 'of a more than ordinary resolution'. 'With one frown', it seems, being 'somewhat overheated with the fire and the company, she drove us all out of the chamber'. She was more than capable of similar iciness towards the king himself when occasion dictated. For when he first attempted to reform the laxity of his wife's household, where French attendants approached her 'without ceremony' and shared her conversation with 'openness and freedom', Charles found himself squarely balked. He had intended that Henrietta should follow the same rules that had applied in 'the Queen my mother's house', only to be told that such regulations 'wounded her maids whom she loved'. She could not, recorded the Comte de Tillières, willingly 'surrender her liberty', and desired that her husband 'would give her leave to order her house as she list'. That she had refused Charles' request was provocative enough, but that she had done so in full public view of his courtiers made the slight all the more intolerable. Later, when he drew her aside to explain her mistake in both 'the business itself' and in making a 'public denial', Henrietta merely compounded the insult. Far from 'acknowledging her fault', the queen launched at once into 'so ill an answer' that Charles refused to record it.

Nor was it long before the queen's wish to assert herself was manifesting itself in the royal bedchamber. 'One night when I was in bed,' the king wrote, '[she] put a paper into my hand, telling me it was a list of those that she desired to be of her revenue.' When told, furthermore, that this was a matter for her husband and to 'remember to whom she spoke', she fell nevertheless into a 'passionate discourse' and declared 'how miserable she was'. Yet even this was not the end of the unhappy exchange. For when Henrietta Maria objected that Charles' mother, Anne of Denmark, had chosen all her own officials, Charles replied that 'his mother was a different sort of woman from her'. During the inevitable exchange of insults that ensued, in which the queen claimed pre-eminence as a 'daughter of France' over a mere Danish princess, Charles dismissed her status as 'nothing very great'. 'Besides', he added, 'she was the third and last' of Henri IV's daughters, 'and therefore of less account'. At one point, after Henrietta had complained that 'business succeeded the worse for her recommendation', Charles had attempted to answer, only to find that 'she would not so much as hear me'. And to demonstrate his indignation at the whole unhappy episode, the king subsequently avoided his wife's company for three whole days, after which he did indeed revisit her bed, though not, as he made clear 'for love of her', but only 'for the love of his people', for whom he must beget an heir.

Not long afterwards, it seems, Henrietta Maria's former governess, Mamie St Georges, was consulted about her young charge's sexual unresponsiveness. Since their very first meeting, when Charles had excluded St Georges from a seat in the royal carriage, he had been convinced that the doughty French matron was mainly responsible for stirring the queen into 'such an humour of distaste against me, as that from that very hour to this, no man can say that she ever used me two days together with so much respect as I deserved'. But now his predicament was such that the Duke of Buckingham was encouraged to sound her out. Though the former governess primly declined to meddle in such matters, rumours persisted that all was not well and that 'bawdy' priests in particular were exacerbating the problem by interrogating the queen – 'by way of confession' – 'how often in a night the king had kissed her'. Almost every day seemed to bring a different religious 'feast' day when Henrietta was told 'you must not let the king approach'. By these means, Charles complained, 'the happy conversation that ought to pass between him and his dear wife, which is the principal comfort of marriage, hath not only been interrupted but wholly squenched and perverted'.

Equally predictably, perhaps, the influence of the queen's priestly entourage had become a source of widespread dissatisfaction in the country at large. Not long after the royal wedding, Buckingham's sister, the Countess of Denbigh, had arranged for the local parson to come and preach at Titchfield for the Protestant members of the queen's household without requesting her permission, whereupon she reacted by walking to and fro through the hall where the service was being conducted, in the company of her French ladies and their pet dogs, talking and laughing, making mock hunting cries, and generally creating so much disturbance that the preacher was unable to continue. Worse still, the same parson would later complain that some of the queen's servants had taken pot-shots at him while sitting on a bench in his own garden. Though de Tillières explained the incident by attributing it to bird-hunting on behalf of two of the queen's lackeys, the residual holes in the garden bench raised lingering doubts, which were not dispelled by a subsequent scuffle between rival Protestant and Catholic chaplains, who had tried to shout each other down in saying grace and thereby forced the king to rise 'instantly' from the table 'in a great passion ... taking the queen by the hand'.

That Easter, during Holy Week, Henrietta and her ladies had gone into retreat at Somerset House, where a long gallery had been divided and equipped with cells and an oratory, and there, we are told, 'they sang the hours of the Virgin and lived together like nuns'. But the climax came when she travelled on foot, 'a distance of a mile', through the streets of London to the Palace of St James, where her private chapel was approaching completion. For the queen this was merely normal Catholic devotion, but public outrage was unremitting. Henrietta's priests, it seemed, had humiliated the king's wife, making her 'dabble in the dirt, in a foul morning, from Somerset House to St James's, her Luciferian confessor riding along by her in his coach'. If, the same account continued, they 'dare thus insult over the daughter, sister and wife of so great kings, what slavery would they not make us, the people, to undergo?'

A similar excursion, two months later, caused even greater consternation when the queen made what amounted to a pilgrimage to the site of the gallows at Tyburn, in response to 'the most holy Jubilee' that the Pope had declared at that time. In the midst of some thirty of her courtiers, she had set to 'walk afoot (some say barefoot)' across Hyde Park before stopping to pray on the public highway – 'so openly that the people noticed and were scandalised' – for the souls of those Catholic saints and martyrs who had suffered at that 'holy place'. Beseeching that God would 'give her grace with the like constancy to die for her religion', she was even rumoured to have prayed specifically for the soul of the Jesuit priest, Henry Garnet, 'who had suffered cruel torture and death on that spot' for his involvement in the Gunpowder Plot twenty years earlier. Nothing, of course, could have represented a greater abomination for English Protestants or a more direct affront to Charles himself, who knew Garnett as a ruthless traitor, instrumental in the assassination plot against his own father. In the aftermath of Henrietta's action, he could therefore 'no longer bear it', it seems, and it was this that prompted him at last to 'deliver his dear wife' from her French attendants.

At this point, it is true, the king himself continued to attribute the various 'unkindnesses and distastes' souring his marriage to the queen's comparative youth and 'the ill crafty counsels of her servants for advancing their own ends'. But the fact remained that Henrietta Maria's coldness and disrespect towards Charles was nevertheless, as he freely admitted, 'too long to set down all'. The nadir duly arrived at about 3 p.m. on Monday, 31 June 1626, when the queen's French attendants were abruptly ushered out of her chamber and she was informed by her husband that her retinue was to be sent home. First outraged and then terrified, she fell to her knees, weeping and imploring the king to reconsider in a manner 'which would have moved stones to pity'. When Charles remained unmoved by her protests, she screamed loud enough, according to one account, 'to split rocks' before rushing to a window, smashing the glass with her fists and clinging to the iron grating in a frantic attempt to hold the attention of the crowd that had gathered in the courtyard below. Appalled by such a shamelessly public loss of control, it was the king himself, it seems, who finally dragged her away, her hair dishevelled, her dress torn, her hands cut and bleeding.

Nor were there any immediate signs thereafter that the queen was becoming reconciled to the loss of her associates. On the contrary, the Comtesse de Tillières, who had heard the entire episode from the other side of the door, feared at the time that she would cry herself to death. 'Never could a similar affliction be seen,' she recorded, adding that Henrietta 'almost died, crying out, despairing, demanding us back with such prayers and tears that if it had been another [man than Charles] assuredly we would have been called back'. In a letter smuggled out to the comtesse a little later, Henrietta confided that the king was even following her to the close stool. To her beloved mother, meanwhile, she described herself as 'the most afflicted person in the world'. Left 'a complete prisoner' and surrounded by Buckingham's relations – 'persons who had shown themselves her enemies since the moment she landed in England' – her 'tears and displeasure' were 'continuous', so that 'she hardly sleeps any more and eats very little'. 'If you do not take pity on me,' she wrote, 'I am beyond despair.'

In the meantime, while Charles attributed his marital ills to a simple surfeit of Gallic meddling, so Henrietta herself had continued to see the malign influence of the Duke of Buckingham at every turn. Notwithstanding the fact that the duke had attempted to persuade his master that the queen's behaviour might be remedied by 'kind usages', there was indeed no curing her hostility. She had not only refused on the one hand to be crowned in a Protestant ceremony or to watch her husband's own coronation from 'a place made fit for her' – a private curtained gallery – but had also flatly refused even to enter Westminster Abbey at any stage during the five hours of solemn ceremonial. Instead, she and her entourage chose to watch Charles' procession to and from Westminster from a nearby house, while, according to one hostile rumour, 'her ladies [were] frisking and dancing in the room behind her'. Even so, the king appeared to bear Henrietta's absence with surprising good grace, even making light of the episode when he met her afterwards by 'putting his two hands to his crown and lifting it a little', like a gentleman doffing his hat.

But when, at the Duke of Buckingham's suggestion, Henrietta was invited to watch her husband's passage to the State Opening of Parliament from the Whitehall apartments of the duke's mother, there followed the bitterest royal quarrel to date. Her absence from the event itself – 'from the same religious scruples' – had once again been countenanced, albeit awkwardly, but her decision to decline the duke's invitation at the last moment on the grounds that it was raining and the journey involved a muddy trip on foot across the Privy Garden – an open space some 100 yards wide – proved a step too far in more ways than she herself had anticipated. She was fearful, it seems, that her hair would be spoilt and her clothes dirtied, and Charles, at least, was initially inclined to acquiesce with her request that she be allowed to watch the procession from her own windows. From Buckingham's perspective, however, the insult to his mother was intolerable, and according to the account of de Tillières, it was the duke who now pushed matters to an issue by asking the king how he could expect Parliament to obey him when his own wife displayed such defiance.

The result was another belated fit of anger from the king, which resulted in public humiliation for his wife and another night-time spat that further confirmed the depth of their difficulties. Ironically, under the advice of the French ambassador, the queen had indeed agreed to attend the Countess of Buckingham's apartments, only to find after her arrival that the king was now insisting that she return. When his message was initially delivered by none other than Buckingham himself, moreover, the queen compounded the king's fury by sending the duke back with a request that she be allowed to stay. Faced with what seemed yet another example of casual disregard for his authority, Charles then dispatched Buckingham once more with an absolute command that she return at once. Though at last she acquiesced, she fumed that night in the royal bedchamber for being thus embarrassed before the entire court. She would rather die, she claimed, than offend her husband, but was unable to come to terms with 'the Duke acting as messenger on this occasion' and could never believe that words such as hers might be considered faults.

In response, Charles told Henrietta that he would no longer torment her with his visits and left the room. Next day, Buckingham himself informed the queen that the French ambassador, Blainville, must no longer enter her presence, and for hours 'pressed her for a promise of acquiescence'. Once again, moreover, it was only under the duke's 'constant pressure and the king's demands' that Henrietta Maria finally acceded. For two nights, the king and queen slept separately before Buckingham finally informed her that unless she begged her husband's pardon with all due humility, he would not visit her again. Indeed, if she had not done so within two days and agreed in the process to the expulsion of her French household, Charles would not treat her as a person fit to be his wife. In consequence, even her most spirited protests, which followed thick and fast, were suddenly rendered hollow. For even a queen like Henrietta was unable to trump an ace of this particular potency. Though, as she continued to maintain, she was guilty neither in word nor in deed, nor even in intention, she would nevertheless formally comply as commanded. One day later, therefore, she duly visited her husband, expressed her regret at the misunderstanding and begged him to think of it no longer. Under the circumstances, it was the closest thing to an outright apology that he could hope for, and that night, as court observers recorded, 'the complete and sincere affection which subsists between the King and Queen was restored'.

The eventual expulsion of the queen's French retinue would, of course, quickly shatter this particular show of domestic harmony, and the formal reconciliation with Buckingham, engineered by the ambassador Bassompierre 'with a thousand pains', lasted a mere twenty-four hours. After two years of marriage, moreover, and in spite of trips to the small county town of Wellingborough and its famous mineral waters, which were said to 'facilitate generation', the queen was still not pregnant. By and large, the royal couple confined their exchanges to arid letters containing little beyond 'dry, ceremonial compliment', and as relations with France deteriorated into the bargain, Henrietta had sought solace increasingly in a mixture of play and self-improvement within the largely separate enclave that she fashioned for herself. On the one hand, she bought a lute and started lessons with 'a certain Monsieur Gouttier, a Frenchman and a famous performer'. There was ongoing support, too, from her two remaining Oratorian priests, Fathers Philip and Viette, who were to become her lifelong companions, though above all, she lavished affection on 'Little Jeffrey', or 'the Queen's dwarf' as he came to be called: a little boy named Jeffrey Hudson, whom Buckingham's mother had first presented to her under the crust of a cold pie, from which he emerged to stun all onlookers. Standing only 18in high at the age of 8, he was described by one observer as 'a marvellous sight … the most perfect imperfection of nature that ever was born'. And when the queen chose to indulge herself with the broader pleasures of court life, there were also lavish masques for her to lose herself in: at one of which, we are told, everyone danced until four in the morning. 'Doubtless', wrote one outraged Londoner, 'it cost abundance' – so much so, it seemed, that 'one Mr Chalmers sold 1,000 yards of taffeta and satin towards it'.

As time passed, furthermore, there were even signs of a thaw in Henrietta's relationships with both her husband and the Duke of Buckingham himself. In May 1627, she had finally accepted Charles' formal regulations for her court, and was described thereafter as 'very happy and cheerful' with her new English companions. In particular, she eventually developed a keen regard for Buckingham's mother and wife. The first, after all, was a passionate Catholic convert, whose Whitehall lodgings were a notorious safe haven for 'the most active priests in England', while the other, Katherine, Duchess of Buckingham, was a lifelong Catholic at heart, who publicly practised Anglicanism only to bolster her husband's position. Described as a woman of 'very great spirit', Katherine was also generous, presenting the queen with 'a costly coach and six horses valued generally at 20,000 crowns'. While the duke's closest relatives did their level best to win her affection, so he too played his part in melting her hostility in a whirl of generosity – the most exceptional example of which was 'the most superb feast' that the French ambassador had ever seen, where each course was accompanied by a separate ballet, with its own scenery and music, and Henrietta was treated to a grand masque depicting the French royal family dispensing peace for all Europe among the Gods.

Under such circumstances, it was hardly surprising, perhaps, that the queen would assume an increasingly brave public face and write to the duke 'most heartily and cheerfully' with 'her best wishes' when he finally set off to make war on her homeland. Even a young woman of Henrietta's indomitable temperament could not, after all, resist the inevitable indefinitely. Yet ultimately, only the disgrace and death of the man with whom her husband always corresponded as 'your faithful, loving, constant friend' would relieve her of his influence and thereby at last cement her place in the king's affections. As Buckingham's ill-conceived and ill-fated military expedition to the Île de Rhé foundered, Charles had written to him 'hoping and longing for your safe return' and assuring him that 'no distance of place, nor length of time can make me slacken, much less diminish my love to you'. Yet optimism swiftly faded, and by the time that the duke returned to Plymouth at the head of the broken remnant of his force, English news-sheets were awash with reports of a 'great slaughter' and 'a rout without an enemy'.

The king, it is true, remained thoroughly enamoured with his friend, insisting that 'all the shame must light upon us here at home' for failing to send reinforcements in time. But his subjects were altogether less indulgent – as Buckingham would discover to his mortal cost on Saturday, 23 August 1628, when he was 'slaine at one blow with a dagger knife' by a morose ex-officer lieutenant named John Felton, who had been passed over for promotion and found himself owed £80 in back pay before finally acquiring a tenpenny weapon from a cutler's shop on Tower Hill with which to demonstrate his disapproval. As he left the parlour where he had been breakfasting, Buckingham was dispatched by a single merciless thrust, delivered 'with great strength and violence', which had passed through his lungs and into 'the very heart itself', leaving him spouting blood from the mouth 'with much effusion'. Though he had pulled the dagger from the wound and made to pursue his attacker, the chase lasted only a few steps before he slumped to the floor. 'I am the Man, heere I am,' called Felton, making no attempt to escape from the crowd in which he had mingled beforehand.

When questioned, the assassin had explained that his motive was nothing less than to 'doe his Country great good service', and there was no denying, as the Venetian ambassador Alvise Contarini observed, that it had been 'very difficult in many parts of the country to prevent bonfires and other rejoicings'. Yet the real beneficiary in many respects was none other than the king's own wife. Upon hearing the news of the duke's death, the queen had visited the duke's bereaved wife – 'an act on her part', noted Amerigo Salvetti, which 'greatly gratified the king'. Yet Charles had been thrilled by Henrietta Maria's support beforehand too, at the very time of Buckingham's military expedition itself, for although she had expressed her regret at the conflict with her homeland, she had also wished the duke 'all success, being more interested for him than for anyone else'. The king had responded effusively. 'My wife and I,' he informed Buckingham, 'were never better together; she, upon this action of yours, showing herself so loving to me, by her discretion upon all occasions, that it makes us all wonder and esteem her.'

The budding reconciliation had begun to manifest itself more visibly too, as Charles, notwithstanding his own shortage of funds, lavished generosity upon his formerly recalcitrant wife. On the one hand, he ordered that Henrietta's debts be paid off to the tune of £30,000, and also gave her lands worth £6,000 per year, so that her income should match that of the late Queen Anne. Even more extravagantly, however, the king saw fit to gift her Greenwich Palace, a favourite resort of his mother, where she had begun building a luxurious, Italianate 'Queen's House' to designs by Inigo Jones. If Henrietta's domestic needs were now catered for with a new diligence, so too, it seems, were her religious tastes, as Charles turned a blind eye to the many English Catholics who now eagerly attended Mass at her private chapel in Somerset House. When Parliament protested at such 'connivance at Popery', the king responded angrily; and when Henrietta asked him to reject a new anti-Catholic Bill that MPs had just passed, he acceded gladly.

All observers acknowledged, however, that Buckingham's death proved the final catalyst in swaying the king to an almost unconditional dependence on his wife that would thereafter span some two decades. Within a fortnight of the duke's assassination, the Venetian ambassador had written to his opposite number in Paris how it was believed 'the queen would henceforward have great influence', and not long afterwards he would confirm that 'every day she concentrates in herself the favour and love that was previously divided between her and the duke'. Amerigo Salvetti, indeed, thought that 'were she not so youthful … it would be an easy matter for her to make the King do whatever she pleased, so much is he attached to her'. The Earl of Carlisle, on a diplomatic mission abroad, heard how he would find his 'master and mistress at such a degree of kindness as he would imagine him a wooer again, and her gladder to receive his caresses than he to make them'.

To all appearances, then, the transformation was a truly remarkable one, as Charles suddenly and unconditionally shifted his emotional dependence upon Buckingham to the nearest available substitute, and Henrietta – newly outgoing and affectionate, and at last finding herself loved and respected – reciprocated warmly. Her nineteenth birthday was celebrated by a tournament, the king on horseback and determined to 'grow gallant every day more and more'. When Charles left London, Henrietta's only consolation was his portrait, 'his shadow at her bedside'. That same December, Thomas Carey informed the Earl of Carlisle that 'the King has now so wholly made over all his affections to his wife, that I dare say we are out of the danger of any other favourites'. Indeed, though she seems to have informed Alvise Contarini around this time that 'she did not pretend to interfere in state affairs', the ambassador was in little doubt that her support was a valuable tool in assisting his efforts to promote the cause of peace between England and France. 'I know,' he informed Giorgio Zorzi, 'that her entreaties have made an impression in addition to my own.' Nor was this all. For boatloads of captured French fishermen were released after 'she exerted herself with much warmth' on their behalf, and the king 'not only reprieved, but pardoned' a condemned Jesuit priest as a result of her intervention.

In the meantime, fresh rumours that the queen was 'breeding child' only served to consolidate her new-found position at the epicentre of her husband's world. Though her first child, a boy born ten weeks prematurely, lived only long enough to be hastily baptised by one of the king's chaplains, Henrietta duly became 'the happy mother of a Prince of Wales' only one year later. This time, moreover, there was no question about the health of the infant. The queen's first child had been turned 'overthwart' in her belly, and she had endured several hours of great pain and considerable danger, as Peter Chamberlen, a leading obstetrician who had pioneered the use of forceps, struggled unsuccessfully to save the situation. Now, however, she could boast a baby boy whose longevity seemed guaranteed. Giovanni Soronzo, who saw the future Charles II in his cradle before he was a week old, observed that 'so far as one can judge from present indications he will be very strong and vigorous'. Though the queen herself regretted aspects of his appearance, she was more than satisfied with the end product of her labour. 'He is so ugly,' she informed her former governess, 'that I am ashamed of him, but his size and fatness supply the want of beauty.'

Henrietta had good reason, moreover, to delight at her new child's arrival, since he was the first heir apparent to be born on English soil since Edward VI. His birth had been accompanied by all the bell-ringing, bonfires and bad verse customary on such occasions, but more significantly still, it had ushered in a new dawn of unprecedented happiness and influence for the queen – one which would consolidate her hold over her husband's heart and confirm her place at the centre of state affairs. 'I wish that we could always be together,' Charles told his wife shortly after the birth of his new heir, 'and that you could accompany me to the Council.' While Charles knew that this could never be – for 'what would these people say if a woman were to busy herself with matters of government?' – there were other, more subtle ways in which the same effect might be achieved. When, more than a decade later, Henrietta had left to raise funds in the Netherlands under the shadow of civil war in England, her husband had galloped along the cliff tops to keep her ship in sight until the last sail had vanished below the horizon. Throughout the trials and disappointment that followed, that same lovelorn dependence had been maintained. By then, the fortunes of war and even the loss of his liberty to the Scots had only served, if anything, to magnify the king's desire for her company and dependence on her counsel. She was indeed, to all appearances, his alpha and his omega – his rock in adversity, his guiding light in the darkness of the times.

But if Charles' ardour was seemingly unconditional, the queen's remained tinged with frustration at her husband's weakness, stricken as he was by a curious – and ultimately fatal – cocktail of stubbornness and vacillation. 'I am most confident that within a very small time I shall be recalled with much honour, and all my friends will see that I have neither a foolish nor peevish conscience,' he told his wife on 30 November 1646 from his quarters at Anderson House, where his Scottish captors were by then lodging him. In love no less than politics, he continued to ignore the warning signs. There was only one fault, she had once told the Duke of Buckingham, that could make her unworthy to be the king's wife, and she was certainly too well bred to be guilty of it. Yet sordid rumours of Henrietta Maria's unfaithfulness had already continued to dog the king for some time. Even upon the occasion of their reunion at Edgehill, indeed, there was mischievous talk of her unseemly familiarity with Lord Charles Cavendish, for whom she was said to have delayed her journey. The Earl of Holland, of course, had also unsettled the king by his more recent appearances in her rooms at Merton.

Now, however, as autumn mists turned to winter fog in Newcastle, even more scandalous whispers were reaching Charles' ears concerning his own friend Henry Jermyn, for whom the queen had immediately requested a peerage upon her reunion with her husband at Oxford in 1643. Born in 1605, he was the second surviving son of Sir Thomas Jermyn – a long-serving court official who eventually became Governor of Jersey – and had followed his father into royal service, attending Lord Bristol's embassy to Madrid in 1622–23, as well as Lord Kensington's mission to Paris to negotiate the marriage of Charles I and Henrietta Maria one year later. He had served too as an MP – for Bodmin, Liverpool and Corfe Castle – though his real talents were always as a courtier, and it was the courtier's gift of gentility, finesse and eagle-eyed opportunism that had first secured his place within the queen's household in 1627. Handsome, discreet, a fluent French-speaker and no lover of the Duke of Buckingham, who had stripped his kinsman Francis Bacon of the Great Seal, Jermyn was ideally equipped to win the queen's affection and maintain her confidence, all of which had been amply demonstrated in 1633 when he displeased the king by refusing to marry the pregnant Eleanor Villiers. Though his prospective spouse was a maid of honour and niece of the deceased Buckingham, Jermyn held firm on the grounds that Eleanor had already slept with two men besides himself. Notwithstanding the fact that Charles banished him to France, Jermyn was back at court once more in February 1636 – as a direct result of the queen's intervention.

It was from this point, furthermore, that his close relationship and increasing influence with Henrietta Maria had become a particular source of gossip. In 1636, William Davenant may have intended an ironic allusion to the pair in his play *The Platonic Lovers*, and Davenant almost certainly depicted Jermyn as the philandering Arigo in his poem 'Madagascar' two years later. But the courtier's activities also gained a notoriety that extended well beyond literary circles and into the murkier corners of court life – the realm of creeping whispers and furtive knowing looks. The private apartments of the monarch and his wife were, after all, a strictly self-contained and forbidden microcosm, where only a carefully chosen elite of gentlemen, ladies and necessary servants might expect to gain entry. Rules that served to insulate the king and queen so securely from the outside world were only likely to foster an extraordinary degree of intimacy between themselves and the immediate circle that surrounded them. Where such intimacy obtained, therefore, so too, inevitably, did rumour – however ill-founded or otherwise.

In particular, it was the closeted world of the queen's Privy Chamber – where Henry Jermyn appeared to hold such sway – that became the focus for a steady trickle of curious tales and half-lit hearsay. One story, recorded sometime after the event, originated with Jermyn's own cousin, Tom Killigrew, whose task was to light the king's way along the corridors that joined his own apartments with those of his wife. Whether at Whitehall or St James's, this process was always conducted during autumn and winter nights at those times when Charles chose to sleep in his wife's bed. On this occasion, however, Killigrew purported to have opened the door to the queen's chamber, only to find her sitting on the bed, almost completely hidden by the broad-shouldered form of his cousin. Acting as quickly and resourcefully as he could, Killigrew is said to have dropped the taper and fallen to his knees, scrabbling about to clear the wax and apologising all the while, in order to buy time for the embarrassed couple. By the time the bemused king eventually entered from the corridor, the queen, it seems, had composed herself and Jermyn had vanished.

Killigrew, ultimately, would become a successful playwright who established a reputation as a witty and somewhat dissolute figure at the court of Charles II. But by the time he came forward with his claim, he was a heartfelt devotee of the Stuart cause and Roman Catholic, who had no reputation for slander or any appreciable grounds for defaming the queen herself. He was a man with a critical eye for the evidence, having witnessed the exorcism of the 'possessed' nuns of Loudun and dismissed the proceedings in a sceptical account of 1635. Though Pepys dismissed him as the king's fool and jester, Charles II nevertheless trusted him sufficiently to install him as Groom of the Bedchamber and Chamberlain to his own wife, and given that Charles himself was rumoured in some circles to be none other than Jermyn's own son, it seems unlikely that Killigrew would have lightly concocted a tale of this kind. The incident, in any case, did not so much incriminate the queen as add one more coal to a slow-burning fire that had long been smouldering in a variety of quarters. In one instance, the Duke of Hamilton is said to have found Jermyn and Henrietta Maria cuddling in a room at Somerset House, while another account suggests that an unnamed earl, playing upon the king's own suspicions, offered to lead him to the queen's chamber at a time when she would be alone with her favourite. Upon bursting in upon his wife, Charles, it seems, found that the pair were indeed together, but merely conversing innocently, leaving him red-faced and stricken with guilt that he should have suspected her in the first place.

By contrast, of course, there were those for whom the queen was nothing less than a model of unalloyed virtue. 'As to faith, or sin of the flesh, she is never tempted,' wrote one particular commentator. 'No one,' he continued, 'is admitted to her bedrooms except ladies with whom she sometimes retires and employs herself on light, but innocent matters.' Written by a papal agent, reporting what he had allegedly been told by Henrietta Maria's confessor, this report, too, must be viewed with due caution. Yet the truly significant feature of the rumours about the queen's fidelity is not so much their accuracy as their very existence – and the high places in which they circulated. In 1643, for instance, Jermyn had been accused by Parliament not merely of political crimes but of what was openly described as 'too great an intimacy with the queen'. In consequence, parliamentary agents had been dispatched to rummage through his apartments at Whitehall – 'in an unprecedented manner' and 'without any respect for the place' – in hopes of seizing incriminating papers and giving 'further offence to Her Majesty'. Though he had been forced to flee to France, his influence remained undiminished upon his return. For not only was he raised to the peerage as Baron Jermyn of St Edmundsbury at the queen's request – on the grounds, ostensibly, that he would thereafter be beheaded rather than hanged, drawn and quartered if he fell into Parliamentarian hands – it was he who accompanied her to France in 1644, and he, thereafter, who mastered her affairs as private secretary. In consequence, wrote Madame de Motteville, he was 'more than ever in the favour of [the Queen] and indeed to a strange degree'. There were further ugly rumours that Henrietta's ninth child, 'a lovely princess' who had been born in the West Country on 16 June after her departure from Oxford, was none other than Jermyn's.

So when the queen's letters began to arrive once more to the king at Newcastle in 1646, she remained a cause for concern for her increasingly hard-pressed husband – not simply because of her ongoing headaches and eye-strain, but also, perhaps, because these ailments now induced her to entrust her correspondence to none other than Henry Jermyn, who rendered them into code on her behalf and likewise deciphered those letters delivered from Charles. Yet the king, master as always of the rose-tinted gloss, continued to take consolation of sorts from the letters of love that his wife still dispatched amid the instructions, exhortations and imprecations that characterised so much of her correspondence. His nagging frustrations were leavened too by the undoubted delicacy of Henrietta's health. The Royalist Francis Bassett, who had seen her passing through Launceston on the way to France from Exeter, had told his wife that 'here is the woefullest spectacle my eyes ever yet beheld on: the most worn and pitiful creature in the world, the poor queen, shifting for one hour's life longer'. Even Theodore Mayerne, who was apt to dismiss many of the queen's symptoms as hysterical in origin, had predicted at that time that she would live for no more than another three weeks, and prior to her departure she had confided to Charles that she was giving him 'the strongest proof of love that I can give'. 'I am hazarding my life, that I may not incommode your affairs,' she continued. 'Adieu, my dear heart. If I die, believe that you will lose a person who has never been other than entirely yours.' And Charles, for the time being at least, did indeed believe as bidden.

In his present circumstances, moreover, the king could perhaps be forgiven for refusing to dwell upon the most unthinkable of all possibilities. For by the beginning of 1647, after eight months in Scottish hands, he was already a changed man. Under strict new orders, 'eight officers never let him out of their sight', his early optimism was now being steadily replaced, under the 'violent importunities' of his enemies, by creeping fears that drained his energy and rendered him increasingly desperate. The pastimes of his early weeks in Newcastle – occasional games of golf in the surrounding countryside, rides along the river to Tynemouth or games of chess indoors – were no more. Instead, for days on end, Charles was occupied only at his desk, managing a constant round of letters: to Henrietta Maria and Jermyn in Paris, to Parliament in London, and to both his enemies and old friends in Scotland. In mid-November, with news from London that an agreement might yet be possible, he had turned to drafting peace proposals, only to be rebuffed by his wife. Thereafter, driven by the queen's accusations that he was destroying by his wilfulness 'all that is dear to me', he had even contemplated abdication. 'I hate it,' she replied by return of post. 'If any such thing be made public, you are undone – your enemies will make malicious use of it. Be sure you never own it again in any discourse.'

As Henrietta and her advisers, including Jermyn, continued to press for his acceptance of Presbyterian settlement, so Charles continued, it seems, to hover near breaking point. 'Good God, what things are these to try my patience!' he wrote. 'I could say much more upon this subject, but I will conjure you, as you are Christians, no more thus to torture me, assuring you that the more ye this way press me, you the more contribute ... to my ruin.' The time for concessions had in any case passed. For some months the Scots and the English Parliament had been forging ahead on a peace settlement entirely independent of Charles, and now they were ready to act. Money would be paid to the Scots for their services in the war, and then they would withdraw. At the same time, the king would be handed over to Parliament in return for a down payment of £100,000, after which, as he informed Henrietta when rumours of the arrangement reached him, 'I shall be an absolute prisoner'.

Under the circumstances, escape appeared the only option, and Charles – once again sacrificing the initiative to the queen – urged her to 'consider well' the idea. As early as June, less than a month after he had joined the Scots, he had pondered the prospect of flight, and by July he was not only convinced that 'I am lost if I go not unto France by the end of August', but imploring Henrietta Maria to make the necessary arrangements. With none forthcoming, he had been left in September to seek help from his daughter, Mary, and her husband, William of Orange. Were his negotiations with Parliament to fail, he hoped a Dutch ship might then arrive in Newcastle, under the pretence of carrying messages, and deliver him safely to Holland. That plan too had failed at first to be implemented, however, and now all hinged yet again upon the good offices of the queen. Once out of the country, he reasoned, the Scots would clash with Parliament, 'and so give me an opportunity, either to join with the weaker party, or frame one of my own'. The Dutch too, it seems, were now willing 'to do what the King commands', and there was also, for good measure, a further rumour for the king to cling to that some 5,000 former soldiers from the Royalist army were gathering, 'high and bold', in and around Newcastle itself.

The queen, however, shared no such delusions, and at the beginning of December she delivered a firm injunction to her husband that he must 'not think of making any escape from England'. 'Everyone here', she wrote from Paris, was startled at the very notion, since a 'general peace' to the Thirty Years' War was imminent on the Continent, after which French aid was sure to be forthcoming. Indeed, their ambassador was already under orders to negotiate a treaty with the Scots to fight jointly against Parliament, in an all-out effort to restore the king. In fleeing now, the letter continued, 'you would destroy all our hopes', and there was also, of course, 'the danger of the attempt to be considered'. Within the month, after all, Charles himself would openly admit to his wife that while 'heretofore my escape was easy enough … now it is most difficult if not impossible'. In such circumstances, Henrietta urged, her husband should only consider such an action as a drastic last resort if the Scots were to declare openly 'that they will not protect you'.

Whether, as some commentators suggested both then and later, the queen really was acting from ulterior motives remains an open question. For by now, Henry Jermyn was not only firmly installed in Paris as her closest confidant and counsellor, he had become in effect a substitute father for her eldest son. It was Jermyn, for instance, who administered Prince Charles' finances and allowed him pocket money out of his French pension. It was Jermyn, too, who delicately tempered the queen's instinct to pamper and cosset her son, and countered the adolescent boy's instinct to rebel against her. Appointing the prince's tutors and deciding what they taught him was only one of many other paternal duties that Jermyn assumed, as he both befriended the boy and did his best to guide him through the troubles of the times. In the meantime, the queen and her secretary became the de facto heart of a Royalist government in exile. Ireland, France, Holland, Rome, Denmark, Sweden, Lorraine and even the Baltic duchy of Courland were all courted in turn by Jermyn from his gilded office in the Louvre, where he sat each day, surrounded by correspondence, ciphers and maps, sifting through reports from his spy network, desperately trying to find a way to save the day while enjoying the constant company and adulation of the queen.

Nor, it must be said, was Charles himself ungrateful to his 'humble servant', who, in concert with the queen, increasingly directed policy. 'Harry,' the king had written in May 1645, 'this is chiefly to chide you that I had no letters from you this last week ... not to hear every day from you ... is a cruel thing failing thereby of my expectation.' The same level of trust and gratitude, with the one notable exception already discussed, was apparent throughout his correspondence from Newcastle during 1646. 'Tell Jermyn from me,' Charles had informed Henrietta in July, 'that I will make him know the eminent service he hath done me concerning Prince Charles his coming to thee, as soon as it shall please God to enable me to reward honest men.' While other Royalist exiles fleeing to Paris resented Jermyn's control of the royal finances – bristling at the fact that he 'kept an excellent table for those who courted him, and had a coach of his own, and all other accommodations incident to the most full fortunes' – the king offered only unconditional trust in all matters, it seems, but religion and the running sore of Presbyterianism.

Yet, notwithstanding a compliant response to the insistent request that he stay put at Newcastle, Charles now chose to exercise his own judgement – albeit in the form of an escape attempt that proved as half-cocked as it was half-hearted. Writing to Henrietta on 5 December, he appeared resigned to his current situation:

> I will, according to thy conjuration, not think of an escape until the Scots shall declare that they will not protect me, and now I see the opinion (I say not thine), that it is less ill for my affairs that I should be a prisoner in my own dominions than at liberty anywhere else ... and therefore will not say more.

On Christmas Eve, however, came news that the Scottish Parliament had passed 'very harsh resolutions', leaving no other recourse than flight. Faced, indeed, with an ultimatum that he must approve 'all the proposals of peace that have been presented to him by the two kingdoms' until which time his 'royal authority will remain suspended', Charles suddenly moved beyond the need to consult the queen. Seeing not a single place in Britain 'where he could remain in safety', he therefore planned to join her in Paris, and though the new French ambassador, Pierre Bellièvre, suggested that it might be 'very difficult for him to return again', and tried desperately to persuade him to 'retire to the Scottish Highlands' instead, Charles remained adamant. A Dutch ship sent by his daughter, which had finally arrived in Newcastle harbour 'under the pretence of being careened', was 'victualled … and new trimmed', and the king, it seems, would brook no delay.

That same day, therefore, the vessel's captain was summoned to Anderson House to meet 'in private' with William Murray, one of the grooms of Charles' bedchamber. Murray had served the king in this capacity since the second year of the reign, in fact, before being arrested as a spy in 1646. Educated as a boy alongside the king, with whom he enjoyed great influence, he had also been employed as an emissary to France. It was this intimate link with his sovereign that had led to his release from the Tower in September as a result of the intervention of the Scottish commissioners, who gained from him an assurance that he would do all in his power to induce his master to yield to Parliament's terms. Like other committed Royalists of his kind, however, Murray plainly considered such assurances unbinding, for he subsequently delivered £100 to the Dutch captain at the quayside Peacock Inn, and on Christmas morning word came back that, if the wind was fair, the ship – a man-of-war 'of 84 gunnes' – would sail on the night tide, 'notwithstanding any opposition from Tynemouth Castle'. Disguised in either 'the habit of a sailor' or as William Murray's servant, the king would thereby achieve his liberty at last.

From the various accounts available, it would appear that late in the night of 25 or 26 December, Murray ventured forth to check whether one of the town gates – either Pandon Gate or Sandgate – had been opened as arranged by Royalists or sympathetic guards with whom Charles had been trying to ingratiate himself, only to find that the gate designated for the king's escape remained secure, since 'a key was set fast and broken' within the lock. Apparently wearing 'gray cloathes', which were intended to render him less noticeable in the wintry murk, Murray then returned to the king's lodging, where he was 'looked upon with suspicion' for 'coming downe the staires at so unusuall a time' and held in the guard house for three hours, during which time Charles concluded that a mishap of some kind had occurred. Whether he had prudently gone to bed in anticipation of a possible surprise visit from either the town governor or the Earl of Leven himself, in order to affect the appearance of innocence, or whether, as Tobias Peaker, another groom of the privy chamber, suggested, the whole enterprise had been abandoned simply because of a change in the wind, remains unknown.

But thereafter 'the suspicion was so great, and the stir so great upon it' that security was considerably increased, notwithstanding the fact that Murray was released after questioning by the town governor. Leven, for example, at once placed his cavalry on the Tynemouth road, and next day ordered the king's guards to 'be strictlier posed than they have been hitherto', with a squadron of the Scottish lifeguards, along with four handpicked officers from each of the other Scottish regiments, 'to watch every night'. For the first time, too, guards were now placed inside the king's apartments, and three government ships – *The Leopard*, *The Constant Warwick* and *The Greyhound* – were stationed to watch the suspect Dutch vessel. Lacking hard evidence to implicate him in an escape plot, Charles was still given leave to play golf on the so-called 'Shieldfield', where he had been accosted some time earlier by a 'distracted' woman who refused to 'hould her peace' and told him that it was better for him 'to be with his Parliament than to be there'. But from this point forth he could do so only with Leven in direct attendance, and even the more eccentric of his supporters became the object of close scrutiny. For when 'a young woman at Morpeth' proclaimed herself to be the king's daughter, Princess Elizabeth, even she, we are told, was subject to interrogation before being 'whipt and sent going'.

Yet the disappointment of Charles' first abortive attempt to escape by no means exhausted either his own or Murray's determination to break loose while any crumb of hope remained. On 28 December, for example, the latter appears to have attended a meeting at The Angel Inn, after which Tobias Parker was dispatched to Hartlepool to 'see what ships were there' now that the Dutch man-of-war, still at anchor in Newcastle, was under suspicion. But the desperation of the hour did not, it seems, produce the man for the moment, since Peaker had proceeded no further than half a mile beyond Gateshead when, in his own words, he began to ponder 'the consequents of that business' and, 'not being willing to be accessory to an action which might prove so prejudicial to the kingdome', turned and rode back to the place he had just passed, leaving his horse at a blacksmith's shop, before proceeding direct to the mayor to tell him the whole business. Leven duly confronted Murray with the incriminating letter, carried by Peaker, enquiring about the availability of ships for a voyage that he was planning. Though, predictably, there was no direct hint in the letter of the king's involvement, his guard was nevertheless doubled – 'both within his residence and without' – that same day.

According to the account of the escape attempt contained in the *Memoirs of the Dukes of Hamilton*, Charles himself had lost his nerve even before the enterprise had been exposed. Wearing a disguise, he had allegedly gone down the backstairs of Anderson House, before turning back in fear of the guards and 'judging it hugely indecent to be catched in such a condition'. If so, it would not be the last time that the king's supreme confidence at the planning stage suddenly melted at the critical point of execution. But when he wrote to his wife on Saturday, 2 January, with the possibility of his death plainly in mind, there was no similar hint of indecision. Indeed, with none of his previous pleadings and self-justification, he laid down what appeared to be his last great requirement from his wife: namely, that she and Prince Charles should 'declare publicly' that his offers to his enemies had been reasonable and 'that neither of you will persuade me to go further, but rather dissuade me, if I had a mind to grant more'. In this way, Charles reasoned, his enemies would not be tempted to replace him with his heir, 'for if there be the least imagination that Prince Charles will grant more, then I shall not live long after'. As such, a public declaration of the sort specified was 'absolutely necessary for my preservation'. With this stark truth, the king concluded. There was no need for further discussion, he reassured his wife, 'for I know thy love will omit nothing that is possible for my freedom'. Nor should she ever 'despair of a good cause', or abandon her labours for their son, 'even as thou loves me, who am eternally thine'.

Just over two weeks earlier, on 16 December, thirty-six carts containing £200,000 had set out from London under a 'large convoy' of Parliamentarian troops, and the day following Charles' plea to Henrietta Maria, they duly reached York. The journey had been long and arduous – 'the waies being very bad' and 'the monies overturned, the boxes dirty' – but the soldiers, though weary 'after many a lang dayes march', were still 'blithe and merry' enough to upset their officers by 'leaping in the churchyard after all their marching so far in the durt'. By that stage, it seems, they had passed beyond fatigue and were in no mood either to dwell upon the purpose for which their cargo of 'good gold and silver coins' was now to be put. Yet they had been responsible, in fact, for the safe transport of nothing less than a king's ransom – though not one to guarantee his liberty, but rather to ensure his transfer from Scottish to

English captivity. For in return for a payment in recompense for all the 'pains, hazards and charges' they had incurred during their involvement in the Civil War, the Scots had agreed at last to deliver the king into Parliament's hands and withdraw from England for good.

For twelve days the money remained in York while English and Scottish treasury clerks counted the coins: several hundred thousand of them at least, and perhaps over a million if, as seems likely, much of the money was in silver. Carefully packed into bags, each containing £100 and secured with the seals of both England and Scotland, the money was then placed, ten bags at a time, into wooden chests, which were once more sealed by both parties. Clearly, neither Scotsmen nor Englishmen were entirely trustful of the other, and it was equally plain that this was no surprise. The wartime alliance between the two old foes had, after all, been a marriage of convenience from the outset, sure to be sundered as soon their separate ends were achieved. So when the job was finished on 15 January, and the carts trundled northwards with their booty to the waiting Scottish troops at Newcastle – 'each one reaching for his share' – the parting was a welcome relief on all sides. Any Scottish qualms about the sacrifice of their anointed monarch had been smoothly allayed by a much-needed injection of Sassenach cash, while for MPs at Westminster, the disappearance of their northern neighbours offered respite, freedom of action and the opportunity to focus without distraction upon their ultimate goal: the bringing to heel of the 'Man of Blood' who, by his stubborn refusal to submit to his subjects' just claims, had racked his kingdom with four long years of civil war.

4

TO ENGLISH HANDS

'For now, it is only the question I shall be a prisoner in England or Scotland. I think to be better used in England, though I have more friends in Scotland.'

Charles I, 15 January 1647

Since at least September, the king had fully recognised the limits of his Scottish captors' patience and that, if frustrated, they would have little hesitation ultimately in handing him over to Parliament. Yet when a group of parliamentary commissioners, consisting of Lords Pembroke, Denbigh and Montague and six MPs, reached Newcastle on 23 January – their horses 'scarce able to hold out' after the long journey – he proceeded to treat them as though he had some choice in the matter, receiving them like petitioners in his Presence Chamber and graciously hearing their message before dismissing them almost casually with the bland assurance that they would have his response after due consideration. Upon their meeting, he had held out his hand to be kissed, 'with affability', and 'seemed very well pleased' with the news that the delegation had been instructed 'to receive the person of the King from the Scots army, and to serve him during the journey' to his house at Holdenby, 60 miles north of London in Northamptonshire. Thoroughly at ease and displaying no hint of malice before a 'full thronged' audience, Charles made clear, too, that all were 'very welcome', since 'none of them were strangers to him', and that their business was 'no less welcome' than they. Eager now 'to remove jealousies and distrusts, and establish a right understanding betwixt him and his two Houses of Parliament', the king even exchanged some 'mirthful passages' with the deputation's head, the Earl of Pembroke, who had so often entertained him at Wilton in the far-off, carefree days of the 1630s.

Still, however, it was not too late for Charles to avoid being handed over to the English. If, as the Scots urged, he was finally to embrace Presbyterianism, he might yet be taken with them to the safety of his northern kingdom. Otherwise, as they made clear with their familiar candour, he would surely be forced to endure the 'strictness' of the English Independents, who would not only deprive him 'of the consolation of receiving the queen's letters and of the visits of his friends', but also treat him like a criminal, posting a watchman 'to sleep in his bedroom' every night – something especially irksome to Charles, since he 'disliked having strangers about him'. But though the threats were compelling, they failed to achieve the desired effect. On the contrary, the king remained adamant, as Montreuil recorded, 'that he would never give his consent', since 'what was asked of him was equally opposed to his peace of conscience and the welfare of his people'. Instead, he would abide with quiet confidence in the fond belief that all would end favourably and the firm conviction that his subjects could never manage without him. Earlier, on 27 October, he had informed Jermyn, Culpepper and Ashburnham that the balance of power between the English and Scots remained in his hands and that, without his authority, 'the two nations must needs fall out'. This remained his view even now. 'Without my establishing,' he declared, 'there can be no peace.'

In Paris, meanwhile, the queen, who had believed until now that the Scots would never abandon their king, shared none of her husband's optimism. Indeed, she wept every day, overcome by the 'unhappy case' of her husband, who 'finds himself abandoned by all before the gates of a prison'. In desperation, she considered a trip to Ireland to muster support for the Royalist cause and toyed once more with the option of retiring to a monastery, though her ultimate destination proved to be Austria, where she complained 'with bitter tears' to her sister-in-law, Anne, of 'the conditions of herself and her husband' and laid the blame for their misfortunes upon France. The French ministers, she declared, had deceived her with empty promises 'of the great things they would do' when peace arrived once more in Europe, only for these 'long delayed hopes' to reduce both her and her husband 'to the utmost extremity'. She had no faith in Charles' continued hope that, once in English hands, the Scots would back down and 'do for him … what they have refused to do when they had him with them'. Nor, it seems, was there any trust in his conviction that those same servants who had failed to liberate him at Newcastle would somehow 'deliver him from Holdenby'.

In the event, Charles was simply left to prepare hurriedly for the latest stage of his restless odyssey. Some four days after their arrival, the parliamentary commissioners repeated their wish that 'orders might be given' for the king's departure, and in the meantime he had destroyed all those papers that 'he could not without some risk of harm carry away with him'. Writing to the Marquis of Ormonde in Ireland, the very last place where his supporters still held sway, Charles ordered him to follow the queen's and the prince's direction, and not to stick at anything 'for want of legal power from the king'. There was a last letter, too, for Henrietta Maria, which confirmed the scale of his predicament. On the one hand, she must believe no future message from him unless it was delivered by an individual of unquestionable loyalty. Nor, at the same time, was she to allow Prince Charles to come to England, no matter what 'threats or entreaties' Parliament might make and irrespective of any fears of her own that she might harbour for him.

Now, most of the old servants who had waited on him at Oxford were to be dismissed, and others – who had neither 'assisted in this unnatural war against Parliament' nor 'adhered to the enemy' – appointed in their place. Nine in number, the leading members of the king's new household consisted of Colonel Thomas Herbert and James Harrington, Grooms of the Bedchamber; Sir Fulke Greville, Gentleman Usher of the Privy Chamber and Cup Bearer; Captain Anthony Mildmay, Gentleman Usher of the Privy Chamber and Carver; Captain Middleton, Gentleman Usher of the Privy Chamber and Sewer; Mr Anstey, Gentleman Usher Daily Waiter; Mr Babbington, Groom of the Privy Chamber and Barber; Mr John Joyner, Master Cook; and Dr Wilson, physician. All, naturally, were loyal Parliamentarians and men of manners and good character who could be relied upon to serve the king with all due respect to his rank. Indeed Joyner, in particular, came with the special recommendation of the House of Commons, since he had served as a captain of distinction in the Parliamentary army. Though the post of cook might therefore seem unworthy of his previous status, he clearly gave good service in this capacity, for he and Herbert alone remained among the king's retainers until his death.

Less conspicuous among the king's new attendants, but in the longer run more significant than most, was a certain Henry Firebrace, who had accompanied Lord Denbigh as his secretary and would come in the months ahead to perform a key role as a double agent, acting ostensibly as a guard whilst secretly ensuring transit of the king's correspondence and assisting in later escape attempts. He recorded later in his *Narrative*:

> Being at Newcastle when the Scots delivered his Majestie to the English, I did (by his directions, to the end that I might with greater Freedome, and less suspition of those, who had him in Custodie) make my application to some of the commissioners that I might be admitted to attend his Majestie as one of the pages of his Bedchamber in which I prevailed.'

Born in 1619 or 1620, the sixth son of Robert Firebrace of Derby and Susan Jerome of Kegworth, Leicestershire, 'honest Harry Firebrace' had been educated at Repton until the age of 14 before his family moved to London and he was apprenticed to Richard Green, a scrivener of All Hallows, Barking. It was the coming of war in 1642, however, that suddenly and decisively changed Firebrace's life, when his sister Rebecca, through the influence of her patroness Lady Villiers, managed to secure a place for him as Lord Denbigh's 'Secretary to the Counsells of War'. Like Denbigh himself a monarchist at heart, the young man thus found himself uneasily attached to a Parliamentarian cause that he would not hesitate to abandon when opportunity arose. That opportunity had now arisen in the most unexpected and significant of fashions, for Denbigh, it seems, had hoped through Firebrace's presence in the royal household to persuade the king to make concessions to Parliament which might preserve the monarchy, or, if this failed, to place Firebrace close enough to the king to assist, if necessary, in saving his life.

Already, then, the king's affairs were entering a new, more critical, more clandestine phase: a point where unrelenting vigilance, espionage, counter-espionage, ciphers, codes and other cloak-and dagger dealings would be constant features. For while Charles I's everyday world had shrunk to a fragment of its former scale, it remained a crucial microcosm upon which the broader political universe still hinged, with the predictable result that its membership became a matter of considerable hard-bargaining. On 1 February, for instance, two days before his departure for the queen's former house at Holdenby, Charles requested, according to the *Moderate Intelligencer*, that some of his former attendants be retained. 'Might he not,' he asked, 'have old servants go along with him and sometimes cast his eye upon if not serve him?' Accordingly, Patrick Maule and James Maxwell were allowed to remain in their old posts as Grooms of the Bedchamber – 'in which place they had many years faithfully served the king' – while one day later, after they had waited on him at dinner, the others 'kissed his Majesty's hand and with great expressions of grief for their dismiss, poured forth their prayers for his Majesty's freedom and preservation and so departed'.

This, however, by no means ended the chess-game process of framing the king's circle of servants. For along with a Clerk of the Avery named Preston, whose task was to supply oats and fodder for the king's horses, a Eurieman and Clerk of the Mouth called John Burroughs, who among other things was to tend the king's table linen, a Cellarman called Lewen, and a Butteryman and Undercook named Catchaside and Andrew respectively, there were also three other figures of much more considerable long-term importance: Francis Cresset, who was appointed the king's Steward and Treasurer; Captain Silius Titus, who became his Equerry and was given £150 for the upkeep of his horses; and Abraham Dowcett, who was installed Clerk of the Kitchen and entrusted with £100 to provide for the king's diet. 'His Majestie hath now other maner of Table and attendance than formerly,' reported one news-sheet at this time, 'a great many honest godly courtiers and good soldiers, Mr Herbert, Sir Fulke Grevill, Captain Mildmay, Carver, Mr Harrington of the bedchamber, Mr Dowcett, Captain Titus, Equerry, etc.' But the writer is likely to have expressed altogether less satisfaction if he had known those cited more fully. For Dowcett and Titus were later to transfer their allegiance wholly to the king's side – taking an active role in smuggling his private correspondence and organising plans for his escape – while Cresset, like Firebrace, was already a secret Royalist.

The very same day that these appointments were made, indeed, there occurred a fleeting glimpse of things to come when one of the king's old servants, a certain Mungo Murray, took leave of the king for his home in Scotland. For while Murray knelt to kiss his sovereign's hand on parting, Charles was seen to slip something into his grasp, after which the Scotsman was accordingly followed, stopped and searched. He had been carrying, it seems, a letter addressed to Montreuil, and was subsequently kept in custody for two days before being released on security. Even so, Murray had become one of the early victims of the game of cat and mouse that would be played out ever more desperately in the coming months. His message, like the many others that were later intercepted, was taken to Parliament for decoding, and though Charles did not make their task easy, the cryptographers involved were never, it seems, unequal to their task. In each case, the coded letters, many of which still survive, consisted of rows of numerals, each denoting a letter, syllable or word, while blank numerals, or 'nulls', were inserted at intervals to render the deciphering process more difficult. For extra security, the king also kept a different cipher for each correspondent, and frequently changed the cipher even when writing to the same correspondent, though this had not prevented the Oxford mathematician, Dr John Wallis, from decrypting the letters famously captured at Naseby, and nor would it foil Wallis' successors.

In the meantime, however, the Scots at least had no more need for such murky dealings. For on the morning of Saturday, 30 January 1647, they paraded their entire cavalry through the centre of Newcastle, then on past Anderson House and out into the countryside. By the afternoon there were just 500 soldiers in the town, ready to hand over to the 500 English soldiers who duly arrived at 2 p.m. It was, we are told, a 'friendly and brotherly parting' on the Scottish side, with the troops under strict orders not 'to plunder any houses, drive away any goods, nor exact … any moneys or provision', though Newcastle's townsfolk were unassuaged by any parting show of goodwill. For them the Scots were 'nothing but Jews', 'people who had sold their king and their honour', and doughty local fishwives cried 'Judas' as the Scots passed by, pipes skirling, while Charles himself added to the biblical theme by taunting his former captors with the jibe that they had sold him 'at too cheap a rate'. Such, indeed, was the level of passion from all directions that newly arrived English officers were said to have been forced to 'blows and threats, to prevent the women of this town from following the Scottish troops and throwing stones at them while they were leaving'.

Inside Anderson House, meanwhile, the Scots' commissioners were taking an apologetic leave of the king. Some, indeed, had tears in their eyes as they told him 'that as he had failed to sign the proposals and treaties, they were obliged to hand him over to the English'. But Charles was predictably unmoved by their professions of regret. Instead, he told them roundly that their refusal to receive him in Scotland was of no importance, 'as even if he had been at liberty, he would rather have gone to those who bought than to those who sold him', though the show of bravado was short-lived, for as the Scots withdrew, their English counterparts 'at once set their guards'. From now on the king's captors were ordered by their superiors at Westminster that they were not 'to allow any letter or paper to be given to him that they had not previously seen'. In consequence, the regular correspondence with his wife that had so far sustained Charles would have to be conducted through secret intermediaries, and while the niceties of his regal status would continue to be observed at Holdenby, his enemies seemed adamant that he would have to remain there 'always', a perpetual prisoner, 'until he has granted everything'.

Yet Charles' departure from Newcastle – more than nine months after his escape from Oxford – nevertheless offered not only welcome relief from a period of unremitting gloom, but even reassurance of a kind. Accompanied by the parliamentary commissioners, their staff and the newly constituted royal household, and escorted by 900 horse, he left on 3 February. The journey of some 160 miles to Holdenby would prove, to all intents and purposes, a veritable royal progress of the old style, passing through Durham, Richmond, Ripon, Leeds, Rotherham, Nottingham and Leicester, with people flocking to see their monarch, pressing forward to be 'touched' for healing of the 'Evil', as the disease of scrofula was then known, and greeting him with cries of joy and prayers for his preservation. For all of 2 miles outside Leeds, indeed, the roads were lined with well-wishers, while at Nottingham none other than General Fairfax, his old adversary, stood ready to honour him. Nowhere, it seems, were the onlookers given 'any check or disturbance' by the soldiers – 'a civility his Majesty was well pleased with' – and the journey as a whole, which lasted a total of thirteen days, proved a much-needed tonic to the king's careworn spirits, 'causing many a smile from his princely countenance'. Just as in freer times, it seems, when he had cheerfully moved from one hunting lodge to another, a change of venue had always lifted the king's spirits, and now was no exception.

At Holdenby itself, meanwhile, painstaking preparations had been made for the king's arrival. By the direction of a Committee of both Houses, Clement Kinnersley, the Yeoman of his Majesty's Wardrobe, had been sent from London with a party of workmen to superintend the fitting of the residence with 'hangings, bedding and other wardrobe stuffe and necessaries'. Upon his arrival, Charles found himself greeted by the Northamptonshire gentry, notwithstanding the county's well-known

Puritan sympathies, as well as 'others of ordinary rank' who 'stood ready there, to welcome the King, with joyful countenances and prayers'. There awaited him, too, lavish provision for his dietary requirements, since he had been granted an allowance of twenty-eight dishes at £30 per day, which was every bit as generous as he had enjoyed in his earlier pomp. Indeed, a household staff of 120 servants brought him everything he needed, except, of course, his freedom – which was denied by a substantial garrison costing £282 a day under the command of Major-General Browne and Colonel Graves – and the consolation of his own Anglican chaplain, of which Parliament had seen fit to deprive him. Ultimately, the king would refuse to attend the prescribed Presbyterian services, spending Sundays alone in his room in prayer, study and contemplation, and when the appointed Presbyterian ministers, Reverends Marshall and Carrill, said grace, Charles would respond by intoning his own Anglican blessing.

Aside from such irritants, however, the king would spend his time at Holdenby in comparative comfort. Re-establishing the ordered life that was always his preference, he read for two to three hours each day, played chess and took vigorous walks with Major-General Browne and the Earl of Pembroke, who invariably struggled to keep stride with the king's rapid pacing up and down the long gravel walk in Holdenby's garden. There was opportunity, too, for him to indulge his particular enthusiasm for bowls, resulting in rides to Lord Vaux's house at Harrowden, around 9 miles away, where 'there was a good bowling-green with gardens, groves and walks that afforded much pleasure', and the Earl of Sunderland's house at the nearer location of Althorpe, 'where also there was a green well kept'. Not altogether surprisingly under such circumstances, Charles soon appeared in excellent health, eating abstemiously at meals, drinking only a little beer and 'wine and water mixt', and enjoying especially good relations with one of his new keepers, Thomas Herbert – a quiet, unassuming character who, as the king's constant companion, eventually gained his complete trust and what may well be considered affection.

Born in York in 1606, Herbert came in fact from a family of merchants and aldermen, who enjoyed not only significant status in their own right but a crucial connection with the Herbert earls of Pembroke. His grandfather had been Governor of the Merchant Adventurers' Company and Lord Mayor of York in 1573, and in 1627 Herbert himself benefited from the 3rd Earl of Pembroke's patronage to serve under

Sir Dodmore Cotton on a three-year journey to India, Africa and Persia. The result was an extraordinary book, entitled *A Relation of Some Yeares Travaile Begunne Anno 1626 into Afrique and the Greater Asia*, which won him lasting fame after its publication in 1634, as perhaps the foremost travel writer of the seventeenth century. Filled with remarkable sketches of dodos, broad-billed parrots, cuneiform inscriptions, the ruins of Persepolis and a host of other curiosities, Herbert's account also displays all the wonder of a young man marvelling at erotic wall paintings in New Julfa or the size of the Shah Abbas' moustache, while revealing at one and the same time a number of keen insights into the many admirable aspects of his own personality as he bounces around, fever-ridden, on the back of a camel, but refuses to turn his thieving nurse over to the Persian authorities for fear of what they might do to her.

Thereafter, he had returned to England by 1634 and retired from court to his Tintern estate, only to re-emerge with the outbreak of the Civil War, during which he served on Parliament's side and performed with sufficient distinction to achieve his appointment in the newly constituted royal household – a role requiring every ounce of his energy, dedication, patience and self-effacing discretion, since it was well known that the king had taken it 'very ill that his old servants were taken from him'. At Newcastle, indeed, Charles had not hesitated to use sharp words with some of the new ones, and Herbert's trepidation at his first interview with his new master, which he relates in his account of his service during the years of the king's captivity, was palpable. Both Herbert and his fellow Groom of the Bedchamber, Sir James Harrington, had in fact been refused access to the king after their initial appointment, and it was only some time afterwards that the former was eventually escorted into Charles' presence by James Maxwell after dinner one night at Holdenby. Kneeling before his master, Herbert was 'enjoined to secrecy' and told to take down a message to Parliament, which Charles proceeded to dictate.

The result was clearly satisfactory, for it was not long after, according to Herbert's own account, that both he and Harrington were admitted as trusted members of the king's intimate circle. Indeed, only a week or so after his initial meeting with the pair, Charles told the parliamentary commissioners:

that he had taken notice of Mr Harrington and Mr Thomas Herbert, and being well satisfied with the report he had concerning them, as to their sobriety and good Education, he was willing to receive them as Grooms into his Bedchamber to wait upon his person along with Mr Maxwell and Mr Mawl, which the Commissioners approving, they were that night admitted and by his Majesty instructed as to the Duty and Service he expected from them.

James Harrington too, then, it seems, was to enjoy a special relationship with Charles, which would last right up to the time around New Year 1649 when their association was abruptly terminated by Parliamentarians furious, it is said, over his refusal to swear to report anything he might hear of a royal escape attempt. At least two contemporary accounts speak of Harrington with Charles upon the scaffold; indeed, and like his colleague Herbert, he was a man of both substance and wide experience. Younger than Herbert by five years, he was born in 1611 in Upton, Northamptonshire, the eldest son of Sir Sapcotes Harrington of Rand in Lincolnshire, and a great-nephew of the first Lord Harrington of Exton, though the early years of his manhood were marked by a restlessness not altogether typical of his class. At the age of 18, he entered Trinity College, Oxford, as a gentleman commoner, though he left two years later with no degree, and subsequently departed the Middle Temple even more abruptly, developing an animus towards lawyers, which found ample expression in his book, *The Commonwealth of Oceana*, published in 1656. In between times, prior to his entry into the royal household, he had enlisted in a Dutch militia regiment – apparently seeing no service – before touring the Netherlands, Denmark, Germany, France, Switzerland and Italy. In the summer of 1635, it seems, he was in Geneva, and subsequently completed his travels in Rome, where, we are told, he 'refused to kiss the Pope's foot'.

Yet his return to England was chiefly unremarkable, for although he came to Parliament's financial assistance during 1641 and 1642, and again in 1645, he appears simply to have settled for anonymity at Rand, living the life of an 'unmarried country gentleman of studious tastes'. Why, indeed, Harrington was eventually appointed to the royal household remains something of a mystery, although his well-known republican views are certain to have convinced many of his reliability, and he had already obtained experience as a servant to Prince Charles Louis, son of Elizabeth, Queen of Bohemia, the king's eldest sister. Herbert describes him, in fact, as 'a Gentleman well accomplished' who 'had waited upon the Prince Elector Palatine in his Chamber, had travelled, Germany, Italy and France, and spake their languages'. Other contemporary accounts confirmed the king's fondness for Harrington, notwithstanding his political views. According to Anthony Wood, for instance, 'His Majesty loved his company' and found him not only 'an ingenious man' but 'chose rather to converse with him than with others of his chamber'. Though 'when they happened to talk of a Commonwealth, the King seemed not able to endure it', Wood makes no suggestion of any resulting hostility, for 'they had often discourses concerning government' and were otherwise apparently of a like mind on all matters.

Even so, it was Herbert who continued to exercise a special influence, displaying both loyalty to the MPs that had appointed him and a personal devotion to the king that made betrayal unthinkable. In recent times, it is true, there has been some variation of opinion upon the selflessness of Herbert's service to his master. In 1678, for example, he published *Threnodia Carolina*, an account of the last two years of the king's life, which has now become a standard source, where Herbert himself appears a model of dedication, being too distraught to be with the king on the scaffold and, on another occasion, bursting into tears when the king seemed upset by some news he had brought. But *Threnodia Carolina* may, some say, have been produced for ulterior motives – an attempt, on the one hand, to give Herbert a good name with Charles II, who did indeed award him a baronetcy, and a ploy to clear the name of his regicide son-in-law Robert Phayre. Nor, of course, would Herbert have been the first to massage his account out of self-interest. Yet many of those appointed to the king's service by Parliament, and many a stauncher Roundhead than he, were converted into Royalists upon closer acquaintance with Charles the man. Herbert himself, to his credit, never professed to any such conversion, preferring instead to maintain a benevolent neutrality, neither aiding nor exposing the king's escape attempts, though delivering more in the process, it must be said, by his prudence and moderation than many of his master's more hot-blooded supporters.

During his stay at Holdenby, in any case, the king appears to have given up all thoughts of escape, though this by no means prevented the efforts of his friends to maintain a secret correspondence with him. Letters, it seems, were brought in by various means, sometimes by ladies who came to kiss the king's hand, or in other cases by those who still came to Holdenby to be touched for the 'Evil'. Among its many other side effects, the war had deprived Charles' subjects of the opportunity to seek the traditional cure from their sovereign, and he was especially gratified by their continued belief in his healing powers. Since the stream of sufferers to Holdenby was surprisingly steady, moreover, so too, it seems, were the opportunities for Royalist interlopers. There were other more systematic attempts, it seems, to keep the king abreast of the wider world's affairs. For during Charles' stay at Holdenby, he was visited by the Countess of Lanark, on her way from Edinburgh to France, who offered 'to do anything in [the king's] service', so that he could maintain contact with his wife.

Communicating with the French ambassador whenever 'passing through London', the countess was already, it seems, part of a courier network in southern England that had been enjoying significant success for some time. For on only two occasions do we hear of letters being intercepted by the king's captors. On 9 April, for instance, Major Humphrey Bosvile, a former officer in the Royalist army, assumed the disguise of a 'rustic' angler, and intercepted the king while he was dismounting by a bridge at Harrowden on his way to Boughton to play bowls. Slipping a packet of letters from the queen into Charles' hands, Bosvile was able to retreat some distance before being exposed by a local miller who had been more vigilant than the surrounding guards and subsequently refused to accept a bribe to remain silent. When apprehended and questioned, Bosvile duly admitted that he had brought letters from the queen, while claiming to know nothing of the contents, except that he had heard from Lady Culpepper that they contained a request from Prince Charles that he be allowed to serve in Flanders under the Duke of Orléans. However, with the kind of neck-or-nothing panache that typified many Cavaliers of his kind, Bosvile could not resist an opportunity for the last word. For when, according to the news-sheet *Moderate Intelligencer*, 'it was demanded of him how he dared to do such a thing as deliver letters to his Majesty, he answered that if he could not have done it in the way he did, he would have done it openly before them all', even if it were to mean 'he had dyed for it'.

Nor would the king himself divulge the letters' contents to the parliamentary commissioners at Holdenby. On 4 March, Nicholas Oudart had observed from Holland that 'the king is so narrowly watched that nobody can privately speak with him nor present to, nor receive from him anything but what his overseers admit'. Yet if

Charles found himself increasingly hemmed in, he was king nevertheless and even his 'overseers' seem to have recognised, up to a point, the moral limitations resulting from this. For when pressed for details about his wife's correspondence, Charles told his interrogators emphatically how 'he was not to give account to any man living', and the issue was pursued no further. Plainly, in the situation pertaining, it was not always clear which party was ascendant. The same kind of ambivalence, resulting from Parliament's reluctance to press home its advantage with the kind of vigour that might be expected, manifested itself in other ways, too, as the prisoner continued to defy, and his supporters continued to offend, with remarkable impunity. Bosvile, indeed, was sent to London to account for his actions and committed by Parliament to Newgate Prison for his troubles, only to reappear at various intervals, making regular escapes from imprisonment in the process, to carry dispatches to France and Holland.

Even more intriguing, however, were the activities and treatment of a certain 'wondrous bold' and 'handsome' lady who was seized and searched at Holdenby a few weeks after Bosvile's exposure. According to an account written at the time by a minor courtier named Roger Corbet, a woman 'calling herself Lady Cave, a gentleman's daughter about Stamford' had received a letter brought from France by a gentleman or his servant, and subsequently approached 'another gentlewoman in these parts', whose name was never revealed, to assist her in delivering it to the king. The letter, it seems, had been written by Jack Ashburnham and delivered by John Browne, a barber of St Ives who had risen to become Ashburnham's right-hand man, while the 'Lady Cave' mentioned by Corbet appears to have been Mary Cave, daughter of William Cave, deputy lieutenant of Northamptonshire, with whom the king had stayed overnight during his flight from Oxford to Newark the previous year. If so, the deputy lieutenant's daughter was an obvious choice for the task. Of sufficient rank to be allowed access to the king and of sufficient loyalty to be entrusted with the task, she was also a member of a family that, to all outward appearances at least, had served the Parliamentary cause without demur up to this point.

But why the services of a mysterious, unnamed third party were required is almost as intriguing as the identity of the other, unnamed, lady herself. It is certainly known that the legendary Jane Whorwood – sister of the Countess of Lanark and one of the most remarkable, unsung stalwarts of the Royalist cause during the king's captivity –

was in the vicinity of Northampton at this time, as she continued to shadow her royal master and serve his interests at every opportunity. This time, it seems, she was at the home of Sir Robert Banastre, former master of the household to James I, and she too was an obvious candidate for the task of conveying Ashburnham's letter. With a view to assisting the escape of Henrietta Maria and Prince Charles to France, she had already arranged in 1644 for some 775kg of gold bullion to be smuggled into Oxford in barrels of soap, and it was not without good reason that she would later be hailed by her contemporary Anthony Wood as 'the most loyal person to King Charles in his miseries as any woman in England'. Equally crucially, she was also the stepdaughter of James Maxwell, one of the bedchamber grooms that Charles had been allowed to retain, and would therefore have enjoyed ample opportunity to gain access to the king's apartments at Holdenby.

In any event, it was the unnamed woman enlisted by Lady Cave who eventually proceeded to a house where an officer of the king's Parliamentary escort named Captain Abbott had his lodgings. Staying there for several nights, she appears to have managed, with the landlady's help, to enlist Abbott's assistance in gaining permission for Lady Cave to kiss the king's hand, as intended, though it was at this point that problems arose. For the landlady, who had been trusted with the secret of the letter, informed her husband, and although he was a Royalist and therefore 'favourable to the design' in principle, he decided that he dared not run the risk of detection. Informed by the husband of what was transpiring, Abbott, who was described for good reason as a 'very honest faithful gentleman', duly informed the parliamentary commissioners at Holdenby, with the result that the scheme was allowed to run its course until the offenders could be caught red-handed.

Accordingly, when Mary Cave arrived at Holdenby on 11 May, she was duly arrested, taken into a room and searched, but managed in the process to slip the offending letter behind a tapestry, so that nothing was found upon her. Left to return home, it was not until two days later, in fact, that Cave was again apprehended after the hidden letter was eventually discovered. Ostensibly a petition referring to some goods lost at sea, it contained on the back, probably written in lemon juice, a ciphered message, in which Ashburnham promised a 'good war for your recovery', involving Dutch and Irish forces led by the heir to the throne. In view of this, the message continued, the king should give no ground to Parliament. There was advice, too, from '389' – the code number for the queen; '389,' the message ran, 'hopes you have burned all your letters and ciphers. If you have not, for God's sake do it. You will still remember the alphabet.'

Though far from unexpected, the message was nevertheless incendiary stuff and more than adequate grounds, if Parliament had chosen to press its case, for Mary Cave and her associates to have been pursued with full rigour. But her claims, under interrogation, that she had not known the contents of the letter were accepted with what can only be described as remarkable blitheness. Indeed, after a brief period of custody by the Mayor of Northampton, during which time Parliament agents arrived to question her, she appears to have been released without punishment. Even John Browne, whom she implicated in her testimony, was also, it seems, spared any formal legal proceedings – presumably on the grounds that he had been acting under directions from his master. In the aftermath of the whole episode, the only action seems to have been a minor pruning of suspect servants from the royal household. By that time, of course, the unnamed female accomplice who had facilitated the whole episode was long vanished.

Thereafter, it appears to have been the king's own servants, including Jane Whorwood's stepfather himself, who assumed the most prominent role in maintaining the steady flow of royal correspondence. Appointed Black Rod in 1622, and acting, after the dissolution of Parliament in 1629, as pawnbroker and financier to the king on the security of the royal jewels, James Maxwell had previously served as Groom of the Bedchamber to both Charles, before he became king, and his elder brother Prince Henry. But he was also known for his entrepreneurial success through his experiments in the manufacture of iron at the mines he owned in the Peak District, and for the exploitation of the patent for the manufacture of pipe clay which Charles had granted him in 1638. With strong connections to the City of London, he had been able to work closely with sympathetic merchants to raise funds for the Royalist cause, and he would not hesitate now, along with Harry Firebrace, to provide whatever further assistance he might on the king's behalf.

Ironically, however, two of the most dedicated smugglers of illicit correspondence proved to be men installed in the royal household by Parliament itself. Francis Cresset, the Steward and Treasurer, was a gentleman of an old family in Shropshire, who had first entered service for the Bishop of Durham and later became attached to the Earl of

Pembroke. After the death of his father and brother, who were both killed while fighting on the Royalist side, however, he was nevertheless able to become an agent in conveying letters to and from the king by remaining attached to Pembroke on the advice of another Royalist agent, the Reverend John Barwick, D.D. In this way he not only escaped suspicion, but was able to obtain, through his master, parliamentary passports for pedlars and others who were carrying secret correspondence. Considered by Pembroke a man in whom complete trust could be placed, Cresset's defection would prove invaluable. Indeed, Cresset, who was accorded his own code letter 'A' in the flow of ciphered messages, would be one of those specially singled out by the king for his 'harty and industrious endeavours in this my service'.

Another whom Charles would 'alwais remember' was Abraham Dowcett, or Doucet, a Frenchman by birth, who seems to have originated from Rouen, where his uncle was governor. Always referred to as 'F' in the king's ciphered messages, Dowcett was in fact a Protestant who had been in the king's service as early as 1629, when he served abroad under the Earl of Holland. But though he subsequently became a Page of the Bedchamber, he presumably took the side of Parliament in some capacity during the Civil War, in order to be appointed in the first place to his new role as Clerk of the Kitchen in the imprisoned king's household. He appears to have lost no time in reverting to his former allegiance when placed in close association with the king. For in a petition to Charles II after the Restoration, he claimed, 'at the hazard of his life', to have served his royal master by supplying him 'with pen and ink when the Commissioners debarred him of them' and conveying 'letters between him and the Queen and other secret intelligence'.

That the king should indeed have been deprived of writing materials at Holdenby seems almost surprising, perhaps, in view of the respect and freedom he was clearly accorded in other respects. But some confirmation of Dowcett's own role is provided in a letter written by Nicholas Oudart to Sir Edward on 18 February 1647. 'They permit him not to speak privately or write to anybody save when themselves are by to heare and see', observed Oudart, though the king, he continued, 'suffers none of the Commissioners to lodge in his bedchamber, but puts out the candle and bolts the door himself'. It was then, it seems, at dead of night and free from observation, that Charles composed his letters, loyally assisted by Dowcett, who was already smuggling ink and paper into the royal bedchamber.

The games of bowls and chess, the brisk garden walks, the lei-surely stints of private reading and the company of respectful, and in some cases loyal, servants did not, however, belie the deeper real-ity of the king's predicament. After seven months of being harangued by Presbyterian ministers, nagged by his wife, berated by her advisers, rejected by both Parliament and the army, and thwarted in escape, the outward calm of the king's days at Holdenby might well have seemed blissful by comparison. But his captors' refusal to grant him his own chaplains, or to make any concessions regarding religion in return for his own on practically every other subject had left him particularly upset and dejected. On 17 February, he wrote to the Speaker of the House of Commons explaining why 'it is fit for me to be attended by some of my chaplains whose opinions as clergymen I esteem and reverence'. Their presence was necessary, he claimed, 'not merely for the exercise of my conscience, but also ever for clearing my judgement concerning the present differences in religion'. Yet a letter making the same request, seventeen days later, asking Parliament to consider 'the divers reasons which no Christian can be ignorant of', fell on equally deaf ears.

Less than three weeks after arriving at Holdenby, in fact, Charles had complained to the French ambassador that 'never was a prisoner more strictly guarded than I am'. 'I must tell you,' he continued, 'I see nothing but ruin to my person through the behaviour of their com-missioners.' Even though he went on to declare that he was 'resolved the rather to perish than ... act against my conscience', there were telltale signs that even his hitherto adamantine will might be about to falter. In Paris too, for that matter, Henrietta Maria appeared at last to have given up all thought of her own future in England, and her mental distress during those early months appears to have been more acute than ever. Giovanni Nani, reporting from the Venetian embassy in the French capital, observed how 'the Queen of England with bitter tears has lamented to the Regent the condition of herself and her husband, and that the long delayed hopes which have been held out of peace have reduced them to the utmost extremity, in which they are lan-guishing at present'.

Nor had Henrietta's renewed efforts to broker a fresh treaty between the Marquis of Ormonde and the Irish rebels provided any consola-tion. A year earlier, the marquis had succeeded in patching together an interim agreement, but since it contained no commitments concerning religion, the papal nuncio, Rinuccini, supported by the clergy, had persuaded the rebels to repudiate it. For his part, the nuncio still cherished dreams of forging a united, independent and Catholic Ireland under the personal protection of the Pope – a prospect which the embattled Ormonde, responsible for the lives and property of the Protestant settlers across the Irish Sea, could never countenance. Instead, he dealt in realities, which encompassed the king's personal circumstances as much as Ireland's. With the Royalist cause apparently lost and a Catholic triumph in Ireland seemingly imminent, Ormonde was therefore already contemplating the unthinkable: the surrender of Dublin into Parliament's hands, which would finally occur in June.

Bereft and beleaguered, with all other options exhausted, even Charles, therefore, was nearing the point where some form of compromise might prove inescapable if a suitable window of opportunity were to arise – which duly happened on 12 May when an approach by a group of Presbyterian peers was made through Bellièvre, the French ambassador. For concern at the growing stridency of Independents, in both Parliament and the army especially, was now increasingly forcing the pace of events. The Scottish presence in northern England at the invitation of their Presbyterian 'allies' at Westminster, had served, in fact, to boost support for the Independents, but the recent withdrawal shifted the balance once more in favour of their Presbyterian opponents, who favoured the king's speedy restoration on terms of their choosing. In London especially, militant Presbyterianism among the clergy and leading citizens was becoming combined with increasing calls for peace and a return to stability, but in the provinces, too, hostility to high taxation and the presence of the New Model Army was leading to similar calls for restoration of the king on specific conditions. No less importantly, fears of the king's possible dethronement were also leading to a resurgence of Royalist sympathies in Scotland, where since March, the Duke of Hamilton and his allies had been controlling the Scottish commission negotiating at Westminster.

At this critical juncture, then, the king was being offered the possibility of rescuing a semblance of respectability from a lost cause, and on this occasion, weakened by the unremitting anxieties of recent months, he responded accordingly. Retreating significantly on the issue that had consistently dominated his thinking, he now agreed to 'confirm the Presbyterian government' of the Church for three years – so long as 'His Majesty and his household be not hindered from using that form of God's service which they have previously' – and to 'consent by Act of Parliament, that the whole power of the militia, both by sea and land, for the space of ten years, be in such persons as the two Houses of Parliament shall nominate'. No less extraordinary was the declaration, amid Charles' pleas 'presently to be admitted to his Parliament at Westminster', that he was now prepared to 'dispatch his directions to the Prince his son, to return immediately to him' and 'undertake for his ready obedience thereunto'. On other matters such as the Covenant, he was, it is true, considerably more vague, though even here he was careful not to close the door on discussion, so that on 18 May, when his answer was announced at Westminster, both the English Presbyterians and Scots commissioners considered his overall response the basis for an accommodation. Indeed, only two days later, the Lords responded to his persistent pleas to come to London to negotiate directly, by inviting him to come for talk to his palace at Oatlands, only just outside the capital.

But in spite of Charles' hopes that the two Houses of Parliament – 'as they are Englishmen and lovers of peace, by the duty they owe to His Majesty their king, and by the bowels of compassion they have to their fellow-subjects' – might look favourably upon his offer and thereby assure that 'the joyful news of peace may be restored to this languishing kingdom', he had acted too late. Since the establishment of Presbyterianism by MPs in January 1645 and the consequent suppression of nonconformity, the cleavage between Presbyterians and Independents had become increasingly a clash between Parliament and the army, where sectarianism among the common soldiery and certain officers was rife. This was by no means the only cause of tension, for as Parliament's financial difficulties grew, so too did arrears in army pay, which by March 1647 appear to have stood at some £2.5 million. The infantry had received no wages for four-and-a-half months, while arrears for the Horse and Dragoons stood at no less than forty-three weeks. To complete the soldiers' tale of frustration, Parliament was now proposing not only to disband part of the army, but to send the remainder to Ireland.

Under such direct provocation, firebrands like the ubiquitous John Lilburne – who, besides forming a 'Leveller' party among civilians, was now actively involved in forming one among the troops of the New Model Army – found a ready audience. Indeed, so successful were Lilburne and his friends that by April, soldiers were electing 'agitators' to present their case and establishing a Council of the Army to direct their affairs. When, moreover, Sir Thomas Fairfax announced on 31 May that he would not draw up his regiments for disbandment, the rift between Parliament and the army became in effect outright, and Lilburne seized the opportunity to set his own inimitable seal upon matters. On the very same day, in fact, though imprisoned in the Tower, he managed to publish his *Rash Oaths Unwarrantable*, in which he castigated MPs as dastardly renegades and suggested that the king's 'seventeen years misgovernment ... was but a flea-biting or as a molehill to a mountain, in comparison of what this everlasting Parliament already is'.

For Oliver Cromwell and other members of the army's High Command, meanwhile, the position was delicate in the extreme. The general had already begged Parliament on various occasions to consider freedom of conscience, and was reluctant on principle to see the soldiers who had won the war subsequently deprived of their wages. Though he had no wish to meddle in politics, he also remained intensely reluctant to see the army's victory thrown away by cynical Parliament men, anxious to strike deals with the king. The prospect of counter-revolution engineered by Presbyterian MPs like Denzil Holles and other 'such incendiaries' was, after all, increasingly conceivable, and remained no less tolerable for a New Model Army, infected with Leveller zeal for free-thinking and equality, than the renewed spectre of invasion by Scottish Covenanters. As one pamphlet put it – echoing Holles' own disdain for servants riding horses – officers formerly 'cloathed in raggs are now arrayed in Scarlet' while men 'used so long to Command ... have forgotten [how] to obey'. But while Presbyterian lords and Parliamentarians bemoaned an upturned natural order, for common soldiers and their hard-pressed commanders, struggling as they were to maintain discipline, the point of no return had already come and gone.

It was in the early afternoon of 2 June, therefore, whilst enjoying a leisurely game of bowls at Althorp in the company of two parliamentary commissioners, that the king first learned of a cavalry detachment approaching Holdenby. Realising what this was likely to mean, he returned at once to discuss the threat with Major-General Browne and Colonel Graves, and all agreed to stand their ground. Browne called his men together to explain the situation, and doubled the guard, though it was not until midnight that the intruders – a force of 500 battlehardened troopers – finally reached Holdenby and mounted guards at all the entrances. By any standards they were a menacing presence, all volunteers from different units and commanded not by a colonel as was customary for a cavalry regiment, but by a cornet or ensign, the most junior commissioned rank. Cornet George Joyce, a member of Colonel Whalley's regiment, had indeed been a humble tailor's apprentice before serving with distinction under Cromwell and receiving a commission by Sir Thomas Fairfax, who would go on to describe him as 'an Arch-Agitator'. Though, as the most junior officer in Fairfax's own lifeguard, his initial announcement that he had business with the king evoked laughter from Browne and Graves, who greeted him at Holdenby, the mirth was short-lived. For, when asked upon whose authority he requested access to Charles, Joyce's response was steely. His own, he replied. After which, the extent of that authority was swiftly demonstrated when the parliamentary commissioners present at Holdenby were at once placed under guard, as the garrison fraternised openly with Joyce's men.

With Browne and Graves decisively undermined, moreover, and plainly smiling no longer, the cornet then proceeded directly to the king's quarters – with all the calm resolve that might be expected from any young man of conviction who had experienced the sharp end of a bloody war against privilege and hidebound tradition. When asked by Charles' attendants who it was that 'in such uncivil manner and so unseasonable a time came to disquiet the king's rest', Joyce's answer through the locked door that confronted him was once again resolute. Displaying what Sir Thomas Herbert, who was present at the scene, described as 'strange confidence' and 'having a cocked pistol in his hand', he made it clear that, while regrettable, the inconvenience could not be helped, 'for speak with him [the king] he would, and that presently'. Though further demands were necessary, as Joyce 'refused to part with either sword or pistol' and 'pressed for entrance', the declarations of Maxwell, Mawl, Harrington and Herbert, the king's attendants, that they 'were resolved to sacrifice their lives' proved unavailing. For the noise, it seems, awoke the king himself, who then summoned Maxwell by the little silver bell he always kept by his bed, and thereafter – 'being acquainted with the business and uncivil carriage of the Cornet' – sent word that 'he would not rise nor speak with him until morning'. Only the king's personal intervention, therefore, temporarily thwarted Joyce. At which point, we hear, the officer 'huffed' and, 'seeing his design could not be effected in the night', duly waited upon the morrow.

When morning came, however, even the regal scorn of which Charles was amply capable could not delay the inevitable. For after the king had risen 'a little sooner than ordinary' and 'performed his morning exercise', he sent for Joyce, who arrived before him 'with no less confidence than if he had been a supreme officer' and 'acquainted him with the commands he had concerning his removal'. The commissioners, who had been apprehended by Joyce's men, were Charles' initial concern, and the officer duly explained to the king's satisfaction that they were 'to return back unto the Parliament'. But when Charles then asked Joyce for 'a sight of your instructions' to establish the authority under which he was acting, the response could not have been more emphatic. Taking the king to a nearby window, Joyce duly showed him his troop of horse drawn up in the inner court and ready for action. 'These sir,' he declared, 'are my instructions' – leaving Charles with no other option beyond a graceful retort acknowledging the checkmate that had befallen him so suddenly. Looking long and hard at the soldiers before him – 'and finding them proper men and well mounted and well armed' – the king told Joyce, 'smilingly', that 'his instructions were in fair characters, legible without spelling'.

Reduced at this stage to little more than a counter in the broader power game being played out between Parliament and the army, Charles retained, then, not only his decorum but that keen sense of his own majesty that would never leave him. According to one account, for instance, even Joyce's flint-faced disregard for convention was not entirely proof against the king's unbending faith in his divinely ordained rank. 'But if I should refuse yet to go with you,' he is said to have asked the officer, 'I hope you will not force me? I am your King and you ought not to lay violent hands upon your King, for I acknowledge none here to be above me but God.' At which, Joyce appears to have lapsed, momentarily at least, into the kind of deference that he had so far shunned so successfully. 'Our desires,' he declared, 'are not to force Your Majesty but humbly entreat Your Majesty to go with us.' Nor was this all. For Charles was also prepared, it seems, to quibble about his destination. 'Now Gentlemen, for the place you intend to have me?' he asked next. When told it was Oxford, he coolly demurred by pointing out that there was 'no good air' in the town. Likewise, when Cambridge was offered as an alternative, Charles appears to have been dismissive, suggesting Newmarket instead, which Joyce duly accepted.

Indeed, the king seems to have mounted his horse only after the
threat of force against the parliamentary commissioners who were
objecting to his removal had been retracted, and even then insisted
successfully that they be allowed to travel with him. Already, it seems,
the commissioners had dispatched Captain Titus, the king's equerry
– 'by an express' – to acquaint Parliament with developments, and
Titus had arrived the very next day, killing his horse in the process,
it seems, since the sum of £50 was subsequently voted for him to
buy another. In the meantime, the commissioners remained adamant
that the king should not be abandoned entirely to the army's control.
On the contrary, 'seeing reason was of no force to dissuade, nor men-
aces to affright', the Earls of Pembroke and Denbigh, as well as Lord
Montague, were now determined 'to attend the King at all adven-
tures'. If the commissioners remained undeterred by the 'violence'
of the army's action, their determination was only reinforced by the
king's own coolness at the unexpected turn of events. For not only did
he insist upon retaining his servants, in order to 'be properly provided
for like a man in his place', he appears to have left Holdenby 'merri-
est of the company' and found opportunity into the bargain for one
more parting thrust at his captors. He was to travel that day, Joyce had
told him, 'as far as Your Majesty can ride', whereupon the prisoner had
declared imperiously that he was fully capable of riding 'as far as you
or anyone else'.

Yet, for all his defiance, when the king left the long gravel drive and
elegant Doric arcades of Holdenby behind him, it would be for the
last time. The cost of building the place had bankrupted Elizabeth I's
Lord Chancellor, Sir Christopher Hatton, and it was there, eleven years
earlier, that Henrietta Maria had pinned a picture of St Catherine to
her bed-curtains upon a visit with her husband. Passing in turn from
his father to his mother to his elder brother and then to him, Holdenby
retained therefore a special significance for the man now leaving it
under heavily armed escort, though 'this very stately house', as events
would soon prove, was 'languishing' like Charles himself under imminent threat. For 'about two years after', Sir Thomas Herbert informs us,
'that beautiful and famous structure was, amongst other his Majesty's
royal houses pulled down, by order of the two Houses of Parliament,
to satisfy the soldiers arrears'. Whereby, adds Herbert, 'the splendour
of the kingdom was not a little eclipsed, as by their ruins is now sadly
manifested'.

The reason for the king's removal, of course, was not in doubt, and least of all to Charles himself. Indeed, the gaping rift between Parliament and the army may well explain his continued high spirits upon departure. But responsibility for the king's seizure is altogether harder to ascertain. For some weeks, in fact, the idea of arresting him had been circulating around the radical Leveller regiments, and it was a notion with which Joyce fully agreed, having stated his readiness only a little earlier 'to do things as were never yet done on earth'. Moreover, he seems to have been acting under instructions from some central committee of the agitators' organisation after learning at Oxford, while engaged with the men of Colonel Rainsborough's foot regiment in securing an artillery train, that orders were being issued from Westminster to remove the king from Holdenby. Rightly fearing, as many in the army were beginning to do, that Charles was to be brought nearer to London so that Presbyterians could strike a deal with him, Joyce appears to have resolved on his own initiative to pre-empt matters.

But it was a heavy responsibility for such a junior officer to assume, and for this reason, it appears, Joyce left his men on 31 May to seek the approval of none other than Oliver Cromwell. That very evening, moreover, Cromwell's approval was indeed obtained, though with the specific proviso that the officer would be disowned if his mission failed. Not altogether surprisingly, of course, it would later be claimed that Cromwell had engineered the whole escapade from the very outset, with Joyce no more than a willing executioner of the general's scheme. The king himself certainly seemed unconvinced when Cromwell told him in person, just two weeks after the abduction, that Joyce had acted wholly upon his own initiative. 'Unless you hang up Joyce,' the king laughed, 'I will not believe what you say!' And there was no denying either that Cromwell was responsible for the pension of £100 with which Joyce was subsequently provided. But Cromwell's respect for the authority of Fairfax, his commander-in-chief, was unimpeachable, and it seems inconceivable that he would have undermined their trust and friendship by acting without consultation. Fairfax's shock and consternation upon hearing that the king was on his way to Newmarket is, moreover, beyond doubt, as he threatened to court-martial Joyce before eventually relenting and promising him the captaincy of the first troop to become vacant.

In any event, the cornet's promotion was well-earned and his pension worth every penny, for his initiative had greatly strengthened the hand of the army radicals, with whom Cromwell had now thrown in his lot. On 10 June, following an army rendezvous on Triploe Heath, twelve senior officers, including General Fairfax, Cromwell and Sir Hardress Waller, and the more radical colonels Pride and Rainsborough, now sent a letter, not to Parliament, but to that other centre of counter-revolutionary activity, the City of London. The letter voiced the army's demand for satisfaction against the guilty men who had misrepresented its aims and tried to disband it. But there was now a call, too, for 'a settlement of the Peace of the Kingdom and of the Liberties of the Subject ... which ... we ... have as much right to demand ... as we have to our money, or the other common interests of Souldiers'. On 15 June, this headlong process of politicisation was stepped up by the so-called 'Representation or Declaration of the Army', which had been prepared by the army's newly created General Council. Leading Presbyterian MPs, including the hated Denzil Holles, were to be purged, Parliament was to be dissolved as a prelude to new elections, and while the declaration steered clear of specific recommendations about the franchise, there was nevertheless a recommendation for the redistribution of seats at the expense of a number of scandalously rotten boroughs. For good measure, there was to be generous allowance for religious toleration, along with the proposal that 'such who, upon Conscientious grounds, may differ from the established forms may not be debarred from the common Rights ... belonging equally to all'.

Common soldiers and their officers were now no longer perceiving themselves as 'a mere mercenary Army, hired to serve any arbitrary Power of State', but as a force 'called forth ... by the several Declarations of Parliament to the Defence of our own and the Peoples just Rights and Liberties'. As the early summer of 1647 unfolded, so MPs fell under heavy bombardment, too, from a stream of Leveller petitions, some of which – as the vote on a proposal that they should be burnt by the common hangman confirms – were attracting support from Independent allies of the army leaders within the House itself. Those leaders, of course, were only too anxious to check the process whereby the Levellers were forging a power base of frightening proportions within the army. But they were no less anxious to outface the Presbyterian 'establishment' which threatened to betray all they had fought so tirelessly to achieve. For they had just acquired the trump card at a time when the cards that remained unplayed daily became fewer as the stakes increased.

'They must either sink us or we sink them', declared one protagonist in the impending fight-to-the-finish over how, and by whom, the
realm should be ruled. Nor had the alternatives ever been so dramatically displayed as on the lawn outside Holdenby House when Charles I
made ready to leave. All around were Cornet Joyce's troopers – 'as good
a law as now I can see executed by any judge in England', thought John
Lilburne – and in their midst the man who had made soldiers of most
of them in the first place, still unbowed by their presence and still insisting, as he would to the very end, 'I am your king'.

5

MORE CONGENIAL CUSTODY

'I am at much more freedom than I were, for my friends have free access to me, my chaplains wait upon me according to their vocation, and I have free intelligence with my wife and anybody else whom I please.'

Charles I to the Duke of Hamilton, 12 July 1647

The royal coach made steady progress from Holdenby, it seems, for by the night of 3 June, the prisoner within and his army escort had reached Hinchingbrooke in Huntingtonshire, 'a fair mansion house' belonging to Colonel Edward Montague, who would be created Earl of Sandwich in the following reign. Throughout the journey to the former nunnery, Charles had ridden in the company of the same parliamentary commissioners who had been ready, if 'in a capacity', to resist his new captors 'to the loss of their lives'. But though they were 'saddened' and 'exceedingly troubled' at their failure in the face of overwhelming odds, the king himself remained buoyant during his short stay, receiving 'honour and heart welcome' before moving next morning to Childerley, about 4 miles from Cambridge, where he was entertained with great hospitality by Lady Anne Cutts, widow of Sir John, the former MP for Cambridgeshire who had died the previous year. On the way, the king's escort had been met, at Fairfax's behest, by two regiments of horse under Colonel Whalley, but Charles himself had refused Whalley's suggestion that he return to Holdenby, with the result that the recently bereaved Lady Anne and the small rural community over which she presided found themselves the unexpected hosts of a royal visitor and an imposing force of Roundhead cavalry.

Over three days at Childerley, Charles was once again restored to full celebrity, as masters, fellows, graduates and scholars flocked from Cambridge to kiss his hand and hail him with cries of '*Vivat Rex*'. More significantly, he was visited, too, by nearly as large a crowd of senior army officers, including Fairfax, Cromwell, Ireton and Whalley, who came not merely to inspect their 'guest', but, rather more remarkably perhaps, to accord him due honour and deference. According to Sir Thomas Herbert, indeed, the king was 'highly caressed by all the great officers, who seldom failed to wait and discourse with him as opportunity offered'. All, it appears, 'behaved themselves with civility and due respect to his royal person', while Charles in turn was 'sometimes very pleasant in his discourse with them'. Fairfax, in particular, was keen to emphasise that the seizure at Holdenby had been carried out 'without his order or approbation', and Joyce was duly replaced with a more senior – and rather more amenable – officer as the king's main overseer. Several officers, it seems, were perfectly prepared, 'so soon as they came into the presence', to kiss the king's hands, and even Charles' attendants seem to have been tendered the respect to which they were entitled. For, as Herbert relates, even the 'private soldiers' were willing 'to oblige all that followed the king with civility'.

Nor should it be forgotten that the military visitors to Childerley included among their number those that can hardly be characterised as anything other than hard-line radicals. Hugh Peter, for instance, was perhaps the epitome of those razor-tongued army preachers who had earned notoriety by their swingeing attacks upon both king and Parliament at this time. Born in Cornwall in 1598, Peter had become a leading Puritan divine before finding it expedient to retire first to Holland in 1629 and then to New England six years later in the company of John Winthrop, the wealthy Puritan lawyer who had helped found the Massachusetts Bay Colony, and to whom he was related by marriage. Whilst overseas with Winthrop, moreover, he had taken a leading part in New England's affairs, only to return a year before the war and subsequently enlist with the Parliamentary forces as a chaplain, acting ultimately as Cromwell's chief propagandist, and gaining special recognition for his inspirational addresses to the troops before battle. Indeed, his sermons against Charles I would lead ultimately to his own execution as a regicide, although he is also believed to have assisted at the king's eventual execution. Charismatic and passionate to an extreme, though loathed for his outspokenness by most who met him, Peter appears to have remained a rule unto himself until he crumbled during his own execution at Charing Cross on 16 October 1660, unable to endure the emasculation and disembowelment that awaited him.

'Never,' declared the official newspaper, *Mercurius Publicus*, 'was person suffered death so unpitied and (which is more) whose execution was the delight of the people.' Yet even Peter would bridle his restless tongue in the king's presence at Childerley in the summer of 1647, as Charles was meticulously spared the kind of browbeating that had accompanied his captivity among the Scots at Newcastle. The two-week stay at his hunting lodge at Newmarket, which followed, proved equally congenial. The lodge itself had been fitted for his reception 'as well as that little edifice would admit', and most important of all he was now allowed his precious Anglican chaplains, the Reverend Doctors Hammond, Sheldon and Holdsworth. Many of the local gentry from Cambridgeshire, as well as those from farther afield in Suffolk and Essex, also flocked to see him in his Presence Chamber, where he seldom failed to dine in public. Most important of all, perhaps, he was now able to resume the ordered routine that suited him so favourably. Basking once again in the prayers and acclaim of common folk who happened to encounter him on the excursions that he was frequently allowed to undertake, he was also given access to his old associates, the Duke of Richmond and Sir William Fleetwood, as well as those servants who had been dismissed from his household at Holdenby. On other occasions, when not on public display or involved in business, he kept his usual hours of private devotion and spent much time on Newmarket Heath 'to recreate himself, sometimes in his coach, but most part riding'. It was a place, observed Herbert, that 'for good air and pleasure, gives place to no other in this great island' – a place 'much frequented by former princes'. After the tensions of Newcastle, it could not have been more suitable for Charles' present purposes, especially when it is remembered that his own father, King James, had taken 'exceeding delight there in hunting, hawking and races, both horse and foot'.

Less welcome, of course, were the overtures arriving from the Scots, which were roundly rejected by the king, not least of all because his apparently infinite sources of optimism were once again beginning to stir. 'This army speaks to me very fair,' he confided to a friend at this time, 'which makes me hope well.' According to the account of Major Robert Huntington, indeed, it was at Childerley that Cromwell

made 'large professions' and 'first gave his Majesty hopes of restaura-
tion', along with assurances 'that he would be continually instrumental
therein'. And the mood, it seems, was infectious, for if Herbert judged
correctly, even the parliamentary commissioners who continued to
wait upon the king appeared 'very cheerful, having as 'twas presumed,
fair hopes as well as promises, that some grandees of the army would
be instrumental and … endeavour a happy understanding between him
and his Parliament'. The broader, altogether more frightening ramifica-
tions of the massive soldiers' meetings of 10 June, at which there had
been threats to march on London, were somehow coolly overlooked,
as of course were Cromwell's private thoughts, as he conversed on ami-
cable terms with the king in his makeshift Presence Chamber. For the
general had, it seems, already decided to take control of an overwhelming grass-roots movement among his soldiers that he had little chance,
or indeed inclination, to stem. The consequences, of course, were to be
momentous, but both Charles and even his well-wishing parliamentary associates at Childerley continued to cast only positive glosses and
high-flown hopes upon the ominous tide of current events.

For this reason, the army's decision to move the king to Hampton
Court appears to have raised his expectations even higher, for he was
sure that the closer he came to London, the easier he would find it to
play Parliament and the Scots commissioners at Westminster off against
each other. When Charles reached 'his own little house' at Royston
on 24 June, moreover, after lodging at various noblemen's houses en
route, events once more contrived to cheer him. For although the
dwelling was 'seldom used … capable but of few attendants, and
meanly furnished', the town itself made every effort to welcome not
only the king but also his followers and servants, 'which then were
numerous'. The army's care and courtesy also remained undiminished
during the two-day stay, notwithstanding the indiscretion of a hapless
colonel who clumsily disrupted a solemn ceremony during which an
emblem of the Garter was being returned to the king by the envoy
of a German prince upon the death of the prince's father. Not even
Charles' scowls, it seems, could force the man's withdrawal until the
royal barber, Mr Babington, who enjoyed 'a better understanding of
good manners', persuaded him to clear off. The colonel who had been
'so malapert as to interpose', had done so, according to Herbert, 'to
the end that he might be privy to the affair, and hear what the envoy
had to communicate to the king'. But he had acted entirely upon on

his own initiative and was subsequently rewarded for his efforts with a 'sound reproof' from none other than Sir Thomas Fairfax himself.

Still well satisfied with his treatment and high in optimism, Charles then moved to Hatfield in Hertfordshire and the 'very noble house', with its 'vineyard, gardens and walks full of pleasure', that had been built during the previous reign by his father's chief minister, Robert Cecil. Here, too, the king was treated 'with great civility and observance', and the very next day after his arrival on 26 June, he was allowed to use the Anglican Prayer Book in public for the first time in over a year, though even this would not match the highlight of his journey that was still to come. For, after leaving Hatfield on 1 July and continuing to follow the movements of the army on their indirect route to London, he passed through Windsor and on to Sion House, where he stopped for dinner with the Earl of Northumberland and his nephew, the Elector Palatine. It was here, it appears, that Charles was at long last informed that permission had been granted for a meeting with his children, who had fallen into the army's hands after the Royalist surrender and were now under the earl's care. Accordingly, after reaching Lord Craven's house at Caversham on the south bank of the Thames on 3 July, where Cromwell visited him several times, he was finally reunited with his children for two whole nights.

Riding hotfoot to Maidenhead to meet them, the king's emotional rendezvous with the Duke of Gloucester and Princess Elizabeth occurred on 15 July at the Greyhound Inn. Both Fairfax and Cromwell were present, and the exchange between the army's Commander-in-Chief and the 11-year-old princess, in particular, was touching enough to be reported four days later in the contemporary newsletter *Moderate Intelligencer*:

> Letters from the Army tell of the greatest joy of his Majesty at the sight of his children (returned Saturday) and mention this, that immediately upon coming to him, the General came into the Presence, which occasioned some carriage in those that attended his Majesty, which was taken notice of by the Princess, who demanded who he was, and understanding it was the General, she went unto him, and with the greatest of civilities, thanked him for the great happiness she at this time enjoyed, the sight of her dear Father, effected by his alone industry and ingagement; for which as she should run no hazard, so it should ever by her be acknowledged; and if ever in

her power requited. He returned humble thanks, saying that he had done therein but the least of those duties he was obliged to serve his Majesty and children in; and having kissed her Highness' hand, both made their addresses to his Majesty.

More interesting still, however, was Cromwell's subsequent reaction to the meeting. Both he and Fairfax had come from Windsor, where they had been preparing the ground for the army's forthcoming peace proposals, and now Sir John Berkeley claimed to have met him leaving the scene of the king's encounter with his children. A cousin of Sir Thomas Roe, who was himself a kinsman of Henry Jermyn, Berkeley was, in fact, a committed Royalist who had undertaken diplomatic missions for the king and given good service in the wars. He had been present, too, at the baptism of Princess Henrietta Anne in Exeter Cathedral and recently spent time with the queen and Jermyn in Paris. But he was known, nonetheless, for his honesty, and for this reason had just been allowed to return from France along with Colonel William Legge, to rejoin Charles' service as a suitable intermediary between king and army. As such, he would prove a valuable witness to events, and his account of the general's emotional response to the sight of the king with his children is far from implausible, not least of all because the softer side of Cromwell's personality is well attested by other sources. Always an inwardly sensitive man, Cromwell is therefore said to have spoken to Berkeley with tears in his eyes, having just witnessed what he apparently described as 'the tenderest sight that ever his eyes beheld, which was the interview between the King and his children'. Never, he added, was man so abused as the king, who was 'the most uprightest and most conscientious man of three Kingdoms'.

And if appearances were any guide, the same sympathy and goodwill were still fully intact by the time of Charles' arrival at Woburn on 20 July. Welcomed both 'honourably and affectionately', he was also reunited now with Jack Ashburnham, who had made his way safely to the Netherlands after his flight from Newcastle and thence to the queen at Paris, where, to the king's annoyance, he had joined the chorus urging him to drop his opposition to the covenant and become a 'King of Presbytery'. Any earlier spat was swiftly forgotten, however, as Charles not only welcomed Ashburnham but promptly installed him, along with Berkeley, at the forefront of negotiations with the army, which lasted throughout the following week. For

Oliver Cromwell's son-in-law, Commissary General Henry Ireton, had not only been busy with the army's peace proposals, but appeared to be favouring a more moderate approach, opposing the excesses of Republican and Leveller extremism, and suggesting instead what amounted to a form of constitutional monarchy, encompassing King, Lords and Commons. Plainly, the ferment within the army had alarmed him deeply, and to this extent he was well suited to the task of forging some kind of workable agreement.

But if Ireton's intentions were statesmanlike, his tone was frequently waspish, and his task was complicated by the ongoing obstructiveness of the king, who appears to have regarded his negotiations with the army as a mere preliminary, believing that the generals had little power to carry out their undertakings and that Parliament was in any case certain to outbid them in terms of its own proposals, which were sure to follow. The result was a clash of personality between the Commissary General and the king, which was clear from the outset, as the military man resorted to sharp sentences, refusing to wrap up a denial in the kind of deferential manner to which the king was accustomed, and Charles opted for the kind of hauteur that hardly befitted his present circumstances. 'You cannot do without me,' Ireton was told by his adversary at the beginning of negotiations. 'You will fall to ruin if I do not sustain you,' the king continued, provoking a predictably unsmiling and emphatic response from the general himself. 'Sir,' he replied, 'you have an intention to be the arbitrator between Parliament and us, and we mean to be it between your Majesty and Parliament.' And when Charles remarked later that 'I shall play my game as well as I can', Ireton was equally quick to counter by reminding him that 'if your Majesty have a game to play, you must give us also leave to play ours'.

In light of such tensions, it was no mean achievement, then, that Ireton's peace terms, known as the Heads of the Proposals, still went much further than those offered by Parliament a year earlier – so much so, indeed, that it was widely rumoured that Charles would be back in Whitehall within a week. While control of the militia was to pass for ten years to a Council of State dominated by senior officers, and church attendance, like use of the Prayer Book, would no longer be obligatory, the king would nevertheless be under no compulsion to take the Covenant or establish Presbyterianism. Though bishops were to be stripped of their temporal authority, Royalists were nevertheless to be treated with commendable leniency, accompanying the offer of a general amnesty for all but five of fifty-eight 'delinquents'. Nor were Ireton's other offers any less accommodating than the king could reasonably expect. Parliament was to be granted the right to raise revenue without royal approval for ten years, and the same newly appointed Council of State would participate with him in the conduct of foreign affairs. In the meantime, the existing Parliament would end within the year, to be replaced by new biennial Parliaments, elected upon an extended franchise operating with new constituencies reformed according to tax assessments.

Under the circumstances, the army's terms appeared to offer Charles – as his own advisers were keen to emphasise – the opportunity to achieve by peaceful means the best he could reasonably hope for: a face-saving way out of a no-hope situation and, more importantly still, the prospect of gradual recovery in the longer term. Indeed, in the hands of a shrewd tactician like his father or eldest son, they could have provided the basis for a substantial restoration of royal authority over years to come. Biennial parliaments in particular, and the added prospect of eventually regaining control of the militia and government appointments, offered considerable scope for party-building and political manoeuvre. Even the bishops and the Prayer Book were to be allowed to continue where desired, affording room for at least the possibility of some kind of Anglican resurgence at a later date. Clearly, both the General Council, whom Ireton represented, and their allies among the leadership of the Independents in Parliament were prepared to risk all at a time when the anger among common soldiers appeared to be growing by the day. For it was to the 'shame of men', some argued, and a 'sin against God' that too many of their leaders were prepared 'to kneele, and kiss and fawne upon' the king, still surrounded as he was by 'deceiptfull Clergy' and immersed 'over head and eares in the blood' of 'dearest friends and fellow commoners'.

So when trusted members of Charles' own circle urged acceptance at all costs, the stakes were apparent. 'Never was a crown so nearly lost so cheaply recovered as his Majesty's would be,' insisted Sir John Berkeley, if only he were to seize the moment and submit without delay. Though few had realised it – and least of all Charles – the intervention of Cornet Joyce at Holdenby had actually been nothing less than critical, depriving him of his best chance of an immediate restoration and introducing the new and volatile influence of the army over his fate. Yet even at the eleventh hour, the king had now been offered a lifeline, only to spurn it. Convinced that once the army understood its own interests it would readily grant both him and his people 'what is their own', he set out to ply the military commanders with promises of peerages and promotion, and was surprised when the bait was duly rejected. Believing that support for him was growing in London and Scotland, he had not hesitated either to send General Fairfax a less than honest promise denying the widespread rumours that he was now trying to cultivate the Presbyterians.

It was Charles' fatal flaw, in fact, that, in failing to reconcile himself to realities, he constantly hoped for more from someone else, depending all the while upon his enemies' divisions and consistently overestimating his personal capacity to exploit to best advantage what he wrongly perceived as a budding counter-revolution in the capital. The attempt by Independents to impeach eleven Presbyterian leaders in the Commons and gain control of the London militia had led, therefore, to a string of events that utterly clouded his judgement at the critical moment of decision. On 21 July, huge crowds had gathered in the City to support the signing of a Solemn Engagement which pledged to uphold the Covenant but secure the king's restoration on the terms set out in his letter of 12 May. Four days later, moreover, there was widespread rioting, which led to the return of the eleven members and the flight of the Independents. Surely enough, on 22 July, Charles' misapprehensions were finally set in stone when John Maitland, 2nd Earl of Lauderdale, approached him with the vain assurance that the Scots were at last willing to secure his authority by invading England.

A more astute politician would at least have toyed with the army's proposals more seductively. Cromwell, Ireton and other officers had urged him to write 'a kindly letter to the army', giving it his blessing in restoring order and disowning the actions of the mob. But when the Heads of the Proposals were formally presented to him on 28 July, Charles was at his most brutally dismissive, notwithstanding the conviction of Bellièvre, the French ambassador, that he could still have carried the army with him. Rather than acknowledge any aspect of their efforts, he subjected Ireton and his associates to what Berkeley despairingly termed 'very tart and bitter discourses'. By the time that Charles finally 'recollected himself' after Berkeley had warned him that if 'he had some secret strength and power that I do not know of, he should conceal the fact', the damage was already done. Lauderdale was promptly barred from further access, on the assumption that he was plotting an invasion, while Colonel Rainsborough went back to the army's 'agitators' to make clear that further attempts at negotiation were now pointless. All that was left, indeed, for the final collapse of the king's strategy was the restoration of the ejected Independents to their place in Parliament, which duly occurred on 4 August when Fairfax marched into London at the head of 16,000 troops, and Denzil Holles fled, along with the rest of the eleven members whose impeachment the soldiers had demanded.

Fairfax's entry had been, in fact, a carefully staged demonstration not only of the army's strength, but of its discipline too. A day earlier, he had drawn up his men on Hounslow Heath – their massed ranks stretching for a mile and a half – and escorted the two Speakers, fourteen peers and 100 or so MPs in review of them. Moreover, not a shot was fired nor a sword drawn when the general's regiments circled the City the next day, or when the returning members were escorted to the Palace of Westminster amid cries for 'Lords and Commons and a free Parliament'. On the contrary, Fairfax's men wore laurel leaves in their hats and church bells pealed, and to complete the triumph, all twenty of his regiments staged a final parade that Saturday, before marching to Cheapside with colours flying, trumpets braying and drums beating. They took, it was said, not so much as an apple, and would gladly have brought the king with them, to place him once more upon his throne, had he not missed the unique and fleeting opportunity placed before him less than a fortnight earlier.

If Charles had grasped the nettle by pledging himself there and then to the Heads of the Proposals, Fairfax, it seems, would not have hesitated, irrespective of Parliament's response. For when Berkeley had asked Ireton and his fellow emissaries how they would respond to any refusal by Presbyterian members to accept their peace terms, he was given to understand quite clearly that the desired outcome would have been achieved by leaving potential opponents no choice, presumably by excluding enough Presbyterians to secure a majority. Thereafter, since the very first clause of the Heads of the Proposals stipulated an early dissolution of Parliament, followed by a general election, the likely result was a landslide victory in favour of a settlement which already had the support of the army, the 'royal independents' and, above all, the king himself. Ironically, of course, the army would indeed purge Parliament only sixteen months later – with unhappy and deeply unpopular results. But while the purpose of this later purge was actually to prevent the restoration of the king, the effect in August 1647 would have been the diametrical opposite.

In the event, Charles had certainly been ill-advised by others. On the one hand, Sir Lewis Dyve, his former major-general of Dorset, who was now a prisoner in the Tower, had grossly overestimated the potential of the forces lately raised in the City, while the Presbyterian Colonel Joseph Bamfield had also hopelessly poisoned the king's mind against Cromwell and Ireton. But Charles, to his great cost, had nursed his grievances and indulged his own indignation at the generals' presumption far too readily. And when he arrived at the Palace of Oatlands – 'a large and beautiful house of the Queen's upon the River of Thames' – on 13 August for what would prove a ten-day stay, he remained stubbornly impervious to the mounting tide of events on every side. Indeed, his mood was said to have been 'very merry' as he travelled from Maidenhead to Woburn on 20 July, and on to Latimers in Buckinghamshire and Moore Park – 'a place of much pleasure' – some 2 miles from Watford. There he dined with Lord Cary, admiring the 'curious gardens' and 'water-works', before making a final stop en route at Stoke, a 'fair house' belonging to Lord Chief Justice Cook. Throughout this leisurely passage, he had continued to busy himself with the niceties of constitution-making, offering little and achieving less, and upon his arrival at Oatlands, which to his disappointment possessed no tennis court, he wrote encouragingly to Ormonde and Digby in Dublin, to the Covenanters in Scotland and to Edward Hyde on the Continent.

Nor did Charles' arrival at Hampton Court, his final destination, on 24 August serve in any way to shake him from his slumbers. Indeed, captivity continued to sit lightly upon him as he was now placed under the charge of Cromwell's cousin, Colonel Edward Whalley. The palace had been made ready by Clement Kinnersley, who ensured that it was 'amply furnished' and suitably prepared for the establishment of the royal court that now re-emerged around the king. 'And a Court it now appeared to be,' remarked Sir Thomas Herbert, 'for there was a revival of that lustre it had formerly', as noblemen mustered in numbers, chaplains performed their duties and 'every one' of the king's servants was 'permitted to attend in their respective places' to execute 'his services in the accustomed form and state'. 'Intercourse was free between King and Parliament,' Herbert also observed, 'and the Army seemed to endeavour a right understanding among different parties: which gave hopes of an accommodation.' Fairfax and the other military commanders were, indeed, said to be 'much at Court' and undertaking 'frequent conference with the King in the Park' and elsewhere. To complete the picture of uncanny calm and affability, we hear too how 'no offence at any time passed among the soldiers of either party'. On the contrary, 'there was an amnesty by consent, pleasing, as was thought, to all parties'.

All in all, it was small wonder, perhaps, that Herbert should speak so glowingly of 'these halcyon days'. Berkeley, Ashburnham and Legge were all on hand to advise as the commissioners from Parliament remained in constant attendance and the stream of visitors from London – including not only various aldermen, but Cromwell, his wife, his daughter and her recently married husband, Henry Ireton – filled the king's spacious Presence Chamber to overflowing. There was ample scope too, it seems, for leisure. 'To John Powell for 4 billiard staves with pins, balls and porte provided for His Majesty … £6 0s. 0d.' runs an entry in the Exchequer Rolls for 21 August, as the king also indulged his love of hunting and tennis, 'a recreation he much desires to use for health'. His children came over for visits – sitting for portraits by the miniaturist John Hopkins – while he, in turn, made at least one trip to Sion House, some 7 miles away, to sup with the Earl of Northumberland, the man still entrusted with the care of young Princess Elizabeth and her brother the Duke of Gloucester. 'The Earl,' wrote Herbert, 'welcomed the King with a very noble treat', which extended, it seems, to his followers, who 'had their tables richly furnished'.

Since Charles had given his word not to escape, he had virtual freedom of movement, too, within the grand confines of Hampton's 1,500 rooms. But he remained, of course, under close supervision and enjoyed little communication with his wife in particular, though he seemed somehow less troubled by this inconvenience than formerly. When Oliver Cromwell and his fellow officers entered London in August, Henrietta Maria had attempted to suborn him with almost unlimited wealth, lands and titles in return for his assistance in restoring her husband to the throne. But she had failed abjectly, and although some of her jewels had been redeemed with the help of a shipment of tin mined in Cornwall before the final defeat of the Royalists, her lack of funds had become increasingly noticeable at her hard-pressed Court in Paris, where she confined herself largely to the consolations of prayer and the company of Henry Jermyn, who continued to immerse himself in the social life of the French capital and to revel in the considerable popularity he enjoyed amid the Parisian elite. So preoccupied was he now with the time-consuming business of courting friends in high places, he had begun to delegate the task of transcribing and deciphering the queen's letters to Abraham Crowley, and there was talk before long, too, that he was diverting some of her funds to his own use. Not altogether ungenerously, therefore, Madame de Mottville described him as a 'rather worthy man', though she was quick to point out, too, that his mind 'seemed very narrow and more fitted for petty things than great ones'. Rumours of his illicit relationship with the queen were also still circulating, though Lady Denbigh at least was prepared to deny them, complaining to her son about the 'untruths' which were as common as ever in letters arriving in England.

There was, indeed, a general atmosphere of recrimination and spite at Henrietta's parsimonious French Court, to which increasing numbers of self-seeking Royalists had gravitated in a vain search for rich pickings. By now she had given so much of her money away to help her husband's cause that her scope for patronage of any kind was all but gone, and violent quarrels were not uncommon among her visitors. When Montrose visited the Louvre, in fact, he, like others, was shocked by the prevailing air of futility and discontent. For individuals like the queen's old friend Chevalier de Jars, whom she had helped release from the Bastille, continued to make trouble, while others in her intimate circle, such as Endymion Porter, struggled in vain to improve the tone. A diplomat enjoying a considerable reputation in the world of art and letters, Porter had acted as a messenger for the queen and was described by Anthony Wood in his *Athenae Oxonienses* as 'beloved by two kings: James I for his admirable wit and Charles I for his general bearing, brave style, sweet temper, great experience, travels and modern languages'. But even the portly Porter was not without his detractors, it seems, since he too had been reduced to self-seeking poverty and his Catholic sympathies were another bone of serious contention, as a parliamentary report of the day, highlighting 'his fat guts, peppered with popery', made manifestly clear.

'I am weary of this place,' Lady Denbigh wrote from Paris to her son, 'the air is not good, and to be deprived of your company and the rest of my children is very troubling to me.' But for the queen, by contrast, even the presence of her own offspring had not been entirely trouble-free. That summer, to Henrietta Maria's great delight, she had been reunited with her youngest daughter after Parliament had ordered the girl's carer, the Countess of Morton, to hand her over into captivity. Unwilling to comply, the countess, dressed in a tattered gown that she had stuffed with pieces of linen to hide her elegant figure, had set off for Dover with the 2-year-old princess, posing as the wife of a French valet. The child herself, meanwhile, had been disguised as a boy and dubbed 'Pierre' – somewhat to her displeasure, it seems, since she exclaimed angrily at one point that she was to be addressed as 'Princess'. Even so, the princess' precocity had not compromised the escape bid, and the beautiful, intelligent, dark-haired little girl, who so much resembled what her mother had once been, eventually made her way safely to a new life in Paris, where her eldest brother was no less taken with her charm than Henrietta Maria herself.

The Prince of Wales himself, however, continued to be a cause of significant concern for his mother. By now a tall, well-made, black-haired 15-year-old, he had at first refused to join the queen from his refuge in Jersey, and it had ultimately required Jermyn to fetch him in person. Upon his arrival, moreover, the teenage boy had hardly proved a social success. Taciturn by nature, and unable in any case to speak or understand French effectively, he made little impression above all upon Princess Anne-Marie, the niece whom Henrietta Maria had earmarked as a prospective bride. On the contrary, the princess treated him with an icy condescension, having set her own sights upon the Habsburg Emperor rather than the penniless heir to a threadbare English throne, who now lay decoratively at her feet as she watched her favourite comedies, or held flaming torches at her side as she sat before the mirror in her chamber applying her make-up. Even the services of Prince Rupert, who had arrived in Paris as general of all the exiled English and now acted as interpreter, were to little effect. Henrietta Maria's final resort of lending her niece the few jewels she still possessed proved equally futile when, at the finest ball of the season, Anne-Marie demonstrated more money than taste by appearing with a vast bouquet of flowers strewn liberally with enormous pearls and diamonds, which dwarfed her aunt's own.

Perhaps it was not altogether surprising, then, that her husband's own predicament should have failed to dominate the queen's thinking in quite the way it once did. One of her associates, Father Cyprien de Gamache, noted how her mind now dwelt increasingly upon devotional subjects as she learned through hard experience that honours, wealth, pleasure and grandeur are evanescent and valueless. In spite of all, she had continued to dispatch couriers like Porter to England, and would still write, exhorting and hectoring in the well-worn way. Dr Stephen Goffe was only one among many whom she urged to beseech her husband not to insist 'too nicely upon terms in the present exigency of his affairs'. But the response had been the familiar one, as Charles complained how the army's offers simply intended 'to cajole him to his ruin', and in the face of such obstinacy, even Henrietta Maria had come, it seems, to face the fact that her future efforts must be made more out of duty than in hope. In spite of all, she had spent her money on her husband's cause, and soon she would be doing away with her servants, her furnishings and her fine coaches, pawning the last of her jewels in Holland, around which time the Venetian ambassador saw her waiting in Cardinal Mazarin's office with tears in her eyes, attempting to enlist his assistance.

For his own part, of course, Charles' apparent reluctance to exchange letters with his wife as freely as he once did may well be partly explained by the uses to which his enemies might put them. The publication of his private letters after their capture at Naseby had taught him, after all, that no man's malice could be 'gratified further by my letters than to see my constancy to my wife, the laws, and religion'. 'Bees will gather honey,' he had added at the time, 'where the spider sucks poison', and in light of this, he had justifiably concluded that all future letters 'may be liable to envious exceptions'. When, moreover, his everyday circumstances were so much more favourable than they had been at his lowest point at Newcastle in particular, it was again only natural perhaps that he should pine less urgently for his wife. For his overseers were now at pains to maintain the semblance of their royal prisoner's liberty as he walked the terraces and gravel ways of the gardens and gazed at the Thames, the familiar river so closely associated with his happiest days.

On such occasions, Jeremy Taylor, his favourite chaplain, was often close by – a source of unerring loyalty and constant consolation, and a companion whose learning and discretion made him more than ever at this time the ideal companion for the beleaguered king. The 34-year-old's literary output would eventually earn him a reputation as one of the finest writers of English prose and the epithet the 'Shakespeare of Divines'. But, as a protégé of William Laud and a resolute supporter of the Royalist cause, he had nevertheless undergone imprisonment after the siege of Cardigan Castle in 1645, and been at his sovereign's side for much of the fighting beforehand. For his further efforts as a Royalist apologist and in particular his pamphlet, *Episcopacy Asserted*, he had also been one of those rewarded, at the king's request, by the University of Oxford, which had conferred upon him the degree of Doctor of Divinity in 1643. Whilst the king had not altogether agreed with his subsequent *Liberty of Prophesying* – a treatise on 'the unreasonableness of prescribing to other men's faith, and the iniquity of persecuting different opinions' – Taylor had nevertheless firmly consolidated his place in the king's affection by the time of his arrival at Hampton Court.

Whether it was this, however, that explains Charles' eventual decision to reward the chaplain with a ring embellished with two diamonds and a ruby, as well as a watch and some pearls and rubies ornamenting the ebony case in which he kept his bible, is far less certain. For the cleric is known to have lived 10 miles from Mardinam in Carmarthenshire, the home of Joanna Bridges, who was rumoured to be the king's natural daughter by the Countess of Lennox. According to one tradition, Charles' later reputation for sexual continence had not applied in his youth, and he had allegedly been led astray – 'under the guidance of the dissipated and licentious Buckingham' – at some time between 1622 and 1627. Although by then in her forties, the thrice-married countess was indeed a prominent member of the circle surrounding both Charles and the duke, and was said 'to be much courted and respected by the Prince', who, along with his father, accompanied her from one place of entertainment to another, turning up unexpectedly in a variety of resorts with a minimum of etiquette and 'an abandon of high spirits'. Certainly, a gift of the kind that Charles eventually made to Taylor was highly irregular, and it is hard to explain why the jewels should be given to a royal chaplain at all, unless they were to be passed on to Bridges herself, whom Taylor would eventually marry as his second wife at some point between 1652 and 1656.

By the time of his arrival at Hampton Court, the king's financial resources were in any case increasingly limited, as a letter from a member of his household, dated 23 August, makes clear. 'What necessity of moneys is here,' the letter begins, 'you have I doubt not sufficiently been advertised by Mr Cresset.' For it was now not only deemed 'full time that his Majesty have a new supply of cloathes and some Jewels and other ornaments for the Royal person', but time too 'for a further supply of Pewter and Pans and Kettles and divers other necessaries for the kitchen', as well as 'Silver for his Majesty's uses and

Linnen and other necessaries which are wanted to accommodate his Majesty'. In reality, as the Exchequer Rolls make clear, the king can hardly have been as badly off for clothes as the correspondent suggests, since two sums of £333 15s and £235 9s had been paid in June to David Murray, the royal tailor, for six suits, coats, cloaks, stockings, gloves and other articles of attire. But four more suits were indeed paid for in August, presumably by outside sources on the strength of a plea for additional funds, along with a further two and some night attire in September: 'a tennis suit of wrought coloured satin lined with taffeta, a night gown of wrought tabby lined with plush, and a grey cloth hunting suit with necessaries suitable'. In other respects, too, the Exchequer Rolls confirm that, if the king's stay at Hampton was comfortable, there remained little if any room for undue largesse. Clement Kinnersley appears to have done a sterling job with the £100 he was paid on account for supplying the king's new residence with 'beds, sheets, carpets and other necessaries'. Yet no jewels or silver were forthcoming to ease Charles' predicament – only three horses, one of which was a 'grey roan', costing £70.

Well before September was out, however, there were far more pressing matters, even than money, for the king to worry about. For as Sir Thomas Herbert noted at the time, amid his descriptions of 'halcyon days' and a newly resplendent royal court, 'the fairest day is seldom without a cloud'. It was Charles' great misfortune that, just as toughness made him stubborn, so appeasement made him over-confident, particularly when both Parliament and the army were competing for his favour, as was now the case. In September, therefore, he turned down Parliament's peace proposals, which were in effect a rehash of the former Newcastle Propositions, explaining now that the Heads of the Proposals 'were much more conducive to the satisfaction of all interests, and may be a better Foundation for a lasting Peace'. But by failing once again to accompany honeyed words with specific concessions, Charles created only an impasse that made the growing influence of the Levellers within the army – and the risk of general anarchy – daily more perilous. Indeed, far from appreciating at once the imminent danger posed by 'active and malevolent persons of the army' – some of whom would soon be wishing to make 'a dead dog' of him – Charles was even prepared to toy with the notion of enlisting their support.

Throughout autumn, as frustration at the failure to achieve a satisfactory peace increased apace among common soldiers, the influence of the Leveller leader, John Lilburne, had grown to such a degree that an outright takeover of the army now seemed conceivable. Lilburne, in fact, had been imprisoned in the Tower since July 1646 after denouncing his former commander, the Earl of Manchester, as a traitor, and had managed to establish contact with another prisoner, the Royalist general, Sir Lewis Dyve, who had been incarcerated since the capture of Sherborne Castle in August 1645. By this means, Charles was kept fully apprised of Lilburne's intention to capture the army, and, no less interestingly, of his wish for an accommodation with the king himself, whose reign remained, in the Leveller leader's opinion, 'but as a flea biting' to the enormities of Parliament. Nor, it seems, was Lilburne the only radical of this mind, for other sectaries were also approaching the throne for assistance, including William Kiffin, the Baptist, who now reported that the king had given him such firm assurances of future goodwill that every effort should henceforth be made to enter into negotiation.

In light of this, Lilburne had therefore actually tried to arrange through Dyve a meeting between Charles and leading agitators within the army, assuring in the process that in pursuit of an agreement, he himself was prepared to pawn his own life. Such was Dyve's unerring confidence in Lilburne's curious new tack that he was happy to report on 5 October how 'within a moneth or six weekes at the farthest the whole army should be absolutely at your Majestie's devotion to dispose thereof as you pleased'. All that was required to guarantee this happy outcome, Dyve urged, was that Charles should send for six or seven notorious army radicals, including Major White, Captain Reynolds and Edward Sexby, and reassure them of his good intentions. Thereafter, neither Parliament nor the 'grandees' who constituted the army's official leadership would be able to dam the irresistible tide of popular feeling. Charles would be reinstated, the common soldier's wish for religious liberty satisfied and the peace of the war-torn kingdom guaranteed at a stroke.

On this occasion, however, not even the king was susceptible to such 'foolish zeal'. Believing, quite rightly, that Lilburne had not gauged the real strength of Leveller support from his prison cell, and fearing too the ongoing strength of the members of the army's General Council, Charles duly demurred. In the meantime, moreover, reports were soon reaching him of a new and altogether more disturbing brand of extremism within the army's ranks. Already Lilburne had written a widely publicised open letter, urging soldiers 'not to trust your great officers at the general's headquarters no further than you can throw an ox'. But others were now directly 'intermeddling with affairs of state' with new and much more far-reaching proposals. In particular, they were reinterpreting the army's declaration in its Solemn Engagement of June in a much more radical light than originally intended. There it had been stated that 'we shall not willingly disband nor divide, nor suffer ourselves to be disbanded or divided', but now it was being suggested that this had not only transformed the army into a corporation independent of the state, but vested ultimate power into its representative General Council – with the effect, as the pamphlet *England's Freedom, Soldiers' Rights* put it, that leading officers 'being only admitted by mutual consent … would have no power but what was entrusted to them by the soldiers'.

By 18 October, furthermore, there had come a challenge that shook the army to its roots and threatened to give a genuinely revolutionary turn to national politics. It came in the form of a paper entitled *The Case of the Army Truly Stated*, written chiefly by the Leveller John Wildman, which alleged that senior officers had been perverting the whole intention of the Solemn Engagement by preventing the agitators from redressing the grievances of the people and warning them not to meddle with matters that did not concern them. Worse still, the grandees were supposedly proposing to restore the king with his royal veto intact and to disband the army with few guarantees against further abuse, and every possibility that the king would choose to take his revenge later on. 'The flood-gates of slavery, oppression and misery are opened upon the nation,' the paper declared, while 'the people's expectations that were much greatened, and their hopes of relief in their miseries and oppressions, which were so much heightened' were now 'like to be frustrate'. In such circumstances, only the most drastic measures could suffice. The present parliament should be dissolved within ten months and replaced with one elected by 'all the freeborn' aged 21 or over, excepting those who had rendered themselves delinquents by favouring royalism. Liberty of conscience, meanwhile, was to be guaranteed and the entire law of England codified into a single volume written in plain English. Last but not least, it was suggested that the army's arrears in pay should be found from the sums that had gone to court parasites and the 'dead stocks' lying frozen in the vaults of City companies.

From some perspectives, of course, both Charles and his supporters could take heart from the growing fissure in the army, and in a news-sheet of 27 September, the royalist William Smith confidently declared his belief that 'the officers of the army will come to an agreement with the King for fear of their own factions and the odium they contract from the kingdom'. As so often, there was also consolation of a kind to be had from Scotland, where fears remained that Charles might yet reach agreement with the Independents and the army. In consequence, the earls of Lanark, Loudon and Lauderdale had travelled to Hampton Court and on 22 October delivered a message to Charles declaring their readiness to 'engage themselves for your restoration and civil interest' in return for 'satisfaction in the point of religion'. The following day, indeed, they returned with fifty horsemen and urged the king's escape to Scotland, though he refused, ostensibly on the grounds that he had given his word not to do so.

In reality, Charles was once again holding out for better terms, particularly since the Scots remained stuck fast to the demand that he sign the Covenant. The Kirk and majority opinion north of the border still demanded as much, and there was the added complication that the Duke of Hamilton was reluctant to commit to invasion while the Scottish army remained under the control of the allies of his foe, Argyle. But prevarication, of course, came at a price of its own, as the realm teetered on what some observers considered to be the brink of anarchy. 'I hear all things are in very great confusion still,' wrote Sir Edward Nicholas from the Continent. 'As the king at first called a Parliament he could not rule, and afterwards Parliament raised an army it could not rule, so the army have agitators they cannot rule,' Nicholas continued, in one of the aptest summaries of the English Civil War produced by any contemporary. 'What will the end be,' he concluded fearfully, 'God only knows.'

As October ran into November, concerns of this kind seemed especially well founded. For in response to the seething discontent expressed by John Wildman and others, the leading agitators were now invited to discuss their proposals before a committee of the General Council, chaired by Oliver Cromwell. In the event, the Lieutenant-General's sympathies were themselves complex, exhibiting all the tension that one might expect between the property owner's yearning for order and the godly officer's belief that the army, for all its turmoil, was nevertheless a gathered church of the saints. As committed as ever to the principle that all forms of government were 'but dross and dung in comparison of Christ', this was nevertheless the country gentleman who had never sounded more conservative than in July, when he had angrily confronted agitator 'saints' bent on a coup. 'Have what you will have, that you have by force I look upon it as nothing' were his words at that time. Nor had he in the interim altered even slightly the same firm conviction that Leveller demands, if carried to their logical limit, 'must end in anarchy': a conclusion that seemed to be borne out all too painfully by the so-called 'Putney Debates' which now ensued.

The Case of the Army Truly Stated had been followed, in fact, by the Levellers' *Agreement of the People*, and it was this blueprint for an entirely new constitution which set, in effect, the agenda for the series of hotly contested discussions beginning on 28 October at the Church of St Mary the Virgin, Putney. Lilburne's Leveller allies, like Richard Overton and William Walwyn, had for some time been pouring scorn on the unrepresentativeness of England's constitution, the iniquities of its laws – particularly those exacting the death penalty for a range of offences against property and those condemning debtors to jail – and the costs of its legal procedures. Initially, their demands had ranged from the stock call for the disestablishment of the Church and the abolition of tithes, to the decentralisation of the legal system and election to all local offices. But by the autumn of 1647, Overton in particular was voicing the need for a new franchise to underpin the sovereignty of the people as a barrier to the supremacy of Parliament. Elaborating the common Leveller claim that the laws were the product of the 'Norman yoke' of William the Conqueror and his tyrannical lords, Overton saw them as 'unworthy a free people', while Walwyn was even prepared to chide Lilburne himself for his faith in that 'mess of pottage', Magna Carta. In their readiness to transcend the letter of the law, moreover, these Leveller leaders found themselves drawing from a well of support which was also spawning even more radical sectarian tendencies. For the fracturing of political authority had encouraged many 'saints' to conclude that the law was being superseded by the spirit – a notion which warranted nothing less than the freedom of the 'godly' over the tyranny of Presbyterian oligarchs and army generals alike.

At Putney, then, only 6 miles away from what the king now perceived as his decreasingly safe haven of Hampton Court, the stakes could not have been higher, as soldiers' prayers alternated with impassioned talk of constitutional reform, and ugly whispers of bringing the royal prisoner to justice continued to grow in volume. Charles had, in fact, been growing increasingly melancholy at his enforced captivity even before this latest assault on his peace of mind, and Lady Fanshawe, who had made one of the many war marriages in Oxford, was only one of many to be much distressed by his sadness about this time. 'When I took my leave,' she wrote, 'I could not refrain from weeping.' For common troopers, as the king well knew, were now 'of their own accord' without 'either authority or countenance' of their generals, engaged 'upon fair pretences'. After she had saluted him and 'prayed to God to preserve His Majesty with long life and happy years', he had stroked her on the cheek wistfully and confided his growing pessimism. 'Child,' he observed, 'if God pleaseth, it shall be so, but both you and I must submit to God's will, and you know in what hands I am.'

On the first day of the so-called Putney Debates, the *Agreement*, with its declaration that the power of the people's representatives in Parliament should be 'inferior only to theirs that choose them', was duly read to the General Council, and Cromwell's attitude appeared conciliatory. He was not, he assured the spokesmen for the *Agreement*, 'wedded and glued to forms of government', and was equally prepared to acknowledge 'that the foundation and supremacy is in the people, radically in them'. The following day, moreover, would witness Colonel Thomas Rainsborough's memorable affirmation, during a gladiatorial contest with Henry Ireton, that the 'poorest he that is in England hath a life to live, as the greatest he' and that, therefore, 'every man that is to live under a government ought first to put himself under that government'. If this were not the case, continued Rainsborough, he 'would fain know what the soldier hath for all this while fought' – a view echoed with equal force by Edward Sexby, who remained totally unconvinced by Ireton's defence of a franchise limited to those who had 'a permanent fixed interest in this kingdom, whether as freeholders or as freemen of corporations'. Was it not, asked Sexby, 'a sad and miserable condition that we have fought all this time for nothing'?

And as the onslaught continued, so the radical agenda expanded accordingly. Unlike the captive Lilburne, who was comparatively well disposed to the king, John Wildman was an outright republican, keen to indulge the kind of temperament that relished conflict and conspiracy, and it was almost certainly he who wrote *A Call to All the Soldiers of the Army by the Free People of England*, which was circulating among soldiers just as the great debate on the *Agreement* was gathering

pace. Denouncing both Ireton and Cromwell in virulent terms, accus-
ing them of leading the agitators by the nose in the General Council
while promoting the king's designs in Parliament, the pamphlet called
upon troops to withdraw obedience from any officer opposing the
Leveller programme. 'Ye have men among you as fit to govern as
others to be removed,' the argument ran. 'And with a word ye can
create new officers.' The time had arrived, therefore, to form 'an exact
council' and join hands in it with the 'truest lovers of the people ye
can find to help you', so that a free parliament might be established 'by
expulsion of the usurpers'.

By now, in fact, 400 men of Colonel Robert Lilburne's foot regiment
had already defied Fairfax's orders to march to Newcastle, threatening
ironically enough to declare for the king, while Leveller propaganda
was suggesting that as many as sixteen regiments, including seven of
foot, were in open support of their programme. Nor, when the debates
at Putney resumed on Monday, 1 November, was there any sign of
passions abating. On the contrary, as Cromwell reopened proceedings
by inviting those present to report any divine guidance they may have
received in answer to their prayers, the result was nothing less than an
open invitation to those who felt that God had withdrawn his presence
from them because their leaders persisted in trafficking with the king.
As Lieutenant-Colonel William Goffe put it, 'this hath been a voice
from heaven to us, that we have sinned against the Lord in tampering
with his enemies', while in the case of a certain Captain Bishop, the
message from above seems to have been blunter still, since, after due
reflection, he had concluded that no good could come from 'compliance to preserve that man of blood, and those principles of tyranny',
which God 'hath manifestly declared against'.

Under such pressure, even the members of the General Council
could not remain impassive, and on 5 November a resolution urging
Parliament to make 'no further addresses' to the king was duly
enacted as a prelude to one final effort by Lord Saye to isolate Charles
from the Scots, and pressurise him into accepting the Heads of the
Proposals. Three days later, it was announced too that a general rendezvous was to be called with a view to settling the 'many distempers
... reported to be in the several regiments'. Plainly, discipline would
have to be restored by a combination of firmer pressure upon the
king and, as events would prove, even more decisive action against
dissenters within the army's ranks. For on 15 November, at Corkbush

Field near Ware, Oliver Cromwell personally oversaw the crushing of the Leveller cause. Faced at last with the need to opt for order over liberty, he had chosen to impose what Fairfax later described as 'an absolute Submission and Conformity to the ancient Discipline of the Army' upon defiant soldiers wearing copies of their cherished *Agreement* in their hats, overwritten with the slogan 'England's freedom and soldiers rights'.

In the process, Cromwell had seen fit to charge, sword in hand, at those members of his beloved New Model Army who resisted the order to comply, though initially only one mutineer paid the ultimate price for his defiance. Up to nine ringleaders were court-martialled on the spot and sentenced to death, after which Fairfax pardoned all but three, who were then allowed to draw lots for their lives. The unlucky loser, as it transpired, was Private Richard Arnold, whose execution was intended to serve as an example to the rest of the troops. Eleven others in their turn were taken into custody for future trial, and this time the result would be the death penalty for two – both of whom were once again eventually reprieved. Even Colonel Rainsborough, whose support for the protestors' cause at Corkbush Field had been the most dangerous of all because of his seniority and popularity within the ranks, was not only spared, but appointed soon after to high office within the navy, though he would die in suspicious circumstances within the year, run through, allegedly, by a Royalist sword during a bungled kidnapping attempt at Pontefract Castle.

Thus were the restless elements within the army, so menacing to the king, duly cowed and tamed. Instead of the *Agreement of the People*, the General Council had retained the Heads of the Proposals as their agenda for peace, and the spectre of 'democracy' had been banished for a century-and-a-half and more. Anarchy was at bay and the imminent threat to the king extinguished. Yet the 'man of blood' himself had already fled the scene. Stirred by fears of summary justice and stricken by rumours that had been quick to penetrate the tapestried walls of Hampton Court, he had realised at last that his plans to bide his time while his enemies flew at each other's throats were no longer viable. Instead, quick decisions were required, and, for once, he took them. For on Thursday, 11 November, leaving his pet greyhound bitch whimpering in his room, Charles I, ruler of three realms, slipped quietly down an unguarded back staircase and out into the squally rain of early evening, to savour his first taste of freedom for eighteen months.

6

'TO SEEK MY SAFETY'

'Liberty being that which in all times hath been, but especially now is the common theme and desire of all men; common reason shewes that Kings less than any should endure captivity.'

From Charles I's letter to the Speaker of the House of Commons, 11 November 1647

On the evening of 5 November, while Londoners enjoyed a spectacular firework display at Lincoln's Inn Fields, the king was already pondering escape from Hampton Court. With his freedom to ride out already curtailed, he had been further agitated by several round-about reports of plots upon his life, and the dismissal of Ashburnham, Berkeley and other of his attendants four days earlier had only served to increase his sense of isolation. As early as 28 September, moreover, the *Moderate Intelligencer* was reporting Colonel Whalley's fears that he 'could no more keep the King (if he had a mind to goe) than a bird in a pound'. The sleep of the Princess Elizabeth had been disturbed, it seems, by the pacing of sentries in Hampton Court's Long Gallery, and when Whalley refused to shift their position until her father had agreed to renew his 'engagement' not to escape, he was met with defiance. 'To renew the engagement was a point of honour,' the colonel was told, according to his own testimony to the Speaker of the House of Commons. 'You had my engagement,' the king continued, 'I will not renew it. Keep your guards.' And with this emphatic response, the prisoner had rendered himself a free moral agent, liberated from all promises made both by himself and others on his behalf. In consequence, even a 'crackbrained Phanatick' like Whalley could appreciate the threat, but his appeal to be relieved of his duties as jailer and custodian was firmly rejected by Fairfax, and he was duly left to cope with neither the resources nor the authority to impose the kind of restraint necessary for his task.

On or about Saturday, 6 November, therefore, Colonel William Legge, who had been allowed to remain in post at Hampton Court, was dispatched to Jack Ashburnham's current residence – an inn at Thames Ditton – with news of the king's intention to escape and instructions that the courtier was to make the necessary arrangements. Surprised by the turn of events and uncertain of his royal master's intended destination, Ashburnham then decided to consult Sir John Berkeley, who was invited to dinner, along with Legge, the following day. But when Legge arrived on Sunday, Ashburnham was still in doubt and found little consolation after asking for Charles' own preferences, which consisted of flight to either the Continent or Jersey. For escape overseas entailed considerable risk of capture en route, and there was the further difficulty of arranging a ship for the purpose, which applied with equal force to any journey to Jersey. Equally, the king's departure would leave his supporters in England leaderless at the very time when friendly foreign powers were in any case far too preoccupied with their own peace negotiations to offer any hope of meaningful action on his behalf.

Nor was any further inspiration on offer from Berkeley when he arrived sometime after Legge and news of the planned escape was broached to him as all three men were about to take dinner. Though he believed that escape by sea might indeed be possible, he remained vague on details and possible destinations, and it was left instead to Ashburnham to formulate his own plan – which he did with growing enthusiasm as the meal progressed. For the king now had access to the commissioners of the Scottish Parliament – Lauderdale, Loudon and the ever candid Earl of Lanark – who had somewhat belatedly made an approach to him at Hampton Court. If these could be persuaded to meet Charles at the Lord Mayor's house in London, Ashburnham reasoned, and a suitable agreement was forthcoming, the support of City Presbyterians might also be enlisted, at which point, a further message could be sent to the House of Lords, proposing a session in the king's presence. Though the army, divided as it was, could be relied upon to mobilise in response, it was nevertheless likely, in Ashburnham's opinion, to take at least ten days to do so effectively, by which time the capital would be secure, the support of the Scots guaranteed and the whole momentum of events decisively shifted in the king's favour.

Plainly, the plan was not without its attractions, for Legge at once returned to Hampton Court, where Charles found it both persuasive and timely, since Major Huntington, one of the attendant army officers sympathetic to his plight, had been fuelling his fears of agitators and offering, by coincidence, to find a 'secure lodging' for him in the City. When Charles approached the Scottish commissioners as recommended, moreover, he found them generally amenable, so that by the morning of Monday, 8 November, Ashburnham and Berkeley were already visiting the army's headquarters at Putney with the intention of laying a false trail by collecting permits enabling them to leave the country and 'return beyond the seas'. Only when Berkeley expressed concerns on the return journey from Putney, indeed, did there seem to be any hint of failure. Suspecting that the army still remained in effective control and concluding, therefore, that bloodshed was bound to result, Berkeley had in fact reached the conclusion that any resultant violence would be blamed upon the king. His misgivings were soon infecting Ashburnham, who, in scrabbling for a new alternative, raised the prospect instead of escape to the Isle of Wight, claiming in the process that he had recently met the Governor, Colonel Robert Hammond, and detected signs that he might prove helpful.

Scarcely more enthusiastic than before, however, Berkeley then returned to the view that it might be preferable for the king to leave the country altogether, at which point Ashburnham himself demurred. Since the army was holding its rendezvous the following week, he objected, Charles would only strengthen the hands of the agitators by flight, and do so, furthermore, before precise terms had been finalised with the Scots. 'The World would laugh at us,' he declared, 'if we quitted the Army before we had agreed with the Scots.' And the fact that the Scottish commissioners were already abandoning the scheme for co-operation, even as Ashburnham spoke, could not have demonstrated his point more conclusively. For, as the two men were grappling with their apprehensions on the road from Putney, the Scottish lords at Hampton Court, anticipating a prickly reaction from their Parliament in Edinburgh, were earnestly informing Charles that while they were prepared to endorse his escape as private individuals, they could not act officially, since any action they undertook was likely to be disowned by the Church party at home.

To complicate matters further, Charles had also raised the possibility of an escape to Berwick, which met with an altogether warmer response from his Scottish audience. The Earl of Lanark, indeed, who had listened in silence until this point, now begged the king to adopt a course which from his perspective offered so many advantages. At Berwick, after all, Charles would still be residing in England and therefore untainted by claims from elements within the army that he had abandoned his kingdom. No less importantly, the town was capable of stout defence and near enough to the border, in any case, for the king to make a prudent withdrawal to Scotland, if necessary. This alone, of course, should have been enticement enough for a man bereft of options and in growing fear for his life, though Charles' memories of previous mistreatment at Scottish hands remained as vivid as ever, and the prospect of delivering himself once more to their protection swiftly palled after Legge had visited Ashburnham on Tuesday, 9 November, and returned with further information about escape to the Isle of Wight.

Although Ashburnham remained of the opinion that Colonel Hammond was likely to be sympathetic upon their arrival, he had now reached the conclusion that Charles should first take shelter with Sir John Oglander at his house at Nunwell in the east of the island, since Oglander was not only a confirmed Royalist but also the island's erstwhile Deputy Lieutenant. From Nunwell, the king could still maintain contact with the army's officers through Hammond, but since the army had no units on the island itself, he would be free from the threat of extremists. As at Berwick, he would be remaining within the kingdom, thereby maintaining the morale of his supporters, and the door would also be kept conveniently ajar for future negotiations with Parliament or indeed the Scots. If, moreover, any section of the fleet were to desert his enemies, its help could easily reach him. Even the prospect of Hammond's possible non-co-operation seemed less than disastrous, indeed, since Ashburnham was convinced an escape from the island to some safe haven abroad was unlikely to prove too formidable.

Less than forty-eight hours after its conception, therefore, the original escape plan involving the Scots had not only been abandoned but entirely replaced by a new alternative, which, while offering the king fresh hope, also no doubt stirred certain misgivings. He had, it is true, made four visits to the island in happier times and was therefore comparatively well acquainted with it, though the last occasion had been all of nineteen years ago. Likewise, though he knew that there were ardent Royalists like Sir John Oglander among the island's inhabitants, he was no less keenly aware that the outbreak of war in 1642 had seen his support quickly submerged when surrender occurred on 24 August after no more than a single shot had been fired. Oglander indeed had noted the king's disappointment at Oxford only a year later. When hostilities began, he observed, the king 'had more Confidence of the Isle of Wight, that they woold have stood for him, than of any other partes of his kyngdome, but now by his experience he fownd fewe honest men there'.

Yet time was of the essence, and after Berkeley had endorsed the proposal and Legge had hurried back to Hampton Court to put it to Charles, everything hinged upon the dependability or otherwise of the island's Governor, Robert Hammond. Still only 26 and a cousin of Cromwell, Hammond had already enjoyed a distinguished career in the service of Parliament – culminating in the command of an infantry regiment in the New Model Army – and stood as living proof that, where talent and loyalty were present in abundance, age was no bar to advancement. He was the second son of Robert Hammond of Chertsey, Surrey, and had matriculated at Magdalen Hall, Oxford, on 20 May 1636, aged 15, before leaving the university without taking a degree. Like many young men of his generation, however, the war would be his making, for in the summer of 1642 he was listed as a lieutenant in the army destined for Ireland, and on 6 July obtained a commission as captain of an infantry company of 200 men, to be levied in London and the adjoining counties. Nor was this the end of his rapid progress, for on 11 March 1643, he was appointed a captain in the Earl of Essex's regiment of cuirassiers, after which he was singled out for special praise during the capture of Tewkesbury in June 1644.

Such were Hammond's merits, in fact, that even an unfortunate incident in the streets of Gloucester that October did nothing to block his progress. For a quarrel involving a certain Major Grey had led not only to a duel in which Grey was killed, but a subsequent court-martial for Hammond himself. The result, however, was a unanimous acquittal on 28 November, on the grounds that the victor had acted in self-defence, and a further promotion to the rank of colonel in 1645. Thereafter, at the Battle of Naseby, Hammond's regiment formed part of the reserve, and he was actively involved in the storming of Bristol and Dartmouth and the capture of Powderham Castle and St Michael's Mount, as well as the Battle of Torrington, which, in February 1646, had effectively ended Royalist resistance in the West Country. Sixteen months earlier, moreover, he had experienced the other side of war after being captured during the siege of Basing House, though when Cromwell eventually subdued the garrison it was Hammond who found himself sent up to Westminster to give account of the victory and he, too, who found himself voted the sum of £200 by the House of Commons to recoup his losses as a prisoner.

Yet just as Hammond's talents stretched well beyond the field of battle, he was likewise no mere mannequin, slavishly following orders and avoiding all contention. As Governor of Exeter in 1646, he acquired valuable administrative experience, and by 1647 had become an influential voice in the framing of army policy. When Parliament required him to serve in Ireland in March 1647, however, he proved refractory, and sided increasingly with his fellow officers during their ongoing struggle with Westminster that summer. According to Denzil Holles, in fact, he 'stood upon his pantoufles' in face of parliamentary pressure and 'stipulated such Terms as no Prince or foreign State that had but given an assistance could have stood upon higher'. On 1 April, he appeared in person at the bar of the House of Commons to answer for his conduct in permitting the circulation of the army's petition against disbandment in his regiment, only 400 of whom were subsequently willing to serve in Ireland, and he also signed the vindication of the officers presented to Parliament later that month, as well as the letter of the officers presented to the City on 10 June. During the crucial army debates at Saffron Walden church in mid-May, moreover, he experienced a well-advertised brush with Colonel Sheffield, who was in favour of accepting Parliament's terms.

By the summer of 1647, therefore, Robert Hammond was to all appearances a hardline critic of parliamentary policy, and in this capacity became one of those appointed to treat with Parliament on behalf of the army on 1 July. But the more aggressive activity of the Levellers soon proved no less intolerable, it seems, than the machinations of MPs at Westminster, and as the summer progressed, threats of force by radical elements within the army were once again raising the colonel's moral hackles, leading him to seek and obtain release from active military service on the grounds that 'he found the Army resolved to break all promises to the King and he would have nothing to do with such perfidies'. Nor was it any small measure of Hammond's residing reputation that on 3 September 1647, no less a figure than Philip Herbert, 4th Earl of Pembroke, who since 1642 had been Governor of the Isle of Wight, duly announced to the House of Lords that Thomas Fairfax, by his authority as commander-in-chief, had commissioned Hammond to replace him. Offering no resistance, Herbert duly requested that the Lords accept his own resignation, and asked them to pass an ordinance appointing his successor, which was accomplished on 6 September.

According to the contemporary account of Anthony Wood, only one day before Hammond's departure for his new appointment, he was introduced directly to the king at Hampton Court by his uncle Henry, who happened to be a royal chaplain. There, it seems, he was recommended to Charles 'as a penitent convert … which his majesty taking well, he gave him his hand to kiss'. It was only the day after, it seems, that Ashburnham had his fateful meeting with Hammond, which convinced him too of the colonel's potential as an ally. Encountering him 'upon the Highway near Kingston' shortly after he had begun the journey to take up his new post, Ashburnham found him 'not very averse to his Majesty'. Indeed, Hammond made it clear, we are told, that 'hee was going down to his Government, because he found the Armie was resolved to break all promises with the King, and that he would have nothing to doe with such perfidious actions'.

If so, then Hammond was hardly alone in his sentiments, for by now, of course, Cromwell and other senior figures within the army were being openly decried for visiting the king to 'kneele and kisse and fawne upon him', and there are other indications, too, of Hammond's comparative moderation. 'He is an Independent,' reported one Venetian observer writing from London to Paris, 'but of those who are in favour with the king, with liberty of conscience, and not of the extreme party.' Equally, a Royalist news-sheet of the day, *Mercurius Elencticus*, noted, albeit grudgingly, that 'Hammond is a Man that hath usually trod in the Circle of a Civill life, and is observ'd not to have admitted of such dangerous Principles, nor been so violent, either against the Cause or Person of the King or others of his Fraternitie'. Even Sir John Oglander, for that matter, who was hardly inclined under most circumstances to speak kindly of Roundhead officers, acknowledged Hammond to be 'a Gentleman and olso yonger sonn to a Gentleman'.

Plainly, then, with a potentially sympathetic Governor in place, Ashburnham's recommendation of escape to the Isle of Wight was not without appeal, though Charles remained hesitant, and as his anxiety grew, he resorted to altogether more suspect sources of counsel. In particular, he seems to have asked the ever-willing Jane Whorwood to pick her way at great danger through the crowded streets of London towards the corner house opposite Strand Bridge, where the astrologer William Lilly conducted his fashionable and lucrative practice. Certainly no Royalist, Lilly had spent the war in the capital waging battles of his own with the Oxford soldier-astrologer George Wharton, with whom he competed avidly in a sordid quest for money derived from fear, loss and uncertainty. His surviving case notes deal with loved ones missing in battle or through exile or imprisonment, requests from Royalists seeking the fate of the king, as well as consultations involving a range of health problems and everyday inconveniences, including the recovery of a mislaid cloak in Covent Garden. In all cases, Lilly consulted his charts, wove complex mathematical webs to confound his clients and, as occasion demanded, called upon other more idiosyncratic techniques of 'philomathy', including the counting of pock marks.

Even hard-headed souls like Thomas Fairfax were not above seeking Lilly's advice, it seems, and though 'he understood it not', the astrologer would nevertheless be taken to the siege of Colchester in 1648 to bolster army morale. Hugh Peter, the radical chaplain, checked that his almanacks were 'lawful and agreeable to God's word', while more moderate Puritan divines were also prepared to accept a clear distinction between what Lilly practised and the forbidden arts of magic and necromancy, since his procedures involved no 'charms, sorceries or enchantments'. Though a certain Dorothy Osborne dismissed him in 1654 as 'worse than an old woman that passes for a witch, a simple impostor', Cromwell was prepared to pay him £250 for his services, while the king furnished him with at least twenty gold coins for a series of consultations with Jane Whorwood, whom the astrologer referred to in his notes as '*Doowrohw Lady*' by reversing her surname. On 2 May 1647, she had sounded him out on an unrecorded matter, but on 3 June, Lilly noted a meeting involving '*domina ex Oxford de amico*' (a lady from Oxford about a friend) as well as a further discussion, three days later, '*de exercito*' (concerning the army). Equally intriguingly, there is a request, in mid-June, for Lilly to determine the likelihood of agreement between Parliament and the army, while in July, just as Charles was involved in talks with army generals, three other unnamed clients consulted the astrologer '*de rege*' (about the king).

Even before Jane Whorwood's final visit to his premises, then, it appears that William Lilly was doing good business from his most prestigious client's predicament, for while Charles would later confess that

'I do not care for him', since 'he hath always been against me', he also freely acknowledged that the widely admired stargazer 'understands astrology as well as any man in Europe'. When Lilly now peered at Whorwood through a reluctantly opened crack in the doorway of his premises on the site of what is now the abandoned Aldwych tube station, he was about to be questioned on the most delicate of all issues. In view of the astrologer's known sympathies, it was a measure of Charles' desperation, of course, that he had decided to consult him at all, and to do so on the matter of his impending escape involved what can only be considered a truly remarkable gamble. Yet whispers of poisoning, talk of trials and the ongoing agonies of determining a safe haven had pushed him to the point of no return, so that now, it seems, he would take any risk for peace of mind.

The interview with Whorwood which ensued is described, moreover, in Lilly's own *History of His Life and Times*, which was dedicated to his patron Elias Ashmole, and to whom he refers here as 'Esquire':

> Upon the King's intention to escape, and with his consent, Madam Whorwood (whom you know very well, Esquire) came to receive my judgement, *viz*. In what quarter of this nation he might be most safe, and not to be discovered until himself pleased. When she came to my door, I told her I would not let her come in to my house, for I buried a maidservant of the plague very lately. 'I fear not the plague, but the pox,' quoth she; so up she went. After erection of the figure [astrological chart], I told her about twenty (or thereabout) miles from London and in Essex, I was certain he might continue undiscovered. She liked my judgement very well; and being herself of a sharp judgement, remembered a place in Essex about that distance, where was an excellent house, and all conveniences for his reception.

Undeterred not only by the threat of detection but by the direct threat of plague as well, Whorwood had, then, once again fully earned the praise heaped upon her as 'the most loyal person to King Charles in his miseries as any woman in England'. She had sounded Lilly out, stood alongside him in his consulting chamber as he 'erected the figure' and identified a safe residence in Essex in accordance with the astrologer's findings – possibly at the Elsenham manor of Alderman Thomas Adams, who had just given Whorwood £500 in gold for the king's cause, or at Barringtons, the Chigwell home of the banker to the

Royalists, Robert Abbott. Years later, Lilly would remember her earthy riposte about fearing the pox rather than the plague as a characteristically strong-willed refusal to take no for an answer when he had tried to bar her from entry. He had, after all, been house-bound by plague for seven weeks, as a result of the loss of two of his servants. But Jane Whorwood was nothing if not intrepid. Thereafter, she had risked all once more, making her way back along the river to Hampton Court, probably cloaked and hooded against the cold and no doubt haunted all the while by the possibility of her betrayal, to furnish the king with the all-important information he required.

By the time of her arrival, however, as Lilly records in the rest of his account, events had already overtaken her. 'Away she went early next morning to Hampton Court to acquaint his Majesty,' Lilly tells us. 'But see the misfortune,' he continues, for the king, 'either guided by his own approaching hard fate, or misguided by Ashburnham, went away in the night time westward, and surrendered himself to Hammond in the Isle of Wight.' The final straw, it seems, may well have been a mysterious letter sent to Charles on 11 November, warning him of an imminent assassination attempt and signed only 'E.R.' Now known almost certainly to have been written by Lieutenant-Colonel Henry Lilburne, the altogether more moderate brother of 'Freeborn' John the Leveller, the letter had been written on 9 November and passed on to the king by Whalley, with predictable results. For, while some of the king's circle considered it a ruse, its contents were hardly able to be lightly ignored, particularly when it is remembered that Cromwell himself had heard similar 'rumours abroad of some intended attempt on his Majesty's person', and warned his cousin Whalley to 'have a care of your guards', since such an assault upon the king's life 'would be accounted a most horrid act'.

Providing specific detail on stirrings within the army and thereby confirming all his worst suspicions, the anonymous letter that Charles now read, ran as follows:

May it please your Majesty.
In discharge of my duty I cannot omit to acquaint you that my brothers at a meeting last night with eight or nine Agitators; who in debate of the obstacle which did most hinder the speedy effecting of their design, did conclude it was your Majesty. And as long as your Majesty doth live it would be so: And therefore did resolve for the

good of the Kingdom, to take your life away and that to that action they were well assured, that Mr Dell and Mr Peters, two of their preachers, would willingly bear them company, for they had often said to their Agitators, your Majesty is but a dead dog. My prayers are for your Majesty's safety, but I do too much fear, it cannot be whilst you are in those hands.

I wish with my soul your Majesty were at my house in Broad Street, where I am confident I could keep you private till this storm were over, but beg your Majesty's pardon, and shall not presume to offer it as an advice, it is only constant zeal to your service, who am,

Your most dutiful subject, E.R.

Whether the offer of help was genuine and whether the house in Broad Street was indeed a prospective safe haven remains unknown, but Charles by now had no need of either, since his own plans were already in place, and he had both the motive and the means to enact them. Now firmly established among the army radicals at Putney as the 'Chief Delinquent' and biblical 'Man of Blood', there was cause enough for escape even had his life not been in direct danger, as he would soon confirm in the letter he left for Whalley after his departure. Whalley's conviction that he could not hold his prisoner, should he wish to gain his freedom, had not receded. 'It was impossible for me to keep the king,' he would complain later, 'he having such liberty and such Bedchamber men about him, his ancient servants.' Nor did the presence of the Scots at Hampton Court ease the colonel's concerns. Ashburnham himself had complained to him that 'no other language is spoken in the court but Scotch', and there was general recognition that Charles' circle was 'so much scottifyed' that 'there would be workings to get the king away'.

Not even added manpower, for that matter, could set Whalley's mind at rest, since the escape occurred, according to a contemporary Venetian source, at the very time that there were 'foot and horse guards being set'. Always a palace rather than a prison, Hampton Court appears, in effect, to have been a honeycomb of private apartments, inter-connected chambers, anterooms, galleries, staircases, towers and turrets. While the prisoner continued to be accorded such deference and privacy by virtue of his royal rank, Whalley's actual control would continue to remain little more than nominal. Unable to keep the king under the kind of 'close watch' that was necessary within his own rooms, and knowing full well that retainers like Firebrace, Maule and Murray were still on hand to assist in any escape attempt, the captor had become to all intents a passive spectator in events that he knew to be unfolding around him. There was, indeed, an almost agonising inevitability about the embarrassment awaiting Whalley as he strove in vain to impose some semblance of genuine security upon Hampton Court's sprawling confines.

The section of the palace in which Charles was housed was demolished, in fact, during the reign of William III, and replaced by Wren's south and east fronts, but a rough plan of the configuration of the original building has been preserved at Oxford, and its external appearance is shown in a picture painted for Samuel Pepys in 1669. At the western end stood the guardroom near the main staircase, and at the other end a backstairs leading down to a courtyard. Sentries were also posted in the Long Gallery, which ran past the back of the king's apartments and into which a number of adjacent rooms opened. Likewise, in the grounds outside stood several towers and turrets connected by other galleries stretching in an irregular line from the palace's south-east angle to the river, where a large building with stairs and a water gate was located. From this, the so-called 'Water Gallery' communicated with another building known as the 'Great Round Arbour', behind both of which lay 'The King's Long Gallery', jutting into the park in an easterly direction at right angles to the other galleries, at the end of which was a room called 'Paradise', described in John Evelyn's *Diary* as a 'parterre ... in which is a pretty banqueting-house set over a cave or cellar'.

Such, then, were the prison walls confining the king as he primed himself for escape on 11 November 1647. It was his custom on Mondays and Thursdays to retire to his bedchamber at the west side of the palace at about 2 p.m. for the purpose of writing letters to his relatives abroad, and to emerge for prayers between 5–6 p.m. Thereafter, he would take supper, comparatively briefly, before returning once more to his bedchamber, at which point guards took up their posts. On the afternoon of the 11th, however, Charles gave strict orders to Maule and Murray, who were on duty in the adjoining anteroom, that he should not be disturbed under any circumstances, and it was only as darkness descended, around 4 p.m., that he contacted them again, calling first for candles, and a little later for snuffers. Close by too, in a chamber next to Maule and Murray, was the king's secretary, Nicholas Oudart, and

Henry Firebrace, who was in one of the several rooms laying between the royal bedchamber and the backstairs themselves.

It was at 5 p.m., in fact, that Whalley arrived at the anteroom to escort his prisoner to prayers, only to be left waiting – 'without mistrust' – for a full hour before telling Maule and Murray that he 'wondered the king was so long a writing'. Clearly lacking the free rein that might have bred an altogether more decisive reaction, he was then met with the almost insulting response that the king probably had 'some extraordinary occasion'. More surprisingly still, when Oudart suggested that his master was writing to the Princess of Orange, Whalley appears to have taken 'some satisfaction for the present'. Indeed, it was not until 7 p.m. that the colonel suggested to Maule that the king might be ill, and that it would be well if he entered to see. Yet Maule was adamant that he dared not disobey the orders of the king, who had in any case bolted the door from the inside.

By now 'extreme restless in his thoughts', Whalley was reduced, it seems, to peeking several times through the keyhole, but could see nothing. Maule, in the meantime, refused even to knock on the colonel's behalf, for, under normal circumstances, the king's jailer lacked even this option in his own right. Only at 8 p.m., in fact, some three hours after his initial arrival, did Whalley feel able to take the initiative, though rather than choosing the simple option of forcing entry there and then, he sought instead the assistance of William Smithsby, Keeper of the Privy Lodgings, who had attended the king at Edgehill in 1642, served as a Groom of the Privy Chamber for thirteen years before that and was now fully involved in the escape attempt himself, having been entrusted by the king with certain pictures and other articles prior to his departure.

Together with one of the king's abettors, then, Whalley now made his way to the royal bedchamber by the back route, through the garden and up the backstairs, meeting no one, it seems, except the sentries posted in the garden, since Firebrace, who had been keeping vigil during the king's departure, had long since withdrawn. According to Firebrace himself, moreover, the night was dark and rainy, but plainly not so dark that Whalley was unable to detect the first conclusive sign of what had transpired. For, as he moved with increasing urgency through several intervening rooms, he found the king's cloak lying on the floor of the one next to his bedchamber. Advancing no farther, he then called for Maule, who still refused to enter until ordered to do so in the name of Parliament. In all, it had taken a further half-hour before the king's attendant did as bid and in doing so confirmed that 'the king was gone'.

Though Maule was at once accused of being an accessory, precise details of how the escape was effected would only emerge in news-sheets over the next week. According to an edition of *A perfect Diurnall*, appearing on 15 November, it had been achieved 'by the backstairs and vault towards the waterside', while the *Moderate Intelligencer* suggested it had occurred 'by way of Paradise, a place so-called in the garden'. It seems, in fact, that as soon as it was dark enough to avoid observation, the king, accompanied perhaps by Colonel William Legge, did indeed pass down the backstairs, along the galleries leading to the waterside and then by the King's Long Gallery to the Paradise room in the park, the door of which, being some distance away from the main building, was unguarded. In the meantime, at about 2 p.m. according to *Mercurius Antipragmaticus*, 'six lusty horses, led by men in different habits', were ferried over from Long Ditton and 'were seen to take an hill adjacent to his Majesty'.

Whether these were employed in the escape remains unknown, but if so, it would appear that Charles and Legge may subsequently have ridden to Thames Ditton and there crossed the river. Sir Thomas Herbert's account, however, only states that the river was crossed at Thames Ditton, which is no more than a mile from Hampton Court, and it remains possible, too, that a boat had been concealed near Paradise and that the two men rowed down to Ditton, mounting their horses there. Certainly, this was consistent with the view expressed in *Major Huntington's Narrative*, which describes how the king:

> caused a boat to be laid by river side, and upon the 11th of November, about the beginning of the night, went alone from the Privy-lodgings, through a door where no guard stood into the park, and so crossing the Thames, landed at Ditton, where Sir John Berkeley, John Ashburnham and Colonel William Legge (sometimes grooms of the Bed-Chamber) were placed with horses.

In this particular account, then, the king was actually unaccompanied as he left Hampton Court, meeting Legge only later, some way downstream from his starting point. But on one smaller point of detail at least there is general agreement: namely, that the king not only left behind him his cloak – probably in exchange for another less conspicuous one

– but also his beloved greyhound, Gipsy. According to the *Moderate Intelligencer*, when the king did not 'come forth' from his chamber after Whalley's arrival, 'there were feares, which increased by the crying of a greyhound again and again within'. This was indeed the 'grew bitch', mentioned in Sir Philip Warwick's *Memoirs*, who held such a prominent place in Charles' affections – so much so, indeed, that he specially requested, upon his escape, that she be sent to the Duke of Richmond.

Besides his favourite dog, however, Charles also left four letters in his wake at Hampton Court – all prominently displayed on his bedchamber table for immediate inspection, and three of which were written in his own handwriting. The first was the warning letter sent by 'E.R.', while the second, addressed to Parliament and reproduced in full below, was intended to unburden his mind of grievances, apportion blame, restate his principles and repeat the plea to be heard with safety and respect:

Charles Rex.

Liberty being that which in all times hath been, but especially now is the common theme and desire of all men; common reason shewes, that Kings less than any should endure captivity. And yet I call God and the world to witnesse, with what patience I have endured a tedious restraint; which so long as I had any hopes that this sort of my suffering might conduce to the peace of my Kingdom, or the hindering of more effusion of blood, I did willingly undergo: But not finding by too certain proofs, that this my continued patience, would not only turn to my personal ruin, but likewise be of much more prejudice than furtherance to the public good, I thought I was bound, as well by natural as by political obligations, to seek my safety, by retiring myself for some time from the public view, both of my friends and enemies. And I appeal to all indifferent men to judge, if I have not just cause, to free myself from the hands of those who change their principles with their conditions, and who are not ashamed openly to intend the destruction of the Nobility, taking away their Negative voice, and with whom the Levellers doctrine is rather countenanced than punished: And as for their intentions to my person, their changing and putting more strict guards upon me, with the discharging most of all those servants of mine, who formerly they willingly admitted to wait upon me, does sufficiently declare. Nor would I have this my retirement misinterpreted, for I shall earnestly and uncessantly endeavour the settling of a safe and well-grounded peace wherever I am or shall be; and that (as much as may be) without the effusion of more Christian blood; for which how many times have I desired, prest to be heard, and yet no ear given to me? And can any reasonable man think, that (according to the ordinary course of affairs) there can be a setled peace without it? Or that God will bless those, who refuse to hear their King? Surely no. Nay I must further add, that (besides what concerns myself) unless all other chief interests have not only a hearing, but likewise just satisfaction given unto them (to wit, the Presbyterian, Independents, Army, those that have adhered to me, and even the Scots) I say there cannot (I speak not of miracles, it being in my opinion a sinful presumption in such cases, to expect or trust to them) be a safe or lasting peace.

Now as I cannot deny but that my personal security is the urgent cause of this my retirement; so I take God to witness that the public peace is no less before my eyes, and I can find no better way to express this my profession (I know not what a wiser may do) than by desiring and urging that all chief interests may be heard, to the end each may have just satisfaction. As for example, the Army (for the rest though necessary, yet I suppose are not difficult to content) ought (in my judgment) to enjoy the liberty of their consciences, have an Act of Oblivion or Indemnity (which should extend to the rest of my subjects) and that all their arrears should be speedily and duly paid, which I will undertake to do, so I may be heard, and that I be not heard, and I be not hindered from using such lawful and honest means as I shall choose.

To conclude, let me be heard with freedom, honour and safety, and I shall instantly break through this cloud of retirement, and show myself really to be *Pater Patriae*.

Hampton Court, Novemb. 11. 1647.
For the Speaker of the House of Peeres *pro tempore* etc.

The third of Charles' letters, meanwhile, expressed gratitude to Lord Montague and the rest of the parliamentary commissioners for their behaviour since his arrival at Hampton Court:

Montague,
First I do hereby give you and the rest of your fellows thanks, for the civilities and the good conversation that I have had from you:

Next I command you to send this my message (which you will find
upon this table) to the two Houses of Parliament, and likewise to
give a copy of it to the General: Likewise I desire you to send all my
saddle-horses to my son, the Duke of York. As for what concerns the
resolution I have taken, my declaratorie message saies so much, that I
refer you to it; and so I rest,

Your assured friend, C. Rex.

The homely tone of the message, and in particular the casual reference to his saddle-horses, hardly accords, of course, with the flight of a
man in desperate fear of his life, and reflects, indeed, the almost routine
nature of the whole escape attempt. Nor, for that matter, is there any
apparent recognition on Charles' part of the deep provocation entailed
by his actions, let alone the ensuing crisis they had spawned. On the
contrary, he is calm, collected, confident and, from his own perspective,
still thoroughly in command of the forces ranged against him.

Yet it was the fourth of the letters left behind by Charles that carried
altogether more significance. Addressed to Whalley, it displays typical
condescension on the king's part and an equally crushing disdain for
the broader consequences of his actions. Not only is the colonel's predicament of no apparent concern, there is also a carefree assumption
that he will continue to service his former prisoner's needs without
either regrets or recrimination. Acknowledging that he had been 'civily
used' by both Whalley and Major Huntington, Charles then proceeded
in his 'parting farewel' to 'desire' of his erstwhile captor that he protect
'my household stuff and movables of all sorts, which I have left behind
me in this house, etc.'. Favourite pictures, including a Van Dyck portrait
of the queen, were to be carefully protected, furnishings safely stored
and the king's whimpering greyhound suitably homed in accordance
with her master's wishes.

The most intriguing section of Charles' letter lies elsewhere,
however. For in a postscript, the king mentions another mysterious
message presented to him by Whalley, which, as would become clear
subsequently, was not the warning letter signed 'E.R.', but Cromwell's
letter to 'Dear Cousin Whalley' that 'there are rumours abroad of
some intended attempt on his Majesty's person'. Assuring Whalley
that it was not, in fact, this letter 'nor any advertisement of this kind'
that had prompted him to 'take this resolution' to escape, Charles

implied nevertheless that it may well have represented something of a final straw, since he was 'loathe to be made a prisoner under pretence of securing my life'.

That Whalley had indeed shown his prisoner Cromwell's letter is clear from the colonel's own testimony to Parliament in the aftermath of the escape:

> And whereas, Mr Speaker, you demand of me what that letter was that I showed the King that day he went away? The letter I shall show you. But with your leave, I shall first acquaint you with the author and the ground of my shewing it to the King.
>
> The author is Lieutenant General Cromwell. The ground of my shewing it was this. The letter shows some murderous designe, or at least fearing it, against his Majestie. When I received the letter I was much astonisht, abhorring that such a thing should be done, or so much as thought of, by any that bear the name of Christians. When I had shewn the letter to his Majestie, I told him 'I was sent to safeguard and not to murther him'. I wisht him to be confident no such thing could be done. I would first dye at his foot in his defence. And therefore I shewed it to him that he might be assured, though menacing speeches came frequently to his eare, our general officers abhorred so bloody and villainous a fact. Another reason, that I might get a nearer admittance to his Majestie, that so I might better secure him.

Ostensibly, of course, Whalley's explanation of his action is by no means unreasonable. But the suspicion that Cromwell may well have wished to prompt the king's escape has a sufficiently long pedigree to merit careful consideration. Even the poet Andrew Marvell, who was more than capable of singing the general's praises when occasion demanded, made direct reference to the episode in *An Horatian Ode upon Cromwell's Return from Ireland* (1650):

> And Hampton shows what part
> He had of wiser art,
> Where, twining subtile fears with hope,
> He wove a net of such a scope,
> That Charles himself might chase
> To Caresbrooks narrow case.

And there was no denying that Cromwell had indeed become increasingly alarmed at the possibility that radical elements within the army
might ultimately become uncontrollable. As such, there was certainly
good reason to remove him from the proximity of Hampton Court,
while keeping him in the hands of army moderates and at a safe distance from both Parliament and the Scots. Nor was there any doubt
that Charles' eventual destination at Carisbrooke Castle upon the Isle
of Wight suited this purpose admirably. For the island was within reach
of London, but cordoned off by the Solent from both extremists and
would-be wooers of the king. With Hammond, a trusted cousin and
colleague, firmly in place there, what could be better than to lay the
trap and make the king's decision apparently his own?

No less a figure than Thomas Hobbes, indeed, would suggest in
Behemoth (1679) that the ploy was staged by Cromwell as part of a
blueprint for obtaining supreme power in the longer term – something
that could never be achieved as long as Charles remained upon the
throne:

> To keep him in the Army was a trouble, to let him fall into the hands
> of the Presbyterians had been a stop to his hopes, to murder him pri-
> vately would have made him odious without furthering his design:
> there was nothing better for his purpose than to let him escape from
> Hampton Court (where he was too near the Parliament) whither he
> pleased beyond sea.

However persuasive the counter-arguments, it is not difficult to see
why such suspicions have remained entrenched to the present day. With
hindsight, of course, it is apparent that Cromwell had not yet given up
hopes of coming to terms with the king, for only the day before his
escape, the Commons had put the finishing touches to a new set of
peace proposals, based on the initiative of Cromwell's own Independent
allies. More significantly still, perhaps, Charles' eventual arrival upon
the Isle of Wight was entirely uncertain at the time of his actual departure. He was, after all, a notorious vacillator and the advice from his
inner circle remained indecisive, since the Isle of Wight, for any apparent advantage it might offer, remained isolated and war-weary, more of
a dead end than escape route and, as one commentator put it, 'just like
other parts of England, a melancholy, dejected, sad place: no company,
no rents, no neighbours seeing one of the other'. Ashburnham, indeed,

had only proposed it initially as a last resort, later claiming to have pressed the king to encourage Henrietta Maria to send a French ship to Southampton, through the agency of the Pitt and La Mott families of the Royalist oligarchy there.

This, according to Ashburnham's own testimony, had actually been achieved before Charles hesitated once more and the ship was eventually dismissed, adding to the ongoing concerns of others in the king's circle. Berkeley, for example, had remained uncertain throughout, warning the king for some time that success required 'three or four ships in several ports', and collaborating in the entire escapade, when the time for action finally arrived, only under his master's unyielding demand for blind obedience. For Berkeley, more than any other, was convinced of Cromwell's genuine concern for Charles' welfare, 'sometimes wishing that he, the king, was more frank and less tied to narrow maxims; sometimes complaining of his son [-in-law] Ireton's slowness in perfecting the proposals and his not accommodating more to His Majesty's senses'.

To suggest, then, that the escape from Hampton Court was engineered by the Roundhead general's invisible hand presents at least two apparently intractable problems. Yet the circumstantial evidence to that effect remains stubbornly intact. Colonel Hammond's appointment as Governor of the Isle of Wight, for instance, was certainly more than curious. Swiftly following his resignation from active military service and alleged visit, as a penitent, to the king at Hampton Court, it was a promotion not only inspired by the army but executed under obvious pressure from the army's leadership. Governors of the Isle of Wight were normally appointed by royal patent, but with the displacement of the Royalist Earl of Portland in 1642, his successor, the Earl of Pembroke, was nominated by Parliament. After which, Pembroke ruled the island throughout the Civil War, acting mainly through his deputy, Colonel Carne.

Though he had become an outspoken critic of the New Model Army by mid-1646, moreover, Pembroke quickly changed his tune in August when the army marched into London, and he had shown no previous signs of dissatisfaction in the execution of his duties. Yet on 1 September 1647, General Fairfax wrote to the Earl of Manchester, Speaker of the House of Lords, that Pembroke had indicated 'his satisfaction in my disposall of the Government of the Isle of Wight to Collonell Robert Hammond', and invited the House of Lords to ratify the appointment.

Two days later, furthermore, Pembroke himself announced to the Lords that Fairfax required Hammond's appointment to the governorship, 'he being a person looked upon by the General as a fit Person for that Trust'. Thus sponsored, an ordinance for the appointment was drafted the same day and, after a largely token amendment by the Commons bringing the process under the nominal control of Parliament, the measure went through without further difficulty, leaving Hammond to be duly initiated into his new post.

En route, of course, he had also apparently stumbled upon Jack Ashburnham and convinced him of his sympathy for the king's predicament. By mid-September, the colonel was firmly installed in his new role, both officially and, it would seem, personally, for he was not without direct connections to the island. His aunt, Jane Dingley, for example, already lived at Wolverton Manor in the village of Shorwell, 4 miles from Carisbrooke Castle, and on 18 September he was duly 'elected & sworne' a burgess of Newport before being made 'Vice-Admiral of the County of Hampshire and the Isle of Wight' on the opening day of the following month. Twenty-four hours earlier, moreover, Pembroke had duly 'retired' amid widespread talk that his departure from the island was a dismissal rather than a resignation. On 19 September, indeed, an anonymous Venetian observer, remaining in London after the closure of his embassy, was in no doubt that coercion had been employed. 'The governorship, held by the Earl of Pembroke,' he wrote, 'has been granted to others, and he with six others of the Upper House is accused of crimes against the state.'

Ultimately, in fact, no such charge materialised, and by July 1648 the earl had once again assumed a role of some prominence as a member of the parliamentary commission negotiating peace with the king at Newport. Yet Pembroke's departure, and even more so Hammond's arrival, was too striking to escape speculation from contemporaries. 'It was observed,' wrote Clarendon, 'that Hammond himself left the army but two or three days before the King's remove, and went to the Isle of Wight at a season when there was no visible occasion to draw him thither.' Sir John Oglander, meanwhile, was even more forthright, observing how 'Hammond was made Commander of the Isle of Wight purposely to be King Charles' keeper'. It was wholly predictable, of course, that the coincidence between Hammond's arrival on the island and the king's should have been aired in the news-sheets of the day. In the *Mercurius Anti-Pragmaticus*, for example, it was noted that the colonel's transfer to the island had occurred 'as if it had been told him by revelation that his Majesty would commit himself to his protection', and that his journey, ahead of his regiment, had taken place 'as if by instinct he had foreseen his Majesties comming'.

At the same time, Cromwell's own movements added further fuel to Sir Thomas Adams' suspicion, expressed from the gloom of a prison cell in the Tower of London, that there had been more than a little 'juggling in the king's being found at the Isle of Wight'. Certainly, the general later explained Hammond's resignation innocuously enough, observing how he had 'through dissatisfaction ... desired retirement from the Army, and thought of quiet in the Isle of Wight'. But Cromwell's visit to the island between 4–12 September, just after Hammond's promotion to the governorship, has never been explained, and Clarendon made clear that he received the news of Charles' subsequent arrival 'with so unusual a gaiety that all Men concluded that the king was where he wished he should be'. Nor, for that matter, did Clarendon hesitate to claim that Ashburnham himself was a confederate of Cromwell's. Both he and Berkeley had, in fact, conducted negotiations, open and otherwise, with Cromwell and Ireton on behalf of the king, and it was Ashburnham, of course, who proposed the escape plan to Charles initially, after his encounter with Hammond near Kingston. As if this were not enough to ensure the persistence of conspiracy theories, moreover, Berkeley would be dismissed from the service of James, Duke of York in 1656, under suspicion of being in communication with Cromwell – for which there is again some circumstantial evidence.

Fears of defection and skulduggery of all and every manner were, of course, by no means confined to the Royalist side at this tense time. The army, too, was rife with rumours that there were those within its ranks whose sympathies were fickle. 'Who knows not,' declared the Leveller John Wildman, 'that the forces in play will be at the King's beck whenever he be in his throne?' If the king's counsel had indeed been primed from without, even this by no means confirms that the counsellors involved were acting in anything other than what they perceived at the time to be his own best interests. Even as Charles left Hampton Court, still hesitating over his intended destination, his fate was therefore ultimately his to decide, and Cromwell's resulting gain no more, perhaps, than might have been expected. He had already, after all, been borne up by Providence throughout his meteoric rise, or so it seemed. Now, perhaps, it was only natural that 'God's Englishman' should have benefited once more from his enemy's impulsive decision to deliver himself to the Isle of Wight and the care of Colonel Hammond.

7

'MADE SAFE FROM STIRRING'

'His Majesty came into our island on Sunday November 14th to my great astonishment … He could not have come into a worse place for himself.'

Sir John Oglander, A Royalist's Notebook

As search parties, mounted and on foot, fanned out into the park of Hampton Court and beyond, and couriers hurried to the army head-quarters at Putney with news of the escape, the king himself was making poor progress. Claiming to know the area well, and therefore acting as his party's guide, Charles' immediate objective was an inn at Bishop's Hutton in Hampshire, where a relay of fresh horses had been prepared. According to the plan, if such it can be called, the intention was to reach the appointed inn about three hours before dawn, but the weather, which was impeding the king's pursuers, was also disrupting his own flight, and Charles and his followers were soon lost in Windsor Forest, well to the west of their favoured route. In consequence, the first streaks of dawn were already showing through a rack of scud-ding storm clouds as the riders galloped through the sleeping town of Farnham, and it was growing light when they arrived at their destina-tion, some 16 miles farther on. Tired, tense, drenched and watchful, they dismounted, grateful for the respite, only to be greeted with word of a further worrying setback. For the servant who had been awaiting their arrival soon scurried out to warn them that a local parliamentary committee happened to be meeting within.

Swiftly changing mounts, they therefore resumed their journey with-out rest or refreshment, still uncertain even now of where precisely they

should be heading. Before long, indeed, Charles requested his companions to pause and discuss the next move, at which point a curious
discrepancy emerges in the accounts. According to some, a further suggestion from Berkeley that they should make for the West Country to
find a vessel to take them abroad was dismissed, in part perhaps because
Sir John had previously undermined the king's trust in his judgement
by urging him so strenuously to accept the Heads of the Proposals.
Yet Berkeley's own *Memoirs* suggest that Charles had not ridden many
miles from Hampton Court before he himself asked about the availability of ships for flight abroad. More significantly still, when Berkeley
explained that he had never ultimately been told to make such arrangements, the king enquired why Ashburnham had told him otherwise. At
which point, we hear, Berkeley confided that his associate was merely
trying to increase his influence with the king at the expense of equally
trusted counsellors.

If true, this brief exchange was certainly remarkable, and especially
so when Charles' reaction, as described by Berkeley, is taken into consideration. 'I think thou art in the right', he is said to have uttered,
placing his hand on Berkeley's shoulder. Regardless of whether the
king behaved as described, there were therefore clearly misgivings
on Berkeley's part about Ashburnham's motives, and tensions within
the fleeing party that could only have added to the more palpable
strains of escape. In reality, however, a strict watch had been imposed
at all ports and harbours in any case, and this was enough to put paid
not only to Berkeley's suggestion of the West Country, but to the
king's lingering preference for Jersey. Almost by default, then, since
Charles 'saw not well whither else to go', Ashburnham's original
choice of the Isle of Wight was allowed to stand. As an added precaution, he and Berkeley were to cross the Solent alone to seek out
Hammond, while Charles and Legge would make for the safety of
the Earl of Southampton's home at Titchfield on Southampton Water.
There, if all went well, the party would rendezvous once more when
Hammond's response had been ascertained, though Ashburnham
ended the discussion on an ominous note. Shouting back towards the
king, as the group separated, he made clear that if he and Berkeley
had not returned to Titchfield within twenty-four hours, it was to be
assumed that they had been taken. If so, the flight should be resumed
without them.

Since Charles was to travel to the eastern side of Southampton Water, Ashburnham opted to lay a false trail by riding over to Lymington, the most westerly of ferry points to the island, which lay some 35 miles away. It was towards evening on Friday, 12 November that he and Berkeley finally arrived. The gales and rain that had blanketed Hampton Court the night before were still in progress, however, making the heaving Solent far too rough to cross that night. Instead, the two impetuous Royalists eventually made the journey early next morning, reaching Yarmouth, a small harbour on the west of the island, without incident. From there, Colonel Hammond's residence at Carisbrooke Castle lay a further 9 miles away, and they duly reached it a little after 10 p.m., approaching by the path from the west. As sentries marched to and from the guard-house, which was built into the massive west gate amid cannon emplacements that lay all along the three-quarter mile outer earthen bank, Ashburnham and Berkeley had therefore duly reached the point of no return when, for good or ill, their quarry's sympathies would be tested once and for all.

But Hammond had just set out, in fact, for a meeting with a group of local gentlemen and militia officers in the island capital of Newport, a mile to the east, leaving his pursuers to hurry after him with news that would swiftly shatter any hopes for peace of mind that he may have wished to achieve in his new role. Overtaking him on the road, it was Berkeley, according to Ashburnham, who made a 'verie unskil-full entrance' into the business at hand by asking the colonel with no attempt at finesse, if he knew who was very nearby. 'Even King Charles,' he continued before Hammond had collected his thoughts, 'who is come from Hampton Court for fear of being murder'd pri-vately.' Whereupon, according to the bungling courtier's own account, his interlocutor 'grew so pale, and fell into such a trembling, that I really did believe he would have fallen off his horse' – a reaction neither Ashburnham nor indeed the colonel himself made any effort to deny later. 'Being herewith exceedingly surprized at present,' Hammond would inform the Speaker of the House of Lords the following day, 'I knew not what course to take', while Ashburnham would describe the Governor as 'very much discomposed'.

Nor, of course, was Hammond's palpable sense of alarm any real surprise, since the Isle of Wight had now been transformed all at once into the centre of a new and potentially desperate maelstrom that threatened to consume him. 'O Gentlemen,' he declared as the full scale of his predicament became apparent:

> you have undone me by bringing the King into the Island, if at least you have brought him; and if you have not, pray let him not come: for what between my Duty to his Majesty, and my Gratitude for this fresh obligation of Confidence, and my observing my Trust to the Army, I shall be confounded.

There was little consolation to be had for Hammond either from Berkeley's bland assurances that no harm would be done by his refusal to receive the king. For if the king should thereby come to any harm, he asked, what would be the response from his army superiors, not to mention the kingdom at large? All he could offer under the circumstances was the decidedly ambivalent assurance that since the king had escaped from Hampton Court to save his life, he was bound to treat him with 'honour and honesty'.

It was a response that could hardly have filled Ashburnham and Berkeley with confidence. They had staked all and the dice had not rolled cleanly. Instead, the whole affair now stood finely poised on the fragile sympathy of an apprehensive and reluctant figure whose earlier resolve they had plainly misjudged – a figure, moreover, who remained at bottom a soldier with soldiers' instincts and, above all, a soldier's inbred loyalty to his commanders. As the two messengers hesitated, moreover, it was Hammond who now took command of the situation, declaring that the king would not produce so many quibbles, if only his message was presented to him. Ashburnham should therefore take it while Berkeley remained at Carisbrooke as a guarantee of fair play – the implications of which the latter plainly grasped all too clearly as he crossed the bridge into the castle walls looming above him. 'I had the Image of the Gallows very perfectly before me,' he later recalled.

Yet there was still a further twist in store, for as Ashburnham was no doubt thankfully riding away, he was recalled once more by Hammond. There followed another discussion, lasting a quarter of an hour, during which the Governor now suggested that Ashburnham, being a more valuable hostage, should stay in Berkeley's place. When this suggestion was refused, a further proposal followed: namely, that all three men should leave for the mainland to inform the king of the protection that Hammond was prepared to extend to him. 'Let us all go to the king, and acquaint him with it,' said Hammond, having plainly recovered himself sufficiently to have weighed his options and frame the basis of a solution to his quandary. Ashburnham, after all, had played his hand and held no further cards, while Berkeley's objections, after his associate had agreed to the Governor's offer 'with all my heart', were largely redundant. 'What do you mean,' he had hissed, 'to carry this man to the king before you know whether he will approve of this Undertaking or no? Undoubtedly you will surprise him.'

'I'll warrant you,' was Ashburnham's only response, however, and even Berkeley's further declaration that he would not enter the king's presence 'before you have satisfied his Majesty concerning your proceeding' did nothing to stop the inexorable flow of events from this point forth. Setting off for Cowes, where Hammond collected Captain John Basket, commander of the castle there, Ashburnham and Berkeley found themselves sucked into a new venture that both knew was likely to end in calamity. By early evening, nonetheless, they had landed near Titchfield, with Basket's servants in tow, at which point Ashburnham duly informed Hammond that the king was at the Earl of Southampton's house. It was no doubt with heavy heart, moreover, that he asked the Governor's permission to break the news of their arrival, for, like Berkeley, he could not have anticipated a grateful reaction. The king had found the waiting long and hard, and, in the interim, put out feelers once again for a boat to France. He would not appreciate his disclosure to a man who had never enjoyed his full confidence in the first place, and was sure to baulk at his servant's presumption in changing plan without authorisation.

The immediate prospect for Jack Ashburnham was nothing less than daunting, therefore. The king's reaction will have come as little surprise to him, for upon hearing the latest development in his bedchamber, Charles' tightly regal composure swiftly evaporated. 'Oh, Jack,' he cried, upon hearing that Hammond and Basket were below, 'you have undone me, for I am by this means made fast from stirring.' His place of retreat had been revealed and what he had intended to be exploratory was now obligatory. According to some accounts, indeed, such as *Major Huntington's Narrative*, the king expressed such 'sharp resentment of his condition' that there was even a 'vain proposal' to kill Hammond at this point – to which, we are told, 'the King did utterly refuse to assent, rather choosing to yield up himself a sacrifice to those blood-thirsty men, who had resolved his destruction and the subversion of the government, than to be guilty of assenting to take away the life of that one vile rebel in cold blood'. Certainly, Ashburnham was desperate enough to have at least mentioned this possibility, if only to rescue some semblance of credibility after his indiscretion. By now weeping copiously, he clearly had no other resort than a show of ham dramatics, from which he doubtless knew the king would rescue him, as indeed he did. 'The world would not excuse me,' Charles is said to have uttered, while pacing to and fro and pondering his options. 'For if I should follow that counsel, it should be said (and believed) that [Hammond] had ventured his life for me, and I had unworthily taken it.'

Both ethics and politics, but above all hard facts, therefore impelled the king to submit himself to what was effectively Hammond's whim. 'No,' he concluded, 'it is too late now of thinking any thing, but going through the way you have forced me upon, and leave the issue to God.' The decision ultimately had been as simple as it was unavoidable, though it had not, it seems, been reached quickly, for by the time that the discussion ended, Hammond was having supper in the parlour downstairs and becoming increasingly suspicious at the delay. Indeed, conversation had eventually faltered to such an extent that Berkeley was left with no other option than to send up one of the household servants to remind his master that the officers were waiting. Even then, another half hour passed before Hammond was finally admitted, duly announced by Berkeley, who was treated to a scolding of his own for his part in the day's mismanagement.

However, as Hammond and Basket entered and kissed the king's hand, the king appears to have received them cheerfully enough, explaining that he had left London because of the danger from extremists within the army 'resolved of my death', and that he was seeking protection until some 'happy accommodation' could be reached with Parliament. Once more, the Governor's response was guarded as he offered to meet the king's 'just desires' in relation to any orders and directions he might receive. But around two hours later, the return crossing was nevertheless underway, and shortly after the party's arrival at the small town of Cowes, with its trimly whitewashed houses and cottages, arrangements were put in hand for the king's quarters that night. Since Cowes Castle, a small fort built a century before by Henry VIII, offered nothing suitable, Charles was to be lodged at the town's one adequate inn, the Plume of Feathers. Here he would spend the night – in an old bed with a carved oak headboard, inscribed, inauspiciously enough, with the text 'Remember thy end'.

And while Charles, as Berkeley informs us, knelt in fervent prayer beside the bed, taking the inscription as a bad omen, Hammond was already at work, as he would be throughout the night, inspecting the dispatches that had already come in during the day, including the order closing the ports, and dictating his own correspondence – the most important item of which was a message informing Parliament of the king's arrival. Carried by Major Edmund Rolph, Chief Officer at Carisbrooke, who was richly rewarded to the tune of £20 for his services, it arrived on the 15th and was greeted with a mixture of relief and trepidation. For while Charles' continued liberty opened a veritable hornets' nest of disturbing possibilities, so too did his apprehension by an apparent tool of the army's General Council. All, no doubt, would become clear over the days to follow, as would Hammond's precise sympathies, though for now at least the only available options were patience, vigilance – and prayer.

Across the Isle of Wight, meanwhile, word of the king's arrival was already spreading. '[That] Sunday morning at church,' wrote Sir John Oglander, 'I heard a rumour that the king was that night landed at Cowes.' Sitting among the other parishioners at Brading Church during morning service, his first reaction, it seems, was to dismiss the tale as gossip, but by the end of the day all doubt had dissolved. For at evening prayer, a servant of Sir Robert Dillington of Knighton, a neighbour of the Oglanders, had arrived to confirm the king's arrival and deliver news of an important meeting to occur the following morning. 'Governor Hammond,' Oglander recorded, 'commanded me, as all the gentlemen of the island, to meet him at Newport the next day by nine in the morning.' So there could be no doubting either the urgency or the gravity of the business at hand, and no question that the meeting in store would be avidly attended by all concerned.

When Hammond appeared at Newport next morning, indeed, he encountered a crowded audience, abuzz with speculation, which he did his best to allay by candour, calm and a commendable focus upon the here-and-now practicalities entailed by a most unexpected and potentially momentous development. After explaining the king's flight from Hampton Court in fear of his life, the colonel then mentioned that only three ferry points were now open, albeit under guard, and that there had been reports of Levellers upon the island. Any such groups found meeting were therefore to be dispersed, and as a further precaution all captains of the local militia were to renew their commissions, so that there would be no question of their authority to act in any emergency. Beyond this, it seems, there was to be an emphasis upon normality and tending the king's present needs as effectively as possible – a priority, which became even more apparent after Sir Robert Dillington's request that the assembled gentlemen might visit the king in person after dinner. Yes, by all means, responded Hammond, it would be a particularly fit time once their royal visitor had dined. 'And truly,' he added, 'I would invite you all to dinner', were it not for the fact that 'I want, extremely, fowl for His Majesty'.

In the meantime, as the hard-pressed colonel cadged food on his behalf, the king and his escort were already underway for Carisbrooke Castle amid a throng of curious bystanders and well-wishers anxious to catch a glimpse of his passing. As he rode through Newport, a gentlewoman plucked a damask rose, the last remaining flower in her garden after the autumn frost, and gave it to him with a pledge that she would pray for his well-being. Others came to let him know that the island's inhabitants, with the exception of the governors of the castles and Hammond's officers, were unanimously for him and that he should not fear. Carisbrooke Castle, after all, was said to be garrisoned with only twelve old men, all of whom were well-disposed to the king, and there was word, too, that Hammond might yet be won over, or coerced if necessary. If the king could bide his time, all would be well, since his cause was just and his subjects still loyal.

If these sentiments, which the king still shared fully, were not enough to buoy his spirits, the designated meeting with the island's leading gentlemen would complete the task admirably. When his visitors arrived, the king had already dined as arranged, but was busy writing in his room and they were left to wait in anticipation for half an hour. His eventual appearance did not disappoint, however, as his visitors kissed his hand loyally before being told in a short speech how he had been 'forced from Hampton Court by Levellers'. 'I have put myself in this place,' he declared solemnly, 'for ye preservacion of my life', adding how it was his sincere wish that 'not a drop moore of Christian bloude showlde bee spilt'. His stay, he implied, would be a short one, lasting only until a political solution had been reached, and in the meantime the burden upon the islanders would be limited. No doubt unaware of Hammond's earlier plea, he even avowed that 'I shall not desior so

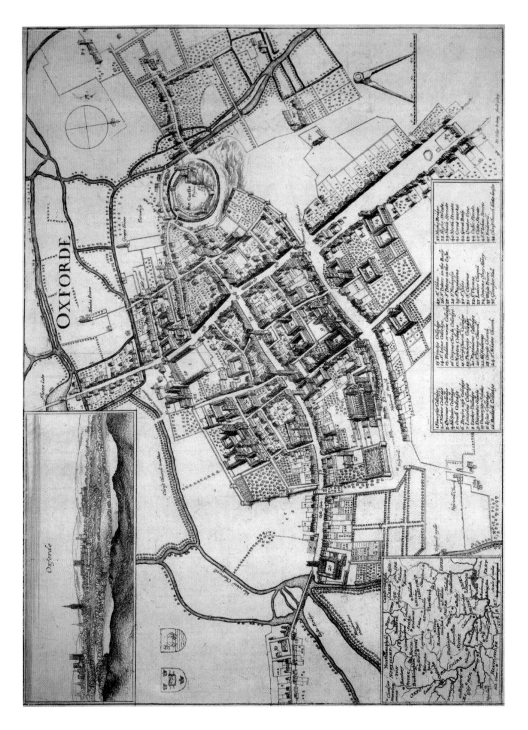

Etching by Wenceslaus Hollar depicting Oxford in 1643. King Charles had made the city his capital after his arrival on 29 November 1642 in the wake of the Battle of Edgehill.

Now for my selfe be confident of my constancy to the Church, for w^{ch}, upon debate, I am dayly more & more confirmed: for now I see cleerly that the Presbiterians disbystle & contradicts bouldly the consent of Fathers & the customs of the Catholike Church: & they wouldthat the Supreme Power is originally in the People, to whom all Magistrats ought to account: As for, ? a long my escaping from hence, I shall not attempt it but by the Queen's advice, 206:2:fo.81:5:38:176:143:154:39:35:11:12:173:279:229:10:53:22:56:44:60:170:110:111:351:404: or such as 45:154: or such as I shall trust to manage that busines, concerning w^{ch}, now that I have declared my Opinion & showen my reasons (as I have fully done in former Letters) I have now no impatience, for I shall not loose, by my owen sylence w^{ch}, was the chiefe care I had in this:

Upon Saterday next I expect the London Propositions; for one of w^{ch}, I particularly desyre advyce, they Demand, not only, the confirmation of their Counterfaict Great Seale, but also, the makeing good of all the Acts wch hath beene done by it: I know, this is not to be granted; for you remember the great consequences that I tould you, in Oxford, depended upon it; but how handsomly to evade it, there is the Question: for this I desyre the Opinions of 331:385:386:387:389. & if thease thinke it expedient, of 357: with as much expedition as may be so

Give this inclosed to my Wyfe, & me a particular   Your most asseured constant frend
account of her healthe   Charles R

Above: Letter from Charles I to John Ashburnham after the king's arrival in Oxford in 1642. Partly written in cipher, it professes Charles' 'Constancy to the Church' and affirms that 'as for my escaping from hence, I shall not attempt it but by the Queen's advice alone or such as she shall trust to manage that business.'

Left: John Ashburnham was with King Charles upon the night of his escape from Oxford, attended him during his escape from Hampton Court, and was instrumental in suggesting the Isle of Wight as a place of refuge.

Portrait of Henrietta Maria, wife of Charles I. Though only 4ft 10in tall, the little queen proved herself more than capable of striking hard-nosed bargains with artful diplomats and money-grubbing arms dealers alike, and exercised a profound influence upon her husband.

Henry Jermyn, Earl of St Albans, in later life, from a portrait by Peter Lely. Tall, broad-shouldered, elegant and refined, and possessing, at only 20 years of age, what the poet Abraham Cowley would describe as 'a soul composed of the eagle and the dove', Jermyn was a bold, self-confident, worldly-wise and watchful man of the moment, who, as Gentleman Usher of Queen Henrietta Maria's Privy Chamber, became the object of scandalous rumours.

> tert. 5:5. Come let us joyn ourselves to the Lord
>
> 1 6 4 3
>
> a Solemn
>
> LEAGVE AND COVENANT,
> for Reformation, and defence of
> Religion, the Honour and happineſſe
> of the king, and the Peace and ſafety of the
> three kingdoms of
> ENGLAND, SCOTLAND, and IRELAND.
>
> in a perpetuall Covenant that ſhall not be forgotten.
>
> We Noblemen, Barons, knights, Gentlemen, Citizens, Burgeſſes, Miniſters of the Goſpel, and Commons of all ſorts in the kingdoms of England, Scotland, and Ireland, by the Providence of God living vnder one King, and being of one reformed Religion, having before our eyes the Glory of God, and the advancement of the kingdome of our Lord and Saviour Ieſus Chriſt, the Honour and happineſſe of the kings Maieſty and his poſterity, and tho true publique Liberty, Safety, and Peace of the kingdoms, wherein every ones private Condition is included, and calling to minde the treacherous and bloody Plots, Conſpiracies, Attempts, and Practices of the Enemies of God, againſt the true Religion, and profeſſors thereof in all places, eſpecially in theſe three kingdoms ever ſince the Reformation of Religion, and how much their rage, power and preſumption, are of late, and at this time increaſed and exerciſed; whereof the deplorable ſtate of the Church and kingdom of Ireland, the diſtreſſed eſtate of the Church and kingdom of England, and the dangerous eſtate of the Church and kingdom of Scotland, are preſent and publique Teſtimonies; We have now at laſt (after other means of Supplication, Remonſtrance, Proteſtations, and Sufferings) for the preſervation of our ſelves and our Religion, from utter Ruine and Deſtruction; according to the commendable practice of theſe kingdoms in former times, and the Example of Gods people in other Nations; After mature deliberation, reſolved and determined to enter into a mutuall and ſolemn Legue and Covenant; wherein we all ſubſcribe, and each one of us for himſelf, with our hands lifted up to the moſt high God, do ſweare;

By 25 September 1643 the Scots had signed the Solemn League and Covenant with Parliament, committing MPs, or so the Scots believed, to the establishment of Presbyterianism in England in return for military assistance. Charles, however, would resolutely resist all pressure to comply with its terms, 'my conscience being irreconcilably engaged against it'.

Sir John Berkeley had taken a prominent military role in the Civil War, becoming Governor of Exeter and commander of the Royalist forces in Devon, before being ordered by the king to attend him in his flight from Hampton Court in November 1647. The fugitives pushed on towards Hampshire and ultimately reached Lymington, where Berkeley crossed the Solent and opened negotiations with Colonel Robert Hammond in the hope of gaining protection for the king.

On 13 November 1647 Colonel Robert Hammond, the 26-year-old Governor of the Isle of Wight, learnt from Sir John Berkeley and John Ashburnham that the king had fled from Hampton Court to save his life from the Levellers. Torn between his duty to the king and his obligations to the army, he finally gave a vague promise to act with 'honour and honesty', on the basis of which Charles I submitted to his custody.

Entrance to Carisbrooke Castle. Although only a mile south-west of Newport, Carisbrooke is almost in the middle of the Isle of Wight, occupying a chalk plateau at about the 200ft contour and dominating the lower reaches of the Bowcombe valley. So complex were its fortifications that their designer, Federigo Gianibelli, hoped that it would be 'one of the strongest places in Europe', though it was far fitter for defence against attack than the successful confinement of prisoners.

The courtyard of Carisbrooke Castle. The king's first bedchamber, which he occupied from November 1647, is behind the second-floor ten-light window, constructed during extensive reconstruction of the building in the 1850s. At the end of April 1648 he was moved to rooms in the now ruined Tudor governor's lodging to the left of the picture.

The bowling green used by Charles I during his imprisonment at Carisbrooke, where on 13 April 1648 he was said to be 'very merry at play' with Governor Hammond. The Governor also created a miniature golf course for the king's entertainment, within the outer defences of the castle, in one corner of which a little summer house was built where the royal prisoner could take shelter from the persistent rain, since the summer of 1648 proved the wettest for decades.

Frontispiece of Eikon Basilike. Eventually published shortly after his death, the book became at once a lynchpin of Royalist propaganda, depicting the king, in effect, as a neotype of the crucified Christ – the princely proto-martyr, politically and morally innocent, cruelly butchered at the hands of his subjects – though as early as August 1649, no less a figure than John Milton was attributing authorship to a 'presumptuous priest', who, in the poet's words, had sought to make 'his King his Bastard Issue Own'.

St. Bartholomew's Church, Holton, where Jane Whorwood and three of her four children were buried, along with her husband and her husband's mistress, Kate Allen, though the graves were destroyed during renovation work in the nineteenth century.

The old Grammar School at Newport where the failed Treaty of Newport was negotiated between the King and Parliament from 15 September to 27 November 1648. Under pressure from army radicals, the purged Parliament annulled the treaty in mid-December, after which preparations were made for the king's trial.

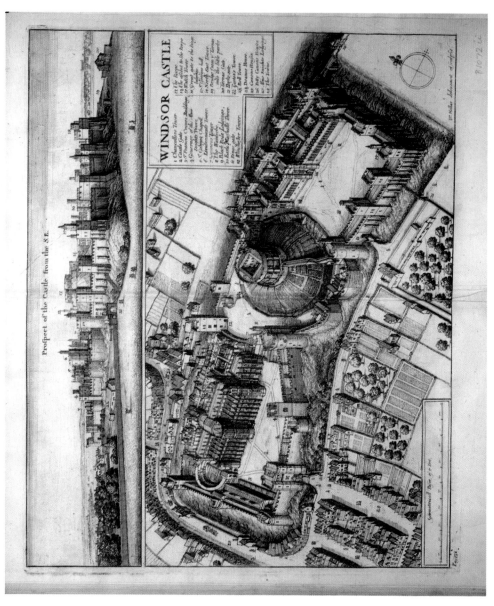

A bird's-eye view of Windsor Castle, produced by Wenceslaus Hollar nine years after Charles I's death. The king spent his last Christmas at Windsor, though without the consolations of the season, for as at Carisbrooke in 1647, all Christmas festivity was strictly banned.

much as a capon from anye of you'. After which, Colonel Legge came forward to read the declaration to Parliament that Charles had left upon his table at Hampton Court.

Overall, the meeting was an undoubted success, and even an anxious enquiry from Colonel Legge, as the audience departed, could not dampen Sir John Oglander's improved spirits. What was to be done, the colonel asked, if a greater number of the Leveller faction arrived in the island than could be resisted by the local people – what measures could then be taken to guarantee the king's safety? 'None that I know,' Oglander replied, 'but to have a boat to convey him from the island.' For even at this stage, notwithstanding damask roses and assurances from Hammond, the background hum of subterfuge and anxiety was understandably still in evidence. Hampton Court might now be far off, but the king's enemies were not at rest. His flight, indeed, had only added to their calls for a more final solution to the problem he personified, and under the circumstances, the primary need was for vigilance and planning, amid a veneer of everyday normality. The king would enjoy the moment as best he could and keep his counsel close – as was demonstrated by his visit to Oglander's country house near Sandown only three days later. '[He] dined with me at Nunwell,' Oglander recorded, 'and during the time he lived in our island he went to no gentleman's house besides. In the Parlour Chamber I had some speech with him which I shall forbear to discover.'

At least the hospitality on offer at Nunwell is likely to have been fit for a royal visitor, since the host appears to have been something of a gourmet. Upon his posting to the island, Oglander had at once increased the number of servants within his household, and he admitted in his memoirs, with no hint of brashness, that 'indeed he kept a very good table'. When the king first visited Oglander on the Thursday after his arrival upon the island, in fact, his host's account book recorded the purchase, for £1, of 'sweetmeates for his Matie', and with the king henceforth a regular visitor, the honourable gentleman even wrote to his mother at Chertsey to enlist her services as a hostess. No expense within his means would be spared, no effort stinted, it seems, in making the king's visits as pleasurable as possible, though Oglander's services, to his credit, were never rendered to curry favour or glean political advantage. On the contrary, he was discretion personified, putting little in writing about the war and even less about the royal captivity. While he remained the staunchest of Royalists, he continued to maintain both an unwavering appreciation of the Crown's shortcomings and the keenest possible awareness that the king's apparent supporters were not, in all cases, to be depended upon.

Intelligent, perceptive, self-effacing and worldly wise, Oglander had been born at Nunwell in 1585 into a family that, as he himself claimed, 'came in with ye conquest out of Normandie'. Thereafter, we hear of him graduating at the age of 18 from Balliol College, Oxford, on 8 July 1603, and becoming a student of Middle Temple the following year: a common entry point on the path to high office for many a gifted scion of worthy gentry stock. Knighted on 22 December 1615, he was appointed Deputy-Governor of Portsmouth in 1620 by the Earl of Pembroke, before becoming Deputy-Governor of the Isle of Wight four years later. In 1625, he was elected MP for Yarmouth on the Isle of Wight, sitting until 1629 when the king opted to rule without Parliament for eleven years. It was during this period particularly that he established his loyalty and value to the Crown, becoming High Sheriff of Hampshire in 1637 and establishing a well-deserved reputation as an energetic collector of Ship Money.

Twice arrested during the subsequent war, Oglander had, however, undergone loss and demotion for the Royalist cause before being treated leniently and rehabilitated in 1645. Thereafter, he had lived quietly, occupying himself with the management of his farm and occasional trips to Bath for his health. But it was no surprise that Charles should have established such a firm link with him at this time. Ashburnham would claim, as we have seen, that he had initially intended Charles' 'concealment' at Nunwell 'until the king had gained experience of the Governor's intention to serve him'. Oglander would continue to visit the king at Carisbrooke even after security arrangements were considerably tightened in January. 'I went most commonly to see him once a week,' his journal makes clear, 'and I seldom went but His Majesty would talk with me sometimes almost a quarter of an hour together.' As a chronicler, it is true, he often accepted as true a good deal of rumour, and his chronology is sometimes defective. But such was his sensitivity and passion for his journal that at times of particular emotion, he is known to have made certain entries in his own blood. 'I could do nothing but sigh and weep for two nights and a day,' he would write after a surge of pessimism for the king's prospects overwhelmed him, and 'the reason of my grief', he added, was that there was no possible place where the king 'could be more securely kept' than where he now found himself.

By the time that Charles' horse first clattered across Carisbrooke Castle's moat bridge, moreover, the same sense of foreboding may well have been dampening his own spirits after the initial good wishes and conviviality of the previous hours. Standing on a commanding chalk plateau above a small village of the same name, about a mile and a half south of Newport, the castle was by any standards a formidable edifice. Indeed, from its 200ft vantage point at the centre of the island, it dominated the Bowcombe Valley beneath, and so complex were its fortifications that it was considered by some to be all but escape-proof. The area contained by the outer *enceinte* covered some 20 acres, within which, at the north-western end, was the castle itself surrounded by a curtain wall. From the high stone keep in the north-east corner of the castle's courtyard, the view encompassed the Solent, the New Forest beyond it to the north, and to the south, about 6 miles away, the hills above Ventnor. To add to the difficulty of any escape, almost no buildings interrupted the mile-long expanse of fields and copses before Newport, which was also easily visible from the castle walls.

From the time of its original construction in the late Roman period, Carisbrooke had certainly undergone extensive development. It was probably the place in 530 where the islanders were defeated by the invading Saxons, who gave it the name of Wihtgarasburh, 'the fortress of the men of Wight', which was later corrupted to Garisbrook. Thereafter, following the Norman subjugation of the isle by William FitzOsborne, Earl of Hereford, the modern castle steadily grew in size and prowess between its foundation in the twelfth century and its reinforcement, under threat of attack from Spain, at the end of the sixteenth century. Most notably of all, in 1597, Federigo Giambelli designed a massive encircling defensive work, or '*trace Italienne*', to encase the entire castle, including the unused eastern bailey. Comprising three-quarters of a mile of stone-faced earthworks within a system of outer ditches, and defended by cross-fire from gunports in the sophisticated arrowhead bastions at the corners, it resulted in a ring of defences that were altogether less vulnerable to artillery attack than the rubble-filled curtain walls of the inner castle. Although the area was large, the skilful placement of the cannon embrasures guaranteed effective coverage by defensive fire, while a 'covered way' just outside the parapet of the earthworks facilitated the safe and rapid deployment of defending troops.

But while the castle's fortifications had been steadily enhanced since the time of its creation, so too had its living accommodation, largely as a result of the efforts of the last of the mighty de Redvers family, Countess Isabella, widow of William de Fortibus, Earl of Albemarle, who lived in the castle in considerable comfort from 1269 and ruled the island as queen in all but name. The Great Hall, for example, was originally built by William de Vernun during his custodianship from 1184–1217, but it was the countess who rebuilt it in the second half of the thirteenth century, and it was she too who added domestic chambers and a kitchen to the north under the curtain wall, as well as the Chapel of St Peter opening out of the Great Hall. Not only did she equip the castle with the first glass in the British Isles, she also, it seems, installed a vast fish tank, and in doing so set a precedent for further improvements by her successors. Towards the end of the fourteenth century, William de Montacute, Earl of Salisbury, built the block at the south end of the Great Hall, which eventually came to form part of the Governor's house, and it was Sir George Carey, Governor from 1582–1603, who undertook further extensive additions prior to the king's arrival in 1647. Under his direction, the Great Hall was raised by a storey and a mezzanine added in Montacute's building, while St Peter's Chapel was dismantled and converted into rooms and lobbies on both floors, thus affording communication throughout the entire range of buildings. A further storey was also added over Countess Isabella's building to the north of the Great Hall, along with a new kitchen and the Chief Officer's House along the curtain wall beyond.

By the time that Charles I first took up residence in his new abode, therefore, it had grown into a particularly imposing structure. 'Carisbrooke Castle, when brought to perfection on my plan,' Federigo Gianibelli had claimed upon his commission, 'will be one of the strongest places in Europe.' From one perspective at least, his proud boast had proved far from hollow. Yet this immense fortification, so well designed for keeping an enemy out, was by no means as ideally suited to the task of keeping prisoners in as many contemporaries assumed. On the one hand, as a result of the porous chalk on which the castle stands, the outer ditches and last vestiges of the Norman moat inside were all dry and comparatively easy to traverse. Furthermore, those same outer defences, which were so daunting for any potential attacker, were still low enough for any escapee to jump from without injury, while their considerable length made the castle's perimeter especially difficult to patrol. Indeed, the only unequivocal asset for any would-be jailer was arguably the high curtain walls of the inner Norman courtyard, where the king now found himself lodged.

There stood within this area, just beyond the stone bridge over the moat and the fourteenth-century drum towers of the gatehouse, a complex of domestic buildings containing the guardrooms and soldiers' quarters. To the left, at the northern side of the courtyard, the officers were lodged in a splendid two-storeyed house built in the 1580s, and from here a central doorway led, by a facing flight of stairs, to the upper floor and to a long gallery between the hall and the curtain wall. The rooms to either side, meanwhile, were illuminated at each level by large bay windows, from which the castle chapel of St Nicholas – a simple, rectangular construction, divided by a choir screen – could be clearly seen. Finally, projecting south into the middle of the courtyard from the north curtain, was the Norman hall itself – complete with further domestic quarters at its southern end – which was to house the newly arrived king in a style wholly fitting for his status. For although no substantial additions or alterations had been made after 1593 and only a skeleton staff was present at the time of king's arrival, the castle as a whole had been maintained in comparatively good condition, so that nothing further seems to have been needed for his reception beyond the provision of suitable furniture, plate and hangings.

The precise location and layout of the royal apartments remain something of a mystery, however, since there are no surviving plans of the hall as it stood in 1647, and extensive restoration of the building in 1856 resulted in the insertion of new windows and removal of the mezzanine floor in the Great Chamber, which, according to some accounts, may have housed the king's sleeping quarters. It certainly does seem from contemporary evidence that the royal bedchamber itself had a room above and a room below, and that it consisted of two bedrooms, one of which opened on to backstairs. Thomas Herbert's *Narrative*, for example, locates the king's Presence Chamber 'under his Majesties bedchamber', and while this need not necessarily place it immediately below the bedroom, it does at least confirm that the bedroom was indeed at an upper level. Likewise, a letter from the so-called

'Derby House Committee' to Colonel Hammond on 7 February 1648 refers to a room over the king's bedroom, which would locate it at the southern end of the hall in the Great Chamber, in accordance also with various other contemporary references to the backstairs.

To complicate matters further, the Great Chamber, which served as the Constable's Lodging before the king's arrival, is today a lofty room, boasting a large Victorian window, with one room below and one above. Yet old drawings, like the one produced by John Livesay in 1798, confirm that before the removal of the mezzanine in the 1850s, this room was itself divided into two storeys. If so, either might have served as the king's bedchamber, though the one corresponding with the present floor of the Great Chamber seems the most likely, since this would be just one stage higher than the Great Hall – which is likely to have served as both royal Presence Chamber and dining hall – and its importance is confirmed by the elaborate medieval fireplace that can still be seen there. From this vantage point, Charles would have glanced out upon the courtyard from the lowest of a set of four windows in a high, gabled building, abutting the remainder of the Constable's Lodging.

Nor was the view an entirely unfamiliar one, for he had visited the castle in happier days and knew it well enough. In August 1618, as Prince of Wales, he had dined at Carisbrooke and 'made divors shots with the ordnaunce'. No doubt he remembered, too, the small, Elizabethan well-house, with its medieval well and treadmill, which had once been turned by prisoners until their replacement by the donkeys that still turn the wheel as a tourist attraction today. The stables to the southern side of the courtyard were untouched, as indeed were the soldiers' quarters nearby, which remained surprisingly quiet, as Hammond's regiment had still not followed him over. The scene, indeed, was almost a tonic after the tensions of Hampton Court: a welcome rest-cure of sorts from the tramp of heavy army boots, the continual flow of worrisome intelligence and the wearisome routines of political gamesmanship necessitated by it. All ferries across to the island had been stopped, except at the three regular entry points of Yarmouth, Cowes and Ryde, and these too were now under guard. But at Carisbrooke, as Major Rolphe was hurrying to Westminster with news of the king's whereabouts, there was little on offer to discourage a consoling illusion of homeliness.

In Parliament, the early precautions taken by Hammond were swiftly approved by both Houses, and it was further resolved that no person who had previously been in arms on the king's behalf should remain upon the Isle of Wight unless he were a native and had compounded for any prior offence. A guard was to be provided by Hammond, servants appointed and £500 allocated for the royal household, though, with the exception of Scots, no stranger or foreigner was to enter the king's presence without specific approval from Westminster. Even so, the king was to be kept on a surprisingly long leash, it seems, for, as he ranged about his new domicile in the company of its custodian, he did not hesitate to pose pertinent questions about the present military strength of the island and the number of its inhabitants. Nor was he disappointed by Hammond's frank responses or the similar liberty he was granted in welcoming familiar faces to Carisbrooke. 'Thither, so soon as the king's being there was rumoured,' observed Sir Thomas Herbert, 'repaired several of his old servants, and some new, such as his Majesty at that time saw fit to nominate', for, over a period of 'some weeks', there was apparently 'no prohibition' in place, leaving those 'desirous to see his Majesty' to do so 'without opposal'.

The early malaise among the remnants of the king's household left at Hampton Court was not, then, long-lived. Maule, Murray and other attendants had been duly questioned about their sovereign's flight, but escaped without punishment, while the staff remaining at the palace merely 'stood gazing at one another', in Herbert's words, until going their separate ways. 'And the master being gone,' he continued, 'the diet ceased, so as with sad hearts all went to their respective homes.' Even loyal Henry Firebrace, it seems, may have taken the opportunity to stay with his wife and daughter in London, though his own account confirms that the respite from royal service was a short one:

> As soon as it was publiquely known where his Majestie was, having received a private letter from him to hasten to him, and with what intelligence I could get after I had acquainted his most faithfull friends about London with my going as his Majestie commanded me; I got leave of the Speaker of the House of Commons, and his pass to go (for I had still kept out of their suspition).

He does not give the date of his arrival, but the list of the royal household, which comprised most of those who had served at Hampton Court, was finally approved in the House of Commons on 23 November, and

£100 voted for the expenses of their journey. The *Moderate Intelligencer*
of 1 December, moreover, announced their arrival at Carisbrooke thus:

> When the new and old attendants came to Court, his Majesty was
> private, but understanding of their arrival, he came out, shewed cheer-
> fulnesse, gave them all his hand to kisse, and said they had done well
> when they brought Hampton Court with them. Mr Ashburnham
> and Colonel Leg are with him, also old servants and chaplains.

The king, then, had even been reunited with the Reverend Doctors
Sheldon and Hammond, and on the very same day that the *Moderate
Intelligencer* was announcing their happy return, the royal coach itself
was being laboriously shipped across the Solent to carry the king in due
splendour along the rough island roads, since, as Herbert relates, 'His
Majesty had free liberty to ride and recreate himself anywhere within
the isle, when and where he pleased.' Making full use of Hammond's
goodwill, he therefore frequently 'went abroad to view the island and to
observe the severall accommodations of it'. In doing so he was also able
to enjoy not only the better-known sights but also the hospitality of
local people. Early in December, for example, he travelled to the island's
western tip to take in the Needles, an impressive line of chalk columns
towering out of the sea, which had once been part of a ridge forming a
link with the mainland of Dorset. From there he visited the small town
and harbour of Yarmouth before finishing the day with a banquet given
by a certain Mrs Urry, probably Alice, the wife of Captain John Urry, at
the village of Thorley, a mile to the south-east.

There is a local tradition, too, recorded much later, which describes
a visit made by the king to the Undercliff area in the south of the
island. While riding one day with his attendants near the little village
of Bonchurch, it was suggested to him that he might acquaint himself
with the small, medieval church there, and he readily agreed. On their
way along the chute that lay on the way down, however, it seems that
the king and his followers overtook a funeral procession making its way
to the churchyard, whereupon the king reined in his horse and sent an
attendant to enquire who was being buried. When the answer came
back that it was Sir Ralph Chamberlain – who 'during his lifetime,
had fought and bled for him, and whose death was indirectly caused by
wounds received in his service' – Charles is said to have responded with
a remarkable show of sympathy. Dismounting from his horse at the

mention of Chamberlain's name, he appears to have joined the mourn-
ers to pay his last respects.

Yet however touching, it was also hardly suggestive of a king in dire
circumstance. On the contrary, the laxity of his general treatment at
Carisbrooke appeared further concrete proof, not least to himself, that
his enemies were finding it increasingly difficult to proceed against him.
Like mice that had cornered the cat, it seems, they were not only at a loss
as to their next step but increasingly divided as the moment for decision
closed in upon them. 'I am daily more satisfied with this governor,' the
king wrote of Hammond on 23 November, and Parliament, too, seemed
anxious to accommodate the prisoner at every turn. On 24 November,
the seals had been broken on the royal apartments, and a generous
supply of furnishings arrived for the king's use within the week. Within
days of his arrival, he had also gone hunting in Parkhurst Forest, 'which
is very plentifully supplied with deer', and was soon hawking whenever
he wished. Before long, equally remarkably, the avidly Parliamentarian
town assembly of Southampton was considering the dispatch of 'a present of Household provition to his Matie at Carisbrooke Castle'. What,
then, could have provided further reassurance of a turning tide as the
king pondered his options upon his island retreat?

There was even the steady trickle of intelligence through the castle's ramshackle security to reinforce Charles' early confidence. Though
Henry Firebrace could not obtain a private interview with the king
upon his arrival, he was nevertheless able to find 'a very convenient
and private place' within the royal bedchamber in which he secreted
certain letters that he had brought. That night, moreover, he was able to
inform Charles of what he had done 'by putting a note into his hand as
he was going to bed'. Nor was this the end of Firebrace's service in this
particular regard, as his narrative makes clear:

> And the next morning, after his retirement, at his private devotions
> (of which he never fayled) I found his paper in the same place; by
> which his Majestie was pleased to express his satisfaction in what I
> had done, and what he had received; and directed the continuance of
> that place and way of converse, which we made use of (for we had no
> better) for many weeks.

Before leaving London, indeed, Firebrace had laid down plans for two
'faithful and unsuspected' messengers to travel between the capital and

the Isle of Wight, in order to maintain a constant means of communication between the king and his friends: an arrangement which could not have been more timely, since the need for such a flow of intelligence was now, if anything, greater than ever, as the latest round of political manoeuvring swiftly gathered pace.

Within days of his arrival at Carisbrooke, in fact, Charles had shown willing to launch a new diplomatic offensive, and while Parliament was digesting the message he had left at Hampton Court, he was already composing, with Hammond's encouragement, a further, more detailed and more conciliatory proposal. Indeed, it was this document that he had been writing when the island's gentry visited him on the Monday after his arrival. Finally dispatched two days later, it opened with the suggestion that talks should be resumed, since he now considered himself 'to be at more freedom and security than formerly'. Though he remained adamant on the issue of the episcopacy and the alienation of their lands, which he deemed not only an affront to his conscience but a breach of Magna Carta, there followed a range of very real, if not particularly novel, concessions. Agreeing, on the one hand, to accept Presbyterian government for three years, with freedom of conscience reserved for all others but Roman Catholics, he also accepted that the long-term future of the Church should be settled by the Westminster Assembly of divines, with the addition of twenty royal nominees. Equally significantly, he was prepared to countenance the appointment of presbyters to oversee bishops' jurisdiction, and to accept the pruning of royal control in at least two key areas. Control of the militia, for example, was to be ceded to Parliament for his lifetime, as was the right to appoint all senior officers of state, and, in the hope that he might be invited to London in person, there were further guarantees that the army's arrears would be paid out of royal revenue, and that the king himself would sign an Act of Oblivion annulling any party's responsibility for the war.

As the proposals were read out at Westminster on 17 November, then, Charles still seems to have harboured hopes of further political progress. But he was enough of a realist to have a number of other ploys in reserve, the most important of which was to open negotiations once more with the army. No doubt emboldened by reports that one of Fairfax's regiments in Hertfordshire had demonstrated in his favour, Charles therefore lost no time in dispatching Sir John Berkeley to the general, with the purported objective of enlisting protection for the newly arrived royal chaplains. In reality, however, Berkeley was to call for a parley between the king and the army's leading commanders, drawing on the stock of goodwill he had gained with Cromwell and Ireton, in particular, during the summer negotiations not long passed. He would travel – 'not without some apprehension', as he himself admitted – in the company of his cousin, Henry, and call upon Fairfax at Windsor, where 'a general meeting of the officers' was in session at the time of his arrival.

Even before Berkeley reached his destination, however, his confidence had been further undermined by two chance meetings en route, the first of which involved a discussion with a messenger of Colonel Hammond's who had been sent to impress upon the generals the need to 'clear themselves of their importunate and impertinent Adjutators'. 'Between Bagshot and Windsor (then the Head-Quarters),' he recorded, 'I met Traughton the Governor's chaplain, who told me he could carry no good news back, the Army being as yet come to no resolution as to the king.' Yet if this particular exchange had not boded well, the next encounter that Berkeley made only a little later on the very same stretch of road not only shredded any remnants of optimism he may have retained, but carried an irony all of its own, for it involved a figure whose unexpected intervention in the king's affairs had already proved so decisive some months earlier. In little doubt thereafter that his mission was effectively futile, Berkeley recalled the meeting and what followed it thus:

As I was half way between Bagshot and Windsor, Cornet Joyce, a great Adjutator, and he that had taken the king from Holmby [Holdenby], overtook me. He seemed much to wonder that I durst adventure to come to the Army. Upon my discourse with him I found that it had been discoursed among the Adjutators, whether for their justification the King ought not be brought to a Tryal, which he held in the affirmative, not that he would have one hair of his head suffer, but that they might not bear the blame of the war. I was quickly weary of his discourse; but I perceived he would not leave me until he saw me in Windsor and knew where I lodg'd.

Nor did Berkeley's eventual meeting with Fairfax and the other generals offer anything other than disappointment, as his description of the encounter makes plain:

After an hours waiting I was admitted, and after I had delivered my Compliment and Letters to the General, I was desired to withdraw; and having attended half an hour, I was call'd in. The General look'd very severely upon me, and after his manner said, That they were the Parliament's Army, and therefore could not say anything to his Majesty's motion of peace, but must refere those matters to them, to whom they would send his Majesty's letters. I then look'd about upon Cromwel and Ireton, and the rest of my acquaintance, who saluted me very coldly, and had their Countenance quite changed towards me, and shewed me Hammonds letter, which I had delivered to them, and smiled with much disdain upon it.

Seeing that this was 'no place for me', Berkeley therefore returned anxiously to his lodgings, where he waited from 4–6 p.m., as the grey evening closed in around him, in the hope that one of his army contacts might call. But 'none of my acquaintance came at me', he noted in his account, 'which appeared sad enough'. In consequence, there seemed no alternative but to send out a servant to scour the town for officers known to Berkeley, who might be willing to throw further light upon the situation. This, at least, proved fruitful, for the servant returned with news that he had met one of the general officers who had 'whispered in his ear' that he would meet Berkeley 'at twelve at night in a Close behind the Garter Inn'.

According to Clarendon's *History of the Great Rebellion*, the officer concerned was Leonard Watson, the army's Quartermaster-General, though Berkeley himself gives no detail about his identity other than to emphasise that he was someone who 'since the tumults of the Army, did mistrust Cromwell, and not long after Ireton', considering them the 'archest villains in the world'. But in spite of Watson's sympathies, he could offer no consolation to Berkeley as the pair shivered in the shadows. 'I came at the hour, and he not long after', Berkeley relates, and when asked what news he had bought, the Quartermaster-General's reply, 'None good', was delivered without hesitation. Ireton, it appeared, had proposed at the army council that afternoon that Berkeley 'should be sent prisoner to London' and that 'none should speak with you upon pain of death'. 'I do hazard my life now by doing of it,' Watson continued. But even this paled into insignificance with the further revelation that the army was now resolved 'to destroy the King and his posterity'. Indeed, from the description of Watson's words given in Berkeley's *Memoirs*, plans to this effect were already in place. 'The way that is intended to ruin the king,' Watson is said to have revealed, 'is to send eight hundred of the most disaffected of the Army to secure his Person, as believing him not so now, and then bring him to a Tryal, and

I dare think no farther.' As such, only one course of action was available. 'This,' he confirmed, 'will be done in ten days; and therefore if the King can escape let him do it as he loves his life.'

Numbed and nonplussed by the sudden change of front by Cromwell and Ireton, Berkeley wound his way back to his lodgings in the early hours, still, no doubt, searching for the explanation of their 'horrid perfidiousness'. In Watson's view, Cromwell in particular had decided 'that if we cannot bring the Army to our Sense, we must go to theirs, a Schism being evidently destructive'. 'And therefore,' Watson reasoned, Cromwell had 'bent all his Thoughts to make peace with the Party that was most opposite to the King'. 'The Glories of the World,' it seems, had hitherto 'so dazzled his eyes that he could not discern clearly the great Works the Lord was doing'. But now 'he was resolved to humble himself, and desire the Prayers of the Saints' and be thereby 'reinstated in the Fellowship of the Faithful'. Against his every instinct, therefore, he would appease the Levellers in the interests of army unity, and he would do so under the banner of divine calling – all of which left Berkeley with few options.

It was clear, in the first place, that two letters should be drafted. One, 'containing a general Relation and doubtful Judgement of things in the Army', was to be sent to Hammond, and the other, written in cipher, was for the king's eyes only, informing him of the midnight meeting outside the Garter Inn, naming the informant who had been present, and 'concluding with a most passionate supplication to his Majesty to mediate nothing but his immediate escape'. With his cousin duly instructed to ride through the night to the Isle of Wight, there was little else for Berkeley to do other than to snatch some meagre sleep before a final visit to army headquarters next morning. The intention was to gain access to Cromwell simply to pass on correspondence that he had brought with him from the king and to receive his response. Beyond this, there was little other point to the journey, if the general's behaviour that day was any guide.

Yet Cromwell's earlier hostility was curiously belied by what followed. 'The next morning,' Berkeley informs us, 'I sent Colonel Cook to Cromwel, to let him know that I had Letters and Instructions to him from the King.' But while the letters concerned appear to have been largely routine in nature, the general's response was not only uncommonly anxious but surprisingly sympathetic to the king's interests. For, according to Berkeley's account, 'he sent me word by the same messenger that he durst not see me, it being very dangerous to us both, and bid me be assured, that he would serve his Majesty as long as he could do it without his own ruin; but desired that I would not expect that he should perish for his sake'. Against all expectation, then, it was plain that Cromwell was still not intent upon burning all bridges with the king. On the contrary, he was playing out a double game, finely balancing the more radical elements in the army with his own more conservative instincts. He would posture publicly and in private weave contrary schemes of his own, watching all the while for openings and right moments. In this respect he was not alone. For, as Berkeley made haste away from Windsor, the king himself was already offering olive branches to other old enemies.

8

'MISERABLE DISTRACTED KINGDOM'

'Many things may be fitly offered to obtain a treaty that may be fitly altered when one comes to treat.'

Charles I to the Scottish Commission in London,
29 November 1647

Notwithstanding Cromwell's parting message, Sir John Berkeley's mission to the army had been a plain and unadulterated failure. When Berkeley took his more than timely leave from Windsor, however, he travelled not to Carisbrooke but to London, to try his luck with those self-same Scottish commissioners that the king both courted and loathed according to circumstance. Soon after his escape to the Isle of Wight, there had been efforts to placate feeling north of the border, for at the time of Charles' departure, it had been understood that he would make for Berwick rather than place himself in the hands of the English army. According to the French envoy in Edinburgh, indeed, the Scottish leaders were nothing less than staggered by the apparent preference he had eventually displayed for the army's Independents by his flight to Carisbrooke, and Montreuil's same letter, written to Mazarin on 10 December, left no doubt either that gossip in the Scottish capital was increasingly disrespectful. Equally certain was the disapproval generated by the rapid publication of the king's message to Parliament, with its proposals for toleration not only of the episcopacy but of the various sects that were anathema to all God-fearing Presbyterians. The king, it seems, was intent upon selling his soul to competing devils in preference to placing his body under Scottish protection, and it would now take every available resource to mend the broken confidence that his recent betrayal had guaranteed.

Certainly, Charles' first efforts to rebuild bridges convinced nobody. On 19 November, he had written to the Earl of Lanark about his offer to Parliament, explaining that 'the end of it is to procure a personal treaty; for which I have striven to please all interests with all possible equality (without wronging my conscience)'. 'I hope no reasonable man will blame me,' he added, before concluding with a justifiably sheepish appeal for continued support, notwithstanding the offence he freely acknowledged he had caused. 'I hope all reasonable men on all sides will concur with me,' he reaffirmed, 'as I expect your Scotch commissioners should do, though I know you must dislike many passages in it.' In an effort to bring peace at any cost to his troubled kingdom, he had therefore been left with no choice from his perspective but to cut his moral cloth according to circumstance, and his would-be allies to the north were to proffer their loyalty accordingly – irrespective of the fact that this loyalty had already been compromised at regular intervals whenever their own self-interest dictated.

As such, it was hardly surprising, of course, that the full scale of Scottish chagrin was barely concealed in their response of 22 November:

> Your message left behinde you at Hampton Court gave Great hopes that your Majesty had gone to some place, where you might be safe from your Enemies, and where your Majesties friends might have accesse to you. But as the place to which you are gone, so your Majesties Message of the 16 hath infinitely disabled us to serve you.

Charles, the complaint continued, had granted 'a full tolleration of Heresy and Schism forever' and 'divested himself of much of his royal power'. He had done so, moreover, in blatant disregard of the more favourable alternative he had been offered. The damage done by his decision was therefore both deep and definitive, it seemed, as the Scots made clear in a further message penned three days later. 'It is of no advantage,' they declared ominously, 'to expostulate what is past, either about the carrying your Majesty into that sad place or the prejudice, your service and we suffer by your Majesties Message.'

So when Berkeley reached London to reassure the seething Scottish commissioners, he was faced with the most delicate of tasks. On

1 December, they had received Charles' flimsy reassurance that his proposals to Parliament were, in effect, nothing more than a ploy to bring his protagonists to the negotiating table. But Berkeley himself now had no explicit authority to negotiate with the Scots, and when he had pleaded for it earlier at Carisbrooke, Ashburnham had strongly opposed the notion. Ashburnham, indeed, had nursed a smouldering antipathy towards Scottish high-handedness from the very moment that they had dismissed him from attendance upon Charles at Newark in 1646, and it was he who now undermined his master's attempts at reconciliation. Already accused by Parliament of treachery in contriving the king's escape from Hampton Court, he wrote from Carisbrooke with an artful justification of his conduct, blaming both Scots and army radicals. 'I was not willing,' he suggested, 'to hazard my honour, nor my life, neither for Scot, nor Adjutator.' The self-same letter was soon being brandished by eager London news-sheets, hungry for titbits to fuel the growing desire to be rid of Scotsmen and Independents alike.

It was the Earl of Lanark, moreover, who greeted Berkeley with a copy of just such a news-sheet upon his arrival in the capital, shaking it under the visitor's nose during his first encounter with the Scottish commissioners and auguring a series of meetings that promised little further warmth over the days ahead. Nor was it any consolation to the Scots that Berkeley, Legge and the royal chaplains had all advised Ashburnham against including the offending reference to the Scots in the first place, for, in Berkeley's own words, 'he liked it so well that we could not make him depart from it'. In consequence, further discussion on Friday, 3 December yielded little, and it was ultimately no small relief for the Royalist representative that he was suddenly recalled to Carisbrooke the following day on what Ashburnham described in the king's name as urgent business. Though his limp apology for abandoning the talks scheduled for Monday was taken 'very ill' by the Earls of Lanark and Lauderdale, Berkeley was at least free of his thankless mission, and at liberty, more importantly, to assist in what he now assumed to be an imminent escape attempt on the king's behalf.

Only the next morning, therefore, Sir John was already dismounting in Carisbrooke's courtyard, travel-stained and exhausted, and hurrying to the king in eager anticipation. Any hope of finding his master poised for departure was, however, utterly dashed when he found himself swiftly informed that he must press on with the very negotiations from which he had been so abruptly called away. Maddeningly composed and in confident good spirits, Charles greeted him 'more graciously than ordinary', thanking him for his dispatch from Windsor, before coolly observing that his current apprehension by the army was actually nothing less than an invaluable political lever, guaranteeing that the Scots 'would take reason' and offer the best possible terms. When asked by Berkeley why he was 'still in the Island', moreover, 'since there were Forces design'd, both by Sea and Land, to secure his Person', the king merely replied that he 'would have a care of that time enough'. Escape would follow, but not before the Scots had been duly won over by treaty. With Ashburnham in close attendance and fully concurring, Berkeley had little alternative other than to comply. 'Against this,' he later reflected, 'I argued the best I could, and when I saw it was in vain, I desired his Majesty would dispatch this Treaty, for his condition would admit no delays.'

In the event, Berkeley was spared the further indignity of returning to the capital, for the next day he fell sick, 'what with my late journeying, and what with my vexation at this way of proceeding'. But the king remained set in his mind, and Mungo Murray and Sir William Flemming, who acted in turn as his messengers in the ensuing negotiations, faithfully wearied many a willing steed as they galloped back and forth to London throughout December, carrying letters loaded with heavy detail on the finer points of church government. The irony was all the more acute when Charles eventually summoned Berkeley to confirm that the Scots were also urging his escape. 'I think you are a Prophet,' the king confided, 'for the Scots Commissioners at London have sent an Express, desiring me to do the same thing in effect you had moved', though it was 'now too late, for they would be come away before another Express could be gone out of the Island towards them'. Plainly, there had been dithering throughout, and by the time that Charles finally saw fit to grasp the nettle, the Scots had temporarily decided to call a halt to the wearisome grind of persuading a misguided man against his prejudices.

By now, in any case, the focus was shifting once more to Parliament. According to a report dispatched to Venice on 28 November, the king's escape had 'caused the Houses and the army much anxiety', though the news of his arrival on the Isle of Wight, which was received on 15 November, produced little stir. On the contrary, the recent order closing the ports was cancelled and Carisbrooke Castle was calmly accepted as the most suitable residence for the time being. Indeed, the only notable sign of recrimination was an order that Ashburnham and his colleagues be arrested for their involvement in the king's action. Within a day, naturally enough, Colonel Hammond had been instructed to appoint 'a sufficient guard … for securing the king's person from any Violence, and preventing his departing the said Isle, without the Direction of both Houses'. Yet Royalist residents of the island, who had duly compounded with Parliament, were, as we have seen, to remain unmolested, and only former soldiers forbidden access to the island's forts and castles. With appropriate warrants from the Edinburgh Parliament, moreover, it would still be possible for Scots to parley with the king.

Such leniency played no small part, in fact, in Charles' decision to send his message of 17 November, offering terms for treaty negotiations, notwithstanding the impact upon both the Scots and his English supporters at home and abroad who were left dumbfounded. 'I could neither comprehend the reason of it,' wrote Edward Hyde to Lord Hopton, '… but I conclude there is some mystery in it that will satisfy me if I know it.' Worse still, Parliament showed little urgency in framing a response, which merely confirmed the impulsiveness of the king's actions and the ongoing distrust of his intentions. In truth, a good deal of committee work was being conducted to produce a common front with the Scots, but by mid-December the Venetian Senate was learning that Charles had still not heard from Westminster, 'as in London everything moves slowly and in disorder', while as early as 6 December, the French ambassador, Bellièvre, was already deciding that the slow progress of events rendered further reports by every mail pointless.

It was upon this same day, furthermore, that the king's own patience finally broke, as he produced an indignant aide-memoire to Parliament that crackled with reproof. 'Had his Majesty thought it possible,' the message ran, 'that his two Houses could be imployed in things of greater concernment than the peace of this miserable distracted kingdom; he would have expected with more patience, their leisure in acknowledging the receipt of His Message of the 16 of November last.' He had made, he complained, so many magnanimous concessions that appropriate goodwill should surely be reciprocated and, in repeating his request for the right to negotiate a 'personal treaty' in London, he appeared to confirm his increasing awareness of the tightening security arrangements at Carisbrooke that were making the castle appear less and less like a safe haven. For, as one newsletter reported on 6 December, 'letters from the Isle of Wight speake of a Guard placed about his Majesty (not to restrain him from going abroad at his pleasure) but to keepe suche from coming to him as may bee hurtful to His person'. Removal to the capital was therefore both politically and personally imperative, and never more so than when another report informed its readers less circumspectly of 'a very strict guard' being placed around the king 'to keep all malignants, and especially those who have borne arms against the Parliament, from having access to his Majesty'.

Charles' fond belief that he could now expect to be trusted by his former enemies and treated to his accustomed dignities at Carisbrooke indefinitely was therefore under open challenge. 'Hee had for a while,' wrote Ashburnham, 'all the satisfaction from the Governour which that place could afford (His flight from Hampton Court being understood by Parliament and Army to carrie greate innocencie with it).' But the army's commanders had soon digested the letter left by the king on his table at Hampton Court and reinterpreted the claim that he was 'retiring my self for some time from the publique both of my friends and enemies'. As early as 21 November, indeed, Ireton was expressing his feelings to Hammond in no uncertain terms:

> For the pretence of the king's keeping himself within the protection of the army by coming into your hands, both reason, and all the circumstances I have heard make me believe, and the king's own declaration, left behind upon his table, doth plainly discover, that he in his going away had other intentions; and his surrendering himself to you was besides his first purpose. And I cannot believe, but it was a second counsel, and that, tho' appearingly a choice, yet really upon some emergent necessity, for the avoiding of a worse, when he someway found himself stopt, and unable to get clear away, according to his first intention.

As if to confirm Ireton's fears, there had been persistent rumours in London since the beginning of December that the queen was in Jersey and the king about to escape there. Talk emerged, too, that Hammond had been forced from the Isle of Wight by the inhabitants, and in such circumstances it was hardly surprising that neither army nor Parliament were keen to indulge their royal prisoner. 'For these last 3 dayes,' said a newsletter of 6 December, 'he hath kept himself more retired, and not stirred forth unless it were aboute the walls and gardens of the castle', while on 9 December the anonymous Venetian source was reporting that guards had been set all around the island 'to prevent his Majesty from leaving or suspect persons from approaching him'. For good measure, the king was also being locked each night in his bedroom, and the keys carried to the Governor, since, as a newsletter put it, 'they now know his Majesty's design was not for that place'. 'Here,' another report ran on 10 December, 'is a melancholy court, walking the round is daily recreation, for other there is none. Hope is superfluous.'

Charles' only consolation from those in authority over him came in fact from Hammond, for in spite of all the current suspicion, and against heavy pressure from Parliament and his army superiors, he continued to trust his royal prisoner. Hammond wrote on 19 December:

> The Kinge stands engaged in his word not to stirre, and doth protest this is the place hee first designed when he apprehended it not safe to continue longer at Hampton Court, and that if he were to chuse anie place within his three Kingdoms hee would not remove hence except to London upon a personall treaty.

Hammond, moreover, continued to resist orders for the arrest of Ashburnham, Berkeley and Legge, which he had received from Parliament as early as 18 November. Only the next day, he invited the Commons to reconsider, since the king's friends had pledged their parole and had acted in good faith by conducting him to the safety of the Isle of Wight, and when Ireton, under Fairfax's authority, applied further pressure forty-eight hours later, the Governor continued to stand firm. Indeed, even when an officer of the Serjeant of the House of Commons arrived in person on 1 December to collect the three 'delinquents', he was obliged to return empty-handed, leaving the arrest warrant to be duly rescinded, upon Cromwell's intervention, on 2 December.

But if the king could still depend upon the good offices of his jailer, Parliament remained unbending and when their response finally came, it arrived as an ultimatum delivered not, as hoped, directly in London but within the confines of Carisbrooke's grim stone walls. The proposals, such as they were, had in any case been continually and forcefully opposed by the Scots, who, on 17 December, had submitted a paper 'in very high language' roundly condemning them. It was only three days later that Parliament finally decided to press ahead, regardless of Scottish opposition, with a deputation headed by the

Earl of Denbigh. Its purpose was to deliver to the king the contents of four bills, which were to be non-negotiable and would effectively divest him of royal power. The first transferred to Parliament for twenty years the control of all armed forces; the second revoked all proclamations against Parliament delivered during the war; the third cancelled those peerages granted by the king during the same period; and the last allowed Parliament to adjourn any session to a place of its own choosing. Only if the royal assent to these measures were granted in advance, moreover, would Parliament then agree to dispatch commissioners to the Isle of Wight to treat with the king in person on other issues, such as the abolition of the episcopacy and the establishment of Presbyterian government.

There was to be, then, no scope for argument and minimal time for manoeuvre, since a deadline of four days was imposed for acceptance. As Berkeley all too aptly observed, the proposals provided 'work enough for abler men than any of us were', while the French ambassador was soon noting how it was being mooted in Parliament that the king was bound to destroy himself just as surely by either accepting or refusing. Berkeley, indeed, was convinced that the bill concerning control of the militia amounted to 'no more nor less than dethroning of the king and enslaving of the People by a Law', since it 'embraced ten times more power than the Crown ever executed', allowing the two Houses to raise soldiers and collect money without any effective restraint. Yet he knew with equal certainty that his royal master's hands were tightly bound, not least because 'his Enemies would deliver his Majesty to the World as obstinate to his own and the Kingdoms ruin if he should not accept this offer'. While Charles might draw up the most ingenious response possible, 'good penning did not signify much at that time'.

When the Earl of Denbigh and his fellow commissioners arrived in Carisbrooke's imposing audience chamber at 2 p.m. on Christmas Eve, therefore, the scene was set for a fateful exchange. Receiving the proposals in good grace, Charles nevertheless confirmed that there could be no immediate answer on matters of such complexity and promised a reply within the next few days. After which, he duly withdrew with his advisers to spend the afternoon poring over the relevant documents in the agonising search for some 'sorry expedient', which would only emerge eventually not within the bills themselves, but from the very Scots who found themselves once more driven to his assistance as the lesser of evils. Even his old nemesis, the Duke of

Argyle, had now been courted by Charles in his effort to rebuild bridges across the border. 'Argyle, howsoever heretofore you and I have differed in judgement,' he had pleaded, 'I believe now that the present state of affairs are such as will make you heartily embrace my cause, it being grounded on those particulars that were never in question between you and me.' And now, as control of the English army by Parliament duly loomed and Presbyterianism teetered under threat from religious Independents, Scottish recalcitrance duly melted under Charles' new-found wish to compromise.

Reaching Carisbrooke on Christmas Day, the Earls of Lanark, Loudoun and Lauderdale therefore lost no time in declaring their dissent to the four bills and entering into private session with the king. The season, after all, was far from merry and Parliament's proposals so wholly 'prejudicial to Religion, the Crown and the Union and Interests of the Kingdoms' that the Scots, notwithstanding the rigours of their midwinter journey, could brook no delay. Nor did the resulting negotiations, conducted behind closed doors though under the very noses of Denbigh and the English delegation, hold back from laying down an agenda that amounted to nothing less than a blueprint for the waging of a second Civil War. As Lauderdale put it, '[W]e did then, at Carisbrooke Castle, receive the King's Commands for engaging Scotland, and raising of an Army for his Delivery and Restitution.' In return, the king duly undertook, at the first opportunity, to recognise in Parliament the Solemn League and Covenant renouncing the episcopacy, and agree to the establishment of Presbyterianism in England for a period of three years, after which a convention of sixty divines would be called to settle the religious issues once and for all.

Additional articles were to provide for further political integration of the kingdoms of Scotland and England, but, above all, the king's right to control the militia, veto legislation and appoint officers of state was maintained, so that even Charles had little hesitation in reaching a decision. By 26 December, indeed, two copies of the resulting agreement had been drawn up and signed: the first being kept by the king, hidden inside a writing desk in his bedroom; the second retained by the Scots and secreted much more elaborately still, at Ashburnham's suggestion, by encasing it in lead and burying it in a garden in the castle grounds until it could be recovered later by their agents. That the treaty had been concluded with the English commissioners so close at hand was, of course, remarkable enough in its own right, but the resulting document was too detailed and bulky to be smuggled confidently through any search that might be conducted as the Scots took ship for London. Although they were eventually treated to nothing more than a snub from the town of Portsmouth on their return journey, their decision to leave the treaty behind them was a thoroughly sensible precaution, particularly when the stakes involved were so high.

After their successful departure, there nevertheless remained for Charles the delicate task of dealing with the unpalatable demands of the English commissioners who remained behind. Berkeley's ingenious recommendation was to accept the four bills, to which there was no alternative, but only as part of a package encompassing four further bills, which, while thoroughly objectionable to Parliament, were 'all most popular, and such as they durst not pass nor well deny'. The first and most important was 'a Bill for payment of the Army, which contained their disbanding as soon as they were paid', while the second proposed 'a period to the present Parliament'. The third, in its turn, was to be framed with the intention of 'restoring the King, Queen and Royal Family to their revenues', and the last with the express hope of settling the ecclesiastical issue 'without any coercive power'. If accepted, Berkeley's strategy would at the very least have bought some time, and he seems initially to have had high hopes for it. 'I shew'd this answer first to Mr Leg,' he later recalled, 'then to Dr Hammond and Dr Sheldon, who seemed to approve of the Expedient, and desir'd Mr Ashburnham would acquaint the King with it.' 'But,' he added, 'I never heard any thing from his Majesty; and I was resolved never to have it obtruded, lest I should appear fond of my own Conceptions.'

Instead, Charles opted for an altogether clumsier, less convincing and less effective policy of prevarication, drafting a paper declaring that, as he was anxious to satisfy all parties, he could not accept proposals with which the Scots were bound to disagree. Equally naively, he would insist that his blank rejection of Parliament's proposals be delivered to Denbigh sealed and that it should remain unopened until its eventual arrival in Westminster. But when, on Tuesday, 28 December, Denbigh and his commissioners filed into the king's presence, they were not to be thwarted so tamely. Sitting with the sealed document in his grasp and attended by his worried advisers, Charles asked the earl, wholly redundantly, whether he had authority to negotiate. When Denbigh confirmed once more that he had not, the letter was duly handed over, irrespective of the fact that there was no guarantee that the sealed message did indeed contain an answer – something which was quickly pointed out to the king after a hurried conference between the commissioners in private. Indeed, as Berkeley put it, Denbigh 'seemed offended with his Majesty' upon his return 'and expressed his indignation in harsher terms than one ought to use to another'.

Whenever he had acted as the king's ambassador in former days, Denbigh fumed, he had never delivered a message to foreign princes without knowing its contents – a comment which elicited an even more acerbic response from Charles to the effect that none of the two score ambassadors he had sent forth on diplomatic business had ever had the temerity to break his seal. Even Hammond was now impatient with the 'long expostulations' that followed before 'his Majesty was perswaded to open his answer', and far from placated by the nature of the contents when finally revealed. On the contrary, Berkeley tells us, the king's response 'so far from allaying the storm … increased it both in the Commissioners and the Governor, who altogether retired from the Castle of Carisbroke to Newport, an English mile from the Castle'. Just as all had fully expected, Charles had unilaterally rebuffed the four bills on the grounds that they would 'not only divest him of all sovereignty' but jeopardise his subjects' rights. 'His Majesty,' the royal reply concluded, 'is very much at ease with himself having fulfilled the offices of both a Christian and a king.'

But if Charles was, as always, secure in his conscience, his stubborn refusal to compromise his scruples would once again come at a cost. As Berkeley had pointed out at the time, the king's decision to respond with 'an absolute Negative' was almost certain to lead to orders that Hammond should 'look more strictly to his Person' and thus hinder any intended escape. Yet even as the Governor was accompanying Denbigh's frustrated party to Newport, the need for flight was plainly imperative, since the ploy to gain time by sealing his response had so signally failed. According to Ashburnham, even Charles himself was by now prepared to consider passage to France, since he had already written to his wife earlier in December, asking her to arrange for a ship to arrive in Southampton, which was now in place and awaiting his orders. At the same time, a certain William Lisle had also undertaken to provide a vessel that could transport Charles away from the Isle of Wight on the initial leg of his journey to the waiting French barque, travelling by night and braving the danger posed by the five naval frigates constantly patrolling the Solent. If these could be avoided and

Henrietta Maria's own ship safely reached, a favourable wind might carry the king without delay to liberty and a long overdue reunion with his waiting spouse.

Berkeley's account suggests, in fact, that all was feverish preparation and bustle from the moment that Hammond and the commissioners departed the castle. Berkeley informs us:

> As soon as they were gone, I went to Mr Ashburnham, who told me that he had newly dispatch'd away a Footman over the Water, to order four or five Horses to be removed from the Place where they then stood, lest they should be found and seiz'd by the Soldiers that were coming into the Island.

Whereupon, the account continues, 'I conjured him by no means to do it, lest the Winds or the Parliament's Frigats might force us in our escape to put ashore, and we should want Horses.' Plainly in some confusion from the rapid progress of events, Ashburnham then dispatched another groom to countermand his orders, only to reissue the same command once more 'within few hours'.

Ashburnham's indecision was not, however, reflected in the king himself on this occasion, for, according to Berkeley's account, 'that night or next morning his Majesty resolved to endeavour his escape'. Seized, it seems, by an uncharacteristic gust of enthusiasm for decisive action, Charles was indeed soon dressing for the journey and eagerly watching the weather-vane on the Chapel of St Nicholas on the other side of the courtyard, if Ashburnham's own, slightly confused, description of events is to be believed. 'All things being prepared and adjusted,' Ashburnham informs us, 'I told his Majestie if Hee was pleased to goe, I did not doubt but carry him away without interruption.' At which, the king 'with great joy ranne to the window to see how the wind stood by the fane, and finding it perfectly faire, made all haste to draw on his bootes (for Hee had libertie then to ride abroad)'.

Indeed, it was only at the very point that Charles was 'readie to go out of his Chamber' that he was finally foiled by a cruel twist of events, for, as 'Hee turned againe to look upon the fane', Ashburnham relates, 'so fatal a mischeefe did attend Him, as it was changed at that instant cleane contrary, and continued so for six dayes together, so as the Barque could not stirr'. 'In the very instant' that the wind 'became cross', moreover, we hear from Berkeley that 'the Governor returned from Newport full of fury, and lock'd up the Gates, and doubled the guards, and went not to bed that night'. Why Charles had not opted in the first place for the much faster means of riding or even walking to Cowes rather than sailing down the River Medina to reach the port remains puzzling. But the return of Hammond in the nick of time had now delivered a killing blow not only to this particular escape attempt but to the generally lax security regime which had made it a possibility in the first place. That day had given the Governor his first direct experience of the king's tortuous dealings, and he did not appreciate what he had witnessed, as was made abundantly clear by the letter to the Speaker of the House of Lords that he now drafted by candlelight:

My Lord, This Day, being in the Presence when the King communicated to the Commissioners of Parliament His Answer to the Bills and Propositions lately presented to Him from both Houses, and finding it so contrary to my Expectation, I thought it my duty to take a stricter Care than ordinary of the Security of the Person of the King, and for removing all from about him that are not there by Authority of Parliament, and to take all other effectual ways and means to preserve His Majesty's Person from departing hence, until I received the further Commands of the Houses. By the Blessing of God, I shall omit nothing wherein I can serve the Parliament, in relation to this dangerous Trust. But yet, my lord, I must humbly beg it from you, because I know it is impossible long to secure the King here, that His Person may be removed as soon as conveniently He may; or else that I may be discharged from my Employment, it being a Burden insupportable for me.

Once more, it seems, Robert Hammond was weary of responsibility, or, more likely, sufficiently convinced of his indispensability to employ the threat of resignation as a surefire tool to gain what he wanted. He certainly showed no hesitation in making good his decision to rid the king of his inner circle, for Ashburnham, Berkeley and Legge were all expelled the very next day, 'the Jealousies of those tymes, iudging it inconvenient to continue them in their attendance'. All, including the king, were dismayed if unsurprised, but all, except the king himself, it seems, knew equally well that 'there was noe expostulating with the Governour about it'. For Hammond was not to be spared a stormy exchange with Charles when news of his decision finally broke and the Governor was duly summoned to the royal presence. To the question whether it became a man of honour and honesty to deal thus with those who had so freely cast themselves upon him, Hammond replied that both his honesty and his honour were in the first place to them that employed him, and that he had the authority of both Houses for his action. Nor, he added, was the king ignorant of the causes of his action, saying, 'If he had done amiss let his head answer for it.'

Plainly, a fleeting flash of royal high dudgeon was wholly unavailing against the Governor's own indignation, and after a sad last dinner with the king that afternoon, at which Ashburnham burst into tears, the king's three most valued supporters duly took their leave: Ashburnham retiring to a Newport inn, while Berkeley, according to his own account, took up residence with Legge at 'an Acquaintance's house of ours in the Town'. Once more, there was talk of future hopes of escape, and contingency measures, probably involving the islanders Edward Worsley and John Newland, were already in hand, as Berkeley's account makes clear. 'Before we took our leaves,' he tells us, 'we acquainted his Majesty, that we had left the Captain of the Frigat, and two honest and trusty Gentlemen of the Island to assist his escape, and that we would have all things in readiness on the other side of the Water.' The local merchant Newland was, indeed, probably the 'acquaintance' with whom Berkeley and Legge now took up temporary residence to wait upon opportunity.

Nor was it long before an intervention from an altogether unexpected source duly materialised. For not more than an hour after his arrival, Berkeley heard 'a Drum beat confusedly' and discovered 'not long after' that 'one Captain Burley, with divers others were risen to rescue the king'. The son of the former Governor of Yarmouth Castle, Burley had in fact been born on the island and gone on to command the naval vessel *Antelope* before being discharged when the fleet declared against the king. Like many of his kind, however, the officer's loyalty remained unwavering and he had thereafter joined the Royalist army, becoming, we are told, an 'officer of good account', serving both as Lieutenant-General of the Ordinance and Governor of Pendennis. Only the king's eventual surrender, indeed, had finally persuaded Burley to return to the place of his birth, 'where many of his kinsfolk were present', and opt for what appeared to be both honourable and placid retirement.

When news came from Carisbrooke, however, that the king's advisers had been dismissed and that Charles himself was to be subject to close restraint, the need for a brash gesture of derring-do seems to have become overwhelming. Sending a lone 14-year-old boy to fetch the town drum to raise a crowd, and crying 'For God, the King and the People', Burley publicly declared before an agitated throng in the middle of Newport his intention to rescue the king and prevent his murder. Though the resulting tumult among his audience proved little more than 'the mere effervescence of otherwise inconsiderate language', there was to be no drawing back. If others followed, Burley declared, he himself would be the first to enter the castle, notwithstanding the fact that his active supporters would ultimately consist of little more than a braying band of women and children – the 'entire muster', we are told, possessing no more than 'one musket among them'.

Sorry-looking though the 'rebellion' may have been, however, it was certainly noisy enough to arouse Berkeley and Legge some way away, who lost no time in making for Ashburnham's inn, where they found him, to both their surprise and alarm, 'making Speeches to those well-affected People, advising them to desist from their vain Enterprize'. The risks entailed by Ashburnham's intervention, as Berkeley wisely appreciated, were considerable, since any involvement – even an attempt to induce calm – was likely to be exploited by the authorities. With this in mind, both Berkeley and Legge prevailed upon their colleague to stop talking and withdraw: a decision that proved wholly warranted in the rebellion's aftermath when, as Berkeley explained, prisoners were 'not only examin'd concerning us, but promis'd Liberty and Pardon in case they would peach us'.

Before their eventual apprehension, however, Burley and his motley crew did just enough to guarantee the wrath of the authorities. Forcing his way through the participants, the Mayor, Moses Read, along with the few guards he had been able to muster, demanded the town drum's return, only to be refused in 'ill language' by the boy in possession. Burley, indeed, was required to intervene on the Mayor's behalf, rebuking his insolent drummer and 'asking him whether he knew who it was he was speaking to'. Yet the disturbance was still, it seems, in progress well into the evening, and Burley, notwithstanding his respectful treatment of Moses Read, would pay a heavy price for his hot-headedness. For reinforcements were required before the gathering was finally dispersed, by which time both the magnitude and threat of the incident had become wildly exaggerated, as Captain Basket of Cowes Castle placed the commanders of the naval vessels in the Solent on standby, and his orders were confirmed by the parliamentary commissioners who heard of the news while returning from Carisbrooke.

By around 11 p.m., in fact, the ships' captains had received a further dispatch from Basket to the effect that the Governor of the island was that night 'besieged by some formerly of the King's party, that had been in Armes against the Parliament ... and that also divers of the Islanders were joined with them'. In consequence, a council of war was hastily convened upon one of the ships, and a decision taken that the vessels should be spread around the Solent 'in such stations as might best prevent the putting off of boats to or from the Island without search'. The fact that, by morning, Burley had been 'committed to a dungeon in the castle he had proposed to attack' and sat there in the company of only three other prisoners was effectively neither here nor there. In such distracted times, the captain's actions were not a matter for clemency, and Parliament was no less determined than local officials that punishment should be swift, visible and condign, so that when Hammond's report was received by the House of Commons, little time was lost in ordering 'that the general, Sir Thomas Fairfax, be required to grant a commission to the governor of the Isle of Wight, to try by martial law the chief actors in this mutiny, or that shall make any further disturbance'.

Ultimately, only Burley himself would be committed to the gallows for his actions, in a trial described by the antiquarian George Hillier three centuries later as 'one of the most peculiar in history'. With a certain Sergeant Wild presiding, whom Hillier freely described as 'a man of infamous character', Burley stood accused of treason, we are told, for no other reason than 'because he opposed those who were committing it'. The outcome of the hearing at Winchester, which began on 22 January 1648, proved painfully predictable. Less than a fortnight later, and following a short reprieve 'because no one in Hampshire could be prevailed on to undertake the executioner's functions', the would-be rescuer of the king was duly put to death by a man called Gregory who had been specially brought from London 'to perform his hateful duty'. After taking leave of his wife and children at the prison door and requesting that he 'be driven speedily to his journey's end, in order that he might obtain endless rest and peace', the victim would finally suffer his fate, as Hillier's description makes clear, in a way that deeply impressed not only onlookers but the king himself, who is said to have been 'materially affected' by the episode:

> On coming to the place of execution, where were already the faggots to consume his bowels and the cleaver to divide his body, Burley requested the 12th chapter of Isiah to be read to him, together with the 8th chapter of the Romans, and the 69th Psalm; and having taken leave of the world, and repeated a prayer he had written for the occasion, which he presented to the sheriff, and which was afterwards published, ascended the gallows, where he was again moved by a minister to be humbled, that the Lord might have mercy upon him, and to confess his sins to God, particularly the treason for which he was to die. Burley said he was a sinner, but no traitor; and on being told what a fair trial he had, and how legally he was condemned answered, it was true the judge condemned him upon the bench, the ministers in their pulpits, and the gentlemen of the county in their verdicts, but still he was no traitor; whereupon he was urged how bloody an act he had agitated in seeking to take away the king through blood; to which he replied, he was happy to die so, and hoped his blood might be the last that should be so shed; when he again prayed fervently, and, concluding with the Lord's Prayer proclaimed with undaunted courage, *Fear God and honour the King*. The hangman thereupon pulled the cap over his face, and the unfortunate man, as he was turned off, called, 'Lord preserve my soul – Lord Jesus, receive my soul'.

In the meantime, however, Ashburnham, Berkeley and Legge had at least been able to avoid implication in Burley's abortive insurrection, and had crossed to the Hampshire coast, where they took up residence at Netley Abbey, the seat of the Marquis of Hertford, and re-established correspondence with the king. Three weeks later, indeed, Berkeley proceeded to Henrietta Maria in France, while his two colleagues remained behind and continued to harbour hopes for a royal escape attempt. Only when the Derby House Committee caught wind of their activities, some five months later, were Ashburnham and Legge finally apprehended and confined in Arundel Castle, after which Ashburnham was eventually exchanged on 7 August for Sir William Masham on condition that he left the country within two months and in the meantime remained at his own house. All in all, it was hardly indicative of any new-found thirst for summary justice on Parliament's part, and while Legge was forced to remain at Arundel, he too was treated with remarkable leniency, as the king's opponents struggled to come to terms with a debilitating predicament arising from the novelty of the constitutional situation confronting them. For how could any confederate of the king, who remained the head of state, be deemed an enemy of the state, particularly when the king himself remained the theoretical lynchpin of the entire legal system?

Yet the alarm generated by Burley's impulse to rescue his sovereign was real enough, and the consequences for Charles, in particular, no less tangible. Over Christmas there had been riotous demonstrations for king and church, almost amounting to insurrections, in Canterbury, Ipswich and other towns, while in London, Christmas decorations appeared defiantly in churches and other public places. Ejected clergy-men resumed their pulpits and used the banned Prayer Book services at the very same time that Royalist newspapers and pamphlets were reappearing openly on bookstalls. While all this was more symptomatic of a widespread nostalgia for the old days of peace than of any genuine upsurge of support for Charles in his own right, it added undoubtedly to the growing undercurrent of anxiety on the part both of Parliament and the army leadership as fiscal oppression and arbitrary imprison-ment continued on a scale to rival anything experienced before the war. While meat and salt had been freed from the hated excise tax in 1647, for instance, it still fell on other articles of mass consumption, making violent attacks on collectors commonplace. But the ongoing legal activities of Star Chamber, High Commission and the county committees were almost as unpopular in their own right, and there was also the nagging burden of free quarter for many communities to bear as a result of the ongoing shortfall in soldiers' pay.

Any attempt to free the king, however ill-conceived, was therefore certain to be greeted with panic at such a sensitive time, and espe-cially so when suspicions of foreign involvement had also been aroused. For on Saturday, 11 December, seven ships of the Dutch West India Company, carrying troops and supplies for Brazil, had been anchored on the island – two ships and two galliots in St Albans Road, and three frigates in Cowes Road. Though, as ships of a nominally friendly state, they had every right to shelter and victual there, they were nevertheless still in place as the end of December approached. When Burley finally made his hasty move, therefore, at least one news-sheet, *The Perfect Diurnall*, was already reporting fears of 'a fearful story of the Prince of Orange with a great fleet of ships to begirt the island', with the predictable result that when further news reached the English frigates off Cowes on the fateful night of 29 December that Hammond was besieged by Royalists, it was immediately feared that 'the Hollanders riding there at Anker might be ingaged with them'.

Ultimately, the commanders of the Dutch vessels would be able to clear themselves under questioning and had left the island with their ships by 7 January. But their mere presence had underlined the vulnerability of Carisbrooke, notwithstanding the fact that within a week of the king's arrival, Fairfax had diverted a troop of horse under Captain Peck to Redbridge near Southampton, with two infantry companies also put on short notice to transfer over to the island, if needed. Nor was it any surprise when, on 30 December, the very day after Burley's commotion, these same companies duly became the advance guard for a new flow of reinforcements, 100 soldiers arriving in the early morning, to be followed soon after by a further 100 from Portsmouth. All, moreover, were of Hammond's own regiment: crack troops of the New Model Army, and, for Ashburnham, Berkeley and their like, an altogether different proposition to the four squadrons of Newport men with whom the Governor had hitherto been holding the island.

Although their arrival was not entirely unexpected, it had clearly been hastened by the current emergency, and the Mayor and Corporation of Newport found themselves later that day in a hastily convened session to make improvised arrangements for the billeting and maintenance of some forty of the soldiers. Moreover, the advent of these troops marked merely the starting point of a much broader extension of precautions. For on 30 December, Fairfax dispatched three senior officers – Sir William Constable, Lieutenant-Colonel Salmon and Lieutenant-Colonel Goffe – to assist Hammond, while on Saturday, 1 January, the House of Commons not only furnished the Governor with powers of martial law but ordered Vice-Admiral Rainsborough to proceed with more ships to the island. Two days later, for good measure, it was also agreed that fifty barrels of powder, 'with Match and Bullet proportionable', should be placed at Hammond's disposal.

Even more importantly, however, the Burley episode had played its part in underpinning Parliament's no-nonsense response to the refusal of its four bills by the king. On 15 January, a measure was passed declaring that the two Houses would 'make no further Addresses or Applications to the King' and 'receive no more any Message from the

King'. To complete Charles' isolation, it was also made treasonable for anyone else to apply to the king without Parliament's express approval: something which elicited a predictably pungent response from the Scots, who promptly discovered that they, too, were to be excluded from free access. Plainly, the facade of Anglo-Scottish co-operation was now as unnecessary as it was unconvincing, and the inevitable renewal of hostilities only a matter of time. Indeed, with any illusions of the Scottish embassy to Carisbrooke over Christmas long since exploded, the so-called Committee of Both Kingdoms, which had embodied the pretence of amity since 1644, was already being superseded by the Committee of Both Houses, or 'Derby House Committee' as it was more commonly known. 'The House of Commons,' wrote Cromwell to Hammond on 3 January, 'is very sensible of the King's dealings, and of our brethrens, in this late transaction.'

The agreement between Charles and the Scots had, in fact, been a foolish bargain from the outset, though especially so from the king's perspective. The Scots, after all, had no prospect of mustering an army capable of matching that of Fairfax and Cromwell, and would have to count on powerful risings in their support. But they were hardly likely to win the hearts and minds of Englishmen by dictating in advance the answers to such delicate questions as the control of the armed forces, the appointment of ministers and the royal veto, and, worse still, by closing the door to liberty of conscience. In effect, Charles' decision to enlist the help of a Scottish army before he had fully exhausted the possibility of achieving a peaceful restoration would prove the most disastrous decision of his life. If he had been in Scotland, with a reasonable chance of escape in the event of his allies' defeat, the gamble might have been less reckless, though he would still have incurred incalculable damage for plunging his kingdoms once more into bloodshed. Yet to count on Scottish help when still a prisoner was tantamount to suicide – both political and personal. For defeat in a second Civil War would leave him friendless and defenceless against a surge of outrage that even his royal status could never withstand.

To compound Charles' predicament, there were clear signs, too, of a reconciliation between Parliament and the army as the breach with Edinburgh widened. About a week after the escape from Hampton Court, there had been talk at Ireton's headquarters at Kingston-upon-Thames that the king might come to terms with Parliament, and the general's response had been duly ominous. Warming himself at his fireplace, he had expressed the hope that so treacherous an agreement might be such 'as we might with good conscience fight against them both'. Now, however, Parliament was no less distrustful of the king than the army, and Cromwell in particular had become anxious to sever links with the king once and for all. The autumn of 1647 had seen him paying court to Charles whilst executing summary justice upon extremists within his army. At one point, indeed, there had been the real prospect of an accommodation between king and army to the exclusion of Parliament. But now, as the growing influence of Scots and Presbyterians raised fears once more of a settlement that excluded his men, Cromwell had come to see Westminster as the lesser of evils.

The general's change of mood may well have been triggered, moreover, by an incident that he is said to have related to Robert Boyle, 1st Earl of Orrery, years later. The son of the Earl of Cork and formerly a staunch Royalist, Boyle had become, by 1655, a keen devotee and trusted confidant of Cromwell, and it was in this capacity that he seems to have elicited from the general the remarkable story of his final disillusionment with the king, which dated to the winter of 1647, when trust, respect and goodwill were still largely intact on the army's part. At that time, indeed, negotiations were still ongoing, when a warning appears to have been raised by an army spy 'who was of the king's bedchamber' that the king had written to his wife that he was bent on abandoning the generals. The offending letter was to be sewn up inside the skirt of a saddle, it seems, and delivered to Dover by an unwitting messenger who would be stopping en route at the Blue Boar Inn in Holborn at 10 p.m. that very night. If Cromwell could intercept him, he could learn for himself, first-hand, of the king's double-dealing.

As Boyle's account develops, it tell us, furthermore, that Cromwell did indeed make his way to Holborn, with his son-in-law Ireton in tow. Dressed as troopers and accompanied by a lone soldier, who was left on watch outside, Cromwell and Ireton duly entered the Blue Boar and supped beer while they waited for news of the messenger's arrival, which occurred at the predicted time, and proved the signal for action. For the two generals now approached their quarry with drawn swords and warned him that everyone entering or leaving the inn was to be searched. When the saddle was cut open, the letter was discovered just as foretold and pored over at leisure back inside the inn, while the messenger, who had no idea of his saddle's contents, was allowed to go on his way. Nor did any shadow of doubt remain as Cromwell and his son-in-law read the incriminating document, which spoke of Charles' courting by both the army and the Scottish Presbyterians, and his apparent preference for the latter. He would, in effect, sell himself to the highest bidder, as convenience dictated and, by implication, abandon even them when opportunity afforded.

'Upon this,' Cromwell is said to have related, 'we took horse and went to Windsor; and finding we were not likely to have any favourable terms from the King, we immediately, from that time forward, resolved his ruin.' No date for the entire incident is given by Boyle, though it seems likely to have taken place after the army's headquarters had transferred to Windsor late in November, and before the agreement with the Scots had been made at Christmas. Certainly, its timing would help to explain Berkeley's chilly reception upon his own arrival at Windsor, and while the tale has its improbable elements – not the least of which is a beer-supping intervention by Cromwell himself on such an errand – it is by no means implausible in its essentials. Albeit in less melodramatic circumstances, various interceptions of royal correspondence were subsequently made by the Derby House Committee, which had assumed effective oversight of the king's incarceration, while an unnamed correspondent to the Earl of Lanark confirmed on 4 January that the queen had been furnished with news in Paris that the king was close to agreement with the Scottish commissioners – 'although she have no certainty thereof neither from the King nor any of your Lordshipes'.

But whatever the cause, the New Year began surely enough with the army and Parliament newly aligned in opposition to the king, and the 'Vote of No Addresses' firmly supported by both parties. Fairfax and the army's general council issued a declaration, in fact, openly endorsing the measure, and while Charles continued to take afternoon walks at Carisbrooke when weather permitted, there could be no doubt that the net was tightening ever closer around him. Now, of course, he was confined entirely to the castle, and the steady arrival of provisions and further servants merely confirmed that no end to his stay upon the island was imminent. 'They intend if it may be,' complained the Royalist *Mercurius Pragmaticus*, 'both to winter him and summer him there.' It was surely no mere oversight that when Vice-Admiral Rainsborough dined at Carisbrooke towards the end of January, he left without seeing the king. For, as Rainsborough's ships continued to prowl the Solent, the prisoner's isolation was now effectively complete.

9

'EXTRAORDINARY INCIDENTS' AND 'GUILELESS STRATEGEMS'

'The King's escape is designed. The manner thus; by one Napier and a servant of David Murray, whom we take to be the King's tailor. The King is to be drawn up out of his bed chamber into the room over it, the ceiling whereof is to be broke for that purpose; and then conveyed from one room to another, till he be past all the rooms, where any guards are at any doors or windows.'

The Derby House Committee to
Colonel Robert Hammond, 7 February 1648

It was no small irony that, as security tightened around the king, so Governor Hammond's anxieties increased accordingly. Indeed, even his family, which had been, like many, so sorely divided by the war, was newly intent, it seems, upon adding to his troubles. His grandfather had been doctor to James I, and for the last two years his uncle Henry had remained Charles' favourite chaplain, notwithstanding the fact that he had been mainly barred from the royal household. But another uncle, Thomas, would be among those who sat in judgement upon Charles in 1649, and now his cousin, William Temple, made his own personal gesture of opposition to the Governor's current role as overseer of the king's imprisonment. For after visiting the Isle of Wight in early 1648 and obtaining a personal audience with the royal prisoner, Temple saw fit to use his diamond ring to etch a Biblical curse, obviously directed at Hammond, upon the window of a local inn. 'Haman was hanged on the gallows he had prepared for Mordecai', ran the allusion to *Esther*, 7:10, which had been used by Royalist pamphleteers over the preceding months to bait the Governor. Plainly infuriating Hammond by his action, Temple was duly brought before his cousin and only released when his travelling companion, Dorothy Osborne, finally opted to take the blame upon herself.

Whether the vigour of Hammond's response reflected the more general pressure weighing down upon him is unknown, but there is little doubt that the respected field officer who had become Governor of Exeter in 1646 at the age of only 25 was now feeling the full burden of the pass to which his meteoric rise had brought him. Under growing pressure from Parliament's executive committee at Derby House, Hammond also found himself subject to a steady trickle of harassment from both Cromwell and, more especially still, Ireton. On 3 January, the former had asked his cousin through marriage to John Hampden's daughter to 'search out and let us know of any juggling [by the king]', while Ireton, Hammond's old field commander and now cousin-in-law, rebuked him for seeking 'ease and quiet' on the island, regardless of his proven battlefield valour and the growing possibility of a foreign attack on Carisbrooke. In some respects, Hammond's naive frankness may well have prompted the taunts, for he had already indicated that the king's removal from the island was 'the thing most desirable for me'. But while Cromwell was tactful, if terse, Ireton was prepared to enlist divine retribution in nailing Hammond to his task. 'Some of us think the king well with you,' the former had affirmed. For Ireton, however, Hammond's duties at Carisbrooke were nothing less than 'God's charge'.

The need for further troops and guns to make the castle safe now became paramount, therefore, as the prisoner's yearning to escape grew more and more acute with every passing day. In the meantime, the number of people willing to help the king indicated both the extent of royalism on the Isle of Wight and the prisoner's continued ability not only to inspire loyalty from those devoted to his cause, but to gain the sympathy of those entrusted with his confinement. Into the first category fell soldiers like Colonel William Hopkins and his son, George, who lived at Newport, as well as the nameless local sailor who would risk all, albeit vainly, to smuggle letters from the king to his wife and children. Sir John Bowring, too, who had become a clerk to the Privy Council at Oxford, had useful connections on the island, and had for some time been acting as a confidant and go-between.

But there were others like Captain Edward Cooke, one of the king's guards, who were won over by his dignity and stoicism in the face of growing adversity. Silius Titus, the royal equerry, had of course already been wooed and won at Holdenby, notwithstanding Parliament's trust in him, and there were also the other members of the king's household who represented, in effect, a Trojan horse, demanding constant vigilance on Hammond's behalf. On 11 January, they were listed in the endorsement of a petition submitted to Westminster for the payment of their salaries for the past year, and still numbered thirty-five. Titus, moreover, was still in place, along with Thomas Herbert, Patrick Maule, Francis Cresset, Abraham Dowcett and Henry Firebrace, as well as David Murray, tailor, and Uriah Babbington, the royal barber. Of those who had attended him at Newcastle, indeed, only Dr Wilson was now absent, while Mrs Wheeler, laundress, Mr Thornhill, Groom of the Great Chamber, Henry Murray, Groom of the Bedchamber, and five others had actually been added to the king's service. More curiously still perhaps, a Gentleman Usher named Richard Osborne, described by Clarendon as 'by extraction a gentleman', would soon arrive as an enemy spy, only to defect. Appointed to wait at the royal table and take care of the king's gloves during meals, Osborne would soon be conveying messages in the fingers of those self-same gloves.

Already, as early as 23 January, Hammond was informing the Derby House Committee that the agents of Ashburnham and Berkeley were at work, and his letter crossed with one, written by the committee three days earlier, to the effect 'that the King hath constant intelligence given him of all things, which he receives by the hands of a Woman that bringeth it to him, when she bringeth his cleane Linnen'. Stout-hearted Mrs Wheeler had plainly lost no time in showing her true colours, then, and she and her assistant, Mary, along with the old man who brought up the coals for their fires, were only three among many who were to persevere in the task of maintaining the king's lifeline to the outside world. On 7 February, moreover, Hammond was sent warning of an escape plan involving David Murray and one of the king's barbers, also named Murray. There were even hints from Cromwell himself in an undated letter to the Governor about the method of transport to be employed:

This intelligence was delivered this day viz. that Sir George Cartwright hath sent 3 boates from Jersey, and a Barque from

Sharbrowe [Cherbourg] under the name of Frenchmen, but are absolutely sent to bring the Kinge (if their plott can take effect from the
Isle of Wight to Jersey, one of which boates is returned back to Jersey
with newes, but it is kept very private).

It was hardly surprising, therefore, that Hammond should have
found himself under increasing pressure from London to make good
the manifest deficiencies in security. By 2 February, the gaps had
grown sufficiently for the Commons to order the preparation of new
instructions 'for preventing the Admitting of any Letters or Papers
to be brought to the king'. By 18 February, Hammond had been
granted what amounted to a free hand to purge the royal household,
though not, it seems, without compensation, since a Committee of
Revenue had been called upon 'to consider of and appoint a satisfaction to those servants ... that are now to be discharged'. He
was to choose 'such persons as shall attend the king not exceeding
the number of thirty' and 'from time to time to place and displace
such of them as he shall think fit', thereby preventing, presumably,
the kind of enduring links that Charles might be able to turn to his
advantage.

But while Maule, Murray and others found themselves excluded
and the royal household shrank to sixteen at the Governor's behest,
Herbert and, above all, Titus retained their roles. Indeed, in a letter to
the Speaker of the House of Commons, dated 2 February, Hammond
had already confirmed his decision that 'four gentleman of approved
integrity' – Herbert, Titus, Mildmay and Captain Preston – were 'constantly to attend the person of the King in their courses by two at a
time who are to be always in his presence, except when he retires into
his Bed Chamber', after which they were 'to repair the one to one door,
and there to the other, and there to continue until the king comes forth
again'. Their salaries, according to a Committee of Revenue report of
21 March, were to be fixed at £200 per annum, and their appointment
sealed, it seems, with the full approval of Fairfax, who, like Hammond,
was prepared to place implicit faith in the reliability of each and every
one. They had been described by a correspondent to the Earl of Lanark,
after all, as 'four of the severest', and both Preston and Mildmay, at least,
were soon making clear to Sir John Oglander that 'they would inform
both Parliament and Army agaynst me', should he now try to see
the king.

In the event, the rumoured escape attempt, which sparked the purge initially, had never materialised. No doubt rejected as impracticable, it had probably centred on the room above the royal bedchamber on the mezzanine storey, which communicated with all the others on that floor. But the subsequent loss of David Murray, the king's tailor, would prove a particularly heavy loss to bear, since the king's appearance was, of course, a crucial element in the maintenance not only of his regal status but his own self-assurance, and the Derby House Committee's accounts clearly imply that Murray had actually come to Carisbrooke for the express purpose of revamping the royal wardrobe. For, in an entry in the Exchequer Rolls, we find that on 16 December, the tailor had ordered a black velvet suit, cloak and cassock, along with a black satin suit and cloak lined with plush with gold and silver buttons. While a total of £1,635 9s 6d would in fact be supplied by Parliament for the king's garments throughout 1648, we hear nevertheless how Charles was 'most affected in sorrowful expressions' by Murray's departure – and by his barber Napier's too in all likelihood, since the same report from the *Moderate Intelligencer* on 3 March relates how he had by then become 'much overgrown with hair'.

Governor Hammond's first concern, meanwhile, was neither coif nor couture. On 12 January, his application to Parliament for the strengthening of Carisbrooke's defences was duly referred to the Committee for the Army, and on 25 January the same committee was authorised to spend up to £1,000 'for repairing some Places in Carisbrooke Castle, where his Majesty is, and some other places that are ruined and decayed'. Even this, however, seems to have been deemed inadequate by the Governor, for on 14 February, the Derby House Committee finally agreed to grant him a further £500 for fortification work, though not before he had also ensured an upgrading of the castle's artillery. Additional cannon had in fact already arrived by the end of January, but Hammond learnt of a number of brass guns left by Waller's artillery train at Poole in Dorset, and finding that twelve of these – two six-pounders, two sakers and eight three-pounders – were serviceable and not in use, the necessary steps were taken to acquire them, with the result that on 7 February, the Mayor and Governor of Poole were ordered by the Ordnance Committee to arrange for their transfer to the Isle of Wight.

There were steps, too, to increase the number of troops on the island. Early in January, for example, Hammond had called a council of war 'about settling and securing the island', and reinforcements had of course arrived in the wake of the Burley episode. But the Governor still found himself uncomfortably reliant on local levies of unproven experience or loyalty, and on 15 February, Parliament saw fit to approve their replacement by '200 of the most trustworthy soldiers, selected by Gen. Fairfax'. Henceforward, strict control of anyone entering the island could be maintained, while the prospect of any successful armed assault virtually vanished. Indeed, with force no longer even a remotely viable option, the king's only remaining weapons were guile, ingenuity and stealth. If ships and soldiers could not bring about his release, then friends, sympathisers and his own boldness were all he had left, and to this extent, as his captor well knew, the members of the king's household would prove crucial.

Nor, indeed, was confirmation of the warnings reaching Hammond about the royal laundry long in coming, for Mrs Wheeler's assistant Mary, who seems to have been related to her, was continuing to hide letters under the carpet of the king's bedchamber at those times that it was empty and unguarded. In response, Charles passed notes of his own like the one below, dated 31 January, containing messages and requesting favours:

> Mary/send this inclosed, to him, from whom you received that, w^ch
> I found yesterday under the Carpet: but there is a seruice of more
> importance, w^ch, I hope, you may doe me, that now, it being late, I
> cannot particularly tell you of: I could best doe it by word of mouth,
> but for too much notice; wch I leaue to your judgement, wherefore
> I fynde you not in my Bedchamber the morrow after dinner, I will
> wryte it to you as well as I can: CR.

After receiving the initial warning from Derby House on 20 January, along with a further one five days later, Hammond had nevertheless seen fit to let such correspondence continue, preferring for the time being merely to place a watch upon the two women. Yet nothing of significance transpired until the appearance off the island in mid-February of none other than Major Humphrey Bosvile, who had escaped from prison after his arrest at Holdenby, to resume his old trade. Travelling under the pseudonym of John Fox, Bosvile would come to achieve such a notoriety that by the following November, all army pickets had been issued a description of him, which spoke of a man 'of a midle stature' with 'not much haire on his face, the haire of his head a black browne long and falling flat downe, his cloathes sad coloured wth great gold buttons over them, a Freeze coat like a Countrey man upon that a Scarlate cloake'. But even by the time of his re-emergence at this juncture, he was already a marked man and dependent, therefore, upon a sailor from his ship to deliver a series of letters 'to a Gentlewoman in the Castle' – presumably Mrs Wheeler – 'or in her absence to Mistris Mary'.

The ploy had not, however, taken into account the anonymous sailor's apparent liking for alcohol. For, having over-indulged along the way, and only remembering the name of Mary, he made directly for the king's apartments instead of going to the servants' quarters, and in doing so found himself apprehended by guards. The messages, when opened, proved to be from none other than the king's wife and his children Elizabeth and James, who were still prisoners in England. Summaries of Henrietta Maria's, in particular, were soon circulating freely in contemporary news-sheets. According to one, she had told her husband that 'during the sad condition' in which he now found himself, 'nothing can bring more comfort to her, then to hear from him', but since she had heard nothing from him 'on the last returne of the dispatch, she feares that the Letters were intercepted'. 'After this,' the report concluded, 'she proceeds in her caballry and mystical lock of numbers, and I cannot heare of any Key that for the present hath Wards enough to unlock it.'

What this final encoded section of the queen's message communicated remains a mystery, but the packet of letters, of which it formed part, was nevertheless enough to ensure that any doubt concerning the activities of the king's laundrywomen had been banished once and for all. Even now, however, there appears to have been no immediate or wholesale clampdown, for while the *Moderate Intelligencer* reported on 25 February that Mary was 'yet in restraint', Charles' letters to her continued for at least a fortnight after her link to Major Bosvile was first exposed. On 13 February, for instance, he referred to her impending dismissal, and actually requested that she deliver another letter, probably to Jane Whorwood. 'I herewith send you the letter, wch I desired you (at your last being with me) to inclose within yours,' Charles wrote. At the same time, Charles even felt sufficiently at ease to suggest that she visit him before her final departure. 'Forgett not, when euer you are discharged,' he wrote, 'to see me, as you did last, before you go; & in the meane tyme, when you haue any thing to say to me, you shall be welcome.'

The king's last known message to Mary was penned on 26 February, and once more reflects the apparent indulgence with which her misdemeanours had been treated by the authorities. 'Since I see,' Charles began, 'that what I wrote last time came safe to your hands, by the satisfactory Answer which I haue receaued from you; I cannot but wryte yet more freely to you.' There followed instructions that Mary should proceed to London, though she was not to go 'before I might speak with you'. Beforehand, too, she was to arrange a meeting with one of the Governor's maids –'she that you think to haue most credit with him' – and 'seeme to her as if you were sory for what you had done'. Thereafter, 'in recompence', Mary was to offer herself, in effect, as a double agent to the Governor, promising faithfully 'nether to giue any letters to me, nor receaue any from me (wch you shall punctually performe) but that you will giue him a true account how you fynde me inclyned: & that you dout not, but to doe him good seruice heerein, so that I may know nothing, but that you come by stelth to receaue my Comands for London'.

Even as Hammond was procuring money, men and guns for Carisbrooke's defence, therefore, he was still apparently treading carefully with regard to the royal household. Indeed, whether from an ongoing residue of sympathy for the king's predicament or unease at the political alternatives posed by his superiors, he was continuing to confine himself to an awkward amalgam of partially effective and token measures. For Bosvile had not been the only individual still involved in smuggling letters to the king, as a letter from a correspondent to the Earl of Lanark – probably none other than Francis Cresset, another of the king's servants – makes clear:

C___ to the Earl of Lanark, Feb. 23, 1648.
If Oudart and Bosvile were not escaped beyond seas, the one into Holland, the other France, they would hardly have escaped hanging here, Oudart having delivered letters to the Duke of York, persuading him to attempt an escape, and Bosvile having received his answer, which was intercepted at Kairesbrook Castle, with severall other letters from the Queen and others.

Born in Brabant in the Low Countries, Nicholas Oudart was, in fact, a lifelong servant of the crown, who had fled to France after the capture of Oxford, and continued to send him reports written with invisible lemon-juice ink. Now, however, he too was obviously broadening his activities, notwithstanding the fact that he was later damned by Sir Edward Nicholas, his employer, as one who 'gettes his desires' through 'obsequious eye service' rather than 'sufficiency or integrity'.

As the self-assurance of men like Oudart and Bosvile grew, more-over, their efforts even developed an element of mockery towards the king's captors, none of which was better demonstrated than by a batch of letters discovered in February. For the packet itself was laughingly addressed to Captain Anthony Mildmay, one of Hammond's quartet of trusted 'conservators' guarding the king, and almost certainly the most loyal Parliamentarian of all: the brother, indeed, of Sir Henry Mildmay, who had taken a leading role in the trial and sentence of Captain Burley at Winchester. Placed under direct suspicion in spite of his complete innocence, he wrote to Sir Henry on 29 February, acknowledging the mischief done against him, and accepting that this was unlikely to be the last assault of its kind. 'You may very well conceive,' he reflected, 'that the malignant party will stil be practising against me, to make me suspected by the Parliament and their Army, hoping to remove me by that means: all other ways they practised.'

Under such circumstances, as Charles balked at his close con-finement and Hammond bristled at the king's ongoing attempts to undermine his best efforts, it was hardly surprising that tensions should have surfaced between the two men. In mid-January, Charles had formally complained to the Governor about his treatment, ques-tioning whether he was now in fact a prisoner and, if so, by whose command. But in the aftermath of the purge of the royal household, an exchange was recorded by Clarendon, which clearly betrayed a new level of antagonism. For as Charles succumbed to the kind of outburst that typically overcame him when he found himself impotent against overwhelming odds, Hammond plainly had difficulty in restraining his own temper. In the king's case, after all, words were by now his only weapons, while for Hammond, who was clearly a man of hard facts and cast-iron realities, the verbal onslaught to which he was petulantly subjected seemed to evoke the muffled irritation of a parent faced with a recalcitrant child.

'Why do you use me thus?' asked the king, in obvious quest of an opportunity to deliver a regal dressing-down after the dismissal of his servants. 'Did you not engage your honour you would take no advan-tage from thence against me?'

'I said nothing,' replied Hammond, apparently forgetting the vague promise he had given earlier regarding Ashburnham and Berkeley.

'You are an equivocating gentleman', came the smarting response, made all the more significant by virtue of the fact that it was probably the closest that Charles had ever come to directly calling any adversary a liar. 'You pretend for [religious] liberty', he continued, but had nevertheless expelled the royal chaplains. When Hammond refused to elaborate upon his decision, the king complained further that he was being treated 'neither like a gentleman nor a Christian'.

Moreover, even the Governor's attempt to break off the discussion before any further deterioration occurred proved unsuccessful. 'I'll speak to you when you are in better terms,' came his reply, only to find Charles unwilling to be parried. 'I have slept well,' he retorted in an effort to imply that he was not the one in the bad mood. When Hammond affirmed that he the king had been treated 'very civilly', Charles' position remained unyielding. 'Why do you not do so now then?' he countered.

Nor, it seems, was this the final attempt by the king to have the last word, though when Hammond, verging on fury himself, accused him of being 'too high', Charles descended into a lame play upon the Governor's words that betrayed his own unease at pressing matters further. If he really was 'too high', as Hammond suggested, then this, replied Charles, was merely 'my shoe-maker's fault' by making the soles of his shoes too thick.

Met with silence, and duly chastened, all that followed was a final pallid plea. 'Shall I have liberty to go about to take the air?'

'No,' replied Hammond, 'I cannot grant it.'

Henceforth, the king would be perceived by his captor more and more as a vexation than a trust: a petty irritant, refusing to accept realities and continuing to demand the kind of respect that he was incapable of earning by personal example. While Hammond would remain respectful and on occasion continue his attempts to save Charles from himself, any hint of divided loyalties that might have been apparent earlier disappeared steadily. The ongoing game of cat and mouse, combined with the king's unending requests for better everyday treatment, made such a reaction all the more inevitable, of course, as even the royal laundry now became an ongoing bone of contention. For although a replacement was found for Mrs Wheeler, Charles remained dissatisfied. 'Whilst I have been here among them, I have wanted linen,' he complained to Sir Philip Warwick in March, though according to the Royalist *Mercurius Elencticus*, the Governor's response was, if anything, decreasingly sympathetic, as he pointed out that the king 'could prevent his fowling so much linen by debarring His walking' and even added tartly how he himself 'wore but two shirts a week', which he considered 'enough for any honest man'.

In fairness to Hammond, of course, many a jailer might well have proved altogether less accommodating – especially so in light of the ongoing subterfuge surrounding his prisoner. For if the royal household had been reduced in size, it was ever more plainly rife with those intent upon deceit. Mary's main assistant in the transit of letters to and from the king had, for example, been Abraham Dowcett, and Dowcett's ongoing involvement in aiding the flow of royal correspondence is confirmed by surviving copies of nine letters – which were made by his friend James Jennings, carpenter to Charles II, and later by Philip Harcourt – along with another twenty that seem to have been burnt by him when he was made a prisoner in May 1648. Anxious by temperament and far from well-suited to cloak-and-dagger dealings of the kind now required of him, Dowcett would seek constant reassurance from the king himself, though his continual misgivings never ultimately overcame him. 'Be confident th^t I will be as carefull as you cane be,' Charles reassured him on 13 January, 'for y^r discovery will prejudice me as much as You, nor will I needlessly employ you in this Kynde.' Six days later, the message was the same. 'Let not Cautiousness beget feare,' Dowcett was urged, '& be confident of me.'

Nor was it surprising that Charles should have taken such trouble to guarantee his servant's continued assistance, for amongst his other duties, it was the task of the Page of the Bedchamber to supervise the king's meals and be present when they were served, allowing for the creation of a system of coded communication, one example of which Charles himself described in Letter VII when Mary was still active at Carisbrooke:

Nor do I urge an Answer to this, but by Sygne: that is to say, your right hand bare, for the recipt of this; then if the last Packett you had from me: which was indeed of importance and haste: went away upon Monday: let fall your handkerchief: if since (for I am confident it is gone) let fall one of your gloves: besides, when you have given this Packett to B. [Mary], tell me newes of fresh Sparagos from

London: and if she tells you that she will be able to observe my directions; then tell me news of Artichokes.

Even after Mary's removal, moreover, Charles still found himself in a
position to leave messages for Dowcett in the royal bedchamber. 'I shall
not blame you,' he wrote in one of his later letters, 'though you hazard
not to fetch this, untill I be gone to Bowles: which is at that hower
every day as I conceive you may come heither without much danger.'
Letters for the queen, meanwhile, were to be forwarded by Dowcett's
wife, who lived at Windsor. 'Deliver the bigger of these two unto your
wife,' Charles instructed in Letter V, 'it is for France, I neede say no
more, you know to whom.' On another occasion, Dowcett's wife
herself wrote to the king without signing her name, implying, albeit
erroneously, that her husband was about to be discharged. For although
he had fallen under increasing suspicion, he would in fact continue in
place for some months – no doubt fearing all the time his imminent
discovery and bearing the brunt, it seems, of the king's determination
to give no hint of proximity to his reluctant messenger, since Charles
had decided, as an added precaution, to behave especially icily towards
him, warning how 'you must not take it ill that I look sowerly upon
you in publick'.
Yet Dowcett remained only one of numerous helpers to the king,
both within and without the castle. Captain Silius Titus, for example,
who had joined the king at Newcastle as his equerry and now acted
as one of the four conservators supervising him, had come over to his
side entirely and enjoyed his complete confidence. Born about 1623
in Bushey, Hertfordshire, Titus was educated at Christchurch, Oxford,
before becoming a student in the Inner Temple and joining the
Parliamentary army at the outbreak of war. But he, like others before
and after, found their viewpoints altered upon personal acquaintance
with the king and experiencing the political upheaval to which he
alone appeared the antidote. Indeed, Titus' conversion to the Royalist
cause would not only place him at the centre of the king's forthcoming
escape attempts, but see him ultimately at Charles II's side at the Battle
of Worcester, and make him the author in 1657 of the celebrated pamphlet, 'Killing no Murder', which not only advocated Oliver Cromwell's
assassination but allegedly left the Lord Protector so gloomy and suspicious thereafter that he rarely slept two nights in the same bed. Such
was Titus' eventual reputation, in fact, that upon his appointment as

one of the grooms of the bedchamber after the Restoration, the new king publicly recorded:

> [T]hat in the years 1646, 1647, and 1648, he was by our royal father intrusted in his affairs of the greatest importance, both in relation to his restitution and in order to escape out of the captivity in which he was held by the rebels, for which he was charged by them with high treason, and forced to fly beyond the seas.

Other, more minor, figures like John Burroughs, Gentleman Harbinger and Clerk of the Spicery, were likewise mentioned by Charles in the fifteen surviving messages that he sent to Titus, and Richard Osborne was another, as we have seen, who played his part on the king's behalf. Educated by Lord Wharton and recommended by him to Hammond, Osborne enjoyed, in fact, the Governor's wholehearted trust, but could not, it seems, resist the king's dignity and kindness, and played an important role in maintaining communication with Royalist sympathisers in London, among whom were: Dr Frazer, former physician to the Prince of Wales; a certain London merchant named Low; and Dr John Barwick, who is said to have shared a weekly letter with the king through Francis Cresset. All had useful connections, and all, it seems, were trusted implicitly. However, another of the king's messengers, the Postmaster Thomas Witherings, 'proved faulty', keeping Hammond informed of conspiratorial activity, while Low was certainly not without his limitations, as Clarendon makes clear, describing him as a 'a man intelligent enough of the spirit' and 'very conversant with the nobility and gentry about the town', but nevertheless 'of so voluble a tongue, and so everlasting a talker, and so undertaking and vain, that no sober man could be imposed upon by him'.

More worrying still was the faith placed by the king in Lady Lucy Carlisle, second daughter of Henry Percy, Earl of Northumberland, and widow of James Hay, 1st Earl of Carlisle. A woman of great beauty and wit, but an arch-intriguer nevertheless, and as heartless as she was cunning, she attached herself to all parties in turn and remained loyal to none. She was an intimate friend of the queen, but betrayed her secrets freely, and after the death of her admirer, Strafford, felt no compunction in attaching herself to John Pym and other opponents of the king. Thereafter, she gnawed deep into the councils of the little party of aristocratic Presbyterians who had taken up arms against the king, only to become anxious later to preserve the monarchy and agree terms with him. Seen by Charles as a useful channel to these self-same enemies, the good lady did not hesitate, nonetheless, to pass his ciphered letters on to the Derby House Committee. 'She has been,' wrote Sir Edward Nicholas, 'through the whole story of his Majesty's misfortunes a very pernicious instrument, and she will assuredly discover all things to her gang of Presbyterians who have ever betrayed all to the ruling rebels.'

Altogether more reliable, by contrast, was Catherine Howard, Lady d'Aubigny, though she too was said by Clarendon to be not only a 'woman of very great wit', but 'most trusted and conversant in those intrigues which at that time could be best managed and carried on by ladies, who with less jealousy could be seen in all companies'. She was the daughter of the Earl of Suffolk and widow of George, Lord d'Aubigny, third son of the Duke of Lennox, who was killed at Edgehill. She had already suffered in the king's cause, coming to Oxford in 1643 with a pass and the consent of Parliament to transact the affairs of her own fortune in person. At the same time, however, she had been asked to convey a small, mysterious packet with great secrecy to London and deliver it to the person who should call for it. Though she did not know it, the lady was actually carrying – concealed in her hair, it seems – the Commission of Array containing the king's authority to arm the citizens of London against the rebels, and when Parliament discovered her mission, she was duly imprisoned before escaping and once again taking up service to the king.

Armed with supporters like these, and notwithstanding the treachery of Lady Carlisle and a handful of others, the king was able to maintain a steady, if restricted, flow of contact with the outside world. But it was one servant in particular, 'honest Harry Firebrace', who now came to assume ever-increasing prominence in Charles' secret activities. The 28-year-old Page of the Bedchamber, who had joined the king's household at Newcastle, was another convert to the Royalist cause who remained totally unsuspected by Parliament, bringing with him from Hampton Court such oddly assorted documents as an official pass from the Speaker of the House of Commons and letters from various sympathetic contacts. But, as security at Carisbrooke tightened, Firebrace, like the assistant laundress Mary, began delivering letters to the king's bedchamber – in 'a very convenient and private place' – while it was empty during the day. Later, while assisting Charles in his preparations for sleep, Firebrace was able to relate where the secret messages were hidden, before collecting answers next day when the king was at prayer.

Nor, as the following section of his *Narrative* relates, were such activities curtailed by the appointment of the four conservators in January:

> At length I found favour in the eyes of those appointed by Colonel Hammond to be Conservators, whose office it was by turns to wait at the King's two dores of his Bedchamber by Day, when his Majestie was there and to lodge their by night, their Beds being layd close to the Dores; so that they could not open until the Beds were removed.
>
> The King constantly went into his Bedchamber so soon as he had supped, shutting the Dores to him. I offered my services to one of the Conservators to wait at the Dore opening into the Backstayre whilst he went to supper, I pretending not to sup; which he accepted of, by which meanes I had freedom of speaking with his Majestie, none being on that side but myself, with which his Majestie was very well pleased, directing me to get that liberty so often as I could, which I procured very frequently.
>
> Then, lest we might be surprised by anyone, too soddenly rushing into the Bedchamber, and so discover the Bedchamber door open (for so it was that we might hear each other the better) I made a slit or chink through the wall, behind the Hanging; which served as well as the opening of the door and was more safe; for upon the least noyse, by letting fall the Hanging all was well.

By such simple means, Firebrace was able to pass on all news entering the castle, and more importantly still communicate plans for an escape attempt, which he himself now hatched.

Once again, the scheme for liberating the king had all the merits of simplicity and was based on the fact that Hammond had placed no sentries in the base court of the castle. If, therefore, the king could extricate himself through his bedchamber window, there would be limited difficulty on a suitably dark night in reaching the great wall on the south side. A reference to a plan made in 1741 shows, indeed, that the ground later occupied by a garden enclosed by a wall was then not only a largely deserted space but served by a ramp affording comparatively easy access to the wall at any point. As such, the only major obstacle, aside from the narrowness of the king's bedchamber window, was the drop of some 12–15ft from the castle parapet to the ground outside, which while falling steeply into the surrounding ditch, nevertheless sloped more gently on its opposite bank. Beyond this lay only the last remnant of the Elizabethan fortifications beyond the curtain wall: a sunken 'covered way', involving a descent of 9ft that could be conveniently negotiated with the assistance of no more than two waiting sympathisers.

In the time-honoured manner, Firebrace was to stand beneath the king's window on the designated night – Monday, 20 March – and provide a signal by tossing something against it, at which point the king would squeeze through and lower himself by a cord given him for that purpose, in order to pass with Firebrace across the court to the great wall. There the page intended to lower him by another cord – this time with a stick fastened to the end for the king to sit upon – after which, matters were to rest with Richard Osborne and his accomplice, the 27-year-old Edward Worsley, who would journey from his home in Gatcombe, 1½ miles away, to wait in silence under cover of darkness. They were to furnish the king with a good horse, riding boots and a pistol, and conduct him to 'a convenient place' on the sea, some 10 miles away, where the ever-willing John Newland would be ready with 'a lusty boat' to carry the royal passenger to Edward Alford's house at Arundel, after which he would make his way to Queenborough in Kent and a waiting ship.

'Every one,' Firebrace recorded, 'was well instructed in his part.' In preparation for his own role in the coming adventure, the king, who had lately been keeping to his room, was once again seen walking around the castle – sometimes two or three times a day – especially around the battlements, where he was shown the point on the curtain wall at which he was to be lowered, and also the location at which he was to surmount the outer wall. Ambling at leisure, apparently aimlessly, Charles was revelling no doubt in the ignorance of his captors, and grew in confidence as the feasibility of the plan became more and more evident: so much so, apparently, that he could not contain either his optimism or, for that matter, the secret itself. For on 7 March, an unknown correspondent, possibly Dr Frazer, was able to pen the following message to an unnamed recipient who, if not the treacherous Lady Carlisle herself, was likely to have been the Earl of Lanark:

Before this comes to your hands *the King will have attempted his escape* (not that hazardous way you may probably have heard of, because it was knowne to some of *your correspondents here*) but by the *assistance of some nowe about him* (and as he *writs*) with great probability of *success*; but till ye here the successe you may please *keep it private*.

Concealing his identity under the signature '349' and producing the italicised words in cipher, the author had nevertheless not only breached security himself but proven conclusively that one of those directly involved in the escape attempt had been guilty of a grievous indiscretion.

Furthermore, another letter of the same date, this time by a correspondent signing himself '409', made its way to the Earl of Lanark, providing additional confirmation that the secrecy so crucial to any escape of this kind had been dangerously compromised. 'I doubt not if designe faile not,' the message ran, 'he will make his escape and be with you before you can hope it. Soe well have I order'd the business that nothing but himselfe can lett it.' It was not without significance, of course, that the message cited the king as the only potential weak link in the scheme, but it was more significant still that the same correspondent was almost certainly another outsider who had been let in on the secret. For although this letter has usually been attributed to Firebrace, its author had sent another message to the king from London on 1 February, when Firebrace was almost certainly well away from the capital. Even more conclusively, the letter of 1 February contains at least one sentence of personal detail that would suggest it was written by another party, almost certainly of significantly higher rank. 'I had another [letter],' it relates, 'which I delivered to your wife concerning my Father.'

In all probability, then, it was the king who had let slip the vital information, for the Derby House Committee was soon aware of developments – most likely from Scottish sources – and writing the following message to Hammond on 13 March:

We have received information, that there are some designs in agitation concerning the King's escape, who is to be carried into France; and that there are two of those, that now attend the King, upon whom they rely for effecting the escape. Who they are we cannot discover, nor yet what grounds they have to expect their service in it; yet we thought it to give you this advertisement, that you might the more carefully watch against it.

Ironically, however, it was neither Charles' indiscretion nor Hammond's pre-knowledge that eventually foiled the king's first escape attempt from Carisbrooke. Instead, it was nothing more complicated than the narrowness of the bedchamber window that the escapee would have to exit at the very outset of his venture. From the remains of the original mullions, it can be seen that the casements were of the same width as the existing ones – about 15in. But a central bar, of which we can still see the evidence by a hole in the sill that has since been filled with cement, reduced the available space to no more than 7in. Only the king's own insistence, in fact, had convinced Firebrace to accept his assurance that he had already tested the aperture by passing his head through, as well as the further claim that where the head could pass, so too could the body.

With characteristic common sense, the page had continued to doubt at first, and proposed a way to make the opening 'a little wider by cutting the plate the casement shut to at the bottome, which then might have been easily put by'. Precisely what Firebrace meant by this is unclear, though it would appear that he intended that the side of the frame in which the casement fitted should be cut, slightly increasing the width between the bar and the mullion. Since the frame itself was iron, this would have necessitated the use of a file, which Firebrace considered feasible, but the king did not, since the whole process would increase his chances of discovery unnecessarily. Not only could he pass through, Charles insisted, he would pass through in entirely the way he predicted, and the mastermind of the escape attempt was, in consequence, not only overruled but 'commanded' to prepare 'all things else' according to the blueprint already laid down. He would have to bow to royal edict, suppress his misgivings and make his way, as arranged, on the fateful, pitch black night of Monday, 20 March, to the designated spot beneath the king's window.

So dark was it, in fact, that Firebrace could see nothing of what was passing above him, but, as his *Narrative* makes clear, it was soon apparent from the king's stifled groans that the very first obstacle to his escape was also to be the last:

In the middle of these hopes, I gave the Signe, at the appointed tyme. His Majesty put himself forward; but then too late found himself mistaken; he sticking fast between his breast and shoulders, and not able to get forwards or backwards; but at that instant, before he endeavoured to come out, he mistrusted, and tyed a piece of his cord to the bar of the window within. By means whereof he forced himself back. Whilst he struck I heard him groane, but could not come to help him: which (you may imagine) was no small affliction to me.

Ultimately, Charles would inform Firebrace that his 'designe was broken' by setting a candle in his window, though there remained no hint in the page's account of the intense frustration he must undoubtedly have experienced at his master's ineptitude. 'If this unfortunate impediment had not happened,' he reflected, 'his Majestie had then most certainly made a good escape.' Yet all that remained for him was to make his way to the appointed place on the castle wall where Osborne and Worsley were keeping their bleak and hazardous vigil, to inform them of what had transpired.

'Now,' Firebrace's account continues, 'I was in paine, how to give notice to those without, which I could find no better way to do, than by flinging stones from the High Wall, where I should have let down the King, to the place where they stayed.' Plainly, to have hailed the two men at 40 yards' distance from the curtain wall was not an option, but though Firebrace could not see his assistants, the expedient seems nevertheless to have 'proved effectual'. For the eerie jingle of harness, receding into the darkness, made clear that they were moving off, leaving his plans in ruin, and he himself, potentially at least, sorely compromised by the evening's activities. He would certainly have to cover his trail carefully upon his return to the castle, and, more importantly still, hope against hope that Hammond, on heightened alert as he was, would discover no trace of evidence that could confirm what had passed.

To Firebrace's infinite relief, however, there was actually 'never any discovery' of the abortive escape of 20 March. Indeed, Osborne was able to return unsuspected to his duties as Gentleman Usher and messages were sent to Legge and Ashburnham, as well as Newland. But within the week, rumours of an escape attempt were circulating in newsletters, and it was even reported that Colonel Hammond had uncovered two of the participants who were now in custody. 'Mention should be made here,' ran one report on 25 March, 'of an attempt to get the King's Majesty from Carisbrooke, which its said was in design, but taken before the form of it could be drawn forth.' Another report quoted a letter sent from Carisbrooke the following day, suggesting that one of those involved 'hath confessed that there was a design to carry away the King, which Collonell Hammond hath examined, and found out two of the actors in the businesse, which are now in custody'. This latter revelation, moreover, was borne out by a letter to the Earl of Lanark, dated 28 March, from an unknown correspondent signing himself '624:123:', which noted that Francis Cresset had in fact been 'discovered by indiscretion and removed, and the business more than suspected'. It was finally confirmed by a letter written by the Governor himself to the Speaker on 22 April, which made direct reference to the departure of 'Mr Cresset, the late Treasurer ... which is now more than five weeks'.

Nor was there any doubt that the authorities were equally keenly aware of the ongoing subterfuge within the king's household. Firebrace, for instance, mentions how 'a letter came from Derby House to Hammond to direct him to have a careful eye on those about the king, for that they discovered there were some who gave him intelligence'. A further letter from Oliver Cromwell to Hammond, dated 6 April, mentions 'a very considerable person of Parliament' who 'saith that Captain Titus and some others are not to be trusted'. Firebrace, too, is directly mentioned as 'the gentleman that came out of the window' on the night of the escape attempt – the precise date of which was also cited – and there is a further reference to Cresset and John Burroughs. All had been frustrated in their efforts on this occasion, but they were undaunted. For, as Cromwell's letter also makes clear, 'the same design is to be put into execution on the next dark nights'.

Judging by a letter from Charles to Firebrace on 8 April, in which he asks 'what is to become of T? (i.e. Burroughs)', some action beyond the expulsion of Cresset had in fact already been taken. Firebrace himself was certainly subject to intensive questioning, as his *Narrative* makes clear:

This was a general suspition, but they could point at nobody. Hammond got his engines to worke and did pumpe me, so as I heard he did others, but at last he tooke me into examination, and when he could make no discoverie he told me the reason.

I acquainted the King with all passages, at which he was much troubled, and told me that, if they had a suspition of me they would not leave till they had ruined me; and would have me gone with all his letters to the Prince (his Son our Sovereigne Lord and Master).

But I told his Majestie I was confident they could prove nothing against me; and therefore begged I might stay to see the issue, and that if the worst happened, they could but put me away: and then, I did not doubt but I should be able, some way or other to serve his Majestie.

Yet both he and Titus were allowed to remain in place until 28 and 25 April respectively, and more extraordinarily still, the chink in the wall by which Firebrace maintained contact with Charles remained in use. Henceforth, indeed, letters for the king's friends within the castle and dispatches to be sent to London were also placed inside it, as the creases from the tight folding of the surviving messages confirm. Incoming correspondence, too, was delivered in the same way, and if Titus' and Firebrace's days at Carisbrooke were numbered, Abraham Dowcett remained to continue in the underhand activities that came so uneasily to him. 'Tell F. [Dowcett] when he sees me pull downe the skirts of my Doublet,' runs one subsequent message from the king, 'then he is to look for something in the pocket.'

So for all the leaks and partial success in piercing the king's communication network, there was still an impunity of sorts surrounding his activities. Hammond and the Derby House Committee remained tantalisingly close to their goal, it was true, but the game of cat and mouse was still in play, thanks in no small part to the privileges still afforded the king by virtue of his regal status, and thanks, too, to the ongoing dedication and boldness of his inner circle, which even the king's own naivety and error-prone judgement could not, it seems, diminish. Far from taking his master's advice, Harry Firebrace and his colleagues remained in place, determined to 'see the issue' through while risking all in the process, and Firebrace in particular was already poised for further adventure. For even before the removal of Cresset around 24 March, he was planning the acquisition of 'some instrument' to remove the offending bar from the king's window that had frustrated his escape only four days earlier.

10

'SWEET JANE WHORWOOD'

'You may freely trust Whorwood in anything that concerns my service, for I have had perfect trial of her friendship to me. I cannot be more confident of any.'

King Charles I to William Hopkins, Master
of Newport Grammar School, 1648

By the early spring of 1648, the prior consolations of life at Carisbrooke had palled markedly. Indeed, as the king watched the rain, whipped by a south-westerly wind off the neighbouring downs, stream over the windows, bringing with it the fusty smell of damp stone, the full desolation of his circumstances became increasingly apparent. The royal coach, shipped so painstakingly from London some months earlier, now lay idle, and the furniture and library, brought from Hampton Court with equal care and consideration, had become little more than the lining of a royal cage. Deprived even of the consolation of his chaplains, the king had been in effect 'chaplain to himself' since December, and, with the continued absence of Ashburnham, Berkeley and Legge, came a creeping awareness that neither time nor the balance of political forces were working to his advantage as once they had done. Hitherto, he had been cushioned not only by his status as anointed king and the conviction that Parliament could not govern without him, but by the knowledge that his enemies were divided and the belief that he could escape whenever he chose. Now, however, the visible impatience of Hammond, the increasing traffic of couriers between London and Hammond's study and, worst of all, the sinister echoes from army headquarters betokening a new unanimity of purpose with Parliament confirmed that royal influence was more marginal than ever.

The feebleness of Charles' own escape attempt had been highlighted, moreover, by the brilliant execution of his son's removal from St James's Palace the following month. All three of the royal children remaining in England – James, Duke of York, Henry, Duke of Gloucester and the Princess Elizabeth – had been detained there in the care of the Earl of Northumberland. But on the evening of Friday, 21 April, agents of the émigré English court in Holland engineered the liberation the 14-year-old Duke of York with a simplicity, finesse and efficiency that could not have contrasted more starkly with the farce that had been played out at Charles' bedchamber window. Under cover of a game of hide and seek, the prince had made his way through an outer door in the palace's park, where Colonel Joseph Bamfield was waiting for him. After a brief stop at the house of a certain Anne Murray, where he was dressed in girl's clothes, James then made his way down the Thames with Bamfield in a skiff, to a boat bound for Holland.

The news of the prince's escape came, of course, as no small relief to his father. But in deepening his desire to be gone from Carisbrooke, it augmented his private sense of failure and pessimism. Calling his servants together not long afterwards to tell them that there was 'no remedy but patience', he also betrayed the same underlying sense of resignation to Abraham Dowcett. 'Servant,' he confided, 'you now see by Experience that my Condition is much wors then you thought it would have beene, but yet it is not so ill as I expect it will be.' Some small satisfaction, it is true, could be gleaned from a gentle goading of his captors. According to the *Mercurius Elencticus*, for instance, he did not forego the opportunity to remind Hammond that the king might one day have power of life and death over him. But this did not prevent the Governor from searching his prisoner's desk for secret papers in late April – an act wholly inconceivable only five or six weeks earlier. Walking in the grounds at a time when the weather suddenly turned chilly, Charles had dispatched Herbert to his room to fetch a cloak, with the result that Hammond was discovered red-handed, accompanied by John Reading, the Page of the Backstairs, who had presumably let him in. Far from embarrassing the Governor, however, this particular incident merely preceded a decision to move Charles to the north side of the castle, adjacent to the walls, and marked only the beginning of Hammond's more direct intervention in the king's everyday affairs, as he now spent hours outside the royal bedchamber in a personal vigil.

Why Hammond had conducted his search remains unclear, though Thomas Wagstaffe, one of the garrison, later revealed that concern had been raised by the king's habit of working late into the night, yet continuing to rise early. For this reason, we are told, 'they diligently serch'd his Chamber, after he was walked out one Morning, and in searching, one lifted up the Hangings, there they found pinn'd up, Sheet by Sheet, within the Hangings, next the Wall, many sheets of this Book'. The book concerned was purportedly *Eikon Basilike*, which Charles is thought by some to have been writing at this time. But, even if true, the object of Hammond's search is almost certain to have lain elsewhere, and Herbert's claim that the Governor was seeking 'some supposed papers of intelligence from the Queen and correspondency with others' is only marginally more convincing, for without any assistance from him, much of the royal correspondence was already being effectively intercepted.

In fact, the most plausible answer is probably supplied by Ashburnham's account, which centres upon the articles of agreement with the Scottish commissioners that Charles was suspected of retaining in his possession. Ashburnham, after being ordered away from the castle at the end of December, had already expressed doubts about the safety of the documents buried in the castle grounds in a lead container, and the Scots, too, had shared his misgivings. As a result, the compromising papers had finally been spirited away to Ashburnham, it seems, 'to provide for His and their security, by placeing them where they may rest concealed till some seasonable opportunity to make use of them'. But Hammond may also have got wind of Charles' own copy of the incriminating articles and attempted to intervene, albeit unsuccessfully, as Ashburnham confirmed some time afterwards. 'Verie happy it was,' he declared triumphantly, 'that His Majestie did send them to mee, for within Ten dayes His Cabinet was broken open, and search made for all his writeings, expressly ayming at those papers.'

In any event, the only recourse for Charles henceforth, it seemed, was the shelter of everyday routine and largely ineffectual musings upon the mechanics of escape. Although he refused the services of Parliamentary chaplains, and his subsequent appeals for a congregation for services according to the Prayer Book were turned down, he nevertheless began each day in private devotion, before spending the rest of the morning, if weather permitted, circuiting the castle with Hammond – usually some seven or eight times around the ¼-mile perimeter of the battlements – before retiring to his apartments to read and write letters. Though he was still prone to frustration and low spirits, there remained other consolations of a kind. Not least of all, Charles seems to have developed a new interest in food, notwithstanding the fact that his meals were reduced from twenty to sixteen courses in early March, as a result of economies. Food prices on the Isle of Wight were high, with corn selling at 10s 6d, according to Oglander, and the king's menu was to be curtailed accordingly. But he enjoyed his meals, and the catering itself remained suitably lavish.

Equally importantly, it was at table that the king became really animated, asking for news of events in various parts of the country, or, when the mood took him, talking 'of morality, and of passages of other kingdoms of old'. On one occasion, predictably enough, he initiated a discussion 'touching the prerogative of Kings, what divers had acted, and the successe thereof', though what followed was neither reverential nor even, for that matter, particularly reverent. For when some of Charles' attendants saw fit at last to air their own views, we hear that 'the discourse broke off with a merry jest'. Indeed, whenever talk at table became charged or heated, the king was always inclined to end it with a touch of humour, and a similar latitude was also extended above all to Hammond's chaplain, young Mr Troughton, who had just come down from university. Charles and Troughton spent many hours, in fact, debating theology – the latter holding forth with all the vigour of the undergraduate he had recently been, the older man exhibiting the kind of wisdom and self-certainty that was characteristic of the don his father had always wanted him to be. But while there was sniping and point-scoring on either side as the pair regularly strolled up and down the royal Presence Chamber after dinner, tussling with each other from prepared positions, at no point was Troughton intimidated or abruptly silenced for his impetuosity – apart, that is, from one occasion, in the middle of an intense exchange, when the king is said to have suddenly unsheathed the sword of one of the officers in the room, only to confer a knighthood on one of the attendants present.

Notwithstanding changes in Charles' physical appearance, which suggested that the prolonged strain was gradually taking its toll, he seems to have retained not only traces of his mordant wit, but even a dash of that schoolboy humour, which is often underestimated in character studies of the private man. With the dismissal of the royal barber at the end of February, the king refused the services of a Parliamentarian replacement and, in consequence, his hair, which was now thinly streaked with grey, grew so long that he was frequently compared to a hermit. But while he was prone to fits of moodiness, brought on by the prolonged bouts of introspection in which he now indulged more frequently, there were still occasional incidents to lighten the gloom. He was overcome by gales of laughter, for instance, when a visitor from London knelt with such enthusiasm to kiss his hand that he fell flat upon his face, and he exhibited hardly less glee when Colonel Hammond himself, accompanying him on one of their regular excursions around the castle, slipped on the damp battlements – a result, no doubt, of the continually miserable rainy weather – and made a similarly ungracious earthward descent.

Playfully interpreting the incident as a 'punishment' for the Governor's 'incivility' to William Hopkins' wife and his 'equivocating to me', there was little apparent malice in the king's amusement. Yet Herbert suggests that Hammond forfeited the king's good opinion of him 'by that uncomly Act' of searching his apartments, and Royalist propaganda was declaring by now that Charles was actually subject on occasion to physical intimidation at his captor's hands. One account, for example, related how Hammond 'in the dead of night came and knockt at his Majesties doore and when the King all amazed, demanded who was there, he told him it was he and he must come in'. When, moreover, 'his Majestie desired him to put of the business till the morrow', the Governor is said to have become insistent, as the rest of the account makes clear:

> [B]ut he replied he neither could nor would, and that if he opened not the doore, he would break it open, whereupon the meeke Prince presently arose, and casting his cloake about him, admitted him; being in he told him, he had an order from the Houses, to search his Cabinet for letters, whereupon his Majestie opening his Cabinet, took thence two letters, and left him to view the rest, which the Traytor perceiving, demanded them also, the king told him he should not have them, and with that word threw them into the fire; when Hammond indeavouring to gaine them, the King tript up his heeles, and laid him on the fire also, whereupon the villaine bauld out for aide, when presently came in a Ruffian and laid hands on the King

in such a rude manner, as he would have strangled him, and striving with him pusht his face upon the hilts of Hammonds sword, whereby it was extreamly bruised, and attempting him further, hit him also against the Pommell of a chaire, whereby his Majesties eye is black and blew, but maugre the utmost of the two devils, the letters were burnt, and Hammond rising up, threatened his Majestie in very approbrious language.

Lord Clarendon, it is true, considered the incident 'somewhat improbable', and Hammond himself vigorously repudiated the charges against him in an indignant letter to the Speaker dated 22 April:

> And considering the strange Reports which have been without the least ground, raised, and as I understand, still continued concerning my Barbarous usage of the King, it may not be unnecessary for me to say to you in my behalf, and I hope among all modest men, the commonsense of this so confident report will in this pleade my excuse, that I have, to the height of my power, given the King upon all occasions, all possible respects answerable to the duty I owe to his person, and the great trust you have pleased to repose in me, and truly, if otherwise, I should be more unworthy than those wicked men who raised this report would make me.

When it was suggested elsewhere, moreover, that the king had given Hammond 'a box on the ear' during the same incident and that the Governor had retaliated with blows of his own, there was even greater improbability involved. For, if Charles was perfectly capable of stretching his captor's patience, there was little to be gained from resorting to violence, and Hammond was far too calculating a character to play so easily into his enemies' hands. On 12 April, a Royalist pamphlet entitled 'The Fatal Blow' described how 'Gaoler Hammond' – 'notwithstanding his most solemn protestations unto his Majesty to treat him well' – had 'impiously and traitorously wounded' the king. But only a day later, it seems, the king was 'very merry at play' with Hammond upon a bowling green that the Governor had built especially for his recreation.

While Charles occasionally bemoaned inferior wine and found his bed linen not overly clean, every possible effort to cater for his comfort continued to be made in other areas. A miniature golf course, for example, was created for the king's entertainment within the outer defences of the castle, in one corner of which a little summer house was built where he could take shelter from the persistent rain, since the summer of 1648 would ultimately prove the wettest for decades. 'From Mayday till the 15th of September,' wrote Sir John Oglander, 'we had scarce three dry days together … His Majesty asked me whether that weather was usual in our Island. I told him that in this 40 years I never knew the like before.' But in spite of the elements, the new structure served its purpose more than adequately. Described somewhat extravagantly in one account as a 'banqueting house', Herbert probably hit the mark rather more accurately by deeming it 'a pretty shed … to rest in, & retyre when the weather was unseasonable', though by mid-July gilders and painters were being employed by Hammond to apply the finishing touches. The king was more than happy with the standard of workmanship, for as one newsletter reported:

> His Majesty often views the workmen, asketh some questions but seldom finds fault with any thing they doe, but saith, that such and such things are well.

From his summer house, too, Charles was able to watch the sea and the shipping, and take in the soft line of green hills which were not visible from his new room, while his bowling green, built at Hammond's specific command on the parade ground to the west of the castle, just inside the outer defences beyond the curtain wall, was considered 'scarce to be equalled'. Work began in February, and on 18 March a news-sheet reported how the 'Bowling Alley', which Charles once again inspected regularly during its construction, 'will be a gallant one when finished'. On 10 April, furthermore, the king was enjoying his first afternoon's play in the company of Thomas Herbert, Anthony Mildmay, Major Oliver Cromwell (a nephew of the lieutenant-general, who was in charge of one of the castle's infantry companies and had been appointed a Groom of the Bedchamber and Cupbearer to his Majesty in February) and indeed Hammond himself. Such was Charles' exuberance during the game, it seems, that, according to at least one hostile news-sheet, he was 'very free in his expressions with the Governour, and others', baiting his opponents in 'merrie discourse', and in particular expressing 'no good opinion of the Scottish nation'.

Credible or otherwise, the same report does, however, suggest that Charles' bowling green chatter was altogether more circumspect where his future political options were concerned:

When he discourses of the conditions and state of things, and what is or may be done, His Majesty speaks extraordinarily warily, and with a great deal of discretion, and still gives solid and well grounded reasons for what he speaks, and it is verily supposed His Majesty is in great hopes that he shall be admitted to come to His Parliament, for sometimes he expresses as much: Also it is thought, that this conceit of His is the cause that he is so much merrier than he formerly hath been. Also, His Majestie enquires much after the proceedings of the Parliament of Scotland, and seems greatly to mislike the Prevalencie of the Clergie under the Presbyteriall Government, as if they carried with them a more uncontrouled and unlimited jurisdiction, then was lately exercised by the Prelates of England.

That Charles should have said even this much in the company of a nephew of Oliver Cromwell and the man who was responsible for his captivity may be questionable, particularly when the specific source for the report remains unknown. But it was consistent with the king's general tendency to be both over-confident and over-talkative in high spirits, and to this extent retains a ring of truth.

More significantly still, it may bear out his underlying trust in the good intentions of the man who had made the game possible in the first place. Though he called down 'a pox' upon the Governor on one occasion, and wrote to William Hopkins on 21 August that 'the devil cannot outgoe him nether in Malice nor Cunning', he knew too that his jailer was a man under pressure: stricken by divided loyalties, averse to the shifty dealings of political negotiation and only inclined ultimately to do what his duty demanded. More soldier than diplomat, it was equally true that if Hammond had grown less sympathetic to the king's behaviour, he had nevertheless maintained his bearing – occasionally under no small provocation – and foregone the opportunity to exploit his position of potential dominance. For the army's Independents, indeed, he was 'not violent Inowgh', and if Royalists saw fit to denounce him as a 'hellhound', 'that baboon' and 'that ape-fac'd blood-monger', his actions consistently suggested otherwise.

Hammond, therefore, was an honourable man, worthy at the very least of the king's grudging respect, if not his gratitude. For ultimately the chasm between the two men concerned methods rather than principles, insofar that Charles would always maintain that the end justified the means in a way that Hammond could never accept. Unsure of his ground and out of place in a time of extreme political and religious passion, the Governor could, in fact, neither comprehend nor countenance the kind of double-dealing that came so naturally to his king, immersed as he was by background, rank and circumstance in tortuous ploys and subterfuge. It was this – and a war-weary soldier's wish for a final, honest settlement, perhaps – that explains Hammond's occasional bursts of irritability, though even he could appreciate ultimately that the king was not, in essence, a vindictive man. In the wake of his search of the royal bedchamber, for example, Hammond learnt how Herbert had raged against the page who had admitted him, only for the young man to be spared dismissal by the king himself who, 'of his goodness', was prepared to pass the matter by 'without either reproaching the Governour, or taking notice thereof'.

The king, in any case, seems to have been less preoccupied with baiting his captors than with his books, his writing and, to a lesser degree, the steady trickle of visitors who still came to him at Carisbrooke. For some still arrived to be touched for the 'King's Evil', others merely to gawk as God's anointed walked the battlements or played at bowls. The doggerel-poet John Taylor, for example, who visited the Isle of Wight during August, described several cases of the king's faith-healing activities, although one newsletter had predicted on 8 May that, with the hot weather coming on, general access to the king for this purpose might have to be stopped, in order to protect his own health. More pressing still in this regard, however, were the security concerns, which continued to nag the authorities. Early in July, for example, Lord Rich had received a permit to visit the king to be touched for 'the Evil', though Walter Frost, secretary of the Derby House Committee, wrote privately on 6 July to warn Hammond that Rich's real business was to consult the king about a Royalist rising in Surrey.

Yet in spite of his closer confinement since January, the single loophole of Charles' supposed healing powers still provided him with some direct access to his subjects. Hopeful sufferers continued, indeed, to make their way to Newport and the surrounding villages from various parts of the country with the intention of talking their way into

Carisbrooke by sheer importunity and waylaying him as he came down to a meal or took his exercise. It was no small irony either that, in his ambivalent position as king and prisoner, Charles now felt under an especially strong obligation to receive them, though not all his visitors were so welcome. Obadiah Sedgewick, for example, a ponderously earnest army chaplain, who had gained notoriety the year before by predicting the end of the world within the fortnight, not only gained access to the king but insisted that he read his recently published *Leaves on the Tree of Life*, droning on into the late hours about this 120-page exposition of a single, markedly abstruse verse of the bible. Only, in fact, when the king tactfully suggested that Sedgewick might benefit from some well-earned sleep did the chaplain finally retire to bed, fondly satisfied that his dogged exegesis of *Revelations* 22:2 had been well received.

Yet, notwithstanding the chaplain's dreary tome, Charles maintained his devotion to more uplifting reading of other kinds. Indeed, since his enemies had left him, as he freely admitted, 'but little of life, and onely the husk and shell', he maintained his spirits by reading widely and took special consolation, predictably perhaps, not only from the Bible, but from Bacon's *Advancement of Learning*, which he kept by him, and devotional works, such as Bishop Andrewes' *Sermons*, Richard Hooker's *Laws of Ecclesiastical Polity*, George Sandys' *Paraphrases on the Psalms of David* and George Herbert's *Divine Poems*. 'Dum spiro spero', he poignantly inscribed in a number of his books: 'While I breathe, I hope'. There were numerous other fly-leaf scribblings, including quotes from Claudian, relating to what Herbert described as 'the Levelling and Anti-monarchik spirits' which predominated at the time, as well as the following Latin distich, affirming that while it is easy to despise life in times of adversity, the man who acts bravely is also able to endure unhappiness:

Rebus in adversis facile est contemnare vitam:
Fortiter ille facit qui miser esse potest.

And there was lighter fare, too, including Spenser's *Fairie Queene*, Tasso's *Godfrey of Bulloigne*, Shakespeare's plays – which Charles annotated – and Sir John Harrington's translation of Ariosto's *Orlando Furioso*. Certainly, the king's library at Carisbrooke could not have been inconsiderable, for Herbert was placed in charge of his books, 'of which the king had a catalogue, and from time to time had brought unto him, such as he was pleased to call for'. A collection of 'Printed Bookes from London' appears to have arrived in mid-April, while Herbert seems to have drawn, too, upon Sir John Oglander's library at Nunwell, since there is a note of the purchase by him of four of Oglander's volumes. There were attempts on other occasions at translation on the king's behalf – of which he had always been fond – including *De Juramento* by Robert Sanderson, whom Parliament had just deprived of the Regius Professorship of Theology at Oxford. Plainly, if Charles could not help his supporters practically, he could at least recognise their sacrifices by the most effective token gestures available to him, which also included reading their propaganda – much of which continued to be smuggled into him, notwithstanding the creation in January 1648 of a Commons committee to suppress all 'unlicensed and scandalous pamphlets'. Usually measuring about 7in x 5in, contemporary news-sheets were a mass of closely printed text and Charles consumed them avidly whenever they came his way.

Whether Charles was actually responsible at this time for penning a full-scale book himself – the so-called *Eikon Basilike*, pages of which, as we have seen, were allegedly discovered by Hammond during a search of the king's apartments – remains open to dispute, however. Eventually published shortly after his death, the book became at once a lynchpin of Royalist propaganda, depicting the king, in effect, as a neotype of the crucified Christ – the princely proto-martyr, politically and morally innocent, cruelly butchered at the hands of his subjects. But as early as August 1649, no less a figure than John Milton was attributing authorship to a 'presumptuous priest' – most probably Dr John Gauden, Dean of Bocking and later Bishop of Exeter – who, in the poet's words, had sought to make 'his King his Bastard Issue Own'. Thenceforward the *Suspiria Regalia* ('Sighs of a King'), as it was originally known, became the seedbed of an ongoing controversy, which was compounded by the admission of Sir Thomas Herbert – who, it seems, first acquired the text – that he 'did not see the King write that book, his Majesty being always private when he writ, and those his servants never coming into the bed-chamber, when the King was private, until he called'.

Yet Herbert remained convinced that his royal master was responsible for the work – not least because the handwriting was 'so very like' what he had seen before – and, according to Thomas Wagstaffe, Hammond, too, provided further testimony connecting the king to it.

Going as usual to the king's room to announce that dinner was ready, it seems that the Governor found him writing on one occasion and lingered behind afterwards to snatch a glimpse of the page, the ink still being wet upon it. What he read was later recognisable as part of *Eikon Basilike* and quite possibly its final chapter, 'Meditations upon Death', which relates to this period of Charles' life. Mixing biblical and classical allusions with political theory, ecclesiastical history, lessons from antiquity and random musings upon Mary, Queen of Scots, the Gunpowder Plot and the Solemn League and Covenant, this particular section contains none of the prayers found elsewhere in the book. But it remains both resolute in affirming the justice of the king's stand – 'We measure not our Cause by our success, but our success by our Cause' – and ends with the hope that those 'whom perhaps ignorance without malice, or some error, less than fatal, hath for some time misled … may find the good grace to bethink themselves and recover'.

In all likelihood, the book was probably the result of joint authorship by both Charles and Gauden. The latter's wife, for example, recalled that sections of his work were at some point read out at Carisbrooke to the king, who 'did exceedingly approve of them' and then 'both corrected and heightened' the text. Charles had certainly been engaged in literary activity while imprisoned at Holdenby, for Major Huntington and other witnesses reported viewing several of his royal 'meditations'. It is known, too, that in 1647 the king also asked Bishop Juxon's help in finding someone to put his 'loose papers' into 'an exact method'. That person, it seems, was Gauden, who, according to his servant William Allen, 'sat up one whole night to transcribe' the king's manuscript before returning it to Carisbrooke, where it was eventually observed by Hammond in March 1648. Bearing on every page, what one nineteenth-century expert considered 'the peculiar stamp of Charles mind and habit of thought', the book provides ample testament, at the very least, to the king's self-image at this time of ordeal.

In imploring God to make his heir 'an Anchor, or Harbour rather, to these tossed and weather-beaten kingdoms', there is full recognition likewise on Charles' behalf that the current troubles have happened for a divinely ordained reason:

> Forgive, I beseech thee, my Personal, and my People's sins; which are so far mine, as I have not improved the power thou gavest me, to thy glory, and my subjects' good: Thou has now brought me from the

glory and freedom of a King, to be a Prisoner to my own Subjects:
Justify, O Lord, as to thy over-ruling hand, because in many things
I have rebelled against thee.

And there is the same ongoing emphasis upon dignity and decorum
in response to provocation that rarely eluded the king, and to which
he makes direct reference in the account of his treatment by the Scots
at Hull:

> [N]o disdain, or emotion of passion transported Me … to do or say
> anything, unbeseeming My self, or unsuitable to that temper, which,
> in greatest injuries, I think, best becomes a Christian, as coming near-
> est to the great example of Christ. And indeed, I desire always more
> to remember I am a Christian, than a King.

By identification with Job and King David, not to mention the crucified
Christ, Charles' image is, of course, carefully sculpted to emphasise his
heroic suffering 'under the colour of religion'. He is presented, indeed,
as a Protestant martyr, not unlike those described by John Foxe in his
Acts and Monuments, which the king read while in captivity. Even the
book's eventual frontispiece, for that matter, which depicted its author
as a humble, steadfast and triumphant imitator of Christ who cast aside
his crown to don a crown of thorns, was plainly intended, as one of
its critics put it, 'the better to stir up the People and vain beholders to
pity him'. For Milton, 'the conceited portraiture before his Book' had
been 'drawn out to the full measure of a Masquing Scene' with the sole
intention of inveigling 'fools and silly gazers'. Yet he too, of course, was a
practised polemicist of some years' standing, and his own *Eikonoklastes*,
written in response to the publication of *Eikon Basilike*, may well have
been a 'work assigned' by the Council of State, to which he had been
appointed around that time as 'Secretary of Foreign Tongues'.

In the event, Charles himself could not have imagined the future
impact of the text as he pondered it from his prison cell in the early
spring of 1648. At this juncture, in fact, he was spending more and
more of his time contemplating the past and considering the critical
events that had brought him to his present condition. On occasion he
explained, and sometimes excused, his actions, suggesting, for example, that if he had called Parliament to any place other than London
on the eve of the outbreak of war, the consequences might have been

quite different. Likewise, he was keen to affirm that when he left Whitehall, he had been driven by shame rather than fear, in order not 'to prostitute the Majestie of My Place and Person, the safetie of My Wife and Children'. He had passed the Triennial Act of 1641, on the other hand, as a 'gentle and seasonable Physick might, if well applied, prevent anie distempers from getting anie head'. When his wife left England, he confessed, it was not her going that hurt most, but the 'scandal of that necessity'.

As his horizons shrank at Carisbrooke, Charles continued, too, to dwell upon the Earl of Strafford's death some seven years earlier, always struggling with guilt and acknowledging his former servant's abilities, which 'might make a prince rather afraid than ashamed to emploie him in the greatest affairs of state'. In allowing his execution, Charles freely admitted, he had chosen what appeared to be the 'safe' rather than the 'just' course, and in doing so exhibited 'sinful frailtie'. But if he had made errors, there was at least the hope that his heir would not repeat them. To his eldest son, indeed, he wrote that his current reflections had been set down with the intention of helping him to remedy the king-dom's distempers and prevent their repetition. The fact that the Prince of Wales had experienced troubles while young might help him even-tually, just 'as trees set in winter then in warmth and serenitie of time' frequently benefit. Upon his accession, the young man should seek to be Charles 'le bon' rather than Charles the Great, discouraging factions, employing his prerogative equitably, and beginning and ending with God alone.

For his absent wife, meanwhile, the king appeared to display less agonising concern than previously. His promise to Prince Rupert in September 1647 that 'next my children (I saye, Next) I shall haue most care of you' might well be seen as a deliberate relegation of her in his affection – particularly when the added emphasis of the repetition and capitalisation of 'Next' is taken into account – and there was certainly little visible sign of the torment that had accompanied the earlier days of their separation. The comparative coolness was, moreover, mutual, it seems, for he now complained to Silius Titus that while others answered his letters, only Henrietta Maria's correspondence failed to reach him. It was 'ill lucke', he observed on 26 April, 'that my Wyfes letter should only miscarry, for I haue had answers to all the others, wch went by that Messenger'. Though the king acknowledged that her messages 'might be betrayd at the Post house', it is hard to ignore a hint of bitterness in his comment. Nor was this the only observation of its kind, for on 21 July, Charles tersely informed William Hopkins that 'the freshest Letter I have had from 40 [the queen] was of above 6 Weeks Date'. Of more interest to him, it seems, was the news that '50', i.e. Hammond, 'fell flat on his back, walking by me upon Wednesday last'.

Across the Channel, to her credit, the queen was continuing her fund-raising efforts in support of the Duke of Hamilton in vain anticipation of a Scottish rescue attempt on her husband's behalf. But her endeavours were dutiful rather than hopeful, and while Henry Jermyn remained a crutch and sustenance to her, there was no doubt about her straitened circumstances and more general wretchedness. When Madame de Motteville visited Henrietta Maria at her favourite Carmelite convent in the Faubourg St Jacques, where she had gone to pray for the safety of her eldest son, the transformation in her fortunes was apparent. Sitting in a little chamber, writing dispatches, she spoke at length of her anxieties and showed her visitor a small gold drinking-cup – the only valuable she had left. 'Her nights are more sad than usual,' reported one of the queen's remaining attendants, and by the time that Cardinal de Retz met her, she was poorer than ever, tending her 4-year-old daughter, unassisted, in a chilly bedchamber. 'I would not let the poor child rise today as we have no fire,' she told the cardinal.

Whether Charles was fully aware of his wife's predicament remains uncertain, in fact, but the considerable volume of his other correspondence at this time continues to beg the question why more letters were not composed for her benefit. As he admitted at one point to Silius Titus, there was 'no greater service' that could be rendered to the crown 'but to get a letter conveyed to my wife for me, and to take care that I may have the answer returned'. Yet, notwithstanding the continual risk of interception, it was not uncommon for the king to write twice a day to some individuals, and nothing like this scale of effort appears to have been dedicated to maintaining contact with the queen. For 1648 alone, indeed, 159 of his secret letters have survived, and since many of them were cover letters for packets of correspondence, and because Charles burnt all incoming messages and stopped keeping copies, his correspondence that year may well have run to almost 1,000 items. Through secret letters, of course, he was still able to play at the game of kingship, encouraging Royalist resistance and proposing rewards for his followers. But there were also attempts to encourage his children and declare his yearning for them, which were by this time notably absent from his dealings with his wife.

Nor can the king's inactivity in this regard be attributed wholly to fears of detection, for not only did such apprehensions fail to curb his other correspondence, he refused in the main to accept that his communications had been fundamentally compromised in the first place. 'I cannot think anyone so great a Devil as to betray me,' he declared with an almost touching naivety at the very time that Lady Carlisle and Mr Low were readily informing the Derby House Committee of his intentions. His faith in the efficacy of his ciphers and disguised handwriting, not to mention his 'letter boxes' in piles of laundry, spaces under the carpets or the back pockets of servants' breeches remained unwavering throughout. Plainly, the letters from his wife, if written, were not arriving as before, but, more curiously still, his own surviving comments suggest by and large that he was not unduly moved by this. Certainly, there was no impassioned effort on his part to overcome the breach himself or establish its cause. A reciprocal cooling, it must be assumed, had somehow occurred and the royal couple were accepting the fact with only occasional and somewhat pallid nods at their former ardour.

In Charles' case, however, the loss of such an important emotional prop had by no means extinguished his interest in at least one other member of her sex, since Jane Whorwood, who had already distinguished herself by tireless service to his cause, now assumed other duties which gave her altogether broader significance in the king's estimation. The daughter of William Ryder of Kingston-upon-Thames – a German-born Scot who had become a surveyor of James I's stables, and, after his death, stepdaughter of James Maxwell, Groom of the Bedchamber – she had married Brome Whorwood of Holton, Oxfordshire, in 1634 at the age of 19, and became well known during the Civil War in the Royalist capital at Oxford. Even before this time, in fact, her stepfather had brought her to court and acquainted her with the king. But it was her role as an underground messenger and, indeed, smuggler that had made her so invaluable initially. It was she, after all, who had smuggled gold bullion into Oxford hidden in barrels of soap, and she likewise who, at scarcely less personal risk, had consorted with William Lilly on her sovereign's behalf. Not only loyal and intrepid but ingenious too, she had been sent, as we have seen, to Hampton Court in late 1647 with half of the £1,000 in gold raised by

Thomas Adams, leader of the City of London's Royalists. Before then, Charles himself had shown no hesitation in entrusting to her care a casket of jewels at the time of his flight from Oxford, and rewarding her subsequently with no little influence for her trouble. Indeed, from a letter written by Sir Edward Nicholas Oudart on 18 February 1647, it would appear that her alleged lover, Sir Thomas Bendish, owed more to her efforts in obtaining his appointment as Ambassador of Constantinople than to the £3,000 he paid to William Murray for the same purpose.

'Had the rest done their parts as carefully as Whorwood,' wrote one of Charles' inner circle to the Earl of Lanark on 27 June 1648, 'the king had been at large.' But by this time, she was already on her way to becoming far more for her sovereign than a gifted secret agent. For in July, Jane was on the Isle of Wight, probably staying with the family of William Hopkins, with whom she soon became close friends, and on 26 July Charles wrote to 'Sweet Jane Whorwood' suggesting that she might circumvent the Derby House Committee rule that only those with their permission could visit him, by having Captain Mildmay invite her to his room. The captain, who slept across the king's chamber door each night to bar his escape, was in fact impervious to his prisoner's charms, and had even described him to his courtier brother, Henry, as 'the most perfidious man that ever lived'. But the intention was for Charles to gain access to Jane by entering Mildmay's room, as if by accident, when she was there. Plainly, the urge to see her was a compelling one, and it was hardly insignificant, too, that he signed this particular letter 'your most loving Charles'.

Among contemporaries, in fact, the term 'sweet' bore none of its modern-day connotations. No more, indeed, than the current use of 'dear' in letters was it intended to betoken any emotional significance. Clarendon and Berkeley, for example, used it to each other as friends, as did royal princes; and 'Sweet Saviour' was a commonplace in prayer. Before long, however, Charles was also describing himself as Jane's 'best Platonick Lover or Servant', and he would eventually send her at least sixteen messages over the next few months, meeting her in secret several more times in the process. In due course, he chaffed when she and Mrs Hopkins were unable to come and see him, and then yearned inordinately for their visits. Likewise, when Jane did not respond to his messages he became testy, and when she suffered some 'barbarity' at the hands of 'a pretended … gentleman', he sent her a 'consolatory letter', following it next day with another in the hope that it would bring 'her Contentment … for her's to me gave so much'.

At the start of August, meanwhile, he would beg her not to leave the island, and on 13 August delivered the following cryptic message to Hopkins:

> Tell N [Jane] when you give this enclosed to her that it is now the best caudle [medicinal broth] I can send her, but if she would have a better she must come to fetch it herself … her Platonick Way doth much spoil the taste in my mind and if she would leave me to my free Cookery, I should think to make her confess so herself.

The double entendre was manifest, and the reference to Jane's 'Platonick Way' smacked plainly of the kind of masqued courtly romancing that was commonplace for the day. 'Caudle', on the other hand, between two Scots, was a homely version of the French '*medecin*', which the king and his queen appear to have used earlier in reference to their sexual love. Though Jane never became the 'Sweet Heart' or 'Dear Heart' that Charles used in his letters to Henrietta Maria, and the 'eternally thine' that he employed with his wife plainly eclipsed the 'you' with which he addressed Jane, the evidence for a romantic link seems hard to deny. Jane too, for that matter, had written of her own need to 'satisfy desires', and by this time her marriage to the violently inclined and unfaithful Brome Whorwood had, it seems, already broken down irretrievably, making it wholly understandable that she should feel free to reciprocate the king's interest. Addressing him as 'my dear friend' and signing herself with the nom de plume 'Your Most affectionate Hellen', she had plainly established a special bond with her sovereign, amply demonstrated by the fact that, though she remained discretion personified, she was confident enough to ask William Hopkins on 13 November to 'present my affectionate love … to my dear friend 391'.

Charles' devotion to, and indeed dependence upon, his wife was, of course, widely acknowledged at the time. For many observers, it conformed admirably with the picture of the grave, dignified family man who had imposed his own brand of moral uprightness upon the profane and dissolute courtly world of his father. 'The face of the court was much changed in the change of the king,' wrote Lucy Hutchinson, 'for King Charles was temperate and chaste and serious, so that the fools and bawds, mimics and catamites of the former court grew out of fashion.' If such a hostile critic to the king on political and religious grounds could write so approvingly of his beneficial influence in at least this one area, it is not hard to appreciate how entrenched this perception had become. Though he openly acknowledged the king's indecisiveness, lack of enterprise and meanness, Clarendon, too, had no hesitation in perpetuating the notion that 'he could never endure any light or profane word with what sharpness of wit soever it was covered'. 'And though he was well pleased and delighted with reading verses upon any occasion,' he continued, 'no man durst bring him any thing that was profane or unclean.'

Where Charles' dealings with his wife were concerned, moreover, even his enemies appear to have accepted his reputation for 'goodness', though they seasoned it, too, with accusations of 'uxoriousness' that they levelled against him at every opportunity. As runt of the royal litter, Charles was, it seems, always vulnerable to accusations of undue dependence on women, dating back to a childhood in which governesses and nurses coddled the 'spindly small and stuttering' junior prince in Scotland in an effort to make up for a long-absent mother gone south to be queen in 1603. The French wife, whom the Royalist newsletter *Mercurius Britannicus* eulogised as 'our sovereign she-saint', was considered by less sympathetic observers to be nothing less than a ruthless, self-interested and unashamed exploiter of this particular weakness – someone whose unnatural primacy in the royal household scorned the patriarchal order.

Before his execution in 1649, Charles would ask his daughter to tell the queen that his thoughts had not strayed from her since their parting at Abingdon in 1644 as she left Oxford. There seems little reason to doubt that Henrietta Maria remained what might be termed her husband's 'fundamental option'. It was her miniature, after all, that he carried with him throughout his misfortunes, concealed in the Garter George he bore upon his breast. But there was, it seems, another side to this most private of men, who frowned upon duelling and gambling and had refused a court post to the Duke of Buckingham's brother, Kit, on the grounds that 'he would have no drunkards of his chamber'. Clarendon's claim, for example, that he disliked 'unclean' language can be countered by a number of instances where, as a young man, he had engaged quite lightly in vulgarity and sexual innuendo. In 1624, during the French marriage negotiations, Viscount Kensington had received a furious letter from Charles addressing him as 'Captaine

Cokescombe', and declaring that he 'would not caire a fart for [the] frendshippe' of the 'Moñsers' were it not for his respect for 'Madam' (Henrietta Maria). One year later, moreover, in a letter to the Duke of Buckingham, we find him employing his father's apparently affectionate, but obscene, term for the duke's wife, mother and sister. For James I these august ladies had been duly dubbed 'counts', i.e. 'cunts', and for his son the same term still applied, while just prior to his marriage, William Montague reported to the Earl of Carlisle in Paris how Charles was swearing how his wife-to-be 'shall haue no more powder till he powder her and blow her up himselfe'.

In their own right, of course, such fragments hardly shatter the traditional image of the king propagated so sedulously by his sympathisers and enshrined in *Eikon Basilike*. But there was talk, too, of sexual licence – and not always from wholly tainted sources. William Lilly, for instance, who was acquainted with Jane Whorwood, remarked in his *Observations on the Life and Death of King Charles I*, published in 1651, how Charles 'rarely frequented illicit beds' and 'prostituted his affections only to those of exquisite persons or parts'. 'As the queen well knew', Lilly went on, 'he rarely forgot' his marriage, and 'when he did wander it was with much caution or secrecy'. Sir Edward Peyton, in his turn, accused the king of courting 'a very great lady' at Oxford in 1643 during the queen's absence, after sending the lady's husband abroad – a charge which coincides curiously in some details with Jane Whorwood's whereabouts at the time and Brome Whorwood's trip to Holland and the Continent in that year. By this time, in fact, Brome had already embarked upon an affair with Katherine Mary Allen, a household servant, and made his journey in an effort, it seems, to avoid involvement in the war rather than at the king's direct behest. Indeed, Jane would much later testify to Chancery that her husband had absented herself from her 'beyond the seas' both 'wilfully and without cause'. But if she was not the object of the king's desire by then, someone else may well have been, and even so notable a commentator as John Milton would later come to relish the 'whispers in court of the king's bad actions ... polluted with Arcadias and romances'.

Certainly, there were grounds for a liaison of some kind on both Jane's and Charles' parts: she as a zealous devotee of the Crown, frustrated and slighted in her marriage, he as a lonely, increasingly careworn man, separated from a wife who, though still loved after a fashion, had nevertheless done more than enough over the years to weaken his fidelity. Though no known portrait of her exists, Jane Whorwood appears to have been a handsome enough woman in her own right, notwithstanding the 'pock holes in her face', which were mentioned by the Derby House Committee when they issued an otherwise favourable description of her in 1648. In the words of her pursuers, 38-year-old Jane was 'a tall, well-fashioned and well-languaged gentle-woman, with a round visage', and she was remembered equally for her flame-red hair, which, though an impediment in contemporary eyes, had nevertheless been one more feature allowing her to turn heads upon her arrival in a small city like Civil War Oxford.

Around that time, John Cleveland of the Oxford garrison wrote a tribute to ideal beauty, enitled *To Prince Rupert*, which contained references to a number of figures, all of whom were real, making the following lines, not altogether implausibly perhaps, particularly significant:

Such was the painter's brief for Venus' face,
Item, an eye from Jane, a lip from Grace.

But it was still, in any case, a woman's actions rather than her com-plexion that stood out as her real measure. Diana Maxwell, Jane's half-sister, who sat for Lely, the court painter, and was celebrated for her good looks, was remembered ultimately only for her greed, while Jane herself, victim of a violent husband and mother of four chil-dren, three of whom had died, was prepared to risk all in service to her principles, operating only 'through a lattice and enveloped in a mist', as the clergyman John Barwick, her fellow Royalist spy, put it. Nor would she be rewarded in the longer term for her efforts. 'My travels, the variety of accidents (and especially dangers) more become a Romance than a letter,' she wrote in 1648. Yet it was others, like Silius Titus, who eventually reaped the reward for their sacrifices on the king's behalf. 'I have ten times ventured my life in His Majesty's service when his affairs were desperate,' Titus later boasted, as promo-tion, financial rewards and a place in Parliament came his way. While Whorwood's namesake Jane Lane, who assisted the escape of Charles II after his defeat at Worcester in 1651, was lavished with a pension from the king and a valuable jewel from Parliament, for Charles I's would-be saviour there was only obscurity and the ongoing mistreat-ment of her husband to look forward to.

In 1657, indeed, two years before she finally achieved a formal separation, Jane Whorwood would be forced to leave home in fear of her life and under constant threats and taunts from the man who was demanding by then that she allow his mistress to reside within her house. Four years younger than his wife, Brome derided her as a 'jade', i.e a worn-out nag, and 'whore', and banned the local vicar, Albert Eales, from seeing her after taking a 'great distaste' to her refusal 'to let Katherine Allen live with in the house'. On one occasion, indeed, when Brome caught his wife going through their park to visit Eales' wife in labour, he 'took her against a tree', it seems, and 'hit and kneed her and banged her head'. Telling her at other times that 'she was old and her breath stinketh', he frequently 'did beat, kick and drag her and strike her', we hear, 'and did sometime batter and bruise and wound her, and did curse and threaten to kill her'. Servants at Holton would also testify before Chancery in 1659 how Brome and Allen had conceived 'a base child', and that he had told his wife how he 'would rather kiss Katherine Allen's arse than touch thee'.

Such behaviour was of long-standing and it was this, of course, that had made an extra-marital liaison – especially one conceived as a patriotic duty – so easy an option for Jane more than a decade earlier. But there is also much more than circumstantial evidence available to corroborate an intimate relationship between the king and his agent, and it is to be found in the two surviving letters that he wrote to her. Both, quite curiously, employ cipher almost throughout, indicating perhaps a more perilous intended route for them, but also indicating, alternatively, that Charles was particularly anxious to conceal their content from all but the intended reader. Certainly, the cipher itself is a relatively complex one, and though it was largely broken in the twentieth century, the deciphering process remained highly dependent upon context and conjecture based upon the likely initial letters of the words concerned. In essence, it involved the employment of single or double-digit numbers for individual letters, apparently assigned at random, and the application of at least two different numbers to every letter, so that the 24 letters of the early modern alphabet (i/j and u/v each being treated as one), together with various 'nulls', i.e. dummies designed to sow confusion, or blanks to serve as word spacings, are represented by numbers from 1 to 70. Similarly, two- or three-digit numbers are used to indicate specific whole words, syllables or proper names, rendering Charles, for example, '391' and Jane '390'.

On this basis, the first of Charles' two letters to Jane, dated Monday, 24 July, was until recently interpreted thus:

> Sweet 390, your two letters ... so to doe: Yet I imagen that there is one way possible that you may get answering from me (you must excuse my plaine expressions) which is to get acquaintance with the new woman (who you may trust for she now convaise all my letters) and by her meanes you may be convayed into the stoole room (which is within my bedchamber) while I am at dinner by which means I shall have 3 howers to embrace and nippe you (for every day after dinner I shut myself upp alone for so long) and while I go a walking she can relive you when however though this should prove impossible (as I hold it will not) yet I am sure this new woman can convay to me what letters you would giue her wherefore you must be acquainted with her.

The 'new woman' was, in fact, an illiterate serving woman who emptied Charles' toilet and had been enlisted by Hopkins to smuggle correspondence. Now, it seems, she was to be called upon to assist in servicing the king's broader physical needs. Quite how 'Sweet 390' was to be allowed entry to Carisbrooke in the first place remains puzzling, of course, given the Derby House Committee's suspicion of her activities, but once inside, her destination was clear: the royal 'stoole room', or lavatory, where she could be 'nipped' and 'embraced' at leisure over a three-hour period.

Likewise, the second of Charles' letters, written on 26 July, in which he proposes that he should intercept her, as if by accident, with a sudden entry into Captain Mildmay's apartments, also mentions his intention 'to get you alone in to my chamber', which was next door, and thereafter to 'smother Jane' with '407'. Whether '407' meant 'embraces', as has been suggested in some interpretations, remains uncertain. But that Charles desired to meet Jane alone in his room and smother her in something is no more in doubt than the way he chose to end the message: 'your most loving 391'. If the conclusion that a sexual liaison was involved is not actually inescapable, it seems more than merely plausible, and accords perfectly with the import of his message two days earlier, which appears itself to contain further material to confirm that not only was Charles intent upon a relationship with Jane that was far from 'Platonick', but prepared to express his urges with a coarseness that belies his prudish reputation.

The king's apparent decision to consort with Jane in his 'stoole room' adds in itself, of course, a less than romantic patina to his behaviour. But the most recent reinterpretation of his message of 24 July adds a whole new dimension, arguably, to the earthiness of his approach to courtship. Certainly, the passage 'you may get answering from me (you must excuse my plaine expressions)' is puzzling both in grammatical clumsiness, and in its reference to 'answering' as a 'plaine expression'. In fact, for 'answering' to be correct, Charles, we now know, would have had to make three separate errors in the cipher, which runs: '26:23:66:50:12:3:222'. Of these seven elements, 26 is twice used on other occasions by Jane Whorwood for 'a', while 66 is employed for 's', and 3 for 'u/v' (as opposed to 'r', which would be required in 'answering'). In its turn, 222 can be deduced to be '-ing', as it is used as a suffix to both 'wallk' [*sic*] in the message of 24 July, and 'do' in Charles' letter two days later. Perhaps more significantly, however, it now seems that 23 was used by both Jane and Charles as a separating device between words and sentences. If so, the word interpreted until recently as 'answering' – consisting, as it does, of the four elements 'a23:s50:12:uing' – must mean something else.

All hinges, then, upon the meaning of the numbers 50 and 12, both of which are employed not infrequently in the king's other correspondence. The former, in fact, can be confidently identified as 'w', and although 12 is more problematic, it was certainly used by Charles for the letter 'y' in both 'Mildmay' and 'conuay'. The result is a noteworthy reinterpretation of the opening sentence of the first of his surviving letters to Jane, which removes all ambiguity and rids us, too, of the other infelicities entailed by inserting the word 'answering'. For now the sentence reads: 'Yet I imagen that there is one way possible that you may get a *swyuing* from me (you must excuse my plaine expressions)'. And since 'swiving' has but one meaning in a seventeenth-century context, the term 'plaine expression' could not be more appropriate when used in association with it. Employed several times in Fletcher's translation of Martial's *Epigrams*, and more frequently still in the pornographic verses of John Wilmot, 2nd Earl of Rochester, it is the contemporary equivalent to the term 'fuck'.

Whether Charles succeeded in his intentions with Jane remains uncertain. His later references to 'her Platonick Way' might well suggest otherwise, of course, and there is no guarantee in any case that his plans to gain access to her were actually fulfilled. She was, after all, a well-known prime suspect for the Derby House Committee at a time when security around the king had already tightened considerably. Nor, likewise, does one prurient expression, or, arguably, even an extra-marital lapse serve entirely to negate our perceptions of Charles as an otherwise sober-minded and generally moral man. His apparent wish to 'swyve' his most loyal helper – in the royal 'stoole room' no less – stands in undeniable contrast to the saintly stereotypes associated with *Eikon Basilike* and heaped upon him by his supporters. Indeed, it might even suggest that beneath the regal posturing and platitudes, there was an all-too-human streak in his make-up, encompassing selfishness and exploitation, which was rather more in keeping with the suspicions of his enemies than the adulation of his admirers.

But the king's gentler, more winning side continued to shine through, and never more so, indeed, than around this time. For, although he was now showing his years, Charles had grown personally during his time in captivity, developing a capacity to give of himself, make friends and win the loyalty of individuals high and low. Over this trying period, indeed, he came to find much pleasure in the company of ordinary people, appreciating more keenly, perhaps, both his own humanity and the sacrifices they were prepared to endure on his behalf. Like his son Charles II, after the Battle of Worcester, or his great grandson Bonnie Prince Charlie after Culloden Moor, he came in adversity, it seems, to relate to his subjects more directly, not only tolerating a subtle relaxation of protocol but even encouraging a greater degree of informality in his relations. The dangers of his situation in the Scots army camp at Newcastle had induced the aristocrats Jack Ashburnham, Henry Jermyn and John Culpepper, writing from Paris, to address him with a freedom and urgency that at first took him aback. But not long afterwards, he was writing to humbler figures like Firebrace, Titus and Hopkins in what he termed his 'slow hand' – a neat secretary script rather than his normal italic – with remarkable ease, openness and consideration. 'All I have to say,' he informed Titus on Sunday, 14 May, 'is that I see you well satisfied with me, so I am you.' To emphasise the closeness of their bond, he did not hesitate to sign himself 'your most assured constant friend'.

Even servants and the wives of those who served him gradually became objects of concern, meriting personal gratitude and encouragement. When Mrs Dowcett, like her husband Abraham, was struggling with her anxieties, she too was consoled and told to be 'confident of me' and 'doubt not of my Carefullnes'. 'I shall observe your dayes, & not trouble you oftener, except upon very urgent occasion,' Charles continued, before mentioning his hope that the 'time will come that you shall thanke me for more than looking well upon you'. Likewise, as Mrs Wheeler, the king's laundress, went about her business, smuggling correspondence to the king, he did not hesitate to extend his personal thanks. 'I know,' he told her, 'that nothing will come amiss when it comes in thy hand.' The spouse of William Hopkins was also treated with a solicitude that Charles had rarely extended to the wives of his great officers of state, when he humoured her son who had taken offence at some unintended slight and reacted with the kind of surliness painfully characteristic of adolescents. 'As for yourself, be sure,' the king promised the whole Hopkins family, 'when I keep house again there will be those, who shall think themselves happy & yet sit lower at the table than you.'

Hopkins himself, indeed, would come to be treated as a trusted confidant and counsellor, notwithstanding his comparatively humble rank as headmaster of Newport Grammar School. A friend of Sir John Oglander, his royalism went back in fact to August 1642, when a Parliamentary mob had sacked his house for signing a Royalist manifesto, after which he had evidently been largely excluded from the civic life of the town, since his name appears only incidentally in the Corporation records. But he too would enjoy a special status in the king's affection, initially getting letters to the king by means of the illiterate serving woman he had procured to empty the king's stool pan, and it was from this modest beginning that Hopkins became another to achieve unimagined intimacy with his sovereign, receiving sixty-two letters between 2 July and 8 December 1648. 'I desire you,' Charles told him on 16 July, 'to make your Queries, or Objections, freely to me', adding in another message only the next day how 'I shall be in pain until you resolve me, because I shall be sorry to be the Occasion of the least inconvenience to you'.

It was manifestly a changing, if not changed, king: one who could enjoy a freedom of intercourse that had never been allowed in his former, more guarded days at court in London, and one, perhaps, more open than ever to the most intimate relations of all. For, though his fortunes had fallen, he was still king and retained the aphrodisiac of power. Never once, it is true, did Charles mention Jane to Henrietta Maria, even assuring her on one occasion that if his wife found out about their relationship, she would surely approve. But he was now 48 and had not seen the queen for four years, during which time the two had grown increasingly quarrelsome over a range of fundamental issues, as communications between them deteriorated. He was lonely and dispirited, confiding to Sir Philip Warwick that his best day-to-day companion at this time was the 'little old crumpling man' who made his fires. He longed, it seems, for the consolations of a woman's voice and a woman's sympathy at a time when he was faced imminently not only with the daunting prospect of another escape attempt but the consequences of both starting and losing a second civil war.

11

'A BUSINESS OF ACTION & NOT OF WORDS'

'Tomorrow I will begin to try the bar: & at night I will begin to give you some account of it.'

Charles I to Henry Firebrace, 23 April 1648

If earnest words were a measure of firm intentions, and the stirrings of a restless kingdom any guarantee of solid support, the spring of 1648 still bore certain signs of hope for Carisbrooke's royal prisoner. In the country at large, as high taxation, food shortages, censorship, sequestration and religious upheaval showed no prospect of abating, there was growing dissent. All the while, from the confines of his bedchamber, the king talked fervidly of escape. The vain attempt in March was casually dismissed and the factors which frustrated it conveniently downplayed. 'I pray you,' Charles wrote to Titus in early April, 'thinke wch way I shall remoue the Bar out of my Window, without noise and unperceaued; and what time it will take me to doe it.' Nor was it long before he himself had found the apparent solution and was urging Firebrace to acquire the necessary equipment. Last time, he wrote, 'the narrowness of the Window was the only impediment for my escape; & therefore ... some instrument must be had to remoue the bar; w^{ch}, I believe, is not hard to gett; for I have seene many, & so portable, that a man might put them in his Pocket.' This gadget – which he referred to as 'the endless screw' or 'the grat Force' – would, he ardently believed, be the key to his freedom. Guards, walls and ditches – no less, of course, than informers and the unwavering watchfulness of Governor Hammond – were to be lightly discarded, just as the subsequent success of his Scottish allies was to be taken as read. For the Scots, along with their Royalist English counterparts, would surely carry the day, as their king, freshly hatched from confinement, swept all before him to assume once more his rightful place upon the throne.

The architect of the previous scheme, meanwhile, had lost no time in concocting new plans. Indeed, immediately after his previous failure, Harry Firebrace had 'sent for Files and Aqua Fortis [nitric acid] from London' in an effort to make the king's passage through his barred window 'more easy'. His agent, as usual, was to be Jane Whorwood, working through the astrologer William Lilly, who not only set out to obtain the necessary acid but also, according to his own account, enlisted a certain G. Farmer – 'a most ingenious locksmith' who 'dwelt in Bow Lane' – 'to make me a saw to cut the iron bars in sunder'. Neither saw nor acid had arrived by mid-April, however, and as the urgency for action increased, so the king's misgivings grew. Writing to Titus on 10 April, he wondered 'whether I shall haue tyme anufe, after I have Supt & before I goe to Bed, to remoue the Bar; for if I had a forecer, I would make no question of it; but hauing nothing but fyles; I much dout that my tyme will be too scant'. The very next day, he was still preoccupied with the same issue, noting now that the bar would have to be cut in two places and worrying about the problem of hiding 'the leade that tyes the Glasse'. Still he bemoaned the lack of a forcer, though now he wondered whether a fire-shovel might be used instead.

By 12 April, meanwhile, Charles was sounding out Titus about the possibility of suborning his guards:

The difficultie of remouing the Bar, hath made my thoughts runne much upon the later Designe: it is this: since for my goeing out at Window, it is necessary that an officer or two be gained; will not they, as willingly, & may they not, more easily, helpe me out at the Dores? And truly in my judgement there can be nothing of lesse hazard then this last Desygne, if any one Officer can be ingaged in it; for then, any Disguyse will make me passe safly through all the Guards; wherefore I pray you thinke well upon it, for I am most confident that I am in the right; yet, for God's sake make your objections freely to what I haue said; or if you do not understand me, tell me in what, & I hope, that I shall satisfie you: howeuer, I pray you lett me haue your Opinion of this, as soone as you may, whether to be Pro, or Con: if this Desygne be resolued on, we need not stay for Darke Nights.

But the nagging doubts and constant pendulation continued, as he returned next day to the pitfalls of files, observing to Titus that 'I know not how fyling can be, without much noise, & time', before declaring that 'I absolutely conceaue this to be the best way'.

In this letter of 13 April, moreover, there was an almost touching reference to Charles' unerring conviction that 'no Cipher of myne hath miscarried', notwithstanding the fact that Cromwell's message to Hammond of one week earlier had specifically mentioned that 'there is Aqua Fortis gone down from London'. The king, it seems, had been prodigal too with secrets of other kinds, as the following extract from a letter to the Earl of Lanark, written by an unknown source on 11 April, makes all too clear:

I receaued a letter very latly from the King ... and I hope ane occasion will be afforded him to escape out of the Castle ... There are foure seruants about him, who are interested to designe and assist in this attempt. There is ane engyne made to pull out the barre of his chamber windowe and so to get out ouer the wall, hauing two gentlemen Islanders of his only to carey him away to his ship.

Worse still, Lilly too had been venting details of his secret mission to the locksmith in Bow Lane, so that within days the Derby House Committee was fully apprised of the details by one of its network of informers. Indeed, in a letter to Hammond of 15 April, the committee's secretary was able to specify not only methods but names and intended escape routes out of the castle. Firebrace, Titus and Burroughs were all mentioned – the last being 'either gone into Sussex, or about to go, to lie ready there at a place appointed' – and there was further reference to 'a boat of four oars', which was to be used to transport Charles from the island. Most striking of all, however, was the final passage, which confirmed once more how hopelessly the plan had been compromised:

The king hath a bodkin, with which he will raise the lead, in which the iron bar of the window stands, to put in the Aqua Fortis to eat out the iron. Then being got out, he will from the Bowling Alley cast himself over the works and so make his escape.

Henceforth, the plot could be monitored at leisure, and as the days ahead unfolded, a steady stream of intelligence flowed from London to Hammond's lodgings at Carisbrooke. 'There is yet a design for the King's escape,' Hammond was warned on 18 April. 'Whensoever he shall attempt it, he will be assisted by Harrington. Of the way we know nothing, nor have assurance, that this is true; but are only so informed.' There was also news at one point of another scheme 'to fire the Castle, by firing a great heap of charcoal that lies near the king's lodging', but it was Firebrace's scheme that particularly exercised the thoughts of the king's captors, and on 21 April, an altogether more detailed letter arrived in cipher from Westminster:

> The Aqua Fortis was spilt by way of accident; but yesterday, about 4 o'clock, a fat plain man carried to the King a hacker, which is an instrument made here, on purpose to make the King's two knives, which he hath by him, cut as saws. The time assigned is May Day at night for the King's escape; but it may be sooner, if opportunity serves. He intends to go first to a gentleman's house at Lewes, in Sussex, who is thought to be a Parliament man. The man, that brings this hacker and dispatches, will go to Newport; and on Saturday morning, or about that time, Dowcett, Harrington, or some confidee, will go out to the man, and bring in all to the King. Therefore, if some occasion be taken to search them, all will appear.

As altered information emerged, so it was passed on without delay, for within twenty-four hours another ciphered letter was supplying Hammond with further news on the movements of 'the fat plain man':

> We have now from the same hand, that the same fat plain man comes no farther than Portsmouth, and from thence sends over his business by some fisherman, or some other such person, which will be received from him by some of the persons above-mentioned.

Yet, as Charles himself continued to demur over the bar to his window, Firebrace opted for a simpler, cheekier escape plan, involving disguise, deception and the inattentiveness of Carisbrooke's guards. Exploiting the number of people still crowding into the castle to be touched for the 'King's Evil', it was proposed that a suitable volunteer might enter the castle among the throng of sufferers, dressed so strikingly that his image would be indelibly impressed upon the guards. Sporting 'a fals beard' and a perriwig, along with a white cap, 'a country gray, or blew coate, a pair of coullered fustian drawers to come over his breeches, white cloth stockings, great shooes' and 'an old broad hatt', the individual concerned would then be greeted loudly by Firebrace's servant, Henry Chapman, who would embrace him as a friend before taking him off for a drinking session within the castle, making sure throughout that his garishly attired guest was noticed by any soldiers on hand.

In the meantime, another outfit of identical clothes was to have been made ready in the king's bedroom for him to put on as soon as he had finished his supper. After waiting for a signal from Chapman that it was safe to leave his room once more – presumably with the connivance of one of the 'conservators' attending his door – the king was then to hide in a small room upstairs, which is likely to have been one of those in the Montacute Tower at the southern end of the great hall. From here, as the other visitors to the castle made their way to the main gate, the would-be escapee was to join Chapman, who was on friendly terms with the soldiers, and simply stroll through the walls to freedom, where horses had been saddled at some distance. With a trial run beforehand, which the king insisted upon, and the abandonment of the false beard, which was another bone of contention after his undignified scuttle from Oxford, all was expected to be plain sailing. Indeed, in a letter of 13 April, Charles informed Firebrace that he liked his 'new Desygne … extreamly well', regardless of the fact that Titus was 'not fully satisfied' with it: something that Firebrace was instructed to 'take no notice of'.

Once again, however, it was not long before the Derby House Committee caught wind of this plan too, and on 22 April, a ciphered letter warned Hammond of a porter:

> who useth to carry up coals for the King's chamber presently after dinner and supper, who is to carry the King a disguise, which the King is to put on, and also the porter's frock, and to lock the porter into his chamber, and come down himself, whilst the servants are at supper; and so pass away.

The porter concerned, though not mentioned by name, was almost certainly that self-same 'little crumpling old man' mentioned by Sir Philip Warwick, and it was his involvement, more than anything else, perhaps, that might have proved the final straw for Hammond. Plainly, the king's household was rotten with subterfuge on a scale that even he had failed to appreciate, and equally plainly, therefore, the prisoner would have to be moved to more secure accommodation in the north curtain wall, where he could be lodged next to the officers' quarters in another barred bedroom, 10ft from the ground, which was to be patrolled by sentries on the bank outside.

For the time being, however, neither guards nor bars were the main constraints upon the king, but the constant flow of information to his enemies, which was now becoming common knowledge within the royal circle itself. On 21 April, the Derby House Committee told Hammond that they had seen a letter from the king in which he had written 'that, although Firebrace and Titus be discovered, yet D. is fast to him, and will do the deed'. 'D', in the committee's view, was likely to be Dowcett, though Firebrace soon got news of the message which had been sent to Hammond, and only two days later was able to inform the king:

> You keepe intelligence with somebody that betrayes you, for ther is a letter of yours sent to the G [Governor]: from Derby House, (in Carracters) where in you expresse [in] words at length that though they do remove Titus, Dowcett and Firebrace, yet you dispair not of your busines (or to that purpose). Therefore pray think to whome you writ such a tie and be carefull God knowes what hurt this may do.

The result was a profession on Charles' part that while he could not actually recall writing such a letter, there was still a distinct possibility that his letters to the queen were being diverted to Derby House by 'the roague Witherings' at the Post House.

Thomas Witherings, who is commemorated today by a postage stamp issued in his honour, was in fact a merchant by background who had been appointed Postmaster of Foreign Mails by Charles in 1632 before establishing three years later what would become, in effect, the Royal Mail letter service after receiving instructions to 'settle a pacquet post between London and all parts of His Majesty's dominions, for the carrying and recarrying of his subjects letters'. It was to run 'day and night between Edinburgh and Scotland and the City of London', and establish post offices throughout the country, aided by the creation of six 'Great Roads'. Henceforward, Witherings had boasted, 'anie fight at sea, anie distress of His Majestie's ships (which God forbid), anie wrong offered by anie nation to anie of ye coastes of England or anie of His Majestie's forts … the newes will come sooner than thought'. It was this same service, employing staging posts at intervals of about 12 miles, that Hammond usually employed to send not only his own routine dispatches, but also those written non-clandestinely by the king.

Whether, of course, Witherings merited the king's suspicions remains unknown, and it was no small irony that he would be accused of Royalist sympathies in both 1649 and 1651, suffering imprisonment and loss of property, indeed, on the first occasion. But the king's distrust is well documented and also, for that matter, makes his readiness to dispatch his letters to Henrietta Maria by that means all the more curious, perhaps. For the bulk of his correspondence, he certainly employed his own secret couriers like Major Bosvile, who had nearly walked into Hammond's trap in February, and Thomas Brookes, whose regular route lay between the Isle of Wight and the English court in France. There was also, moreover, at least one other undercover courier – possibly the ubiquitous 'fat plain man' – who, according to the following Derby House letter of 22 April, was entrusted to pick up some letters from the king at Portsmouth and take them to Scotland:

If therefore you cannot intercept those letters in the Isle of Wight, if you can send a faithful man, confident and discreet, to Portsmouth, who may be there on Sunday night, and diligently observe and enquire for such a man, who hath also a horse under him worth £30 or £40 (the colour we know not) and continue there till Thursday, he will certainly find such a man coming out of the town with all the King's letters, whom he is to apprehend; and you are to send up all the said letters.

But the fact that their movements and contacts were so well known renders even Witherings' possible disloyalty largely irrelevant. On 4 May, for instance, the committee told Hammond that 'the messenger, who last came, was so hard put to it by our intelligence, and your vigilance, that he was forced to leave his sword and pistol behind him, and durst not bring his letters to town', though 'one Doctor Frazier met him about Windsor, and took the letters of him'. As if the indiscretions of the king, not to mention the shenanigans of Lady Carlisle and the treacherous Mr Low, were not enough, even those whose intentions could not be doubted were occasionally careless with their trust. Harry Firebrace, for example, sometimes confided injudiciously in the Earl of Lanark, and Richard Osborne, Gentleman Usher in Daily Waiting on the King, is known to have complained on one occasion how Mrs Wheeler was using unreliable couriers in her letters to him. Personal names, moreover, were represented in messages by a code of single letters that remained uniform to all the king's correspondents, and the complex numbering system for key words meant that, unless Charles himself was gifted with a truly phenomenal memory, he was having to keep a code key in his possession that was always liable to discovery.

Even more significant than the random indiscretions of the king and his circle, however, was the remorselessly watchful espionage network at the government's disposal. The replacement of the Committee of Both Kingdoms by the Derby House Committee, after the breach between the Scots and Parliament in January 1648, had led, amongst other things, to the creation of an altogether more elaborate security system, supervised by members of both Houses of Parliament, and Independents and Presbyterians alike. Henceforth, the committee would meet at 3 p.m. every day of the week, including Sundays, supplied continually by its secretary, Walter Frost, with an abundant stream of information from a varied array of anonymous agents, whose numbers were so considerable that their expense accounts would eventually become a serious financial issue. Mingling in streets, taverns, post-houses and army camps, these nameless figures were all too often disconcertingly well-informed, and almost certainly assisted in their activities by at least one informer from within Carisbrooke Castle itself, for the size of the royal household made it easy to infiltrate, and its day-to-day intimacy rendered secrets hard to conceal.

Yet, notwithstanding the king's removal to more secure accommodation, preparations for his second escape attempt continued to proceed steadily, so that on 13 April, Titus was asked 'to make good tryals and giue me good instructions', regarding the 'cheefe instrument' to be used in the venture: namely, one of the files that had already been smuggled to him. Charles still knew not, according to the message, how the filing could be done 'without much noise, & tyme', and Titus was to arrange, too, 'the prouyding of a Ship' to carry the escapee 'beyond the water', regardless of the fact 'that many of my frends thinkes London the fittest place'. The only other considerations, it seems, were matters of fine detail, for on 21 April, Firebrace was asked to provide his master with 'a paire of gray Stockings, to pull over my Bootehose, when tyme shall serve for our great Business'. Indeed, when Charles contacted Firebrace one day later, the stockings appeared to have become his main preoccupation. 'I haue the Aqua fortis,' he declared, 'but I can find no stockings, wherefore doe not forgett to give me them to Morrow.'

Plainly, the more serious business of breaching his window and reaching the castle walls was to be left mainly to the ingenuity of others, and it was for this reason that on or about 23 April, Firebrace penned the following message relating to the king's new accommodation:

In the backstaires window are two casements, in each two barrs, one of the barrs in that next the door shall be cutt, which will give you way enough to goe out I am certaine. The top of the hill comes within a yard of the casement, soe that you may easily step out and creep close to the wall, till you come to a hollow place (which you may observe as you walke tomorrow) where with ease you may go downe and so over the outworkes. If you like this way it shall be carryed on thus. Hen. C. [Chapman] shall cutt the barr and doe up the gap with wax or clay soe that it cannot be perceiv'd. I have already made it loose at the top, soe that when you intend your busines, you shall only pull it and t'will come forth, you must supp late and come up so soone as you have sup't, put of your Geo: and on your gray stockings, and upon notice to be given you by H.C. come into the backstaire and soe slip out, we shall meet you, and conduct you to your horses and from there to the boate. I have tould him of it and hee'l undertake it, therefore leave some of your files that he may try too morrow when you are at bowles. If you intend to try this way I think it not necessary to tell any of it beside Z [Worsley].

That Firebrace saw fit to add the last comment was no doubt further testament, of course, to his master's fatal proclivity to reveal his secrets, and there was more than a little irony in Charles' decision to repeat the self-same warning to Firebrace in his reply, which was left as usual in the chink used by both men for communication. 'Let none know of this way but only Z', he wrote in a less than convincing effort to maintain the appearance of directing events, adding the further order that Firebrace 'must be sure that horses be reddy on the other side of the water'.

By now, however, the king's indiscretions were beyond concealment, and the intensity of his denials served only as further proof, it seems, of that unhappy fact. In the aftermath of the Derby House Committee's message to Hammond, informing him of the interception of 'a letter in the king's hand' and citing Firebrace, Titus and Dowcett as his assistants in an escape plan, he had protested his innocence rather too loudly. 'As they tell it,' he declared to Titus, 'I will take my Oath it is a lye.' His profession to Firebrace had been nothing short of passionate. 'Be as confident of my discretion as honnesty,' he wrote, 'for I can justly brag that neither man nor woman ever suffered by my Tongue or Pen, for any secrett that I have ever been trusted withall.' The alleged letter, he claimed, had only been concocted in the first place 'to make the fair pretence' of dismissing Titus and Firebrace.

Yet the accuracy of the information now lodged at Derby House 'by an honest man' – probably Mr Low – who had allegedly read '4 or 5' of the king's letters, was beyond dispute, and the only remarkable consequence was that Firebrace and Titus continued to labour so diligently on his behalf when their own departure from Carisbrooke was by now imminent. Far from abandoning him, indeed, every effort was being made to expedite the king's escape in the limited time remaining, and all attention now focused upon the backstairs window that Charles would be able to access at night, with the collusion, he hoped, of pliable guards. At only a yard from the ground, as a result of the slope of the earth mound around the curtain wall, as opposed to the 10ft of the bedroom window, the advantages of this particular route were obvious even to the king himself, who now sent files to Firebrace in order that 'I may be sure not to stick'. Even the hazard of sentries on the bank outside might, it seemed, be surmounted by studying the rota of guards each night and bribing the most amenable.

Charles, in fact, seems to have taken a personal interest in identifying suitable candidates among the soldiery, and on 23 April sent the following message to Firebrace:

I hope this day at diner, you understood my lookes, for the souldier I towld you of, whose lookes I lyke, was then there, in a whyte Night-cap; &, as I thought you tooke notice of him.

And before long a payment of £100 had indeed been made by Dowcett to each of three soldiers on the understanding that they would turn a blind eye when the moment for action finally arrived. There was the prospect, too, of pardon for any officers that might assist, as Charles made clear to Titus, who was in overall charge of this particular aspect of the operation:

> Cap: Titus Let those Officers, you tould me of, know, that as my necessity is now greater than euer; so what seruice shall be done me now, must haue the first place in my thoughts, when euer I shall be in a Condition to requite my Frends, & pitty my Enemies: I comand you (when you can doe it, without hazard either to yourself or them) that you send me, in particular, the names of those who you thus finde sensible of their duty, & resolued to discharge the parts of true Englishmen; Lastly, asseure euery one, that, with me, present Seruices wipes out former faults.

But Titus' departure was actually to occur the very next day, and on 26 April, as Firebrace, too, finally received his marching orders, there was one last hasty exchange of notes all round. Firebrace, for instance, was urged to 'harten' Dowcett, whom Charles found 'somewhat feare-full in your absence', and there was a further request that he should take the opportunity to 'inquyre well, whether, or no, Witherings hath plaid the knave'. 'Exact Secresie', Charles urged, was to be maintained at all costs, and horses made ready on 'the othersyde of the Water ... for it were a wofull thing to loose an opportunitie heere, for falt of preparations there', while every effort was to be made to ensure that Osborne, who was remaining behind, 'rightly understand the Desygne of the Backestaires window, as lykewais that other of my window; that *I may leaue or chuse as I shall for occasion*'. Plainly, the king was even now maintaining some semblance of control over proceedings on the eve of the projected escape bid, for, as he informed Titus, 'we are hammering upon a way ... wch if it hit, we shall be sooner ready, then, it may be, you can imagen'.

Four messages were, in fact, sent to Titus on four consecutive days, and the 'promiscuous frequency' of Charles' letters says much about the man who wrote them, since writing gave the feeling of doing, as he himself half-admitted to Titus. 'I importune you with papers having little to say,' he confessed, as he fussed over detail and refused either to delegate or determine. Only Jane Whorwood, it seems, enjoyed his unalloyed confidence, though even she had tested his devotion by apparently 'applying herself' on his behalf to Lord Howard of Escrick who was soon to join the Derby House Committee. Asking Titus to reassure her that 'I am in no ways disgusted with anything I have heard concerning her', he assured him, too, of his confidence that Jane, who was now being referred to as '715' as well as 'N', 'will not deceive your trust'. Trust, as she herself confided, was at an especial premium at this time. 'I could wish I had an hour's discourse with you to discover the villainies I have lately met with,' she had informed Firebrace before urging him to 'take my counsel and act upon it'. 'None,' she declared, 'is worthy of that high trust but ourselves.'

By 27 April, however, the king had hidden in his bedchamber a surprisingly impressive escape kit, including files, nitric acid and the key to a new and difficult cipher devised by Firebrace himself. Though Dowcett and Osborne now remained his only reliable allies within the castle, preparations outside continued to proceed smoothly. Firebrace, for instance, was at first allowed to bide a few more days in Newport to arrange the forwarding of letters, while Titus took lodgings in Southampton and proceeded to arrange the relays of horses necessary for the king's escape. For the time being, according to Firebrace's account, the king 'did not want constant intelligence as before', but he continued nevertheless to pass out dispatches 'with the like good success as formerly', and John Newland was on standby, as before, with a small boat. Almost inevitably, moreover, on 30 April, Jane Whorwood appeared, as arranged, aboard a ship at Queenborough in the Isle of Sheppey, intent upon carrying Charles from the Medway to safety in Holland. Risking all as usual, she probably chartered the vessel in London, and now, like her counterparts, stood poised for what was set to be the ultimate triumph.

Yet on 2 May, as the last pieces of the plan clicked snugly into place, a courier from London was riding post-haste to Carisbrooke with a message from the Derby House Committee informing Governor Hammond of 'an intention to get the King away to-morrow at night or Thursday morning', since a ship 'is fallen down from hence to Queenborough, whereabouts she rides to waft him to Holland'. Nor was this all, for the dispatch also contained the following detail:

A merchant is gone from this town last night or this morning to acquaint the King that all things are ready: four horses lie in or near Portsmouth to carry the King by or near Arundell and from thence to Queenborough. A Parliament man or one that was one who liveth near Arundell, is to be the King's guide. The man is supposed to be Sir Edward Alford. The merchant that is come down to the King at Portsmouth is a lean spare young man. The place by which the King is to escape is a low room through a window, or a window that is but slightly made up. He hath one or two about him that are false.

Even alternative plans of escape, which may well have been discussed by Firebrace and Charles, were mentioned:

Have a special care of the King's bowling, lest he be suffered to escape under cover of bowling; which is the next plot. If this be prevented they will then have a ladder set up to the wall against the bowling alley and horses and a boat ready; and try that way.

As Parliament monitored the situation with increasing vigilance, so the king himself was struggling more and more with the window bars that had already, it seems, foiled a planned escape on 2 May and another on 4 May. As he reported to Firebrace, the space in his new window was no wider than that in his old bedchamber:

I have now made a perfect tryale, and find it impossible to be done, for my Boddy is too thicke for the bredthe of the Window; so that unless the midle Bar be taken away I cannot get through: I have also looked upon the other two, and fynde the one much too little, and the other so high that I know not how to reach it without a Lether [ladder]; besides I do not believe it so much wyder than the other, so that it will serve: wherefore it is absolutely impossible to doe any-thing tomorrow at Night: But I comand you harteley and particularly to thanke in my name A: C: F: Z: [Cresset, Legge, Dowcett, Worsley] and him who stayed for me beyond the workes; for their harty and industrious endeavours in this my service, the which I shall alwais rem[em]ber to their advantage; being lykewais confident that they will not faint in so good a worke; and therefore expect their further advyces herein.

It was Dowcett, in fact, who later testified that he had waited in vain 'almost three hours under the new platform', and, notwithstanding the impact on his already threadbare nerves, there had been further progress almost a fortnight later when, after a consultation with Osborne, the king wrote thus to Titus:

> Now as for our great businesse I desire you to begin to wait for me on Monday next and so after, every night for a week together, because one night may faile and accomplish it, being both trouble-some and dangerous to send often to you. And for the time here, you must know that it is my chamber window by which I must descend (the other being so watched) that it cannot be cut, wherefore I must first go to bed so that my time of coming from my chamber may be about eleven at night. For the rest, you with Worsley must compute how soon I can be with you … also where I shall take boat and where land, likewise you must give me a pass word that I may know my friends in the dark.

In the meantime, Jane Whorwood found herself stranded on board ship at Queenborough, still awaiting 'the good houre of meeting with our Friends', and apparently uninformed of the abortive escape attempts of 2 and 4 May, since she expressed 'griefe and wonder' that no one had yet come. Marking time in the tidal mudflats of Swale, she had become unwell either from a rogue oyster or the sea itself, and found herself cut off from the king's message by an outbreak of violence across Kent and in the fleet. But while Jane remained composed, the patience of her ship's captain, a certain J. Browne, was wearing increasingly thin. For he had already been arrested and imprisoned twice by town mayors at Hull and Northampton in 1647, and was understandably wary of a third confinement, if the following message, squeezed into a 6in square note before being countersigned by Jane and sent to Firebrace on 15 May, is any guide:

> We doe very much wonder y^t in all this weeke, wee haue heard nothing from yo^u; all ye time past, we haue been in readines to depart; but now lye under a contrary winde; & some suspicon hauing neglected a faire winde; therefore wee could not omitt to give yo^u notice y^t wee intend to remoue into Margarett (Margate) Roade, & therefore haue sent upp the bearer heerof, that if they bee not come out before this arriues yo^u, you may let them know itt, y^t soe they may come to the Reculuers, or Birchington where I shall not faile to meete them; but, in case they should bee come forth

before yo^u receiue this then I shall lye at one ferry comeing into this Isleland, & ye bearer att his return atte another, soe to prevent theire comeing hither & to guide them to ye other place. I haue nothing else but to intreat y^t yo^u faile not to send word punctually how y^r busines stands, & what speed hath been since their departure by this bearer who is faithfull & honest & will be heere too morrow night, and to remain.

The plan now, then, was that the fugitives should meet the ship at either the Reculvers or Birchington, which stood at respective distances of 9 and 4 miles from Margate, or alternatively at what is likely to have been Elmley Ferry, a spot connecting Sittingbourne with the Isle of Sheppey. Yet two days later, Browne's ship remained at Queenborough, and it was still there on Monday, 22 May, by which time it had already fallen under the suspicion of William Cooke, acting captain of the forty-two-gun *Henrietta* of the 'Thames and Medway guard', which had the task of guarding against smugglers of fullers earth, gunpowder, illegal oyster hauls and treasonable correspondence hidden in coal. Cooke, as luck would have it, was, like many in Kent and in his fleet, suffering from divided loyalties. Though he had served for more than forty years, he appears to have been amenable to turning a blind eye to what was plainly a nefarious enterprise.

Yet what Jane Whorwood referred to as 'our late contest with Captain Cooke' had demonstrated all too clearly the growing danger of delay. She was still sick, it seems, for the letter she wrote to Firebrace at this time was not only smudged and completed with a blunt quill, but written in lines that sloped uncharacteristically. The treacherous Mr Low had, it seems, once again been asking searching questions and encouraging her 'to sift' Firebrace, with the result she had been forced to trail a false scent in a letter to her husband, sent through Low's own courier, which she knew would be opened and read. 'I left a letter for [my] bedfellow sufficient to satisfy [Low]', she informed Firebrace, and although its contents are unknown, it is likely that she wrote to suggest that she was heading for Holland after a delay through sickness. But her message to Firebrace also contained another attempt to 'lay an importunity' on him 'of hastening on the business'. 'Pray make all the speed you can,' she urged, 'for I lie at very great charge and am in more discontents and fears through this prolongation.' However, she added too that he was to be confident, as ever, 'of no fail in N'.

The same, however, was not to prove true of the man upon whose liberty all efforts now centred, not to mention those assisting him within Carisbrooke itself. Charles had finally informed Titus on Monday, 22 May, in fact, that he would at last be ready two nights later, since the suborned sentries were set to be on duty at that time:

> As you haue advised, Wednesday next may be the first night I shall endeavour to escape; but I desyre you (if it be possible) before then to assure me that you will be ready by that night, and send me a pass word, wch you have not yet done.

And though the Derby House Committee was, as ever, closely on the trail, they remained uncertain at least of the precise date chosen for the attempt, as Walter Frost's letter to Hammond on 23 May makes clear:

> The design, of which I last wrote, still goes on. The ship lies in the Isle of Sheppy. I have again written to Col. Rainsborough of it. The time is to be Thursday, Friday or Saturday night next, if opportunity serve them right, or about the 4th of June: the ways as formerly resolved on, of which you have.

Nor did a rescheduling of the guard duty roster, whether by accident or design, represent any insurmountable problem in its own right, for although the three bribed soldiers found their sentry duty altered from Wednesday, 24 May, to Sunday, 28 May, they were all kept together, and as soon as the king heard of this he merely asked Titus to inform Jane Whorwood that he would now be arriving at the ship on 29 May. On all other fronts, in fact, the escape attempt seemed to be unfolding to plan, as Titus made ready his first relay of horses at Titchfield on Southampton Water, and a fishing boat took up position in 'a private creek' near Wootton Park. As the appointed hour arrived, moreover, Edward Worsley and Richard Osborne were waiting just beyond the castle's outworks with two horses, 'bridled and saddled', while just to the east of the castle, in a large marl pit, a further party of horsemen stood ready to conduct the king through Wootton Park on the first stage of his journey. The bar in the bedchamber window had, indeed, been eaten away by nitric acid – notwithstanding the fact that the first consignment from London had, as the Derby House Committee correctly reported at the time, been 'spilt by way of accident' – and

Abraham Dowcett was duly on hand, as arranged, to lower the king down from his bedroom window and guide him to the waiting horses. By the time Dowcett had led him to the waiting horses, the worst, it seemed, would already be over, though the route to Queenborough through Arundel, Lewes, Tonbridge and Maidstone was choked with soldiers from Fairfax's army.

All was set for midnight, and, as the king waited, the tension was palpable. Though he was well and had been playing bowls daily, he was continuing to betray signs of change and lassitude. 'Mr Herbert and Mr Harrington, his privy chamber men, are weary of their places,' reported *A Perfect Diurnall* on 22 May, 'for their duty is great.' Still Charles refused to cut his hair, though he had received a case of 'very dainty instruments' for the purpose, and by now it was very long. He had maintained, too, his ban upon incoming dispatches, feeling perhaps that the outside world had less good news than ill to offer. Whether, indeed, he had any inkling that failure at this juncture would mark the end of his escape efforts and initiate a steady decline into fatalism and resignation is unknown. But he had now been dogged by failure for many long months and the prospect of final frustration now was bound to drain his already limited resources of natural optimism further – especially if failure was spawned by betrayal of the kind that now occurred.

For it was at 11 or 11.30 p.m. that two of the three sentries involved in the plot went to Hammond's chief officer, Captain Rolph, and confessed. Only two days earlier, uneasy about the island's security, Hammond had requested that Rolph be promoted to the rank of major. There were still, after all, only two companies in the castle garrison, and the Governor clearly felt the need to spread some of the burden that fell upon him personally, particularly with news of mutiny in the fleet and rumours that some of its members had sailed away to join the Prince of Wales in Holland. Describing Rolph as 'an honest faithful and careful man' and one 'who taketh a great deal of pains, and deserveth encouragement', Hammond saw him, in fact, as the extra pair of eyes and ears that he needed so desperately. This opinion was fully vindicated when Rolph now 'dealt with' the bribed sentries and brought them before his superior without delay. The response, as Hammond made clear in his subsequent message to the Speaker, was to allow events to unfold and thereby apprehend as many of the culprits as possible in one fell swoop:

[T]he design had long been in hand, and kept from me until yester-
day when two of the soldiers who had been dealt with came to me
and acquainted me with the whole business (which I am confident,
though I had no knowledge of it, they would have had some difficulty in effecting); I suffered and advised them to carry it on as if I
had not known it, that so I might discover the whole business with
the less pretence of excuse to those unworthy men who were to assist
the King in this escape.

And though accounts of what followed are confused, it was a ploy that
worked to near perfection. One correspondent in the castle suggested
a final loss of nerve on Charles' part. 'The rope falling,' he wrote, 'the
Kinge attempted itt noe further.' According to Clarendon, however, the
king was actually leaving his window at midnight, when 'he discern'd
more Persons to stand thereabout than used to do, and thereupon suspected that there was some discovery made; and so shut the Window,
and retired to his bed'. More credible still is Hammond's own account,
which suggests a blunder on Dowcett's part that led to his arrest and
that of Floyd, the third sentry who had kept his engagement with
the king:

> But being over cautious in securing all places in more exact manner
> than formerly, Mr. Dowcett, by happening on an unusual guard, who
> at the first apprehended them to be of his own party, but upon exam-
> ination finding other answer than he expected, made a discovery,
> which so soon as I understood immediately I secured Dowcett and a
> soldier who was the chief instrument in this design.

As Dowcett was marched off to the guardroom, a pell-mell pursuit
of Worsley and Osborne now ensued, as a manuscript account drawn
up by the former, and later employed by George Hillier, makes clear.
Though 'they received unhurt', according to Hillier, from 'the fire
of a party of musketeers' that were 'supposed to have been placed in
ambush by Hammond himself', Worsley and Osborne finally reached
the waiting fishing boat only to find that 'the master refused to let them
embark', since they had come without the king. 'On this,' the account
continues, 'they were compelled to conceal themselves in the adjacent
woods for several days, and procure sustenance in the night by the assistance of a kinsman of Mr. Worsley, who eventually provided a vessel

to take them from the South side of the island.' The troopers who had first pursued them to the beach had seen their riderless horses and the retreating fishing boat, and wrongly assumed their quarry had got away. As Firebrace suggests in his *Narrative*, the pair would ultimately make their way to London, where he himself 'obscured and preserved them'.

In a volume of topographical notes collected in 1719, however, the author suggests that Charles himself may have had a luckier escape then either Clarendon or Hammond suggested. 'As the king was getting out,' the account states, 'a sentinel unluckily espied him, and fired and waked the watch, and so he was prevented; but the sentinel who fired was afterwards accidentally shot, no person can tell how.' Whether the account is wholly reliable remains more than a little doubtful, in fact. But Hillier suggests that a stone near the south porch of Carisbrooke Church formerly marked the burial place of a different sentry – none other than Floyd – who appears to have been shot for his efforts on the king's behalf. If so, he was the only individual to pay the ultimate price, for Titus made his way to London, and while John Newland was arrested upon his return to Newport, we nevertheless find his name mentioned subsequently in Carisbrooke's accounts in connection with the supply of biscuit and sea-coal for the castle garrison. Plainly, there was no suppressing the entrepreneurial instincts of a good businessman.

Jane Whorwood, by contrast, was still at Queenborough with the ship on 31 May when she wrote to Firebrace:

> I received on the 29th a note from W: [Titus] that he would that day be with mee (he and I faine would have understood the other partyes being at the despatch thereof at Tunbridge in Kent) but this faile thereof hath put me into great perplexities; pray send this enclosed away instantly; and informe mee of all occurrents in relation to our Mr. [Master] more particularly what you conceive to be the occasion of this delay. For longer than one week it will not be possible to abide here without manifest and impatible inconveniences.

However, it was not until 1 July that Charles finally wrote to Titus, asking him to tell Jane 'that I was and am very much grieved' that 'I did not wait on her according to my promise'. Thereafter, it seems, she was left to return to London to nurse her disappointment in the company of the little band of royal servants who now found themselves finally shorn of all options, as Governor Hammond savoured his victory. For his diligence in thwarting the king's plans, Parliament would eventually award Hammond £100, but in the immediate aftermath of the plot, he had entered the royal bedroom, offered his sovereign a bow and examined the window that had foiled his escape. Finding the window bar, in his own words, 'to be cut in two in the middle with aqua fortis', he shook his head in studied perplexity until Charles could stand the silence no longer. 'How now, Hammond,' Charles asked, 'what is the matter, what would you have?' 'May it please your Majesty,' came the reply, 'I am come to take my leave of you, for I hear you are going away.'

Yet the Governor's smugness still belied and may even have resulted in part from his own ongoing problems. The Isle of Wight, after all, as he himself reported, remained vulnerable, with 'only one ship guarding the island and that about to re-victual'. But it was accusations from Richard Osborne regarding Major Rolph that were soon marring the lustre on Hammond's recent triumph. For in a letter to his old patron Lord Wharton, dated 1 June, Osborne detailed incriminating conversations that he had allegedly had with the major in the officer's room at Carisbrooke, in which there had been talk of plans to assassinate the king without the knowledge of either Hammond or the Derby House Committee:

> He informed me that to his knowledge the Governor had received several letters from the Army, intimating the King might by any means be removed out of the way, either by poison or otherwise, and that at another time the same person persuaded me to join with him in a design to remove the King out of that Castle to a place of more secrecy, proffering to take an oath with me, and to do it without the Governor's privity, who he said would not consent for losing the allowance for the house, his pretence to this attempt was, that the King was in too public place from which he might be rescued, but if he might be conveyed into some place of secrecy, he said we might dispose of his person upon all occasions as we thought fit, and this he was confident we could effect without the Governor's privity.

This plot to do away with the king was in fact the reason, or so Osborne claimed, for Charles' escape attempt in the first place, and although Hammond, out of apparent self-interest, had allegedly steered clear of involvement, the charge was serious enough for Rolph to be called before the Commons on 23 June. He brought with him, furthermore, a long letter from the Governor stating that, 'though through weakness he be unfit to travel', he had nevertheless been sent to London, to inform the House of the great untruths told by Osborne. There was a denial, too, of the Governor's own 'inhumane abusing the person of the king' and another request that he might be relieved of his:

> intolerable burden (which God and a good conscience only supports a poor weak man to undergo) either by a removal of his Majesty's person from hence when to your wisdoms it shall seem safe and fit or by better providing for it by a person or persons more able to undergo it.

'Neither Osborne, Dowcett nor any other', Hammond claimed, had suggested that the king's life was in danger, the whole thing being evidently 'a device' of Osborne's own making 'to inflame the people'.

But in spite of a pamphlet published on 18 July, entitled 'His Majesty's Declaration', which had been fraudulently manufactured by a Roundhead propagandist named Tobison, Osborne's accusations would not be lightly dismissed. Published to quieten the people of London after the accusations against Rolph were made public, Tobison's pamphlet suggested that the king had at no stage experienced concerns about his safety, either from poison or any other design. On the contrary, he was so confident of Governor Hammond's honesty, in particular, that he considered himself as safe in his hands, as if he were in the custody of his own son – a claim which eventually led Charles to make the following declaration to Firebrace on 1 August after he had been sent a copy:

> As for Tobison's report, it is such a nonsense; noboddy can beliue it; for although the king does not suspect the Governor would Murther him; must it therfor follow, that he likes his basse Imprisonment, certainely he hath not beene bred up, in such a Cedentary lyfe, that he lykes to be Coopt up; nor is he of so indifferent a disposition, as to be content to have noboddie about him that he can with anie reason, trust.

In the meantime, when he appeared before the Lords on 27 June, Osborne had defended his accusation, and after requesting that Worsley and Dowcett be called as witnesses, was bailed at the sum of £5,000.

Even more significantly, Dowcett's eventual testimony, delivered in writing on 3 July from the Peter House prison where he was incarcerated, not only corroborated Osborne's claims, but was deemed convincing by the committee of the Lords examining it. Dowcett testified:

> My Lords, I am ready to make an oath, that Mr. Richard Osborne told me the King's person was in great danger, and that the said Rolph had a design on foot for the conveying his Majesty's person to some place of secrecy, where only three should go with him, and where they might dispose of his person as they should think fit; which information from Mr. Osborne, and the assurance I had of his Majesty's intention forthwith to come to this Parliament, was the cause of my engagement in this business.
>
> 2. I am ready likewise to depose that the said Rolph came to me when I was a prisoner in the Castle, and in a jeering manner asked me 'why the King came not down according to his appointment?' and then with great indignation and fury said, he waited almost three hours under the new platform, with a good pistol charged to receive him if he had come.

On these grounds, the House saw fit to impeach Rolph for high treason, and he was accordingly taken from his lodgings, where he was now lying ill, and lodged in the Gate House Prison. Thereafter, a petition presented by his wife, which was recommended by the House of Commons, came to be rejected by the Lords, and although Rolph's impeachment was cancelled, he found himself, nevertheless, committed for trial at the Winchester assizes on 28 August. It was only after a strong declaration on his behalf by the presiding judge, moreover, that Rolph was finally acquitted and released on 9 September. Returning to Carisbrooke, he at once resumed his duties as Hammond's chief officer, though the sum of £150 compensation, agreed by MPs, was blocked by the Lords.

Even today, the initial suspicions surrounding Rolph and his subsequent rough treatment remain a matter of some dispute. Clarendon, for example, described him as follows:

> [A] captain of a foot company, whom Cromwell placed there as a prime confident, a fellow of low extraction, and very ordinary parts, who, from a common soldier, had been trusted in all the intrigues of

the army, and was trusted as one of the agitators inspired by Cromwell to put anything into the soldiers' minds upon whom he had a wonderful influence.

As a former shoemaker from Blackfriars, Rolph typified, in fact, the kind of individual cast up into seniority by the vagaries of a new kind of war, in which established norms and the entire social order were being challenged on a day-to-day basis. Thrusting, enthused, irreverent and deeply disillusioned with the status quo, such men were more than capable, when occasion required, of considerable ruthlessness. Clarendon, like the Committee of the House of Lords itself, was therefore readily satisfied that Rolph had indeed been determined that 'the King might be decoyed away, as he was from Hampton Court, by some letters from his friends, of some danger that threatened him, upon which he would be willing to make an escape; and then he might easily be dispatched'. In Clarendon's view, Osborne had informed the king of this and been ordered 'to continue the familiarity with Rolph and to promise to join with him in contriving how his Majesty should make his escape', before making Rolph's villainy the means of getting away.

Yet Osborne, too, had his detractors, as a letter of July 1648, evidently written by a member of the Carisbrooke garrison, makes abundantly clear:

His carriage and language saintlike when he was in the company of religious men, but when associated with vain persons he was as vain and foolish as they, spending his precious time in tippling, singing and unprofitable discourses ...

No man inveighed more against the King's actings and interests than he, insomuch that he was blamed by some, and suspected by others (well affected) upon this ground, as conceiving that a man may be faithful to his trust, and conscientiously discharge his duty, without bitter reflections upon the adverse party.

His expression in the praise and commendation of the army and their late acting and proceedings were hyperbolical, as if he had been one of their greatest friends; whereas, it appears he was one of their most malicious enemies.

From this, it seems, Osborne was inclined to over-act his double game. Yet there is little doubt that Rolph was wholly taken in by his ploy and may very well have confided to him the designs of the army to seize the king's person, notwithstanding the fact that Charles himself made no mention in letters prior to 28 May of being in any danger, as was certainly the case at Hampton Court. When Charles was quizzed by Hammond on Osborne's claims, moreover, he appears to have remained non-committal, because, as Osborne himself put it, 'his maxim is never to cleare one man to the prejudice of another'. In the event, both accuser and accused were left at liberty to nurse their consciences, the former heading to Holland, where he would eventually receive a personal recommendation to the Prince of Wales from the king. 'If Osborne (who has been in trouble for me about one Major Rolphes business) comes to you,' wrote Charles, 'use him well for my sake.' The letter was dated 6 November, and it was a typically generous gesture from a man who, by then, had little else to offer former servants than kindly worded testimonials. For in the tumult and confusion of the preceding summer, both his cause and his options had finally faltered irrevocably.

12

'NEITHER PEACE NOR HONOUR'

'And their fault who have appeared in this summer's business is certainly double to theirs who were in the first, because it is the repetition of the same offence against all the witnesses God has borne.'

Oliver Cromwell, November, 1648

On the evening of Sunday, 21 May, a travel-stained and agitated rider had entered Carisbrooke on a lathering post-horse to demand an interview with the Governor that could not be delayed. Introducing himself as Job Weals, a physician from Kingston-upon-Thames, he declared that he carried an urgent message from army headquarters. But his unexpected entrance was accompanied by a fainting fit, which left him blaming the rigours of his journey and insisting upon a drink of hot water before he could get down to business. It was not the way army couriers handled urgent matters, and it was not enough to convince Robert Hammond that all was in order – particularly at a time when another civil war, arranged through the secret agreement forged with the Scots at Christmas, was daily gathering pace. Though a correspondent had warned the Earl of Lanark on 11 April that the king was 'as impatient of your long delays as you are sorry for the occasion', in Wales and England, Royalist troops had nevertheless begun to muster, while at Pembroke, Colonel Poyer boldly declared for the crown, sparking further risings in Essex, Kent and Surrey the following month. Even, indeed, in London itself, Parliament had now become increasingly vulnerable to the whim of the mob, as army columns marched forth to restore order in the country at large.

While Hammond listened to his visitor's claims, therefore, he did so warily, awaiting confirmation of his suspicions. For Weals now told of an extraordinary plot both to seize the king and kill the Governor by 4 a.m. next morning. A fleet, he claimed, was off the island, and moving into the Solent that evening, ready to land troops during the night. On the excuse of attending a fair to be held at Newport the following day, a mass of people were also to arrive from the mainland to assist the enterprise, aided by signal beacons to raise the islanders and wreak general confusion. As such, declared Weals, there was but one course to follow. Hammond must hand over the king to him and allow the royal prisoner to be conducted to Major Lobb, commanding Portsmouth. Only thus could Charles be secured and disaster averted.

Yet for tales of this kind to convince, even remotely, they would have to be backed by the kind of written authorisation that Weals could not produce when asked. Instead, his response to Hammond's request for his papers verged on the farcical. They were, he said, quilted up in his waistcoat and for Lobb's eyes only. When the Governor persisted, the game was soon up. For the imposter was carefully searched and found to be carrying various petitions from Surrey, along with a message about navy victualling which, with great effrontery, he had intercepted from the Portsmouth to London post on his way down. Were it not for the tension in the country at large, Weals' foolishness might well have served as nothing more than a recipe for merry tales in the castle's guardroom, but in May 1648 there was little scope for laughter either there or elsewhere. On the contrary, there was seething anger that the stubborn man confined at Carisbrooke – the 'man of blood' so detested by so many – had once more brought his subjects to a reckoning of arms.

Yet the causes of the new conflict were by no means all of the king's own making. That so many of the revolts of 1648 occurred in formerly Parliamentarian counties amply reflected, on the one hand, the growing realisation of property-owners that what many had once taken to be a godly cause was no longer worth the sacrifices it entailed. For most, moreover, the absence of reform or indeed a settlement of any kind in the many months since the conclusion of hostilities merely compounded the broken promises of 1642. From his parish of Earls Colne in Essex, the clergyman Ralph Josselin noted in early 1648 that this was 'a sad dear time for poor people' with 'money almost out of the country', while other observers like John Milton, who had formerly defended the Parliamentary cause with such enthusiasm, were by now yearning to see 'Public Faith cleard from the shamefull brand of Public Fraud'. For in the country at large, there was equally widespread dissatisfaction with the imposition of Presbyterianism from Westminster, as only eight of England's forty counties made any significant effort to support the new order. When Sir John Holland boldly declared that he would as readily 'live under the tyranny of the Turk as the tyranny of the clergy', he had merely echoed a common note ringing out well beyond the narrow circle of the gentry.

As such, it was hardly surprising, perhaps, that the widespread demonstrations in London that culminated in rioting on 26 March should have coincided with the anniversary of the royal accession. Though there is no evidence from his surviving letters that the king himself was anything more than a bystander amid the current upheavals, it was no surprise either that the tension at Carisbrooke continued to heighten daily. For Hammond's attempts to improve the castle's fortification had not run smoothly, and the twelve guns ordered from Poole on 7 February took nearly three months to arrive, since the town's governor had pleaded that the guns were too old, and produced a certificate from his gunner to confirm as much. No less frustratingly, Hammond had been forced to point out on 22 April that only half of the £1,000 promised by Parliament had actually been paid. There was, he complained, an urgent need for 'an able ingeneere, who may provide what further security, wth reasonable charge, may be given to this so considerable place', and there could be no delay either in providing the castle with a granary and adequate store of corn.

Above all, however, there was a pressing requirement for extra men, over and beyond the 300 that had been available since March. For the castle to be manned effectively, at least two more companies were essential, and though Hammond's existing troops were proving difficult to pay, a further appeal went out to the Derby House Committee on 22 May, in the wake of Job Weals' visit, by which time the naval guard on the Isle of Wight was down to only one ship, as a result of the mutiny in the fleet on the Downs. Worse still, the Prince of Wales was now at sea with a Royalist fleet from Holland and intent upon an attack, to be co-ordinated with a rising of the king's supporters on the island itself. The heir to the throne was to be joined, it seems, by the 'revolted shipps' from the Parliamentary fleet, which, according to a letter from the Derby House Committee on 30 June, 'hold intelligence with some in the isle' and 'doubt not to effect their design'. Among those involved, according to evidence taken in April 1651, was none other than 'younge Oglander, Sir John's son', along with 'most of the gentlemen in the Isle of Wight'.

Under such circumstances, Hammond's requests could hardly be delayed further, so that by 15 June, two companies of Colonel Ewer's regiment, stationed at Gloucester, were duly ordered to the Isle of Wight, where their landing was expected to occur some ten days later. On the same day, it was ordered, too, that Hammond be supplied with additional munitions taken out of Sussex, which were to include 'an Hundred of Hand Granado Shells' and 200 demi-culverin from Arundel Castle, though even this, it seems, would not entirely quieten the Governor's anxieties. 'Horse would be of excellent use here', he suggested on 23 June, and two days later he was pressing his case to the Derby House Committee once more. 'I doe believe,' he wrote, 'if I had saddles & armes, & there were any way for their certain pay, I could raise a good troope of horse out of the well affected of the island.'

Plainly, the situation remained delicately poised. For in May an army mutiny in South Wales, which Royalists skilfully exploited, had sparked a chain reaction, and although resistance was largely crushed by Thomas Horton at St Fagan's near Cardiff before Cromwell finally arrived, the survivors' spirited defence of Pembroke Castle delayed him for two months, leaving Fairfax to deal on his own with further trouble in the south-east. Nearer to Carisbrooke, moreover, events were continuing to assume an ominous hue. 'The saylors in the ships here,' reported a local newsletter on 20 July, 'as also the people in the Island, doe not cry for King and Parl. but for King and the ships.' The Governor of Portsmouth had not hesitated in response to bar the suspect vessels from harbour, as Hammond did his best to raise his local cavalry troop, among whom, it seems, were various parish ministers like a certain Mr Evans, whom one newsletter saw fit to single out as a volunteer of particularly 'active spirit'.

With the Governor fearing the worst, it was only to be expected, of course, that efforts should have increased to curtail his prisoner's contact with the world outside. 'Here is ane imposibilty of sending to the king', a Scottish agent complained on 24 June, as Royalist pamphlets recounted sorry tales of his being 'bolted and rebolted in an out room in Carisbrooke Castle where he hath blowd his owne fire and turn'd up his own bed'. By now, if Clarendon is to be believed, the prisoner's hair was 'all gray, which, making all others very sad, made it thought that he had sorrow in his countenance', and there was no end either to the abundant rumours of foul play, which circulated constantly in Royalist circles. A letter to the Earl of Lanark, for instance, dated 20 June, suggested that the king had prevailed upon Hammond to take some exercise, only to find his upper-storey apartment collapse inexplicably as he made his way to the nearby bowling green.

Nor, on the other hand, had Charles abandoned all talk of escape, as the illiterate serving woman, whose toilet duties took her daily into the royal bedchamber, continued to carry secret correspondence to and from Newport, where the ubiquitous Major Bosvile was now waiting to organise its distribution. By this means, indeed, the prisoner seems to have been able to re-establish contact with the queen herself, for on 1 July he thanked Titus for helping to bring this about. 'I know not,' he declared, 'whether my astonishment or my joy were the greater; for indeed I did dispaire of hearing any more from you, or any other of my frends, during these damnable tymes.' It was around now, too, that the king first struck up his correspondence with Sir William Hopkins, the Master of Newport Grammar School who had originally engineered the appointment of the king's intrepid toilet maid. Certainly, Charles' delight was palpable upon finding that a new and reliable means of communication had been established through Hopkins' ingenuity, as he made clear to Firebrace on 29 June, emphasising how this new 'way of conueyance' was 'safe, unsuspected, & not tyed to dayes'.

Even more important for the king's flagging morale, however, were Hopkins' efforts to secure his liberation, for on 10 July the schoolmaster had already sent word of a plan through the agency of a lady designated by the number 47, who is likely to have been his own wife. She had succeeded, we are told, in obtaining a private interview at Carisbrooke, and the paper from her husband that she brought with her outlined proposals to raise the island's Royalists, surprise the garrison, arrest Hammond and convey the king away by means of a boat. Though the scheme was neither novel in conception nor any more plausible in essence than previous proposals of the kind, it did at least involve Henry Ley, 3rd Earl of Marlborough, who had been General of the Ordnance and Admiral in Command at Dartmouth, which was enough, it seems, to stir Charles' hopes anew, as he made clear in a letter dated 14 July. 'I do well approve of Marlborough to be a chief

Conductor, as for matter of Action,' he wrote, 'for I am confident of his Courage and Honesty; so, if the business is well laid, he may do as well as any other.'

To his credit, Hopkins had also taken pains to arrange a system of couriers to London, whereby the king was able to communicate with Firebrace, whom he now proceeded to disguise under the name of David Griffin. Learning, perhaps, from past mistakes, Charles was equally careful to avoid any mention of Hopkins himself, observing only that his dispatches had been conveyed by an 'unknown way', while another correspondent, designated '52' and most probably Nicholas Oudart, was also contacted abroad. Most significant of all among the new stream of correspondence, however, were ciphered letters involving Jane Whorwood, or 'Hellen' as she now became known. For even at this point, as is clear from his letters on 24 and 26 July, Charles was keen to devise plans for her to achieve a private interview with him in his bedchamber, which, by some extraordinary artifice or other, she actually seems to have achieved little more than a month later, at which time Hopkins was asked to 'thank her for the visit she stole upon me yesternight'. 'For seriously,' the king added, 'I could hardly believe my own eyes when I saw her.'

The same puzzling lapses in internal security, which had dogged Hammond since his appointment as the king's captor, were still, then, glaringly evident, and without the Governor's tireless personal vigilance, it seems likely that Charles might well have stirred up far more trouble than he actually managed, both in the wider world outside and within the castle itself. Plainly, the king's guards were at best half-hearted in their efforts, if not outright sympathisers with his cause, and the same deference to his regal status, not to mention the abiding hope that he might yet agree to reasonable terms, was even now intact. For Charles, therefore, Hammond alone remained the unshakeable stumbling-block to his plans, and in a letter to Hopkins on 16 July, in which he designated himself '39' and the Governor '50', he plainly implied as much by pointing out 'that unless you secure 50. the Seizing of all the rest of the Horse will not (in my Opinion) do the Work; because he will sooner get help to recover his Loss , than you will be able to force 39. out of his hands'.

One week later, the same preoccupation with the Governor was again in evidence when Hopkins was asked to consider some means of apprehending him:

As to the maine Business; I will only aske you; do you not meane; (when your preparations are made) as well, to seek an Oportunety, by laying a traine for 50:, as to lay houlde of one when he gives it to you?

Within the fortnight, Charles' respect for his captor's tenacity, coupled to his ongoing fears for securing the island, had actually put paid altogether to his intended escape. For in a letter to Hopkins of 26 July, his misgivings were already 'of such waight' that he found himself unable to give a 'determinat resolution concerning it', and by the next day, as he made clear to Hopkins in another letter, these same misgivings had finally consumed his hopes entirely concerning 'the greater designe'.

As Charles grudgingly accepted his impotence, all was left to depend, in fact, upon the success of Royalist efforts on the mainland, bolstered by no more than a 'letter of credit' entrusted to his 15-year-old son. The Scots, it is true, were finally to cross the border on 8 July, and three weeks later Parliament once more approved the idea of a treaty with the king. But Scottish troops were little match for Cromwell's, and it was equally clear that any subsequent agreement with Westminster would be wholly on Parliament's terms, since the news for Charles on all other fronts was nothing less than calamitous. While Colchester held out for the Royalist cause, there was still a straw of sorts to clutch at. But, as the king made clear to Titus on 1 July, this final lifeline would not be long-lived. 'We heere do beliue all the Gallant honnest Men in Colchester infallibly lost, though yet they hould out,' he told Titus despairingly. Nine days later, he was informing Firebrace of further 'ill Newes come hither concerning the Earl of Holand', who had been captured in Hertfordshire following an abortive rising at Kingston in Surrey.

So when three parliamentary commissioners – the Earl of Essex, Sir John Hippesley and John Bulkeley, MP for Yarmouth – arrived at Carisbrooke late on 5 August after a crossing delayed by stormy weather, the king's only effective bargaining counter was the fragile allegiance of the Scots. As a gesture of goodwill, the commissioners had brought with them not only Titus but Babington, the royal barber, and a proposal that while negotiations were in progress, Charles might reside at Newport, experiencing the kind of liberty he had previously enjoyed at Hampton Court. Yet that same night, the prisoner wrote once more to Hopkins to speak of 'a New Conceipt of myne, concerning our great Business', which would prove to be nothing more than a further feeble escape effort, delayed until Parliament's peace proposals had been delivered officially. 'As soon as I heare what the 3 London-Commissioners say to me,' he told Hopkins the day after their arrival, 'I will perform the Promise I made to you Yesternight; in the mean tyme you shall do well to keepe all affections straight.'

Nevertheless, at their first formal meeting on Monday, 7 August, the commissioners seemed heartened by the demeanour of the king, 'from whome', it was reported to Westminster by one of those present, '(if conjecturs grounded on my one observations, & the sence of such as frequently Convers with him, faile me not) you are likely to receive a Complying Answer'. On Thursday, 10 August, moreover, such optimism appeared well-founded, for, in a crowded Presence Chamber, the king formally congratulated his visitors upon presenting 'a fair beginning to a happy peace'. When Parliament first voted to negotiate on 29 July, Charles had been pessimistic. 'I have not great hope that much good will come of it,' he reflected, 'because I do not believe that those who come to Treat will have Power to debate, but only to propose.' Besides which, he added, 'what capacity a Prisoner hath to Treate as yett I know not'. Yet debate had ultimately proved unnecessary, since the commissioners had offered an amenable basis for the initiation of meaningful talks, and the king reacted accordingly. He concluded:

> There might be some that would oppose this Treaty being Gainers by the War, and therefore desired the Continuance of it … Others may think Me revengeful, but, for My Part, I am so far from seeking any, that if a Straw would hurt them, I would not stoop to take it up. God forgive them; for I do.

The 'Treaty' of which Charles spoke was not, in fact, a settlement in its own right, but merely, in accordance with the contemporary meaning of the term, an agreement to negotiate. No actual resolution of the conflict was ever, indeed, likely to ensue, since Parliament's position remained essentially the same as the one it had adopted at Hampton Court in 1647 and subsequently at Carisbrooke shortly after Charles' arrival. Nor was Parliament's superficial generosity prompted by any substantive threat from Scotland. Rather, it was fear of the army and ongoing distaste for the more radical religious elements within it that brought Presbyterian MPs to the negotiating table, while for Charles the talks offered little more than a welcome respite from the wretchedness of incarceration at Carisbrooke, and further opportunity to indulge his fantasies of freedom. Certainly, the prisoner was glad to be leaving, as he made clear while taking a final walk around the castle's grounds. For upon encountering the 9-year-old son of the castle's master gunner, marching up and down a battlement with a wooden sword, he asked the boy what he was doing with 'that terrible weapon'. When the lad replied that he was defending the king 'from all your enemies', the response was a warm one. 'I am going away from here and do not respect to return,' he replied, before patting his protector on the head and giving him the ruby ring that held his cravat. Nor, indeed, would his imminent departure prevent him from further attempts at flight thereafter, as he had already made clear to Titus on 22 May. 'Assure all my friends in my name,' he confided, 'that if ... there shall be any Treaty made me by the Parliamentary party I would only have use of it in order to my escape.'

Even by then, however, Charles had received further cruel tidings. For between 17 and 19 August, after a hurried march north, Cromwell had brilliantly routed the much larger Scottish army of the Duke of Hamilton at Preston. At a cost of fewer than 100 casualties, Parliamentarian forces had either killed, wounded or captured some 8,000 enemy troops, and to compound his agony, the news of this defeat would be blurted out while the king was at bowls with none other than Hammond. After a brooding silence, Charles could not help turning to the Governor and complaining that this was the worst news that ever came to England, provoking the not unjustifiable response that if Hamilton had been the victor, he would soon have controlled the thrones of both England and Scotland. 'You are mistaken,' came the royal retort, 'I could have commanded him back with the motion of my Hand.'

Nor was there any more consolation on offer elsewhere. With Scottish support neutralised, it was useless, for example, for Charles to look to France, where Cardinal Mazarin, deeply embroiled in continental peace negotiations, merely contented himself with maintaining polite relations with the English Parliament. When the Scots first crossed the border, he had prudently recalled his ambassador Montreuil from Edinburgh, and upon breaking his journey in London, Montreuil's efforts to obtain an interview with the king at Carisbrooke had proven wholly ineffectual. For a pass from the House of Lords enabling him to visit the Isle of Wight had been promptly overruled by the Commons, and by the time that Colchester fell on 27 August, England's second flash of civil war was already well and truly over. Henceforth, the king could rely only on his wits in securing some small scrap of respectability from what he openly described to Titus as 'a mocke Treaty'.

With his familiar flair for casuistry, Charles could continue, of course, to stretch the resources of his enemies, riven as they still were by rancour and division, though this is not to say that he entered the forthcoming negotiations at Newport in wholly bad faith. For in expressing his doubts to Hopkins about the prospects for the treaty, there remained fleeting undertones of hope. 'I pray God, I be mistaken' was his concluding observation on what he always considered the most likely outcome, but in one letter, penned on 18 August, he again implied to Hopkins that he was continuing to consider the possibility that talks might yet prove productive. 'As for 64 [the treaty],' he wrote, 'if reall, 41 [the Prince of Wales] will doe nothing in prejudice.' As late as 3 October, he was still instructing his eldest son to await the outcome of the treaty before employing force on his behalf. 'As for my Directions to you at this time,' Charles wrote, 'the issue of this Treaty must be your chief Guide.' In the meantime, his heir was to 'cherish the Fleet as much as you may' but 'stay where you are, until you hear farther from me, or that you find you cannot hear from me'.

Ultimately, of course, it would take far more than human wit and paltry grains of goodwill to bridge the gulf between the king and his enemies. Yet throughout August and September, as both sides busied themselves with preliminaries, Charles was able to take some comfort at least from a relaxation in his physical circumstances. Before long, in fact, the original instructions to Hammond about the king's imprisonment were being steadily dismantled by Parliament, and, after giving his parole for the duration of the treaty and twenty days thereafter, Charles was once more accorded the freedom to move within the island. On 31 August, moreover, he again submitted a request for the reinstallation of many of his former servants, and while Dowcett, Ashburnham and Legge were forbidden to return, others like Firebrace, Titus, Cresset and Captain Burroughs found themselves restored to their former duties. There was even a recall, indeed, for Mrs Wheeler, 'with such maids as she shall choose', including the faithful Mary, though Babbington, the king's barber, found himself replaced for some reason by Thomas Davis at Charles' own request.

When minor moral victories were so hard to come by, it was not altogether surprising, perhaps, that all those involved in the previous escape attempts, with the exception of Osborne – who is likely to have gone abroad – should have been included on the royal wish list of servants. On 22 August, Charles asked Firebrace to thank Cresset and Burroughs 'for their Newes and bid them be confident that the King in Nomination of his attendents ... will not forget one of those who were discharged for his sake'. In the interim, Firebrace was to ensure a steady flow of contact with the outside world, as Charles made clear to him on 29 August:

> You being one of the Kings list I suppose you will repair hither, wherfor I desyre you that before you come away, you leaue such order behinde you, as I may not loose my intelligence: desyre E: [Lady Carlisle] from me that speedely and carefully she send away those two letters I haue sent for M: and G: [the queen and Prince of Wales].

But while Charles was plainly still intent upon corresponding with his wife, nor had he forgotten his tie to the ever-faithful Jane Whorwood, who was now once more close by. Her first letters to him since her sojourn at Queenborough had arrived on 15 July, and two more followed four days later, along with one sent by the queen, from whom he had previously heard in May. By now, indeed, Jane was actually in residence at Hopkins' house in the centre of Newport and ready to serve her sovereign in the new more intimate capacity already discussed, notwithstanding a letter to Firebrace, dated 27 July, in which she intimated that even her courage had initially faltered at the danger involved in the king's invitation. 'As to the satisfaction of him in the contents of it,' she confided, 'I could not soe suddenly challenge [produce] an answer', adding that she 'was willing to decline' the king's request until she had finally 'in some sort acquir'd the meanes to do it'.

Doubtless, she was now making some effort to disguise her appearance, since her pock marks and in all likelihood her red hair were known to her pursuers, but it seems likely to have been only the assistance of Mrs Hopkins, who retained the guards' – and presumably Hammond's – confidence, that finally convinced Jane of the possibility of gaining access to the king. Her eventual arrival served, it seems, as a fillip to Charles' spirits every bit as potent as the news of the impending treaty. In a letter to Colonel Nathan Rich, dated 9 August, Hammond noted how the king had 'clipped his beard and asked the Governor if he saw a new reformation in him'. Furthermore, the flow of Charles' messages to Jane became so torrential that she was soon experiencing difficulties in answering. 'Tell N when you deliver this enclosed,' he instructed Hopkins, 'that I see she will in time learn to answer letters.' On 17 August, there was further evidence of the urgency of the king's wish to communicate with her. 'My haste this day to return N a speedy answer,' he told Hopkins, 'made me slip something which since I have remembered, and therefore again I put you to this trouble hoping that by the morrow at night I shall have answer from her of both together.' Three days later, he was playfully informing the headmaster in mock annoyance that:

[A]gainst [Jane] and your wife I have a quarrel for being here yes-terday and not seeing me, but an easy satisfaction will content me though some I must have. For news I refer you to N expecting an answer from both you and her, by tomorrow morning before Noon.

Writing twice daily on occasion, Charles actually produced double the letters that Jane could manage in reply, uncomprehending, it seems, of the other pressing duties she was executing on his behalf, and telling her on 26 August, 'that she shall have no more pardons without answering more punctually to my letters, beginning with this enclosed'.

In all likelihood, Jane's access to the king was also eased by the fact that Hammond himself was at last beginning to relax at the prospect of his prisoner's release from Carisbrooke, which, though eventually delayed until September, was nevertheless now imminent. Indeed, Newport town hall was already being prepared for the treaty negotia-tions, and Hopkins had made his own home at the grammar school available for the king to dwell in, 'which by Mr Kinnersley of the wardrobe was fitted so well as such a place would afford, albeit of small receipt for the Court'. No doubt to Hammond's considerable relief, too, extra troops had now been provided, as requested, and quarters reserved at the various inns for both parliamentary commissioners and royal attendants. To meet the expense, some £10,000 was borrowed from the City of London, while Hammond himself benefited to the tune of £500 a year from a personal pension that was now granted to him for services rendered. This was not the limit of his good fortune, for he was also allotted a further £1,000 in delinquency fines and treated to a payment from the army of £40 a week for the period of the treaty.

The Governor had confided to his friend Colonel Rich how he had been 'impatient of my load and sought rest, but found none'. Though now free in principle to allow the king greater liberty, he had indeed proved disinclined at first to lessen his vigilance too drastically. He pressed Speaker Lenthall, for instance, to clarify his prisoner's new privileges. Did they extend, on the one hand, to 'horses and riding abroad'; and was Charles, for the time being, to be allowed 'letters or any [person] whatever to come to him'? Since 'I was not there', he wrote, how was it possible to know the full extent of the king's liberty at Hampton Court which he was now ordered to restore. Indeed, it was not until 27 August, when Charles finally offered guarantees of compliance, that Hammond achieved the 'rest' he was seeking. 'His Majesty,' he informed Lenthall subsequently, 'is now free from restraint.' The Royalist poet John Taylor, who had once described the Governor as 'coarse, rigid and barbarous', soon found himself encountering a changed man, newly relaxed and amenable in his altered circumstances – 'a gentleman of quality [with] the humbleness of dutiful service'.

At Newport, meanwhile, the impact of Charles' arrival would prove considerable. It was on 7 September that the royal coach, duly dusted down for the impending talks, eventually made its way from 'Avalon' – as some of the newsletters were now calling Carisbrooke – and on through the late summer hedges to the island's capital for what would be the last political negotiation of the king's life. Though the town awaiting him numbered no more than 3,000 inhabitants, it was nevertheless abuzz with expectancy, for in spite of its size, Newport was revelling in the new-found celebrity that matched its air of growing prosperity. A compact, well-ordered market town, living comfortably off its fisheries, leather-working and brewing trades, its streets were paved and its water mains freshly laid, while its older buildings, half-timbered and plaster-fronted, nestled proudly among newer shops and inns of bricks and timber. It had been a corporate borough for forty years by now, and its mayor and corporation were keener than ever to guard the privileges that dated back to the town's original charter in the twelfth century. They were no less eager, of course, to enjoy the increased profits accruing from the arrival of so many troops and official newcomers, notwithstanding the fact that for the broader populace this also meant extra taxation 'towardes the Charge imposed on the towne for the quartering of troopers & foote souldyers & for fier & Candle for them'.

Nor, it must be said, were all the new arrivals entirely desirable in their own right, for Newport's hostelries were soon teeming with both high and low life from either side, and trouble swiftly escalated between Royalists on safe conducts and Parliamentarians claiming bragging rights after their ultimate victory. It had taken John Taylor four hours to cross Southampton Water to Cowes, before arriving in the capital 'embroidered all over with mire and mud'. But he lost no time in voicing support for his 'heroic and unconquered' king, and denouncing those 'buzzards of incredulity' whom he found denouncing the royal touch for scrofula. 'Here come many to this place,' reported the *Moderate Intelligencer* on 10 September, 'who look upon us, as if they desired the annihilation of all that have served the Parliament.' On Sunday, 22 October, predictably enough, a footman of the king's household twice came to blows with a Roundhead soldier, after which the George Inn witnessed even rowdier scenes than usual, as its Royalist patrons, who had already made the place notorious, celebrated the event. 'That night,' it was reported, 'his Majesty's Health went round lustily in the George-Seller, whither some of the Cooks and others came over from the Court.'

The George, indeed, would witness further disorder on 9 November when Cavaliers, angered by concessions forced upon the king, created such an uproar that four files of musketeers were eventually sent to arrest them and bring them before Hammond. When confronted, the troublemakers drew swords and pocket pistols – 'insomuch', we are told, 'that a bloody conflict began to ensue' – and fighting continued for half an hour before the troops stormed the room and sent the surviving occupants under escort up to Carisbrooke Castle. In all, five men – two Royalists and three Roundhead troopers – lost their lives, though many courtiers, it must be said, also took full advantage of the more gentle recreations offered by the island. For on St George's Down, 1½ miles outside Newport, was a bowling green and 'ordinary', or social club, which had long been a happy haunt of local gentlemen and now found itself the resort of numerous well-heeled newcomers, whose richly adorned ladies self-consciously decked the capital's streets, preening and posturing and eagerly competing to meet the king – though one at least, 'conceitedly decked with black patches or ambitious spots on her face', found herself snubbed by him for her brazenness.

In the meantime, general expectations for the treaty remained mixed. 'Some are of opinion, little will be done, others contrary,' reported the

Moderate Intelligencer from Newport on 17 September. It was mainly left to Lord Lisle, one of the parliamentary commissioners, to cheer the optimists as best he might by producing a piece of prophecy, which received coverage in *Mercurius Pragmaticus*. For a curious Latin inscription and English couplet had, it seems, been found at Carisbrooke twelve years earlier and lately entered the peer's possession. The couplet spoke of a king 'cloth'd all in White' who 'shall crowne this land with Peace in th' Isle of Wight', but more significantly still from Lisle's perspective, the numerals among the Latin inscription, when added together, came to 1648. In a credulous age where optimism of any kind was now more than ever at a premium, this alone was enough for hope – though not, it must be said, for all, and certainly not at Nunwell, where Sir John Oglander sounded an altogether more cynical note about the treaty's prospects. 'They tell us,' he observed wryly, '… wee shale have Peace, and the Issue of blooud will be stopt, fayre weather, and all thinges accordinge to owr hartes desire.'

The foul weather that actually followed would indeed provide a better guide to the treaty's eventual outcome than any prophecies or cryptic inscription conjured up by interested parties. For the rain was unabated, and while Charles nevertheless insisted upon equipping himself with riding boots in anticipation of enjoying the freedom of the island once more, the elements continued to frustrate. Thursday, 7 September, had in fact been designated a day of general thanksgiving for the victories of the Parliamentary armies, but Oglander's description leaves little doubt of the limited meteorological scope for festivity of any kind:

> It wase from morninge to Nyght, the horridst rayny Daye as ever I sawe, Insomuch as Insteed of reioycinge, many had heavy heartes, to see theyre Corne spoyled, and wisched it had bene a daye rather of humiliation, then of Joye, and Merriment, To Conclude there was almost no travelinge on the Earth, both by reason of the flouds and Bogges in the hygh wayes that the rayne, and travelinge made.

Nor was Oglander the only commentator to bemoan the late summer gloom, for John Taylor – known, appropriately enough, as the water poet by virtue of the fact that he was once a Thames boatman – again found himself the victim of the Cowes road, that 'boggy quagmire, miry, rotten, filthy, dirty slow, through over, or into which I must pass'.

So soaked and windswept, indeed, were the parliamentary commissioners at the time of their arrival on Thursday, 14 September, that the volleys of shot and civic junketing on offer did nothing to prevent their creeping to bed at the earliest opportunity. Nor would a prayer drafted by the king at that very time have done anything to lift their spirits further. Not long before, he had experienced a lucky escape in a riding accident when he broke his bridle by reining in his horse too hard while travelling down a steep hill. But his close scrape had neither vanquished nor tempered his truculence, and in opting to treat Saturday as a fast day for the success of the treaty, he used the church service for the occasion as a means of delivering an invocation to the Almighty, loaded with accusation. 'If the guilt of our great sins,' his prayer ended, 'cause this Treaty to break off in vain, Lord let the truth clearly appear who those men are, which under pretence of the publicke good doe pursue their own private ends.'

Somewhat less contentiously, there were also offerings of prayers from Parliament's commissioners before they set out to commence treaty talks on Monday morning. Arriving at the town hall at 9 a.m., they then sent word to the king of their arrival and duly awaited his coach, accompanied by his attendants, 'and His Footmen, and Coachman, with new suites laid with broad plate silver-lace, two in a Seame'. Whereupon the Parliamentary delegation proceeded to the treaty room and took up their places on either side of the lower end of a large negotiating table, and opposite the king who was to occupy a chair of state beneath a canopy at the table's head, with his secretaries close at hand, discreetly lodged behind a curtain. Should the king wish to consult his advisers on any point, he was to be allowed to withdraw into a chamber, standing to one side of the treaty room – an arrangement which also applied to the Parliamentary representatives, who were given access to a similar vestibule.

For up to forty days – the pre-agreed limit for the talks – this setting would provide the backdrop for what promised to be the most fateful negotiations of the king's life. Business was to be conducted by an exchange of papers rather than open discussion, and it was made clear to Charles on the opening day that, while the earlier propositions submitted to him at Hampton Court were to be the basis for discussion, priority must be given to four bills that Parliament considered crucial. They concerned the withdrawal of royal proclamations issued against Parliament during the war; the establishment of Presbyterianism;

control of the militia; and the governance of Ireland. All were deep-seated bones of contention, raising issues that struck at the very core of Charles' values and beliefs, and all were to be effectively non-negotiable, notwithstanding any residual displays of defiance the king might yet attempt. For although he had agreed by only the second day to cancel his wartime proclamations, he nevertheless deigned in his answer to omit a loaded phrase in the commissioners' original proposal, in which they declared that Parliament had been 'necessitated to undertake a War in their just and lawfull Defence'.

Once more, then, Charles was willing to dig in his heels – and to such a degree, in fact, that the Wednesday session developed into a heated wrangle, culminating in an adjournment without decision. As the king retired to his room, moreover, one of his secretaries accosted the commissioners' leader, the Earl of Northumberland. 'My good lord,' he declared, 'remember how gracious this good prince hath been to you, and do you compassionate his distresses, and the strait he is now in.' 'Sir,' came the reply, 'in this it is impossible for me to do any thing, for the king in this point is safe as king, but we cannot be so.' Northumberland's point was incontrovertible, for without such an acceptance of Parliament's grounds for fighting, the risk would remain that the king might later find grounds for punishing his enemies. There could indeed be no scope for compromise, therefore, and though Charles continued to chafe, and postponement followed postpone-ment, on 25 September he was finally forced to concede a position that he had never been capable, from the very outset, of maintaining realistically.

Even now, however, the main potential sticking point was still to come. For, after dinner that same evening, the commissioners settled down to draft their proposal on the future of the Church, which was both completed and delivered to Charles by 8 p.m. No more time had been needed, since the terms were so straightforward: the complete abolition of the episcopacy, and the establishment of the Presbyterian Directory of Worship in place of the king's beloved Book of Common Prayer. On this occasion, too, there was to be not the slightest scope for resistance, as Charles himself appeared to acknowledge when he told the Bishop of London and his other advisers next day that 'the Parliaments commissioners stand upon positives' and would insist upon 'a positive answer to things whither he will pass them or not'. Two days later, moreover, he was proved right, for his desultory attempt to circumvent the religious issue by suggesting that all outstanding issues be settled by direct negotiation with Parliament in London was swiftly and roundly rejected.

The king's delaying tactics were by now, of course, a wholly familiar and thoroughly worn-out option, and on Friday, 29 September, the commissioners arrived at 10 a.m. to confirm as much, freshly buoyed by news that Cromwell had crossed the Scottish border and that the English fleet, duly restored to loyal service, had sailed for Holland to attack the Prince of Wales' would-be armada. Though they were left to cool their heels for most of the day, by 4.30 p.m. they had delivered the following response: 'We humbly desire Your Majesty's Answer to our Paper concerning the Church, delivered in to Your Majesty the 25th of this instant September.' One more week of hair-splitting would follow over the issue of episcopal lands and the virtues of the Book of Common Prayer, but by the time that Governor Hammond invited the commissioners to dinner at Carisbrooke on 6 October, all seemed largely over. Four days earlier, Parliament had rejected an appeal, delivered by Titus, for direct talks in London, and when the increasingly weary round of talks reopened on Saturday, draft after draft of the king's reply on religion was discarded until he was finally reduced to tears.

All Charles might now hope for, it seemed, was one last attempt at escape, and as he retired to his room, thoroughly exhausted by a day of frustrated negotiation and an evening absorbed by touching visitors for the 'King's Evil', he confirmed his intentions in the following letter to Hopkins, dated 7 October:

> Though I doubt not of your Care in expediting that business, whereof I spoke to you this morning; yet I cannot but tell you, that you cannot make reddy too soon, for, by what I have heard since I saw you, I fynde that few dayes will make that impossible, which now is fesible; wherefore I pray you, give me an account as soone as you can; *First*, where I shall take Boate? (spare not my walking, in respect of security). Then, how the Tydes fall out? or whither, incase the Wynde do serve, it be necessary to looke to the Tydes? what Winds are faire? what may serve? & what are contrary? Consider also, if a Pass from 50 [Hammond] may not be usefull. *Lastly*, how soone all will be reddy. To all this a speedy Answer is expected.

His word of honour that he would not escape was plainly no more binding than ever, when, from his perspective, the sole beneficiary was an ungodly enemy, and as he listened next day to the Dean of Canterbury expostulating drearily on the lessons of *John* 5:14 during morning service, Charles' mind was doubtless preoccupied with his latest project.

In the meantime, as was made clear to Hopkins on 8 October, every effort would have to be made to lull the commissioners into a false sense of optimism. 'You will hear to Morrow,' Charles revealed, 'that I have given full Satisfaction concerning the Militia, with which I have acquainted no living Soul but yourself.' A fresh breeze of compromise and accommodation was soon seen to be sweeping through other areas of negotiation. Having agreed to consider Parliament's proposals on Ireland, Charles even produced a somewhat more forthcoming response on the thorny issue of the Church, which caused John Crew, one of the commissioners, to rush off a hasty letter to the Derby House Committee. Once Parliament's attitude on the other proposals had been finally confirmed, Crew suggested, a definitive agreement on the Church would not be long in following. The ever-watchful Venetian correspondent in London was equally confident of Charles' new preparedness to compromise. 'The ease with which he gives way to the determination of Parliament,' wrote the Italian, '[was] giving hope of a speedy conclusion.'

Yet Charles was all the while urging Hopkins 'to haste the work I have set you upon'. 'Lose no time and give daily an Account how you proceed therein,' he wrote on 8 October, before freely acknowledging on the following day the double game he had been playing:

Notwithstanding my too great Concessions alreaddy made, I know, that unless I shall make yet others, which will directly make me no King; I shall be, at best, a perpetuall Prisoner: besydes if this were not, (of which I am too sure) the adhering to the Church, (from which I cannot depart, no not in show) will doe the same: &, to deale freely with you, the great Concession I made this day, was meerely in order to my escape of which, if I had not hope, I would not have done: for then I could have returned, to my straight Prison, without reluctancy, but now I confess it would breake my hart, having done that, which only an escape can justefy. To be shorte, if I stay for a demonstration of their further wickedness, it will be too late to seeke a remedy; for my only hope is; that now they belive that I dare deny them nothing, & so be less carefull of their Guards: wherefore, as you love my safety;

let us dispach this business as soone as we can, without expecting Newes from London; & lett me tell you, that if I were once aboard, & under saile, I would willingly enufe, hazard the 3 Pinaces; To conclude, I pray you belive me, (& not the common voice of Mankynde), that I am lost if I doe not Escape, which I shall not be able to doe, if (as I have said) I stay for further demonstrations; therefore for Gods sake hasten with all diligence you can.

Certainly, the final sentences betrayed a new desperation, indicating for the first time, perhaps, a man now nearing breaking point. Just under a year ago, he had left his pet greyhound whimpering in his chamber at Hampton Court, and for all of eighteen months before that, he had been a prisoner in his own kingdom, resisting what now appeared inevitable even to him. From this point forward, therefore, as he admitted to Firebrace, he was bent on granting 'whatever they could aske, saving his Conscience and the damnation of his owne Soule (wch his Matie once told me, he thought they aymed at)'. Nor, it seems, was Charles' assessment of his plight a matter of histrionics, as he made clear to Hopkins the following afternoon, before a treaty session due to commence at 4 p.m. 'What I wrote yesternight,' he confided, 'was not to ad Spurs, but really to give you the true state of my condition.' Clearly, the point of make or break had at last been reached, and everything now depended upon the Prince of Wales in Holland. 'The procuring of a Dutch Pinck, would make all sure,' Charles reflected.

Even Jane Whorwood, for that matter, was now to be excluded from his escape plans. 'Upon my word,' he told Hopkins in a postscript to his letter of 9 October, 'N. knows nothing of this Business, nor shall: not out of any mistrust, (for I cannot be more confident of any), but to keep my Rule, of not putting such a great Secret as this, than is of absolute Necessity.' Seven days later, his exhortations to Hopkins were becoming more impatient than ever. 'The Businesses of the Church and my Friends come so fast upon me,' he told the schoolmaster, 'that I cannot promise you a Week; therefore lose no time.' Next day, indeed, he was more emphatic still. He wrote after supper that evening:

Excuse my impatience that I desire you to give me an account where the business sticks; for I assure you, that I shall have but few Days free to Act my Part. I need say no more; but let me know what is possible to be done, and then it is for me to judge.

His friends abroad, he added to Hopkins, 'desire my Freedom (if it be possible) more than myself; being confident thereby in a great measure, to alter the Face of Affairs'.

Ostensibly at least, there was still time enough for action, since Sundays and the designated monthly Fast day were not included in the forty days allowed for the treaty, and talks would not therefore end officially until 3 November. On 4 November, moreover, it was actually decided by Parliament that negotiations should continue for another fourteen days, though the pealing of bells throughout the island when news of the extension became known proved premature. For the extra two weeks of talk proffered not so much the prospect of peace but merely an added opportunity for Hopkins to make good the king's escape before he could be transferred back to Carisbrooke once more. In a letter written on 9 November, the schoolmaster duly confirmed that John Newland was once again to be relied upon for the supply of a boat, notwithstanding certain doubts expressed about his honesty, which were shared, it seems, by Charles himself, who nevertheless recommended that the merchant be trusted 'without any more Tryals than to know of him how he can pass the Examination of the Sea Guards'. 'Though you dare not be too confident (for which I cannot blame you) of Newland,' he wrote, '… I cannot thinke any Man so great a Divel, as to betray me: when it is visible that he will gaine more for being Honnest then being a Knave.'

Three days later, meanwhile, Charles was asking to be informed 'of the Tydes and of the Horse Guards both how they are placed and what Rounds they ride', notwithstanding the fact that in spite of his best efforts on this occasion, he had yet again been found out. For in a letter from Newport dated 6 November, the Derby House Committee had already heard of 'a design laid for the conveying of his Majesty's person away'. This time the committee had more exact knowledge of the scheme, which they conveyed to Hammond on 13 November:

We have information from a good hand that there is an intention for the King to make escape; the time to be on Thursday night or Friday night; That he intends to land on this side at Gosport; that only two are to be in his company, a little ancient man with a shrivelled face, and a lusty young man of about 26 or 27 years of age.

Whether Newland was indeed the 'good hand' who had told all remains unknown. But the committee was certainly able to supply Hammond with further details on 18 November:

> To escape all suspicion from you, he [the king] intends to walk out a mile or two, as usuall, in the day time, and there horses are laid in the isle to carry him to a boat. If he cannot do this, then either over the house in the night, or at some private window in the night, he intends his passage.

But Jack Ashburnham, at least, would suggest that it was not so much betrayal as reluctance to assist that finally put paid to the king's escape. For Ashburnham had, it seems, received orders from Charles 'to provide a Barque at Hastings in readiness to carry Him into France, and to send horses againe to Netley, and lay others betweene that place and my House [near Battle]'. 'But within twenty dayes or thereabout,' Ashburnham's *Narrative* reveals, 'His Majestie sent mee the Relation of his Condition, which Hee expressed to be very melancholy, some persons very neare Him having refusd to serve Him in His escape, and so gave mee order to discharge the Barque and horses that waited for Him.'

Typically enough, the king would display little compunction when he eventually explained his intended breach of parole in a letter addressed 'to all my people of whatsoever station quality or condition', which he had planned to leave behind him after his escape was made. Probably written just before 16 November, it was a characteristic piece of self-justification, neatly omitting the duplicity which he openly admitted in his correspondence with Hopkins, and excusing his own broken promise by emphasising the allegedly broken promises of his captors:

> And certainly my condition in point of freedom is farre different from what it was at Hampton Court. Witness the strict guard round about this Island, and the troop of horse always attending, or rather watching me when I go abroad.
>
> Since therefore, none of these conditions are kept to me upon which I gave my word, I cannot be truly said to break it, though I seek my freedom. Besides, the Governor made me declare before the Commissioners, that continuation of guards upon me freed me

from my word, whereupon he took away the sentinels at my door, but never moved those of more importance, which was enough to confess the truth of what I declared, but not sufficient to take away the justness of my plea which cannot be avoided, except by the total taking away my guards, the difference of a few paces position, nearer or farther off, not making me less a prisoner.

The sentries to which Charles took exception had been posted out-side his bedchamber in Newport's grammar school, which still stands as a private residence in St James's Street at the corner of Lugley Street. But according to testimony presented by Hammond in a letter to the Speaker of the House of Lords dated 7 November, the king was, at best, telling no more than half the truth. Fearing in advance that the posting of guards might be used by Charles as a pretext for breaking his word, Hammond had indeed, it seems, pressed the king for his opinions and found him prepared 'to make scruple' over the issue. Yet Hammond was also at pains to suggest that the guards had only been set 'to keep off People from pressing into his Lodgings' and 'to preserve his Majesty's person from violence'. Thereafter, the Governor explained:

He [Charles] concluded himself to be obliged by his Parole if the said Centinels were taken away: which I then promised should be done before the Commissioners. And accordingly it was immediately observed.

Ultimately, the whole issue of Charles' promise would be largely miti-gated by the fact that no actual escape attempt was ever forthcoming, and by 6 November, John Crew was still hopeful of the king's good faith. 'We shall use our uttmost endeavours here,' he informed John Swinfen of the Derby House Committee, 'to bring the King nearer the Houses, and you will doe good service at London in perswad-ing the house to come nearer to the King.' But two weeks later, Jane Whorwood was making the case for his escape more urgently than ever. Hearing of ominous stirrings within the army, she had managed to obtain a pass to revisit the Isle of Wight on 21 November, having already warned Charles of a plot 'to dispose of his M:'. The feeling among his friends in the City, she told him, was that the king should 'thoroughly concede, to prevent Dangers incumbing'. But her own advice to Charles was escape, for as she herself put it, 'if Good be not intended him, no condescension of his can abort it'. He should make his bid for freedom, moreover, 'on Thursday or Friday next' and 'not from the top of the House by the help of Ladders', which had been urged 'by some near him', but 'by all meanes out of some Door'.

It was not the first time that the advice from Charles' 'most affectionate Hellen', as she signed herself, was ignored. Perhaps, as Ashburnham suggested, it was a lack of enthusiasm amongst his other friends that had left him unwilling to take the risk, or, more likely, a combination of weariness and submission to the inevitable that finally blunted his enthusiasm. He had failed so often and for so long that even defeat may now have seemed preferable, so long as it afforded him fleeting repose of a kind. Certainly, when he addressed the commissioners on Saturday, 25 November, as treaty talks finally broke up, there was little evidence of that obdurate defiance that had sustained him over many long months. Instead, there was merely resignation, self-pity and a pallid warning to his enemies of the consequences of their actions:

> My Lords, you are come to take your leave of me and I believe we shall scarce ever see each other again, but God's will be done, I thanke God, I have made my peace with him, and shall without feare, undergoe what he shall be pleased to suffer men to doe unto me. My Lords, you cannot but know that in my fall and ruine, you may see your owne and that also neere to you; I pray God send you better friends than I have found.

At the outset of talks, Charles had seemed renewed. 'The king is wonderfully improved', noted the Earl of Salisbury, as his sovereign assumed once more the trappings of royalty. The royal coachmen had been furnished with new livery, and orders issued from the king's pen with new confidence and vigour, as he encouraged efforts to discover silver in Somerset, requested a favour from the Governor of Newfoundland, granted safe conducts to John Kerckhoven and Lady Stanhope to return to England and appointed Sir Simonds D'Ewes keeper of the royal libraries and medal collection. Even his healing powers had gained a new efficacy, it seemed, when Elizabeth Steben, a 16-year-old gentle-

13

MISCHIEF, BLOOD, ABDUCTION, DEFEAT

'We know not but this may be the last time we may speak to you, or the world publicly. We are sensible unto whose hands we have fallen; and yet we bless God we have those inward refreshments, that the malice of our enemies cannot disturb. We have learnt to own ourself by retiring into ourself, and therefore can the better digest what befalls us.'

Charles I to the Prince of Wales, 29 November 1648

A little before eight on the evening of 30 November, Henry Firebrace entered the king's chamber to confirm that his worst fears had been realised. Carisbrooke Castle was now occupied by 2,000 infantrymen who had landed on the island the same morning, and 'some souldiers with pistolls in their hands' had been noticed 'busily prying about the House, where the King was lodged'. When the Royalist risings flared in summer and the New Model Army girded itself for the challenge, it had been agreed at a momentous prayer meeting at Windsor 'that it was our duty, if ever the Lord brought us back again in peace, to call Charles Stuart, that Man of Blood, to an account for that blood he had shed, and mischief he had done to his utmost, against the Lord's Cause and People in these poor Nations'. Thereafter, Fairfax's army had gone on to pacify the south once more, while Cromwell's northern force had little more than mopping up to accomplish. But the current mood remained bitter as well as confident: bitter because of abiding suspicion that Parliament was bartering away the reforms that had been dreamed of for so long and fought for so hard; confident because victory on the field of battle had been so comprehensive. In consequence, on 16 November, the fateful decision was taken that the king should be brought to trial and a remonstrance drafted to limit the term of the present Parliament's existence.

When, moreover, Charles told Firebrace that they could nevertheless depend upon Hammond's protection, since he would soon be back from a trip to London on personal business, he was swiftly informed of the Governor's arrest at Farnham for not 'rendering such ready obedience to orders as was required'. Hammond had refused, in fact, to hand the king over without orders from Parliament, and consequently been transferred to Reading on parole, leaving Charles with only the slenderest hope that John Newland's boat might somehow be reached through the chaos of the troop takeover in the November gloom. 'Commit yourselfe to the mercie of the sea, where God will preserve you,' Firebrace urged, though the king drew back once more. Instead, he called for further information from the Duke of Richmond, the Earl of Lindsey and Captain Edward Cooke, an officer from Hammond's regiment who had secretly defected. Cooke, it was agreed, would use his links to the notorious Major Rolph in an effort to glean whatever intelligence might be available before proceeding.

The captain's return brought little consolation, however, for Rolph could only guarantee that the king 'shall have no Disturbance this Night', while Charles himself, notwithstanding the entreaties of his advisers, remained adamant that escape was impossible. Indeed, when they argued that he could exploit the confusion caused by the army's arrival, and even sent Cooke out through the swarming soldiers to prove as much, Charles continued to demur, as a result of 'the great Difficulties, if not Impossibility of accomplishing it'. He feared, too, that 'in case he should miscarry in the Attempt', it would only serve to 'exasperate the Army and dishearten his Friends', and even when Cooke subsequently returned from Carisbrooke with further desperate news, the king would not budge. Hammond's deputy, Captain Thomas Boreman, had been threatened, it seems, 'with immediate Death if he but so much as whispered with any of his own Servants', and was in no doubt that 'there were some great Designs on foot', though 'he knew not what they were'. When quizzed, he had conceded that the abduction of the king was 'not improbable' – a prospect fully confirmed by the throng of soldiers continuing to mill about the king's lodgings in Newport upon Cooke's return. For guards had now been set not only around William Hopkins' house and at every window, but within too – even, in fact, 'on the King's very Chamber-door, so that the King was almost suffocated with the Smoak of their Matches'.

Faced with so critical a situation, Charles chose to place the burden of decision squarely upon the captain's shoulders. The officer had faced 'such Extremity of Weather, the Wind blowing very high, and the Rain falling very fast' that he was drying himself by the fire when the king asked of him: 'Ned Cooke, What do you advise in this Case?' Nor would the king accept Cooke's 'humble answer' that 'he suspected his own Judgement too much to offer any Advice, considering both the greatness of the Danger, and the Person concerned in it'. On the contrary, Charles now pressed Cooke in a manner that left no further scope for evasion. 'Ned Cooke, I command you to give me your advice' were Charles' final words, to which the captain, according to his own account, responded as follows:

> Supposed I should not only tell your Majesty, that the Army design'd suddenly to seize your Majesty; but by concurring Circumstances should fully convince you, that it would be so; Also, that I have the Word [password], and Horses ready at hand, they not being far off, in readiness under the Pent-House, a vessel attending at the Cows, nay hourly expecting me, myself likewise both ready, and desirous to attend your Majesty, and the Darkness of the Night, as it were, fitted for the purpose; so that I can foresee no visible difficulty in the thing; which I suppose in all its particulars to be the true state of the present Case: The only remaining question is, If so, What will your Majesty resolve to do?

It was plainly the most unequivocal invitation to bold action that Cooke could have offered. The key was control of the sentries' password, to which he had access, and the bustle of activity outside, which might still be exploited to steal the king away against all the odds. Cooke himself had already passed to and fro, employing his so-called 'Leaguer', or full-length military cloak, and his aim, presumably, was that Charles might use the same garment to effect his escape. He had also carried out the same ploy with the Duke of Richmond, to show the king how it might be done. However unlikely, therefore, Cooke, who was an experienced soldier, of course, remained convinced of the possibility, and Richmond and Lindsey were equally persuaded that the gamble was worth the try. Yet, after a short pause, Charles finally quashed all hope. 'They have promised me, and I have promised them,' he replied, 'and I will not break first.' When, moreover, Cooke expressed further concern at 'the Greatness of your Majesty's Danger, and Unwillingness to obviate it', the king's familiar refrain remained unaltered. 'Never let that trouble you,' he declared, 'were it greater, I would not break my word to prevent it.'

With that, Charles retired to his bed, saying that he intended to take his rest for as long as he could. 'Which Sire,' responded Cooke, 'I fear will not be long.' Under the circumstances, there was little else for the captain to do than return to his own lodgings, though he did not go to bed all night, he tells us, in spite of the fact that the army's noose was tightening all over Newport 'with such Secrecy and Quiet, that not the least Noise was heard, nor the least Cause of Suspicion given'. Over at Netley on Southampton Water, as the wind shifted momentarily over to the south, there were some, it is true, who thought they heard 'drums, and guns, and noises from the Isle of Wight'. But it was not until daybreak next morning that Charles finally heard a 'great knocking' at his dressing room door, and found 'some Gentlemen from the army … very desirous to speak with him'. In an instant, before the king was even allowed to rise from his sheets, they had 'rushed into his Bedchamber' and 'abruptly' informed him of their orders. 'From whom?' Charles asked. 'From the Army,' came the reply. When Charles then asked where he was to be taken, he was told, 'after a short whispering together', that his destination was Hurst Castle. 'Indeed, you could not have named a worse,' he rejoined.

Yet there was further vexation to come. Lieutenant-Colonel Cobbett, whom by now Charles realised was the leader of the newly arrived troops, added insult to injury by refusing to show him his orders from General Fairfax. Instead, the prisoner was forced into his coach so quickly that he was left no time to eat the breakfast arranged by Firebrace. Indeed, when Firebrace had arrived to tell him it was ready, he found 'these wretches' already leading the king downstairs to hurry him away'. 'I kneeled downe, and kissed his hand,' Firebrace tells us, 'at which he stopped to give me leave to do so, when they thrust him; saying, Go on Sir, and so thrust him up into his coach which was set close to the door.' But even this was not, it seems, the end of the king's indignity, for thereafter, as Firebrace relates, 'one Rolph, who had before attempted to murther him; impudently (with his hat on) stept up into the coach to him; but his Majestie with great courage rose up, and thrust him out; saying it is not come to that yet: Get you out'. 'Thus disappointed,' Firebrace continues, '[Rolph] took his saddle horse, which was there for his Majestie and got upon him; and so using insulting words, rode by the coach side.'

Permitted by Cobbett to take only those servants 'as are most useful', Charles nominated Herbert and Harrington and 'scarce a dozen more for other service'. Herbert, in fact, had been absent for three days, being 'sick of an ague', but now 'arose and came speedily to his Majestie' as soon as he was summoned, along with others that included Mr Lewin 'of the Celler and Buttery', Mr Catchaside 'of the Pantry and Ewry', Captain Joyner, who was retained as Master Cook, and Mr Muschamp 'of the Wood Yard'. The Duke of Richmond, how-ever, was ordered away from the party, only 2 miles into its journey from Carisbrooke, 'scarce being permitted to Kiss his Majesty's hand'. In spite of his sadness, he might have done well to count his blessings, for Charles and his party were headed first to Worsley Tower, one of the bleaker spots near Yarmouth, where they were to await the boat that would eventually take them on their choppy journey to Hurst Castle, which, though only 1½ miles in total, nevertheless took all of three hours to accomplish.

Hurst Castle itself, moreover, would prove every bit as unattrac-tive as Charles himself had declared upon learning initially that it was his destination. Its governor was the singularly unprepossessing Lieutenant-Colonel Ayers, whose appearance did not, it seems, belie his demeanour. 'His look,' we are told, 'was stern, his Hair and Beard were black and bushy [and] he held a Partizan in his Hand, and (Switz-like) had a great Basket-hilt sword by his side [so that] some of his Majesty's servants were not a little fearful of him.' Though he 'quickly became mild and calm' after an unexpected reprimand from Rolph, and was subsequently 'very civil to the King both in his Language and Behaviour', this did little to offset the broader inconveniences of the place he oversaw. For the royal accommodation was 'neither large nor lightsome', making it necessary for its occupant to read by candlelight

even at noon. The air, too, in this 'dolorous place' was 'equally nox-
ious' by reason, Sir Thomas Herbert tells us, 'of the marish grounds that
were about, and the unwholsom vapours arising from the Sargasso's
and weeds the salt water constantly at tides and storms cast upon the
shoar, and by the fogs that those marine places are most subject to'. The
only place for exercise, it seems, was the causeway joining the castle to
the coast of Hampshire, some 2 miles in length and 'over-spread with
loose stones a good depth, which rendered it very uneasy and offensive
to the feet'. Here alone, when weather permitted, was Charles allowed
to trudge the pebbles each day at 11 a.m., conversing with Herbert
and Harrington, or sometimes the Governor or Captain Reynolds, his
assistant. With three or four soldiers always in attendance, he could look
out mournfully across the Solent at the low grey outline of the Isle of
Wight and ponder at length the squadron of Parliamentary vessels further barring his passage to freedom.

On 8 December, Charles wrote to Hopkins, asking to be com-
mended to Jane Whorwood and declaring that, though 'closely kept',
he was also being 'civilly used'. Only two days earlier, however, his situation had become even more perilous when the army finally purged
Parliament of its opponents. The Commons' decision on 5 December,
by a vote of 129 to eighty-three, to continue negotiations with the
king had proved in fact the final straw, and sparked the descent upon
Westminster of Colonel Pride and his musketeers, who blocked the
stairs into Parliament and excluded some 110 recalcitrant MPs. After
which, around 160 more proceeded to resign in protest, so that by
the middle of January, the remaining 'rump' would have difficulty in
achieving even a quorum of forty. Compliance was guaranteed, resistance unthinkable. Henceforth, indeed, Parliament was nothing more
than a broken reed, pointing limply in whichever direction the army
might choose to blow; and what the army now wanted incontrovert-
ibly was the trial of Charles I.

A week or so later, the new status quo was confirmed by Harrington's
dismissal from the king's service. During a conversation with Governor
Ayers and a gaggle of officers, he had enlarged, it seems, upon the
wisdom displayed by the king in both his arguments with the commissioners and in his learned disputes with Presbyterian divines. More
provocatively still, Harrington had further maintained that but for the
intervention of the army, the Newport Treaty might well have succeeded. This, it seems, was enough to guarantee his discharge after

he had refused a request to retract his claims. Plainly, the leeway once afforded the king and his circle was no longer available, and though deeply resentful of the outcome, even Charles himself appears to have 'blamed Harrington for not being more wary among men that at such times were full of Jealousies and very little obliging to his Majesty'.

Nor were what Herbert termed Charles' 'melancholy apprehensions' helped by the visit of Colonel Thomas Harrison, one of Fairfax's aides, who would eventually join the committee that determined the form of the king's trial. Tried himself as a regicide after the Restoration, Harrison was plainly a man for the king to fear, as the declaration to his fellow committee members, which eventually led to his execution, made all too clear: 'Gentlemen, it will be good for us to blacken him what we can; pray let us blacken him.' So when Charles was awoken by the noise of the drawbridge being lowered at midnight and learned next morning of Harrison's arrival, he became convinced that an assassination attempt was imminent. Herbert, indeed, claims to have wept upon seeing 'his Majesty so much discomposed', and lost no time in discovering the nature of Harrison's mission from Captain Reynolds.

Much to Herbert's relief, however, Harrison had merely arrived with orders that the king be removed to Windsor. Far from being murdered, then, Charles actually found himself buoyed for the moment by the news of a stay at one of his favourite castles – 'a place he ever delighted in' – and on 19 December, he and Lieutenant-Colonel Cobbett, escorted by a troop of horse, duly made their way along the shingle spit path from Hurst to the mainland, after which they headed for the New Forest and thence to Winchester, where a warm welcome was in store from the mayor, local gentry and common people who flocked to see the king in great numbers, 'some out of curiosity to see, others out of zeal to pray for his enlargement and happiness'. There was all due formality, too, outside Alresford the following day when the commander of a cavalry squadron lining the road, 'gallantly mounted and armed', gave the king an appropriate bow with his head – 'all *a Solade*', as Herbert put it. The officer concerned was, in fact, none other than Colonel Harrison, whose arrival at Hurst had previously caused such alarm, and at Farnham, just before supper that evening, Charles saw fit to confide his earlier concerns to him. 'The law,' Harrison replied, 'was equally obliging to great and small.' For this reason there had never been cause for the king to fear assassination.

But while the colonel's reassurance was welcome, this would not prevent a final vain attempt at rescue by the king's supporters, notwithstanding the fact that he himself was by now finally drained of will and wholly resigned to his fate. Upon taking his leave of Parliament's commissioners on 25 November, Charles had effectively admitted as much, consoling himself only with the thought that he might be ultimately vindicated by events. 'In my fall and ruin,' he had told them, 'you may see your own.' But his defeat was no longer in question, and in accepting as much, he was now prepared to submit to what 'God shall be pleased to suffer men to do to me'. In his exhaustion, it seems, he no longer dreamed of 'Dutch pincks' or other waiting boats that Firebrace had said were 'always ready'. Nor for that matter was there any more consolation to be had from Jane Whorwood's pleas or Ashburnham's promises of horse relays ready from Netley to Hastings to ease his escape to the Continent. He had handed himself over to 'God's people, now called the Saints', as they were described by Oliver Cromwell, and they – 'by providence, having arms' – were wholly in the ascendant.

In the meantime, Charles had not forgotten his friends at least. On 5 December, indeed, his laundress Elizabeth Wheeler – now 'Lady' since her husband's knighthood at Newport – had taken letters from Hurst to Firebrace and Oudart, and conveyed greetings to Jane Whorwood, who was in London. They were inconsequential in tone and had been sent, as Charles himself admitted, 'like poor men's gifts to great persons to gain by giving', for the king, it seems, now valued human contact more than schemes for escape. From these few letters, he hoped 'to gain many' in return, and once more, on 17 December, he appealed to Firebrace that he should 'not be behind hand' with Jane 'in civility' and should 'put her in mind' to answer his letter as soon as possible. Hopkins too received further messages – now signed 'I' by the king – urging him to encourage Jane 'to correspond with me speedily and often'. But when word arrived of another attempt to free him, he showed little of his previous enthusiasm, making clear indeed that any initiative would have to spring from others. For though, as he confirmed to Oudart en route from Winchester, he 'liked well the instruments you name', he left no doubt that 'you at London must lay the design' and 'I can only expect it'.

In the event, it was only fitting perhaps that the final escape bid should have proved so desultory. Lord Newburgh, the 27-year-old groom of the king's bedchamber, had already offered to abduct the king as he exercised along the causeway at Hurst, but the transfer to Windsor had occurred too soon. Now the ever-resourceful Newburghs were again intent upon spiriting the king away as he rested some hours at Bagshot Park. Equipped with a fast horse that Charles knew well from hunting, a breakneck dash through surrounding woods would enable him to elude his captors, or so his friends believed. But the horse, in spite of its reputation as the swiftest in England, went lame, and a wary escort colonel at the head of 1,200 cavalrymen was not to be outwitted by this or any other means. On the contrary, he would hold his prisoner fast and deliver him, as planned, on 22 December – just before the 'former' feast of Christmas – to the now cheerless palace of Windsor, the nation's chief castle and main headquarters of the army.

Though the king found himself lodged in his 'usual bedchamber', the chill in the weather outside amply reflected the coldness of his reception within. By now the Thames was frozen and the battlements cold. As Charles walked them with Colonel Whitchcott, his last jailer, he did so without even the consolations of the season, for as at Carisbrooke in 1647, all Christmas festivity was strictly banned. Perhaps as a gesture to his captors, he made sure to dress for the day itself, and was consoled in part no doubt by messages from those close to him, since Jane Whorwood and Lady Newburgh both sent letters dated 25 December. Indeed, Charles informed Firebrace that he had received 'two letters from N', before another arrived through the agency of Hopkins, to which the king 'enclosed an answer' on 30 December. Three days later there was even a message from the queen, delivered on this occasion by Lady Wheeler, who remained to the end a particularly 'trusty messenger' of the king.

But the letters were the last of their kind, and in losing contact once and for all with Jane Whorwood, he found himself beset once more by taunts and provocation. The first few mornings after his arrival were spent in prayer and 'other exercises of piety', and the afternoons with Colonel Whitchcott. He also attended church in St George's Chapel. But the place seemed naked now without the banners of the Knights of the Garter that had formerly hung above the choir stalls, and when Hugh Peter, the ranting Puritan, was selected to preach, the king walked out in protest, though there was no real hiding place on offer. For while most of the common soldiery, in Sir Thomas Herbert's opinion at least, 'gave no offence either in language or behaviour', there were those, it seems, who lost no opportunity to snipe. One unpaid trooper of the garrison saw fit, indeed, to task the king over his diet of £15 a day, and dubbed him 'Stroker' – a sneer at the royal practice of touching for the 'King's Evil'.

Likewise, though Charles 'had liberty to walk where and when he pleased' both 'within the castle, and in the long terrace without, that looks towards the fair college of Eaton', there was now, more than ever, a bar to contact with the outside world. 'None of the nobility nor few of the gentry,' Herbert tells us, 'were suffered to come into the Castle to see the King, save upon Sundays to sermon in St George's Chapel.' For, prompted by the 'easy possibility of escape', Parliament had personally required of Cromwell 'speedy care of the close securing of the king's person and preventing of recourse to him'. The Newburghs, it seems, had conveyed a master key to Charles, affording him passage to the river and a waiting boat, but it had been discovered on his person, and no similar lapse in security was to be repeated. Instead, oaths were at once administered to those around the king, forbidding their assistance in his escape, and the prisoner was swiftly transferred to 'James's Palace' – now suitably shorne of its former 'saintly' title – on 19 January.

'Whilst his Majesty stayed at Windsor,' wrote Herbert, 'little passed worth the taking notice of.' Yet Herbert's account of some of the king's experiences during this period still captures some of the more personal dramas that occurred within the royal household as altogether more momentous events unfolded in the political world beyond. On one occasion, for instance, we hear how Charles reacted to the loss of a table diamond attached to one of his watches, which, 'as his custom was', he wound up every night before retiring to bed. Next day, 'for near an hours space', Herbert tells us, the king 'walked upon the terrace, casting his eye everywhere' but refusing to confide in the officers of the garrison who 'imagined he had lost something'. Ultimately, the jewel would literally come to light that evening – 'by good providence' – after Charles saw something sparkling in his chamber from the glow of 'a good charcoal fire' and the 'wax light burning'. Herbert, in spite of the king's distress at losing the jewel, had been bidden earlier 'not to vex himself about it', but was now delighted to be able to retrieve the item and present it to his master.

Rather more dramatically, Herbert was also involved in an accident that, as he readily admitted, 'might have proved of ill consequence, if God in mercy had not prevented it'. The groom was lodged, it seems, 'in a little back room near the king's bedchamber, towards Eaton College', adjoining a back stair that 'was at this time rammed up with earth, to prevent any passage that way'. In his efforts to keep himself warm – 'for the weather was very sharp' – he had laid the pallet on which he slept 'somewhat too near the chimney', where two baskets were filled with charcoal. The result – 'either from some spark of the charcoal, or some other way he knew not of' – was a fire which soon reached Herbert's pallet-bed and caused him to run 'in amazement' and 'in a frightful manner' to the king's chamber. Yet Charles remained unruffled throughout, notwithstanding the fact that his own door had been bolted from within, as he always ordered. Plainly, the personal danger to which he had been subjected was not inconsiderable. But once the fire had been 'stifled with clothes' and 'confined to the chimney', he responded with characteristic indulgence. Nor, for that matter, did Charles chide Herbert on another occasion when he appears to have 'over-slept his time'. Instead, he bought him 'a gold alarm-clock' from the Earl of Pembroke's watchmaker – a certain 'Mr East of Fleet Street'.

Yet perhaps it was weariness as well as kindness that explains Charles' generosity. For, as weightier events bore in upon him, the more minor mishaps of his household are certain to have appeared more inconsequential than ever, and the continuing affection of his servants all the more precious. Certainly, the same lassitude that had previously overcome Charles at times of crisis was still much in evidence on more important fronts. Sir John Temple, for instance, remarked upon the king's striking indifference to the ongoing preparations for his trial, which were proceeding apace. Though his life now hung unequivocally in the balance, he hid in trivia, even ordering that some melon seeds should be kept aside for planting in spring, so that he could enjoy them at harvest time. Desultory talk of long-dead hopes now became his only play at politics, it seems. 'He hath a strange conceit of my Lord of Ormond working for him in Ireland', Temple observed on 3 January, noting also how 'he hangs still upon that twig'.

Even the final exercise of regal pomp, for that matter, was largely reduced to parody, when the royal coach, drawn by six horses, left

Windsor on 19 January. For although the roads beneath the castle's keep were lined with musketeers and pikemen, they were only there to foil the king's escape, as he passed in silence largely hidden amid Colonel Harrison's squadron on his last journey to London. The bumpy, ice-rutted road through Brentford and Hammersmith was the same he had taken seven years earlier when fleeing the capital, and now, as he returned largely unnoticed, he was in little doubt that his flight had been in vain. 'I do expect the worst,' he had written at Hurst, acknowledging the pass to which he had come, and even then aware, perhaps, of how his whole adult life had ultimately been but a prologue to what was now at last unfolding. 'I will rather die,' he had declared in 1638, 'than yield to the impertinent demands ... of these traitors.' After two wars against the Scots, the acrimony of the Long and Short Parliaments, a bloody Irish rebellion, two civil wars involving five major battles and countless skirmishes, not to mention six or more abortive attempts at peace, he was about to make good his declaration.

Less than two months earlier, Ireton and Cromwell were still intent upon his survival, and even as late as Christmas, they were prepared to spare him as the figurehead of a new government. Even bad Old Testament rulers had, after all, been spared from prosecution, and had not David, as Cromwell declared publicly, refrained from killing Saul? But when Charles confided to his son that his conscience was 'dearer to me than a thousand kingdoms', he showed both his measure as a man and shortcomings as a ruler. Made no more compliant by protracted suffering, he had sealed his fate politically, though in the process his humanity had become more apparent, and nowhere more so, indeed, than in his dealings with his own children. The contrast between the austere, distant figure whom Hendrick Pot had painted standing at the other end of a long table from his wife and heir was now in fact subtly but decisively altered. He had worried continually about his offspring's safety and done his best to spare them from his troubles. 'Dear Daughter,' he had written to Princess Elizabeth in 1648:

it is not want of Affection that makes me write so seldom to you, but want of matter such as I could wish; and indeed I am loath to write to those I love when I am out of humour (as I have been these days past) lest my letters should trouble those I desire to please.

No doubt, too, it was love for his children that helped sustain the king as death drew ever nearer. A quarter of a century earlier, on 3 April 1625, John Donne had preached before his sovereign that 'the Holy Church of God ever delighted herself a holy officiousness in the Commemoration of Martyrs'. Eight months later, at Charles' coronation, the text had been the twenty-third verse of Psalm 21: 'Be faithful unto death and I will grant you the crown of life.' At Holdenby, he had requested a copy of *The Crown of Thornes*, and it was no coincidence either that *Eikon Basilike* would include a poem, 'On a quiet conscience', apparently written by the king himself:

> Close thy eyes and sleep secure,
> Thy soul is safe, thy body sure.
> He that guards thee, he that keeps
> Never slumbers, never sleeps.
> A quiet conscience on thy breast
> Has only peace, has only rest.

So when eventually Charles took his seat beneath the massive hammer-beamed roof of Westminster Hall on 20 January 1649, he was as prepared as any man might be for the trial to come. It was the place at which the Earl of Strafford had been condemned on his behalf less than eight years earlier, and upon his entrance, Herbert tells us, 'a hideous cry for Justice, Justice' went up among certain soldiers and officers, 'at which uncouth noise the King seemed somewhat abashed, but overcame it with patience', just as he would the ordeal that followed, refusing the right of the court to sit in judgement and keeping his hat on throughout as a token of defiance. 'I would know by what power I am called hither,' Charles famously declared at the outset of proceedings. 'Let me know by what lawful authority I am seated here, and I shall not be unwilling to answer.' On the same day, Lady Anne Fairfax shouted vainly from the gallery how Cromwell was a traitor and that her husband, the army's commander-in-chief, would take no part. 'Shoot the whores,' came Colonel Hacker's orders to his guards, as other women joined in the outcry.

But the outcry was in vain, and the court's response to the king's own pleas would ultimately prove just as unyielding. For one week later, he was finally condemned, 'lifting up his eyes to heaven' and 'smiling' when judgement was pronounced, or so Herbert informs us, after which, according to Purbeck Temple, he was whisked away in a sedan chair along King Street, 'as they carry such as have the plague'. Just as his wife had declared at the time, Sir Thomas Fairfax, sick and ashamed, had indeed refused to attend the court, and on 29 January, after spending the morning in efforts to delay the execution, there were reports that he planned a rescue at the head of 20,000 volunteers. By then, Henry Hammond, the favourite royal chaplain, along with forty-seven 'ministers of the Gospel of the Provinces of London', in an ecumenical coalition of goodwill, had also approached the army's leaders, praying 'that God would modify your hearts towards the king ... or else interpose his hand to rescue his royal person out of your power'. But God's hand remained unmoved, notwithstanding other rumours of revenge after an informer – 'troubled in conscience' – apparently warned Parliament that 'some have entered into an oath, taken the Secret and entered into an Engagement with their blood to murder the Commissioners that judged the king'.

In the meantime, however, Charles quietly prepared for the inevitable. Upon his return from court, he had been transferred after dark to Whitehall Place and thence to St James's for his last two nights, out of earshot of the scaffold-building that was now underway. There were prayers to be said, sermons to be heard, papers to be burnt and a final touching meeting with his children. She must not cry, he told his daughter, for he was to be a martyr, and the Lord would one day settle the throne upon her eldest brother. Then, when Elizabeth became distraught, he comforted her further. 'Sweet heart, you will forget this,' he told her, before expressing concerns that his youngest son, Henry, might be made a puppet ruler in his place. 'I will be torn in pieces first,' came the 9-year-old's reply – a response which is said to have reduced the hardened veterans in attendance to tears.

But while Charles had expressly ordered that only his children be allowed to visit, there was, according to Sir Thomas Herbert, at least one other person for whom he intended a final thought. For 'that evening', it seems:

> the king took a ring from his finger which had an emerald set between two diamonds and delivered it to Mr Herbert and bade him, late as it was, to go with it presently from St James to a lady living then in Channel Row, and give it to her without saying anything.

The street concerned, better known as Cannon Row, was in fact the dwelling-place of Elizabeth Wheeler, the former royal laundress and courier, who was married to the newly knighted Sir William, and Herbert specifically referred to 'the king's lavander' as the recipient in a letter to Sir William Dugdale three years after his *Narrative* was eventually completed. 'She was wife to a knight,' he told Dugdale in 1681, 'and if it be desired I will give you her name and shall satisfy you herein.'

Yet in the original manuscript of 1678, Herbert had annotated that the recipient was none other than 'the wife of Brome Whorwood Esq., daughter to James Maxwell's wife by Rider, her former husband' – a claim that, in spite of Herbert's later denials, the Oxford chronicler, Anthony Wood, would also always subscribe to. Wood, moreover, was close to Herbert, and no less a figure than Jack Ashburnham remained convinced that 'his authority is not to be made light of'. Why Herbert also went so far as to emphasise to Dugdale later that 'it was *not* Mistress Jane Whorwood to whom I gave the ring His Majesty sent me, as you find related in my short narrative of some occurrences' is, of course, even more intriguing. For in 1681, there was still further reason for concealing any possibility of a link between Jane, whose husband had by then been accused of Whig sedition against Charles II, and the regal martyr saint who had died more than three decades earlier.

The fact that Cannon Row was also the address of Lady Anne Everard, who had collaborated closely with Jane Whorwood since 1642, may also be of no little significance, of course – not least, because she had already been investigated by Parliament in April 1648 for receiving 'papers or other matters of value' from the king. But far more tantalising still is a reference in an inventory of 1684 relating to a 'ring box with an emerald ring and two diamonds' which appears to have been in the possession of Jane's daughter, Diana Master, who had continued to live at Holton House after her mother's flight from her husband in 1657. Had Elizabeth Wheeler, on the other hand, indeed been the recipient, as Herbert was at pains to suggest, there is also the puzzle of why she made no reference to it in her own will. Certainly, her husband, who predeceased her, made proud boast in his own bequest of 'the sword wherewith the late king of glorious memory knighted me' at Newport.

But while the mystery of the recipient may abide, at least no doubt remains concerning the fate of the man to whom it had once belonged. For on 30 January, he strode briskly – 'marching apace' – to the scaffold across St James's Park, accompanied by Bishop Juxon, Colonel Tomlinson and Thomas Herbert, all surrounded by Colonel Hacker's halberdiers, alert to any threat of disorder. Herbert, in fact, would describe his master's final passage to the executioner's block as 'uneventful', though other sources suggest that the king's dog, Rogue, was taken from him and that a joiner who had helped construct the scaffold insulted him upon his way. Certainly there was weeping, particularly among women, but whether soldiers mocked and spat, as some suggested, and the sky turned dark from the flight of ducks above St James's lake remains doubtful. The image of a *Via Dolorosa* for a martyr king was clearly no less appealing to future propagandists and romantics than the apocryphal tale of 'the faithful red haired figure' who allegedly 'stepped forward to greet him' as he left for Whitehall.

In the event, the king's death, though anything but prosaic, proceeded largely without incident. The scaffold, draped in black, was equipped with four staples attached to hooks and pullies which were intended to restrain him in the event of a struggle, though they proved unnecessary. 'Hurt not the axe that may hurt me,' he commented when someone on the scaffold bent down to test the blade's sharpness. And while Bishop Juxon had to remind him to make the traditional declaration of faith, he was still sufficiently composed to utter his most famous saying of all: 'I go from a corruptible to an incorruptible crown, where no disturbances can be, no disturbances in the world.' Nor, in doing so, did he hesitate, for the stutter that had troubled him throughout his life now deserted him.

Thereafter, at a little after 2 p.m., having been on the scaffold for all of fifteen minutes, Charles finally knelt before his heavily disguised executioner. Richard Brandon, 'a man out of Rosemary Lane', who had become Common Hangman of London after inheriting the post from his father Gregory, had certainly balked at the prospect of regicide when first approached. But it was he who had beheaded the Earl of Strafford almost eight years earlier, and he who was later purported to have confessed to dispatching the king himself, assisted, we are told, by 'one Ralph Jones, a Rag-man', who also hailed from Rosemary Lane, and in return for a suitably princely sum of £30 – 'all paid him in half crowns, within an hour after the blow was given'. For such a fee and in such company, it was no surprise perhaps that the killing went unbotched. On the contrary, the axe's descent severed the victim's neck unusually cleanly, at the third vertebra, sending him painlessly and at long last to the liberty and lack of 'disturbance' that had eluded him for so long.

EPILOGUE

Of the king's servants who had counselled and sustained him during his captivity, some like Silius Titus and Abraham Dowcett promptly fled to Charles II's court in Holland, though Sir John Berkeley made his way instead to Paris, to assume the post of temporary governor to the Duke of York before eventually becoming co-proprietor of New Jersey prior to his death in 1678. Mocked by the Earl of Clarendon for spinning unlikely tales of his exploits, which, the earl suggested, he may well have come to believe – and remembered by Samuel Pepys as 'the most hot, fiery man in discourse, without any cause' – he was nevertheless spared the prolonged harassment and suspicion that awaited his counterpart, Jack Ashburnham, who found himself detained in the Tower of London during the Commonwealth and three times banished to the Channel Islands, as the authorities sued him for debts contracted for his late master, and fellow Royalists raised suspicions with the new king in March 1650 about his loyalty. Only ten years later, in fact, was Ashburnham finally restored to full favour, serving as a diplomat under Charles II and representing Sussex as a Member of Parliament between 1661 and 1667.

Henry Firebrace, on the other hand, returned phlegmatically to the Earl of Denbigh's household before seeking preferment at the Restoration court and achieving a series of promotions, which left him Clerk of the Board of the Green Cloth and the recipient of a knighthood in 1685. Dying six years later at the ripe old age of 71, wealthy, respected and the father of five children, whose descendants included the poet W.H. Auden, he was altogether more fortunate than Sir William Hopkins, who was eventually rendered bankrupt by his hospitality to the king at Newport, and finally forced to sell his house and leave the island. Unlike Henry Jermyn, moreover, Hopkins did not even live to see the coronation of Charles II, let alone enjoy the courtier's subsequent fame and fortune. Still unmarried at the time of his death in 1684, Jermyn would in fact become Lord Chamberlain and ambassador to France in the new reign, and emerge not only as one of the most influential figures in the popularisation of Classical architecture in Britain but as Grand Master of the Freemasons, whose success in the next century is largely attributable to him.

For the queen, whom Jermyn had attended so attentively, however, there was further grief aplenty over the years ahead. By 1658, indeed, Henrietta Maria was 'so wrapped up in melancholy' that even Oliver Cromwell's death left her incapable of 'any very great rejoicing'. Though she greeted her eldest son's coronation with bonfires and a joyous *Te Deum* at her home of Colombes, other disappointments lay in wait. After sixteen years of exile, her only wish was 'to see yet before I die all my family together, who will no longer be vagabonds'. But in this she was frustrated, for Elizabeth, her daughter, had already died in 1650 at Carisbrooke, after taking a chill in the rain upon her father's bowling green, and barely three months after her eldest son's succession, Prince Henry had followed his sister to the grave with smallpox at the age of only 20. Princess Mary, too, would be dead from the selfsame disease before the year was out.

Though the queen would eventually come to toy with London's social whirl after a fashion, she remained in essence what Samuel Pepys described as 'a very little plain old woman' after seeing her in her widow's weeds. Ultimately, the last four years of her life were spent at home once more in France – at Colombes, where Jermyn was one of the most frequent of her very few visitors. Wealthier, more overweight than ever and thoroughly gout-ridden – 'full of soup and gold', as the poet Andrew Marvell put it – he would not forsake her, though her company was gloomy. For 'as she advanced in piety', Madame de Motteville recalled, 'so also she held back from speaking on almost all things'. Indeed, during the last years of her life, de Motteville observed, 'she had become scrupulous on this', 'weighing her words' carefully and appearing 'very detached from life', particularly after her first-born son had cut her allowance by a quarter, making it impossible for her to maintain her old court. Sick of doctors and their medicines, she was resolved to think of them no more, 'but only of her salvation', after a 'dangerous illness' had left her coughing blood in March 1666 and a further ailment that June had 'made her extreme weak from diarrhoea'. By September she was dead.

In the meantime, the man who had kept her husband imprisoned at Carisbrooke had encountered his own, somewhat less protracted, end. For some months after Robert Hammond's displacement, the Isle of Wight had been virtually ruled by Major Rolph, with the help of Captains Basket and Bowerman. Nor, to his almost certain relief, does Hammond appear to have taken any part in state affairs during the opening years of the Commonwealth, since he was weary, disillusioned and anxious to be free from the burdens to his conscience entailed by high office. Yet in August 1654, he was offered what amounted to the poison chalice of membership of the Irish Council. Surely enough, just as he had done six years earlier, he agreed to compromise his peace of mind in loyalty to a higher cause. Arriving in Dublin to take up his post with as much of his residual diligence as he could muster, he died there from a fever in early 1654 – barely five years after he had finally parted company with his former royal captive.

AUTHOR'S NOTE

The contemporary sources employed in this book, which are comparatively numerous, are all mentioned as and when they appear in the text, though specialist studies produced by modern authorities are still surprisingly scarce for a topic of such fascination and importance. Nevertheless, six individuals remain worthy of particular mention: Professor Charles Carlton for producing his admirable biography of Charles I; Dr Sarah Poynting for her meticulous work on Charles' cyphered correspondence; John Fox for the light he has thrown on the activities of Jane Whorwood; John Barratt for bringing Civil War Oxford to life so colourfully; Katie Whitaker for her sensitive exploration of the relationship between Charles and his wife; and the late Jack D. Jones, former Curator of Carisbrooke Castle Museum, whose knowledge of the king's incarceration there has not been rivalled. My sincere thanks are also owed to Mark Beynon, Lauren Newby, Caitlin Kirkman and the rest of the team at The History Press, whose support and diligence have been invaluable. To all concerned, I raise my glass at journey's end.

INDEX

Abbott, Robert, 139
Abingdon, 10, 15, 16, 236
Adams, Sir Thomas, 138, 151, 234
Agreement of the People, 126, 129
Alford, Sir Edward, 212, 257
Allen, Katherine Mary, 237, 239
Allen, William, 229
Anderson House, 46, 48, 68, 76, 78, 85
Andrewes, Bishop Lancelot, 237
Andrewes, Michael, 14
Anne of Denmark, 59
Anstey, John, 82
Antelope, 188
Arundel, Sussex, 191, 192, 212, 256–7, 261, 272
Ashburnham, John, 9, 14, 30, 31, 35, 38, 39, 40,
    42, 46, 51, 53, 81, 92, 93, 111, 117, 130, 131,
    132, 133, 136, 139, 140, 143, 148–9, 150, 151,
    154, 155, 156–7, 158, 162, 168, 177, 178, 179,
    180, 181, 183, 184, 185, 186, 187, 188, 189
    191, 193, 199, 206, 215, 218, 220, 242, 278,
    290, 292, 302, 309, 312
Ashmole, Elias, 138
Astley, Sir Jacob, 23, 27, 28, 30
Aubigny, Catherine, Lady, 210

Babbington, Uriah, 82, 199, 278
Bagshot, Surrey, 171, 303
Bamfield, Colonel Joseph, 116, 219
Barwick, Dr John, 209
Basket, Captain John, 157, 158, 190, 314
Bellièvre, Pierre, 75, 97, 114 179
Berkeley, Sir John, 111, 114, 115, 117, 130, 131,
    132, 134, 143, 149, 151, 154, 155, 156, 157,
    158, 159, 170–4, 175, 176, 177, 178, 181, 182,
    184, 185, 186, 187, 188, 189, 191, 193, 196,
    199, 206, 218, 234, 312

Berwick, 46, 132, 133, 175
Birchington, Kent, 258, 259
Bishop, Captain, 128
Blackfriars, 267
Blue Boar Inn, 195
Bosvile, Major Humphrey, 91, 92, 202–3, 204,
    205, 251, 273
Bowerman, Captain, 314
Brading Church, 159
Bristol, 13, 24, 25, 134
Brookes, Thomas, 251
Browne, Captain, 258, 259
Browne, John, 92, 94
Browne, Major-General, 87, 99, 100
Bulkeley, John, 275
Burley, Captain John, 188, 189, 190, 191, 192,
    193, 202, 205
Burroughs, John, 84, 209, 216, 247, 278, 279

Carey, Thomas, 67
Carey, Sir George, 164
Carisbrooke Castle, 148, 150, 155, 156, 159, 160,
    162, 163–6, 167, 168, 169, 170, 175, 177,
    178, 179, 180, 181, 182, 183, 189, 190, 193,
    194, 196, 198, 201, 204, 207, 210, 214, 215,
    217, 218, 219, 226, 227, 229, 231, 240, 245,
    248, 252, 254, 256, 260, 263, 264, 266, 267,
    269, 270, 271, 272, 273, 275, 276, 277, 280,
    281, 282, 283, 286, 289, 295, 296, 299, 303,
    313, 314
Carlisle, Countess of, 209–10, 212, 233, 251, 279
Carlisle, Earl of, 67, 237
Cave, Mary, 92, 93, 94
Cavendish, Lord Charles, 69
Chamberlain, Sir Ralph, 168–9
Chapman, Henry, 249, 253

Charles I,
appearance, 48, 273
Eikon Basilike, 228–30
escape attempt of March 1648, 211–17, 245
escape attempt of May 1648, 245–8, 251–64
Hampton Court, residence at, 109, 116–7,
    121–2, 130–1, 139–49
Holdenby, residence at, 86–7, 88, 90–2, 95–6,
    99–102, 105
Isle of Wight, journey to, 133–4, 148, 153–9
Newcastle, residence at, 44–9, 50–4, 69, 72–3,
    75–8, 85–8
Oxford, flight from, 9, 28, 35–6, 37–41
Oxford, residence at, 10, 14–15, 26–7
pastimes, 14, 87, 108
personality, 22, 24–5, 42, 49, 50, 54, 56, 114,
    122, 175–6, 185, 221–2, 242–3, 247, 254, 268,
    290–1, 293–4
political attitudes, 19, 22, 73, 81, 112, 113–4,
    115, 170, 175–6, 230–1, 306
reading, 227–8
relationship with children, 110–11, 306–7
relationship with Governor Hammond, 187–8,
    205–7, 222–3, 225–6, 274–5
relationship with Jane Whorwood, 92–3, 138,
    233–5, 237–42, 243–4, 279–80, 308–10
relationship with wife, 11–12, 15, 53–5, 56
    57–9, 61–5 66–7, 68–9, 72, 73, 74, 120, 231–3,
    235–7, 243–4
religious attitudes, 32–3, 52, 53–5, 97–8, 170
surrender to Scots, 32–5, 39–40, 42–3
Windsor, residence at, 303–6
Charles, Prince of Wales, 22, 51, 52, 67, 119, 166,
    209, 231, 261, 268, 271, 278, 286, 288, 295
Childerley, 107–8
Clarendon, Earl of, see Hyde
Cobbett, Lieut.-Colonel, 298, 299, 301
code used in correspondence, 85, 241
Colchester, Essex, 137, 275, 278
conservators, 205, 208, 211, 249
Constable, Sir William, 193
Cooke, Captain Edward, 199, 296, 297, 298
Cooke, William, 259
Corbet, Miles, 40
Corbet, Roger, 92
Corkbush Field, 128–9
Covenanters, 20, 24, 28, 34, 35, 40, 44, 50, 99, 116
Cowes, 157, 158, 159, 166, 187, 190, 193, 282
Cresset, Frances, 84, 94, 95, 121, 199, 204, 209,
    216, 217, 257, 278, 279
Crew, John, 287, 291
Cromwell, Major Oliver, nephew of the
    Lieutenant-General, 224, 225
Cromwell, Oliver, Lieutenant-General, 23, 41, 99,
    100, 103, 104, 107, 108, 109, 110, 111, 114,

116, 117, 125, 127, 128, 129, 135, 136, 137,
139, 146, 147, 148, 149, 151, 152, 172, 173,
174, 175, 181, 194, 195–6, 198, 199, 208, 216,
247, 266, 267, 269, 272, 275, 277, 286, 295,
302, 304, 306, 307, 313
Culpepper, Lord John, 14, 51, 53, 54, 81, 242

Davenant, William, 69
Denbigh, Countess of, 59, 118
Denbigh, Second Earl of, 80, 83, 102, 182, 183,
    184–5, 312
Derby House Committee, 166, 191, 194, 196,
    197, 198, 199, 201, 202, 210, 213, 216, 217,
    226, 233, 234, 238, 240, 242, 247, 249, 250,
    251, 252, 254, 256, 260, 264, 271, 272, 287,
    289, 291

Dillington, Sir Robert, 159, 160
Dingley, Jane, 150
Dover, Kent, 57, 119, 195
Dowcett, Abraham, 199, 207, 208, 217, 219, 242,
    248, 250, 254, 255, 256, 257, 261, 262, 265–6,
    278, 312

Edinburgh, 48, 91, 132, 175, 179, 194, 250, 277
Eikon Basilike, 220, 228–30, 237, 242, 307
Elizabeth, Princess, daughter of Charles I, 50, 77,
    110, 117, 130, 203, 219, 306, 308, 313

Fairfax, Sir Thomas, 23, 25, 35, 37, 86, 99, 100,
    103, 104, 106, 107, 110, 111, 114, 115, 117,
    128, 129, 131, 136, 137, 149, 150, 170, 171,
    181, 190, 193, 194, 196, 200, 202, 261, 272,
    295, 298, 301, 307, 308
Farmer, G., locksmith in Bow Lane, 246
Farnham, Surrey, 153, 296, 301
Firebrace, Henry, 82, 83, 84, 94, 141, 142, 167,
    169, 199, 210–11, 212, 213, 214–15, 216–17,
    242, 245, 246, 247, 248–9, 250, 252, 253, 254,
    255, 256, 257, 258, 259, 263, 265, 273, 274,
    275, 278, 279, 288, 295, 296, 298, 299, 302,
    303, 312
Flemming, Sir William, 178
Floyd, sentry at Carisbrooke, 262, 263,
Frazier, Dr, 251
Frost, Walter, 226, 252, 260

Garter Inn, Windsor, 172, 173
Gauden, Dr John, 228, 229
George Inn, Newport, 282, 293
Glemham, Sir Thomas, 9, 28, 36
Gloucester, city of, 134, 272
Gloucester, Henry, Duke of, son of Charles I,
    110, 117, 219
Goffe, William, Lieutenant-Colonel, 128, 193

Goffe, Dr Stephen, 120
Goring, Sir George, 23, 27
Graves, Colonel, 87, 99, 100
Greville, Sir Fulke, 82
Greyhound Inn, Newport, 110

Hamilton, James, Duke of, 71, 78, 97, 106, 125,
    232, 277
Hammond, Dr Henry, 108, 184, 308
Hammond, Colonel Robert, Governor of the
    Isle of Wight, 132, 133, 134–6, 139, 148,
    149–50, 150–1, 152, 154, 155–6, 156–8, 159,
    160, 161, 166, 167, 168, 169, 170, 171, 172,
    173, 179, 180, 181, 185, 186, 187–8, 190, 193,
    194, 197–8, 199–200, 201–2, 204, 205–7,
    209, 211, 213, 215–6, 217, 218, 219–20, 221,
    222–6, 228–9, 232, 245, 247–8, 249, 250, 251,
    254, 256, 260, 261, 262, 263–4, 265, 266, 268,
    269, 270, 271, 272, 273, 274, 277, 278, 279,
    280–1, 282, 286, 289–90, 291, 296, 314
Hampden, John, 198
Hampton Court, 109, 116, 121, 125, 126, 129,
    130, 131, 132, 134, 136, 139, 140, 141, 143,
    144, 145, 148, 149, 151, 153, 154, 155, 156,
    159, 160, 161, 166, 167, 168, 170, 176, 177,
    180, 181, 194, 210, 218, 233, 267, 268, 275,
    276, 281, 284, 288, 290
Harrington, Sir John, 227
Harrington, James, 47, 82, 84, 88–90, 100, 248,
    261, 299, 300, 301
Hastings, Sussex, 9, 290, 302
Heads of the Proposals, 112–4, 115, 122, 128,
    129, 154
Henrietta Maria, wife of Charles I, 10–13, 15, 32,
    34, 35, 49, 50, 51, 53, 56–65, 66–7, 68–72, 73,
    74, 75, 78, 82, 93, 96, 102, 117, 118, 119–20,
    149, 186, 191, 203, 231, 232, 235, 236, 237,
    243–4, 251, 313
Henry, Duke of Gloucester, see Gloucester
Herbert, George, 227
Herbert, Sir Thomas, 82, 84, 87–9, 89–90, 100,
    102, 107, 108, 109–10, 116–7, 122, 135, 143,
    165, 167, 168, 199, 200, 219, 220, 222, 224,
    226, 227–8, 261, 299, 300, 301, 303–4, 304–5,
    307, 308–9, 310
Hillier, George, 282, 293
Hinchingbrooke, 106
Hippesley, Sir John, 275
Hobbes, Thomas, 19, 148
Holdenby House, 80, 82, 83, 86–7, 88, 90–1, 92,
    93, 95, 96, 99, 100, 102, 103, 105, 106, 107,
    108, 113, 171, 199, 202, 229, 307
Holland, 12, 55, 73, 74, 91, 92, 107, 120, 193,
    204, 219, 237, 256, 259, 261, 268, 271, 286,
    288, 312

Holland, Earl of, 15, 69, 95
Holland, Sir John, 271
Hooker, Bishop Richard, 227
Hopkins, Sir William, 218, 22, 225, 232, 234, 235,
    240, 242, 243, 273–5, 276, 278, 279, 280, 286,
    287–9, 290, 297, 300, 302, 303. 312–3
Hopton, Sir Ralph, 18, 179
House of Commons, see Parliament
House of Lords, see Parliament
Howe, master gunner at Carisbrooke, 277
Hudson, Jeffrey, 64
Hudson, Michael, 9, 30, 36–8, 39–40, 46
Huntington, Major, 229
Hurst Castle, 298–9, 301, 302, 303, 306
Hyde, Edward, 10, 27, 34, 150, 151, 172, 199,
    205, 209, 210, 223, 234, 236, 262, 263, 266–7,
    272–3, 312

Independents, 30, 31–2, 41, 50, 51, 53, 81, 97, 98,
    104, 113, 114, 115, 125, 136, 145, 148, 175,
    177, 183, 225, 252
Ireland, 10, 20, 21, 34, 35, 42, 43, 74, 81, 82, 97,
    98, 134, 135, 147, 285, 287, 293, 305
Ireton, Henry, 107, 112–3, 114, 115, 116, 117,
    127, 128, 140, 151, 171, 172, 173, 180, 181,
    194–5, 198, 306
Isle of Wight, 132, 133, 134, 136, 139, 148, 149,
    150, 151, 152, 154, 155, 159, 162, 163, 167,
    170, 173, 175, 178, 179, 180, 181, 182, 185,
    190, 197, 198, 200, 201, 221, 226, 234, 251,
    264, 271, 272, 278, 283, 292, 298, 300, 314

Jersey, 69, 119, 131, 154, 180, 199, 200
Joyce, Cornet, 100–1, 102, 103, 105, 107, 113, 171
Joyner, Captain John, 82, 299
Juxon, Bishop Henry, 229, 310

Kent, Royalist risings in, 258, 269
Killigrew, Tom, 70–1
Kingdoms Weekly Intelligencer, 30
King's Evil (scrofula), 226, 248, 286, 304
Kingston-upon-Thames, Surrey, 18, 136, 151,
    194, 233, 269, 275
Kinnersley, Clement, 86, 116, 122, 280

Lanark, Earl of, 46, 125, 131, 133, 176, 177, 183,
    196, 200, 204, 212, 213, 216, 234, 247, 252,
    269, 273
Lauderdale, Earl of, 114–5, 125, 131, 177, 183
Legge, Colonel William, 111, 117, 131, 132, 133,
    134, 143, 154, 161, 177, 181, 187, 188, 189,
    191–2, 215, 218, 257, 278
Lenthall, William, 40, 281
Levellers, 104, 122, 126, 135, 144, 159, 160, 173
Lewes, Sussex, 248, 261

Lilburne, Henry, Lieutenant-Colonel, 139
Lilburne, John, 31, 98–9, 105, 123–4, 126, 127-8
Lilly, William, 137–9, 233, 237, 246, 247
Lindsey, Second Earl of, 35, 296, 298
Lisle, Lord, 283
Lisle, William, 185
Lobb, Major, 270
Loudon, Earl of, 125, 131
Louis XIV of France, 21
Lymington, Hants., 155

Manchester, Earl of, 123,149
Marvell, Andrew, 147, 313
Mary, sub-laundress to the king at Carisbrooke,
    199, 202, 203–4, 207-8, 210, 278
Maule, Patrick, 84, 141, 142–3, 167, 199, 200
Mazarin, Cardinal, 33, 43, 45, 120, 175, 277
Medina, River, 187
Mercurius Pragmaticus, 196, 283
Middleton, Captain, 82
Mildmay, Captain Anthony, 82, 84, 200, 205, 224,
    234, 240, 241
Mildmay, Sir Henry, 205
Milton, John, 228, 230, 237, 270–1
Moderate Intelligencer, 83, 91, 120–1, 130, 143, 144,
    168, 201, 203, 282, 283
Montague, Lord, 80, 102, 145–6, 237
Montreuil, Jean de, 32–3, 34, 35–6, 39–40, 43, 44,
    45, 46, 47, 81, 84, 175, 277
Montrose, Earl of, 23, 24, 35, 41, 43, 49, 118
Murray, Anne, 219
Murray, Mungo, 84–5, 178
Murray, David, 122, 197, 199, 201
Murray, Henry, 199
Murray, William, 46, 76-7, 141, 142, 167, 200, 234

Netley, Hants., 191, 290, 298, 302
Newark, Notts., 25, 26, 28, 35, 41, 42, 43-4, 46,
    92, 177
Newcastle, 30, 44, 48, 50, 51, 54, 69, 72, 73, 74,
    75, 76, 77, 79, 80, 82, 83, 85, 86, 88, 108, 111,
    120, 122, 128, 199, 208, 210, 242
Newcastle, Marquis of, 36
New Forest, 163, 301
Newland, John, 188, 212, 215, 256, 263, 289,
    290, 296
New Model Army, 28, 32, 44, 97, 98–9, 129, 134,
    149, 193, 295
Newport, Isle of Wight, 150, 155, 159, 160, 163,
    185, 187, 188, 189, 193, 198, 226, 248, 256,
    263, 270, 273, 275, 278, 279, 280, 281, 282,
    283, 289, 291, 297, 298, 300, 302, 309, 313
Nicholas, Sir Edward, 210
Northumberland, Earl of, 110, 117, 209, 219, 285
Nunwell, 133, 161, 162, 228, 283

Oglander, Sir John, 133, 134, 136, 150, 153, 159,
    161-2, 200, 221, 228, 243, 272, 283
Ormonde, Marquis of, 21, 23, 28, 34, 42, 82,
    96–7, 116, 305
Osborne, Dorothy, 137, 198
Osborne, Richard, 199, 209, 212, 215, 252, 255,
    256, 258, 260, 262, 264–8, 279
Oxford, 9–10, 13–14, 15–17, 21, 27, 28–9, 30, 31,
    32, 34, 35, 36, 37, 39, 46, 50, 69, 72, 82, 85,
    86, 89, 92, 93, 101, 103, 121, 127, 134, 137,
    141, 162, 198, 204, 208, 210, 228, 233, 234,
    236, 237, 238, 249, 309

Parliament, 10, 11, 18, 19, 20, 21, 22, 23, 25, 26,
    30–1, 33, 34, 35, 38, 39, 40, 44, 46, 47, 50,
    51, 52, 54, 57, 62, 66, 72, 73, 74, 76, 77, 79,
    80, 82, 83, 85, 87, 88, 89, 90, 92, 93, 94, 95,
    96, 97, 98-9, 101, 102, 103, 107, 109, 112–3,
    115–6, 117, 119, 122, 123, 124, 125, 126,
    127, 128, 133, 134, 135, 137, 143, 144, 146,
    147, 148, 149, 150, 158, 159, 161, 162, 166,
    169, 170, 172, 175, 176, 177, 178, 179–80,
    181–2, 183, 184, 186, 187, 190, 191, 192,
    193–4, 194–5, 196, 198, 199, 200, 201, 202,
    205, 210, 218–9, 225, 228, 230, 238, 252,
    257, 264, 266, 269, 271, 275, 276, 277, 278,
    282, 284–6, 287, 289, 295–6, 300, 304, 308,
    309, 312
Peck, Captain, 193
Pembroke, Earl of, 80, 81, 87, 95, 102, 135–6,
    149–50, 162, 305
Pembroke, Royalist rising at, 269, 272
Pendennis Castle, 188
Pepys, Samuel, 70, 141, 312, 313
Peyton, Sir Edward, 237
Plume of Feathers Inn, 158–9
Pontefract Castle, 129
Poole, Dorset, 201, 271
Porter, Endymion, 118
Portsmouth, 162, 184, 193, 248, 251, 256–7, 270,
    272
Poyer, Colonel, 269
Presbyterianism, 20, 21, 22, 30, 31, 32–3, 35, 41,
    43, 48–9, 50, 51, 52, 54, 56, 73, 75, 81, 87,
    96, 97–8, 99, 103, 104, 112, 115, 116, 126,
    131, 145, 148, 170, 175, 182, 183, 195, 196,
    209–10, 252, 271, 277, 285, 300
Preston, Captain Robert, 200
Preston, Lancs., 277
Putney Debates, 126–8

Queenborough, Kent, 212, 256–7, 258, 259, 261,
    263, 279

Rainsborough, Colonel Thomas, 35, 103, 104, 115, 127, 129, 193, 196, 260
Read, Moses, 189
Reading, 16, 296
Reading, John, 219
Reculver, 259
Redbridge, Hants., 193
Rich, Colonel Nathan, 280, 281
Richmond, Duke of, 9, 296, 298, 299
Rolphe, Major Edmund, 159, 166, 314
Rumler, Johann Wolfgang, 14

Saffron Walden, Essex, 135
St Albans, 38, 39
St Albans Road, 192
St James' Park, 310
St James' Palace, 50, 60, 70, 219, 308
Salmon, Lieutenant-Colonel, 193
Sanderson, Robert, 228
Sandys, George, 227
Scotland, 10, 20, 23, 35, 73, 76, 84, 114, 116, 125, 236, 250, 251, 286
Scots, 20–1, 28, 30, 31, 32, 33–5, 39–40, 41–2, 42–3, 44–8, 50, 52–3, 68, 72, 74, 75, 77, 78–9, 80, 81, 83, 85–6, 97, 98, 99, 108, 109, 128, 131, 132–3, 140, 145, 148, 167, 175–8, 179, 181, 182–4, 194, 195, 196, 213, 220, 224, 225, 230, 232, 235, 242, 245–6, 252, 269, 272, 275, 276–7, 306
Sedgewick, Obadiah, 227
Sheffield, Colonel, 135
Sheppey, Isle of, 256, 259
Solemn League and Covenant, 20, 22, 31, 43, 47, 48, 49, 51, 52, 98, 111, 112, 114, 125, 183, 229
Solent, 148, 154, 155, 163, 168, 185, 190, 196, 270, 300
Southampton, 149, 169, 185, 193, 256, 260, 282
Southampton, Earl of, 31, 35, 154, 157
Steben, Elizabeth, 293
Strafford, Earl of, 54, 209, 231, 307, 310
Swinfen, John, 291

Taylor, Jeremy, 120–1
Taylor, John, 226, 281, 282, 283–4

Thames Ditton, 131, 143
Thorley, Isle of Wight, 168
Titchfield, Hants., 59, 154, 157, 260
Titus, Captain Silius, 84, 102, 199, 200, 208–9, 216, 217, 231, 232, 238, 242, 245, 246–7, 249, 250, 252, 254, 255–6, 258, 260, 263, 273, 275, 277, 278, 286, 312
Triploe Heath, 104
Troughton, Mr, 221

'Vote of No Addresses', 196

Waller, Sir Edmund, 20
Waller, Sir Hardress, 104
Waller, Sir William, 13, 16, 201,
Walton, Colonel Valentine, 40
Warwick, 17
Warwick Castle, 44,
Warwick, Sir Philip, 144, 207, 244, 249, 293
Watson, Leonard, 172–3
Weals, Job, 269, 270
Whalley, Colonel Edward, 100, 106, 107, 116, 130–1, 139, 140–1, 142, 144, 146–7
Wharton, Lord, 209, 264
Wheeler, Mrs Elizabeth, 199, 202, 203, 206, 243, 262, 278, 302, 303, 309
Whitehall, 14, 58, 62, 64, 70, 71, 112, 231, 308, 310
Whorwood, Jane, 92–3, 94, 136–7, 137–8, 138–9, 203, 233–5, 237–42, 246, 255–6, 258–9, 260, 263, 274, 279, 288, 291–2, 300, 302, 303, 309
Wildman, John, 124, 125, 127–8, 151
Winchester, Hants., 190, 205, 266, 293, 301, 302
Windsor, 110, 111, 171, 174, 175, 178, 196, 208, 251, 295, 301, 303, 304, 306
Windsor Forest, 153
Witherings, Thomas, 209, 250–1, 255
Wolverton Manor, 150
Wood, Anthony, 14, 90, 93, 118, 136, 309
Worsley, Edward, 188, 212, 215, 253, 257, 258, 260, 262–3, 265

York, James, Duke of, son of Charles I, 24, 50, 146, 151, 204, 219